ARTILLERISTS AND ENGINEERS

THE BEGININGS OF AMERICAN SEACOAST FORTIFICATIONS
1794 - 1815

by
ARTHUR P. WADE

B.Sc., United States Military Academy, 1943
M.A., Fairleigh Dickinson University, 1965

A DOCTOR'S DISSERTATION
submitted in partial fulfillment of the requirements for the degree
DOCTOR OF PHILOSOPHY

Department of History
KANSAS STATE UNIVERSITY
Manhattan, Kansas 1971

Library of Congress Cataloging-in-Publication data
Artillerists and Engineers/ Arthur P. Wade
p.   cm.
Includes bibliographical references and index.
Library of Congress Control Number: 000000000000
ISBN 978-0-9748167-2-2 (pbk.)
1. Military History, 2. Artillery I. Arthur P. Wade

Printed in the United States of America by lulu.com

Reprinted with permission
CDSG Press
1700 Oak Lane
McLean, VA 22101-3322 USA

CONTENTS

MAPS AND ILLUSTRATIONS

The Coast Defense Study Group

The Coast Defense Study Group (CDSG) is a non-profit corporation formed to promote the study of coast defenses and fortifications, primarily but not exclusively those of the United States of America; their history, architecture, technology, and strategic and tactical employment. Membership in the CDSG includes four issues of the organization's two quarterly publications the *Coast Defense Journal* and the *CDSG Newsletter*

The primary goals of the CDSG are the following:
• Educational study of coast defenses
• Technical research and documentation of coast defenses
• Preservation of coast defense sites, equipment, and records for current and future generations
• Accurate coast defense site interpretations
• Assistance to groups interested in preservation and interpretation of coast defense sites
• Charitable activities which promote the goals of the CDSG

The CDSG publishes two periodicals, the *Coast Defense Journal* and the *CDSG Newsletter*. Original articles and source documents on aspects of military, coastal or harbor defenses are published in the *Journal;* the *Newsletter* has organizational news and business, and items of a more timely nature. The *CD Journal* and the *CDSG Newsletter* rely on the submission of articles, reviews, site visit reports, notes, comments, letters, inquiries, etc., from the membership of the CDSG. The CDSG Press provides copies of back issues of the CDSG publications, past meeting notes (which often contain a number of reproductions of important source documents and maps of the harbor defense area visited), and reproductions of important books and manuals. Also, the CDSG ePress provides CD/DVD of important coast defense documents from the U.S. National Archives. The organization also hosts an annual meeting at different harbor locations during which the group tours the remaining harbor defense structures in the area.

For contact information, a membership form and more information on American seacoast defenses as well as our current publications and books, please visit our website - www.cdsg.org

PREFACE TO THE COAST DEFENSE STUDY GROUP EDITION

The huge concrete, camouflaged, gas proofed, and computerized gun batteries constructed in the United States during World War II first sparked my interest in seacoast defenses. Most of the batteries, plotting rooms, fire-control towers, and mine casemates still survive, and their size and heavy construction demonstrate the power of America's last seacoast defenses. After I explored and read about the World War II defenses, it was logical for me to turn my attention to the concrete long-range gun batteries, anti-aircraft emplacements, and protected fire-control switchboard buildings built during World War I, which were often constructed among the concrete disappearing gun batteries created at the turn of the century. These complex structures were often built adjacent to, and sometimes inside of, the multi-story, casemated brick and granite fortifications everyone associates with the period of the American Civil War. These sites sometimes also included masonry gun batteries and magazines protected by heavy earth coverings, which I later learned were built during the 1870s. I soon learned that the casemated masonry forts were part of the Third System of seacoast fortifications, which implied that two other systems preceded them. However, when I finally visited examples of First and Second System forts, I was confused. Some of them were large, one-story masonry works, with dry moats and drawbridges, a few were two or three story casemated structures, and others were tiny earthworks, which held just a few guns. In my puzzlement, I turned my attention back to the Third and later systems of seacoast defenses which made more sense to me.

It was not until the bicentennial of the Second System of seacoast fortifications in 2007 that my interest in the early systems was reawakened. And then I learned of doctoral dissertation on the subject which not only made sense of the first two systems, but documented their importance to the history of the United States and to the systems of seacoast defenses that followed—"Artillerists and Engineers: The Beginnings of American Seacoast Fortifications, 1794-1815," by Arthur P. Wade, a West Point graduate, completed at Kansas State University in 1977.

Reading Colonel Wade's dissertation was a revelation to me. Wade exhaustively researched the topic in the surviving manuscript records of the Secretary of War, Adjutant General, Army Commands, and Military Posts. He had also examined hundreds of primary sources, which had been published by the federal government, libraries and individuals. Newspapers were another primary source he sought out. These sources were the basis for his twelve chapters, in which he includes lists of harbors to be defended and the status of each, and the stationing of companies of artillery and infantry. The notes for each chapter document the sources of all the data included in each, and the appendices provide compilations of material too detailed for the text. Finally, the huge bibliography includes all of the primary and secondary sources.

My first thought after reading Wade's dissertation was that it had to be published. But I soon found that some of my colleagues in the Coast Defense Study Group had discovered the dissertation years earlier, purchased copies, and suggested that the CDSG publish the work. However, they found little interest among their peers in publishing a work on First and Second System fortifications. I contacted these pioneers—Glen Williford, Bolling Smith, and Ken Thompson, among others, and found each still supporting publication. I approached Terry McGovern and Mark Berhow of the CDSG Press, and we went to the CDSG Board of Directors, which was enthusiastic about the project.

Even then, gaining permission to publish the dissertation (especially as Col. Wade was deceased), scanning and editing the text, and creating an index has taken months of volunteer work. But it was worth the effort, and now anyone interested in the learning about the beginnings of America's seacoast defenses will be able to purchase a copy of the definitive work on the subject.

For anyone who is interested in early federal seacoast forts, Wade's dissertation can be considered to be without peer in chronicling the early artillery and engineer regiments and seacoast fortification construction. It is well-researched in primary documents, placed in proper historical context (including the disdainful political basis for officer appointments), detailed, and well-written. The extensive bibliography is extremely useful, and has led to the discovery of the fine collection of the papers, including wonderful fort drawings, of the early 19th century Military Philosophical Society at the New York Historical Society in NYC. In the preparation of histories of the early fortifications of the United States it is necessary to address all of the contemporary forts in the harbor, as well as the evolution of successive earlier forts and ordnance programs for a full understanding.

And, modern-era concrete enthusiasts should remember that the multi-tiered brick and granite forts of the Third System were rendered obsolete by rifled guns during the Civil War, returning the designs of forts and batteries to earthen berms protecting guns and crews through World War II, strongly akin to the early forts discussed by Wade. To be a truly historically complete and all encompassing (in terms of American) "coast defense study group," the CDSG is filling in a great hole in its published repertoire by reprinting Wade's outstanding dissertation.

Joel W. Eastman with comments from Mark M. Berhow
January 12, 2011

AN ABSTRACT OF A DOCTOR'S DISSERTATION

At the end of the Revolutionary War the seacoast defenses of the United States consisted of a scattering of forts and batteries of varying sizes constructed by the individual states. Early in the 20th century the federal system of seacoast fortifications was generally considered the finest in the world. This dissertation examines the beginnings of that federal system, from 1794 to the end of the War of 1812.

In 1794, faced with possible war with Britain, the federal government assumed responsibility for the construction and manning of seacoast defenses from Maine to Georgia. Construction was entrusted to French-born engineers, and a Corps of Artillerists and Engineers was raised to garrison the fortifications and to provide a source of native-born military engineers. The program was stimulated by the Quasi-War with France in 1798-99, but distrust of alien influences led to the dismissal of the foreign-born officers of the Corps of Artillerists and Engineers. Nevertheless, by 1801 the so-called First System of fortifications construction had been substantially completed. The Jefferson administration reduced the size of the Army in 1802, but retained a regiment of artillerists and created the Corps of Engineers, whose mission was both to construct fortifications and to train cadets as engineers at the newly-authorized United States Military Academy. Over the next four years, however, many companies of artillerists were deployed to occupy the Louisiana Purchase, and seacoast garrisons were reduced to a minimum. Beginning in 1806, Britain's flouting of neutral maritime rights again threatened war, and Congress appropriated funds for additional seacoast fortifications. New construction activity was stimulated by the Chesapeake-Leopard incident in 1807. This era of coast-defense construction from 1806 through the War of 1812 was to be known as the Second System. Almost all design and construction was supervised by officers of the Corps of Engineers, most of them young graduates of the Military Academy. The Chief Engineer, Jonathan Williams, introduced new theories from France, and during this Second System the basic fortifications design, hitherto founded on the works of Marshal Vauban, began to reflect increasingly the perpendicular walls and casemated guns advocated by Montalembert.

By the eve of the War of 1812 the defenses of the Atlantic coast and those below New Orleans were substantially completed and manned by regular troops. But the United States was determined to seize Canada to force Britain to acknowledge American maritime rights, and when war was declared the regular garrisons were withdrawn from most coastal forts to join the field armies poised to invade Canada, leaving the fortifications to be manned by local militia companies.

Britain was too involved in the Napoleonic Wars to reinforce her troops in North America until 1814, although the Royal Navy raided the New England coast, blockaded many ports, and ranged the Chesapeake Bay with relative impunity. In 1814 additional British ships and troops were sent to America and conducted several full-scale amphibious attacks on the coast, one of which resulted in the capture of Washington. Only four American seacoast fortifications were attacked: Fort Washington on the Potomac capitulated without firing a shot, but Fort McHenry at Baltimore, Fort Bowyer at the entrance to Mobile Bay, and Fort St. Philip below New Orleans all offered strong defenses and drove off the attacking fleets.

Concluding from the wartime experience that strong seacoast defenses were a necessity, the nation embarked in 1816 upon a system of permanent fortifications that lasted until the advent of long-range aircraft and nuclear weapons made surface coastal defenses obsolete.

AUTHOR ACKNOWLEDGMENTS

The original inspiration for this work stems from two sources. In the mid-1950s Colonel Frederick P. Todd, then Director of the West Point Museum and a founding member of the Company of Military Historians, pointed out to me that the story of American seacoast fortifications prior to 1816 had never been told. Some fifteen years later Dr. Stetson Conn, the Chief Historian of the Army, in a foreword to E. Raymond Lewis's survey, *Seacoast Fortifications of the United States: An Introductory History*, published in 1970 by the Smithsonian Institution, expressed the hope that a definitive history of the coast defenses would someday be written. While this work hardly aspires to that classification, it is an attempt to tell the story of the most neglected and least-known period in the long history of American seacoast fortifications: the era of the First and Second Systems.

Anyone attacking this subject must acknowledge, as I do here with gratitude, the many contributions of the late Colonel Robert Arthur, Coast Artillery Corps. Colonel Arthur's researches into the colonial origins of the seacoast fortifications produced many exhaustive articles on the subject in the old *Coast Artillery Journal* of the 1920s, and it is regrettable that these were never collected into a bound volume.

Because of the fire in the War Department in 1800, which destroyed most of the official records prior to that date, the history of the Corps of Artillerists and Engineers has been pieced together largely from manuscripts held by the United States Military Academy Library. I am particularly grateful to the Librarian, Mr. Egon A. Weiss; to the late Mr. Joseph M. O'Donnell, the Archivist; and to Mrs. Marie T. Capps of the Map and manuscript Division, for their assistance and encouragement.

My thanks go also to Dr. Stephen T. Riley and the outstanding staff of the Massachusetts Historical Society for the productive days I spent with the Pickering Papers. Mr. John D. Stinson of the New York Public Library was most helpful in orienting me on the pertinent manuscript holdings of that great institution. Ms. Freda L. Church of the Society of Architectural Historians very kindly put me on the track of several important recent articles on individual fortifications. For an enjoyable and rewarding visit to the vast holdings of the U.S. Army Military History Research Collection at Carlisle Barracks, Pennsylvania, I am indebted to Colonel James Barron Agnew and Miss Joyce Eakin.

The great bulk of the primary sources for this work, particularly for the years after 1800, is located in the National Archives. For the thirty-odd reels of microfilmed records that I acquired and pored over for more than a year, I can only express my appreciation to the hard-working but anonymous staff of Microfilm Publications of the National Archives and Records Service. I can, however, specifically acknowledge the assistance of Mr. Gary L. Morgan of the Cartographic Archives Division in selecting maps and charts to illustrate my story.

Not the least of both primary and secondary references for this work came from the holdings of the Farrell library at Kansas State University. Mr. Arne Richards of the Documents Division was always ready with information and advice. Where relatively obscure works in Atlantic seaboard repositories were needed, I could always count on the knowledgeable assistance of Mrs. Ellyn M. Taylor of the Interlibrary loan office.

Finally, in the actual writing of this paper I have benefited greatly from the advice, assistance, and moral support of my principal advisor, Professor Homer E. Socolofsky, whose vast knowledge of the American West extends, I found, to the shores of the Atlantic Ocean. Professor Donald J. Mrozek pinpointed several potential areas of weakness, and tried to tone down my pronounced pro-Federalist bias. To them and to other members of the Department of History at Kansas State University I must express my appreciation for their patience in dealing with this lengthy work.

INTRODUCTION

Over twenty years ago, while on duty at the United States Military Academy, I began researching the early years of the United States Army, the tenuous three decades between the dissolution of the Continental Army and the outbreak of the War of 1812. As I read first into the secondary literature of the period 1784-1812, I found several good surveys of the history of the Army, particularly those by William A. Ganoe and Oliver L. Spaulding, and one more detailed treatment of that era by James R. Jacobs. These works, particularly the latter, covered the Harmar, St. Clair, and Wayne campaigns of the 1790s and the successive reorganizations of the Army prior to 1812. Until the late 1960s, these were virtually the only published works treating the origins of the Regular Army, as it came to be called. More recent works, particularly those by Francis Paul Prucha, S.J., and Richard H. Kohn, have explored the role of the Army in advancing the frontier and the position of the Army in the rising political factionalism at the end of the 18th century. Several other full-length studies have discussed the early Army in connection with the founding and early years of the United States Military Academy.

Neglected almost entirely in all works covering the first three decades of the nation's military establishment has been the Army's role in the defense of the maritime frontier. While in recent years considerable interest has grown up in the great seacoast fortifications of the latter 19th century, and particularly in their architectural restoration, almost nothing has been written on the early years of the coast defenses, the periods of fortifications construction prior to 1816 that were known subsequently as the First and Second Systems.

During the colonial period of American history the colonies made varying efforts, some adequate but most rudimentary, to fortify their major harbors and to provide some basic defenses for their differing lengths of seacoast. These early fortifications were repaired and improved during the Revolutionary Wars and some of them—Fort Moultrie in Charleston and Fort Mud below Philadelphia, among others—rendered capable wartime service.

These forts were built and manned by state forces, with only the barest of assistance from the Continental Congress; as might be expected, their size and effectiveness varied widely. Through the years, local historians have been surprisingly successful in recreating the stories of many of these seacoast forts during the colonial era and the years of the Revolutionary War; many articles have been published in state and local historical journals over the years, and others have been stimulated more recently by the approaching Bicentennial celebrations. But this interest in the early fortifications seems to lag after the end of the Revolutionary War, not only because of the end of hostilities but also because, shortly thereafter, the responsibility for the defense of the seacoast became increasingly a function of the new federal government.

Ordinarily, the history of the federally-supported seacoast fortifications, as recorded in documents and maps, would have been available in the files of the War Department and would have found its way into the National Archives. Unfortunately for posterity, the records of the War Department for the period 1785-1800 were destroyed in a fire in November of 1800. Certain received copies of orders and correspondence for that period have survived, of course; some have been included in the *American State Papers,* while others are widely scattered in order books and correspondence books of subordinate commanders, held today by various state and local historical societies and libraries. Happily, many of the scattered records of 1798-1800 are being brought together in the new edition of the *The Papers of Alexander Hamilton* being prepared and edited by Harold C. Syrett. But there still remain large gaps in the pre-1800 records, and the story of the so-called First System of seacoast fortification, lasting from 1794 through about 1801, will probably never be told in full. And because of that fact, few historians have desired to tackle the detailed story of the Second System, from 1806 through the War of 1812, in any detail.

A seacoast defense system consists of forts, guns, and men—three elements which form the theme of this work. Short monographs have been written on several of the fortifications of the first two systems, and there are half a dozen authoritative works, both old and new, that make some reference to the ordnance of the period, but almost nothing has been done on the officers and men who made up the garrisons of the coastal forts during the early years. Nor have I found any adequate history of the Corps of Engineers as regards its role of fortifications design and construction prior to 1816. The objective of this work is to integrate the stories of the forts, the guns, and the men into a single narrative.

Looking back at the entire history of American seacoast defense systems from the vantage point of the Bicentennial Year of 1976, it is almost beyond argument that, eventually, the United States constructed, armed, and manned one of the finest systems of coastal defense in the world. There is general agreement that, by the 20th century, the United States led the other major powers in the development of that combination of military architecture, ordnance production, and gunnery techniques required for the defense of key points along an enormously long maritime frontier. Those who visited American seacoast fortifications from Maine to the Philippines, before they were dismantled after World War II, will remember the massive concrete walls, with their galleries and casemates, and the gigantic guns of up to 16-inch caliber that were ready to defy the largest capital ships of the time. Hopefully, some of those visitors may have wondered how these great forts originated.

The answer to that question involves, of course, more than just the matters of who built the forts, who produced the guns, and who provided the garrisons. More basically important is the developing politico-military philosophy within the United States from which the seacoast defenses stemmed. How and why did the United States, in the 1790s a strongly antimilitary nation generally opposed to a standing army, embark upon the difficult and expensive project of fortifying its seacoast? Why was reliance placed on masonry walls rather than the wooden walls of a fleet? Clearly these decisions were not based on a single decision by the Executive or a single resolution by the Congress, nor was there at the beginning any long-range plan developed by far-seeing statesmen. Rather, as with most American institutions, the seacoast defenses evolved as specific answers to specific crises.

We are concerned in this story with a period of two decades in the early history of the United States, an era which, John Fiske's theory notwithstanding, was probably the true "critical period" of the new republic. During these years there were, of course, many internal political problems to plague the new government and its citizens, but there were also four distinct externally-imposed crises, threats by a foreign power that were very real and immediate to the American people at the time. First there was the multi-crisis year of 1794, when war with Britain over the maritime rights of neutral nations seemed both inevitable and imminent, while at the same time the tiny regular military establishment was thoroughly committed against the Indians of the northwest and almost all available militia was being assembled to put down a "rebellion" in western Pennsylvania against the Administration's whiskey tax. Then came the "quasi-war" with France in 1798-1799, when invasion of the Atlantic seaboard by ships and troops of the French Republic was expected momentarily. Third was the alarm of 1802 and early 1803, when all signs seemed to point to a French descent upon the mouth of the Mississippi and an attempt to reestablish a French colonial empire in North America. And finally there was the crisis of 1807-1808, triggered by the *Chesapeake-Leopard* incident, which threatened to bring immediate war with Britain—war that was, in fact to be deferred only until 1812.

During each of these four crises, public attention necessarily focused sharply on the need to defend at least the most critical portions of the long and exposed maritime frontier. How Congress and successive political administrations reacted to these four crises is the story of the First and Second Systems of American seacoast fortification. It is also to a considerable extent a microcosm of the entire history of American seacoast defense.

CHAPTER I
THE GENESIS OF NATIONAL SEACOAST DEFENSES
1794

In 1794 the United States was in its eighteenth year of independence, its fifth under the Constitution. The Continental Army had been disbanded for a decade, and since June of 1784 the national military establishment, beginning with one under strength regiment, had been concerned primarily with three objectives: protecting the advancing line of frontier settlement from Indian and possibly British encroachment; safeguarding the military stores left from the Revolutionary War; and being ready to take possession of forts along the Canadian frontier as soon as their British garrisons should withdraw, under the terms of the definitive treaty of peace signed in 1783.(1)

For two years the fledgling United States Army had consisted solely of the so-called first American Regiment of Lieutenant Colonel Commandant Josiah Harmer, made up of quotas from Pennsylvania, New Jersey, New York, and Connecticut. Although basically a regiment of infantry, three of its companies were designated and organized as field artillery. Then in 1786 this tiny federal force was temporarily augmented to deal with Shays's Rebellion in Massachusetts, and after the crisis had passed two companies of artillery raised for the emergency were added to the permanent establishment, being combined with the two older companies into a battalion of artillery under the command of Major Commandant John Doughty. This battalion, authorized by an act of 20 October 1786 and retained after the emergency by legislation of 4 April 1787,(2) was the first separate artillery organization of the Regular Army. In 1790 two of its companies were sent to Georgia to garrison the East Florida frontier, while the remaining two companies took part in Harmar's indecisive campaign against the Miami Indians in 1790, and were involved in the disaster to the army under Major General Arthur St. Clair on 4 November 1791. In the latter action the new Major Commandant, William Ferguson, was killed.(3)

The St. Clair massacre prompted a strong reaction by Washington's administration and by Congress, and in 1792 the Army was more than doubled and placed under the command of Major General Anthony Wayne. Extensive recruiting began immediately, and the two artillery companies in Georgia were ordered to the Ohio River frontier to join Wayne's army. Unofficially at first, and then by an order of 4 September 1792, the new force was designated as "The Legion of the United States." Divided into four sub-legions, the Legion included infantry, riflemen, dragoons, and artillery. Henry Burbeck of Massachusetts, the senior captain, succeeded Ferguson as Major Commandant of Artillery.(4)

General Wayne's objective was to organize, train, and discipline the new legion in the months ahead, so that in 1793, or 1794 at the latest, he could lead it into the field against the victorious Miami tribes and their allies. How Wayne accomplished this mission, and soundly defeated the Indians at Fallen Timbers on 20 August 1794, is one of the brightest chapters of early American history. That story, however, is not to be recounted here. For while Anthony Wayne and the Legion were preparing the climactic encounter that would open the Northwest Territory to settlement, a quite different threat was facing the population of the Atlantic seaboard. As would happen again and again over the next century, sudden international crises abruptly turned public attention from the Indian problems to the immediate and vital need to defend the seacoast.

The Threat to the Seacoast

The year 1794 marked a new low in the postwar relations between the United States and Great Britain. Not only was Britain supporting the tribes facing General Wayne in the Northwest, she was also pursuing a maritime policy which threatened American shipping and the neutral rights of the new nation. The fact that Britain's policy was only one facet of her war against Revolutionary France brought scant consolation to Washington's administration; it was, in fact, particularly irritating to the pro-French faction, the anti-Federalists, of the government in Philadelphia. Ironically, the French had been the first offenders; by early 1793, convinced that American neutrality was actually favoring Britain, France had begun seizing American ships and confiscating their cargos–scores of American ships lay under embargo, mainly at Bordeaux, for nearly a year. But every time that France stepped on American toes and seemed about to rouse concerted bipartisan action in Philadelphia, the British committed some even more distasteful acts against American rights and sensibilities, transferring American ire to the old enemy.

The real difficulties started in the West Indies. In normal times France reserved to her own ships the trade with her Caribbean colonies, but with the Royal Navy harassing French trade routes and the colonies facing starvation, France relaxed the old restrictions and welcomed American merchantmen. Such an opportunity was not to be missed, and American ships by the hundreds sailed for French colonial ports. The reaction in London was swift and predictable: Britain activated at once the policy she had enunciated in 1756, that neutral nations in time of war might not open trade routes not previously used in peacetime. Britain's first move, on 8 June 1793, was to issue an Order in Council authorizing the seizure and reimbursed confiscation of all neutral food cargos destined for ports under French control. Five months later, on 6 November, as a British fleet and army were sent against the French West Indies, a more restrictive Order in Council authorized the seizure of vessels carrying the produce of a French colony, or supplies destined for such colony. This meant that private French property in neutral American bottoms could be seized, conflicting directly with the American position that "free ships make free goods." Moreover, this Order in Council was not promulgated until December, and its sudden application caught the better part of 300 American vessels, unarmed and unsuspecting, in or near French colonial waters. About 250 of these ships were seized, with what seemed unusual callousness on the part of Royal Navy captains; roughly half of these were condemned by admiralty courts in the British West Indies, and many of the crews were either thrown into miserable jails or, worse, impressed into the Royal Navy. This was a rude shock to American ship owners, who had been enjoying much-needed prosperity since the opening of Anglo-French hostilities, and their cries of outrage sounded the length of the seaboard.(5)

For the moment, at least, the United States was united in anti-British wrath. The frontier regions had long been convinced that only war could stop British support of Indian depredations along the Ohio; now the seaboard population was raging that only war could end British interference with vital American shipping. But to declare war against Britain would be to invite attack by the Royal Navy, at the very least by destructive raids on American harbors and seacoast towns. Any reaction to this threat would have to be almost purely defensive, for the only armed force the nation possessed, beyond its rudimentary state militias, was even then preparing to meet the Indians in the Northwest Territory. Nevertheless, plans were hastily formulated to begin construction of six warships, and Congress began at once to explore the problem of how best to defend the ports and the long and exposed maritime frontier of the country against British naval raids and possibly even full-scale invasion.

Initial Seacoast Defense Legislation

In view of the continuing cool relations with Great Britain after the Treaty of Paris, it is surprising that none of the plans for a postwar military establishment considered the necessity of defending the maritime frontier. Before the war the individual colonies had made their own arrangements, such as they were, for defending their coasts and harbors; Boston, Newport, Philadelphia, and Charleston had constructed coastal-defense fortifications, some of them quite elaborate, but after the fall of Quebec in 1759 almost all efforts ceased. After 1775 the states continued to provide their own seacoast defenses, and the postwar planners of the Confederation era seemingly assumed that the individual states would continue to perform this function if necessity required.(6)

There had, in fact, been one brief consideration of seacoast defenses immediately after the war. A committee including Alexander Hamilton and James Madison had solicited the views of senior officers of the Continental Army as to a proper peacetime military establishment, and the Chief Engineer, the French Major General Louis Duportail, had mentioned the subject in passing. Duportail was adamant that the engineers and the artillerists of any postwar army be united under one head, insisting that their "preliminary knowledge" was the same. He recommended a peacetime force of two regiments of artillerists and engineers, but added that "if the United States are to have fortified harbors, what I am proposing will be insufficient."(7) But even Duportail's two regiments were considered too great a strain on American postwar finances and the idea of additional troops for seacoast defense received no consideration. The committee finally recommended one regiment of artillery "into which regiment the engineers will be incorporated, the consolidated body to be called the Corps of Engineers."(8) But even this modest force failed to gain acceptance, and in the end the only artillery of any sort in the peacetime establishment consisted of the two companies in Harmar's First American Regiment.

By the beginning of 1794, then, there was hardly a coastal fortification in serviceable condition from Castine to Savannah; indeed, only Castle Island in Boston, Goat Island in Newport, and Mud Island below Philadelphia had fortifications even worth repairing. Nor was there in the federal military establishment of 1794 any source of trained soldiers to man the heavy guns of a coast-defense fort. The four artillery companies with the Legion, Major Burbeck's battalion, were artillery in little more than name; they manned the tiny howitzers in the field and the light guns in the frontier forts, but technically they were little more than infantrymen, entirely untrained either in constructing seacoast fortifications or in serving the heavy guns required by seacoast artillery.

On 20 January 1794, at the height of apprehension over possible raids by the Royal Navy, Congress appointed a committee to investigate hurriedly the problem of defending at least the principal harbors of the Atlantic seaboard. The committee studied the matter for five weeks, calling upon such expert advice as was near at hand. As a first step, the committee faced the delicate political problem of deciding which of the major ports should have priority for construction of defenses; after that came the greater problems of constructing adequate works, and of manning them properly.

Reporting to Congress on 28 February, the committee recommended 16 harbors and ports as requiring first-priority defenses. Perhaps wisely, no priorities within the 16 were specified; they were simply listed from north to south along the seaboard:

Portland, Maine District	New York City
Portsmouth, New Hampshire	Philadelphia, Pennsylvania
Cape Ann, Massachusetts	Baltimore, Maryland
Salem, Massachusetts	Norfolk, Virginia
Marblehead, Massachusetts	Ocracoke Inlet, North Carolina
Boston, Massachusetts	Wilmington, North Carolina
Newport, Rhode Island	Charleston, South Carolina
New London, Connecticut	Savannah, Georgia

The report added that the fortifications to be erected should be sufficient to protect the ports and harbors "against surprise by naval armaments," rather than against full-scale invasion, and concluded that "the parapets of the batteries and redoubts should be formed of earth"–probably a wise decision in view of the need for haste. The committee also recommended that instead of requiring the several states to man their own defenses, the fortifications to be erected should be garrisoned by "troops in the pay of the United States."(9) It was the early acceptance of this principle that paved the way for the creation of a federal corps of artillerists and engineers.

If the selection of the areas to be defended was a political decision, the types of works to be constructed and the weapons to be emplaced in them were matters reflecting the state of the art of seacoast defense at the end of the 18th century. In general, there was during this period very little difference in design between seacoast forts and frontier forts–both almost always reflected the basic designs immortalized by the French Marshal de Vauban in the late 17th century. The key feature of the Vauban system was the bastion built onto each corner of the four- or five-sided fort, allowing the defender to sweep with fire the walls–or "curtains"–between the bastions. Another Vauban signature was an elaborate system of outer works, designed to keep the enemy, and particularly his artillery, away from the main fort. The Vauban system was adopted by almost every military engineer of the western world during the early 18th century; French-speaking engineers worked from Vauban's own works, while English-speaking engineers could utilize the translation and updating of Vauban's works published in London in 1746 by John Muller as *A Treatise Containing the Elements of Fortification*. Essentially, all fortifications of the Vauban school were "horizontal" structures; they presented to enemy artillery the least possible visible target, and were designed so that enemy cannon balls would either bury themselves in the outer earthen slope, or would ricochet from the slope to pass harmlessly over the main fort. Forts emplaced to protect the seacoast or navigable rivers usually had external batteries of guns behind earth embankments close to the shore, known as water batteries; while the larger guns of the main fort engaged enemy ships at long range, the guns of the water batteries provided a heavy volume of close-in fire of smaller calibers.

A major factor in designing coast-defense forts was the possibility that enemy ships might land sailors or marines some distance away, and attack the fort from its landward sides. For this reason all-around defense had to be provided, which explains to some extent the continued reliance on the Vauban system, even to including a ditch or moat around the main fort. Where land attack was unlikely, as against a fort on a small island, the fort was often designed as an unbastioned "star" of five or more sides. In theory, the main fort would be sited on high ground, so that its guns could employ plunging fire, dropping solid shot onto the decks of enemy vessels with increased force; at the same time the water batteries, firing almost horizontally, could ricochet shot off the surface of the water into the sides of the wooden ships–a particularly effective technique using "hot shot," solid shot heated to a glowing red in furnaces at the batteries. As to the material from which the main fort was constructed, much depended upon availability both of time and locally available material. Generally the most effective material for the seaward faces of coastal forts was plain earth, providing it was adhesive enough to retain its form. Lacking good quality earth, the defenses could be faced and shored with timbers, but timbers would be smashed by solid shot, while adhesive earth tended to absorb the shot with little damage. As time permitted, more elaborate walls could be constructed of brick or stone, but in 1794, considering the need for haste as well as economy, American military experts felt that good adhesive earth, properly sloped and then sodded or seeded with a tough binding grass, was the best material available.(10)

The guns to be mounted in these earthen forts depended entirely upon availability. A considerable number of guns, howitzers, and mortars, of both European importation and American manufacture, remained in War Department stores after the Revolutionary War, but most of them were too light for coast-defense purposes. Military opinion held that 24- and 32- pounders—designated by the weight of their solid shot—would be most useful, but a return of ordnance stores in December 1793 showed no 32-pounders in storage. On hand, however, were 15 24-pounders (12 iron and 3 brass) and 36 iron 18-pounders, the next largest size. Although some of the available heavy mortars and field howitzers, which fired hollow explosive shells, could be used in an emergency, it was clear that additional heavy guns would have to be cast at private foundries as soon as possible. The mixture of brass and iron weapons in the American inventory at this time was about equal, but brass weapons were on the way out. Brass gun–"brass" being about what was later known as "bronze"–were more expensive, but there was less danger of their bursting. Lack of the ingredients for brass during the Revolution had forced increasing reliance on iron, which was plentiful and of good quality, and all of the guns cast for the 1794 emergency were of iron. Although brass field guns came back during the Civil War, for the seacoast artillery iron, first cast and later wrought, became the standard in 1794, and no other metal was ever used for heavy American seacoast cannon.(11) Wooden carriages for the cannon were usually constructed at the forts in which they were to be mounted, for there was no standardization of height of parapet or width of embrasures in the forts of this period. Although of many designs, gun carriages were of two basic types in 1794: "barbette" carriages, very similar to field carriages, for guns mounted to fire over a parapet, and "casemate" carriages, for those relatively few guns that would be mounted to fire through an embrasure in the walls of the fort.

The early 1794 Congressional committee report went into surprising detail as to the requirements for fortifications at each location, including magazines and blockhouses or barracks for the troops. Obviously the committee had received expert advice, but no sources were acknowledged. Undoubtedly the Secretary of War, Henry Knox, former Chief of Artillery of the Continental Army, had been consulted, and Knox probably sought advice in turn from several former French officers who had returned to the United States after the outbreak of the French Revolution. The wartime Inspector General, Baron von Steuben, assisted in defense surveys in New York, apparently at his own expense.(12) In sum, the committee report estimated that the 16 ports and harbors would require a total of 445 guns to be manned by 26 officers and 670 men. Having located about 150 guns in the several federal arsenals, the committee decided to authorize the casting of 200 new cannon; the remaining 95 needed could be provided by the states involved. The assumption that 445 guns could be manned by 670 soldiers was curious, suggesting that these men were to be primarily caretakers; whether full gun crews were to be made up from local militia companies, or from some unspecified federal source, was not indicated. The report did state that if the proposed forts were to be garrisoned by troops from Wayne's Legion, then their cost was included in War Department estimates for 1794; if new troops were to be raised, the cost would be just over $90,000 a year. The committee's unfamiliarity with the complexities of heavy artillery was apparent: "It will not escape notice," the report concluded, "that the proposed troops are not artillery, but infantry. It is, however, supposed, that some of the artillery officers in service might be used on the present occasion, and that part of the infantry officers might be chosen for the purpose, who would soon acquire a tolerable degree of knowledge in the use of cannon."(13)

Congressional debate on the proposed legislation began on 5 March, based generally on the committee recommendations, but adding to the list of sites four localities: Wilmington, Delaware; Alexandria, Virginia; Georgetown, South Carolina; and St. Mary's, Georgia. The bill passed both houses and the President signed on 20 March the first legislation for defense of the maritime frontier in American history, "An Act to provide for the Defence of certain Ports and Harbors in the United States."(14) The act designated the sites for fortifications, authorized the President to employ such federal troops as necessary to garrison the proposed forts, provided for cession by the states or purchase from private citizens of the necessary land, and authorized the procurement of 200 new cannon, half to be 32-pounder guns and half to be 24-pounders. In a companion appropriations bill the next day, Congress set aside $76,000 for construction of fortifications, including land acquisition, and $96,000 for the purchase of guns and ammunition. In May, after vigorous representation by its citizens, the town of Annapolis in Maryland was added to the priority list; the following month, after the hard facts of construction expense had been assessed, Congress passed a supplemental appropriation of $30,000.(15)

It was now up to the Secretary of War to find qualified engineers to prepare detailed plans for the proposed works, and to superintend their construction. As Henry Knox well knew, almost no native Americans were qualified for such specialized work. The Corps of Engineers of the Continental Army had been composed almost entirely of French officers, from General Duportail down, and the artillery officers who had served under Knox were not experienced either in construction of seacoast fortifications or in the techniques of heavy artillery. The one officer of the Legion with some background was Major Commandant Burbeck, whose boyhood had been spent with his father in Royal Artillery coastal garrisons, but Burbeck was fully occupied with the Legion on the eve of a critical campaign, and there is no evidence that he was considered.

Secretary Knox's search, however, soon unearthed the fact that there were in the United States in early 1794 perhaps a dozen Frenchmen who had served as engineer or artillery officers either with Rochambeau's forces or in the Continental Army. They had returned to France after the war to resume their professional duties in the army of Louis XVI, and had soon found themselves embroiled in the egalitarian turmoil of the French Revolution. By 1792 at least two of these officers, and probably others, were serving with French forces in Santo Domingo, and during the spring and summer of 1793 they fled to the United States to escape the long arm of the Terror. These and others made their presence known to their old friend General Knox, and this unexpected availability of French talent persuaded the Secretary of War to employ seven of the former officers as engineers for the construction of the newly-authorized fortifications. Beginning on 29 March, Knox offered appointments as "temporary engineers" for specific sections of the coastline to the following:

> Etienne Bechet de Rochefontaine - New England
> Charles Vincent - New York City
> Pierre Charles L'Enfant - Philadelphia and Wilmington, Delaware
> John Jacob Ulrich Rivardi – Baltimore and Norfolk
> John Vermonnet - Annapolis and Alexandria
> Nicholas Francis Martinon- North Carolina
> Paul Hyacinthe Perreault - South Carolina and Georgia

Of these, Rochefontaine and Rivardi were to prove the most effective, and both would become officers in the federal establishment. L'Enfant had already achieved some prominence in designing the new Federal City on the Potomac, but he had also shown himself unable or unwilling to stay within the cost estimates provided by Congress.

Secretary Knox sent very detailed instructions to each of these gentlemen, including their relations with the governors of the states concerned, and passed on the detailed recommendations of the Congressional committee, although he was careful to give some leeway to the experts within the limits of the funds appropriated. Knox decided that these engineers should not become part of the military establishment, at least at that time, and pointed out that "it is explicitly to be understood by you, that the employment is only temporary, and not conferring or involving any military rank whatever."(16)

These seven temporary engineers scattered to their assigned regions during the summer of 1794. Their success or failure would depend not only on their own abilities, but also upon the degree of cooperation they received from state authorities and local landowners. The matter of ownership of the land under certain forts and jurisdiction over the forts, particularly when not actually manned by federal troops, posed constitutional problems that in some instances lingered for years. To some extent, then, these foreign-born engineers became pioneers in federal-state relations; in the absence of precedents, they succeeded or failed through their own personalities and persuasiveness.

Subsequent writers have referred to the defenses constructed during the decade beginning in 1794 as the "First System" of American seacoast fortifications.(17) As will be seen, fortifications construction during this decade was based on two entirely separate impulses, generated by two different threats to the national security. For convenience, the construction effort that began in 1794 will be called the First Phase of the First System.

Initiation of the First-Phase Fortifications

The progress of fortifications construction during this First Phase can be traced in general terms through the reports of the Secretary of War to the appropriate committees of Congress. Although the War Department records were destroyed in a fire in November 1800, the Congressional copies were preserved, including two comprehensive reports prepared by Secretary Knox just before he left office at the end of 1794. The adequacy of Knox's reports, of course, depended upon the degree of completeness and accuracy of the reports submitted to him by the seven temporary engineers.(18)

Stephen Rochefontaine, as he quickly anglicized his name, accomplished his basic surveys from Portland to New London during the spring and summer of 1794, an outstanding effort considering the distances involved. A summary of Rochefontaine's work is instructive not only as an illustration of the French engineer's talents and energy, but also as a brief indication of the state of existing fortifications, many dating from the colonial period, on or near which the new forts were to be built. In Portland, in the Maine District, for example, Rochefontaine decided to build upon the ruins of old fort Allen, constructed on Munjoy's Hill in 1776, and gained approval of the selectmen to purchase four acres containing the ruins for the sum of $68. His plan provided for repairing the fort as an enclosed work with parapets supported by stone walls and sod, adding a brick barracks with a bombproof powder magazine underneath; the fort would be connected by a covered communication way to a water battery near the harbor edge. It was Rochefontaine's idea that the water battery would mount 10 heavy guns on seacoast carriages, while the main fort would be armed only with 6- and 12- pounders mounted on "travelling" carriages–probably so as to be moved to threatened points along the nearby coast. (Fort Allen retained its old name until 1797, when it was renamed Fort Sumner, in honor of newly-elected Governor Increase Sumner of Massachusetts.)(19)

In Portsmouth, New Hampshire's only port, Rochefontaine decided to rebuild an old colonial ruin dating back at least to 1665. Known after the Glorious Revolution as Fort William and Mary, it was located on New Castle Island in the harbor; it had been demolished by local patriots in 1775, although during the Revolution the ruins had been dignified by the name of Fort Hancock. The old site commanded the entrance to the Piscataqua River, and on it Rochefontaine erected a work of masonry and sod, with a small citadel or barracks, designed to take seven heavy guns on seacoast carriages. (The fort was still called William and Mary locally, but federal authorities simply referred to the "works at Portsmouth" until 1801, when the name of Fort Constitution was adopted.)(20)

Three sites on the Massachusetts coast north of Boston had been selected by Congress, each based on colonial ruins. For the defense of Cape Ann, the selectmen of Gloucester were insistent that Rochefontaine rebuild the ruins on Fort Point near the head of Gloucester harbor. He complied with plans for a fort to mount eight guns on seacoast carriages, with a separate citadel, but the fort was not named, no money was appropriated after 1795, and no further work was done in Gloucester harbor during the First Phase.(21)

In Salem Rochefontaine had his choice of three colonial ruins, and in consultation with the town meeting he selected Fort William on the west side of the harbor entrance, which was ceded to the United States later in 1794. Rochefontaine erected an enclosed work of masonry and sod with a brick citadel and magazine, designed to take six medium guns on seacoast carriages and four light guns on travelling carriages. (The fort was called Fort William, at least locally, until 1799, when it was renamed Fort Pickering in honor of Salem's famous son, Secretary of State–and former Secretary of War–Timothy Pickering.)(22) In Marblehead, again, the selected site was the ruins first called Fort Head and later Fort Sewall, on Jack's Point at the western side of the harbor entrance. The town meeting ceded the public land, and added an adjacent lot for $310. Rochefontaine rebuilt Fort Sewall as a battery of masonry and sod with a brick citadel, designed to mount six heavy guns on seacoast carriages and four light guns on travelling carriages.(23)

Congress had envisioned a major fortifications effort in Boston Harbor, not only because of the importance of that port, but also because there were two existing fortifications from colonial days in above-average condition. About 1701 the earlier work on Castle Island had been demolished and a substantial new fort constructed of brick cemented with mortar made of burnt oyster shells; named Castle William, after William III, it eventually mounted over 100 guns, and prior to the Revolution it had been the second most powerful fortress–after Louisbourg in Nova Scotia–in the British colonies. A second fortification, old Fort Warren, had been erected on Governor's Island. Congress planned to refurbish Castle William to take 36 guns and to mount 12 guns on Governor's Island, and had earmarked nearly $9,000 for the two sites. But the commonwealth balked at ceding the islands to the United States, partly because Castle William was being used as a prison and the governor did not think it proper to allow federal fortifications to be erected there.(24) The War Department lost interest in Boston for the moment, and after providing some $2,000 for limited repairs to Castle William, turned the problem of defense of the harbor over to local authorities. (The refurbished fort was briefly named Fort Adams after Governor Samuel Adams, but in 1799, in the next phase of construction, it became Fort Independence.)

The harbor of Newport, Rhode Island, at the entrance to Narragansett Bay, had been fortified in the latter months of the war, particularly after the French forces left for Yorktown in 1781. The colonial fort on Goat Island had been armed by the state, named Fort Washington, and in 1792 mounted ten guns, including three 24-pounders; separate batteries were erected at Pawtuxet, and on North, Brenton's, Field, and Kettle Points. The 1794 Congressional report called for eight guns on Goat Island, but Henry Knox thought this inadequate, and instructed Rochefontaine to refurbish Fort Washington to take 16 guns, 18- and 24-pounders on seacoast carriages. In addition, Rochefontaine constructed a battery at Howland's Ferry, at the north end of Rhode Island, for eight 18- and 24-pounders on seacoast carriages, and designated two positions behind the town for guns on travelling carriages.(25) (In 1798 Fort Washington was renamed Fort Wolcott in honor of the late wartime governor, Oliver Wolcott.)

Congressional plans for the mouth of the Thames River in Connecticut called for fortifications at New London and across the river at Groton. Even before Rochefontaine's plans were completed, the citizens of New London turned out to repair the wartime Fort Trumbull, which Knox described as a citadel "surrounded with Batteries and Glacis to cover it from the direct fire of Ships of War and to scour the entrance of the harbour ... with Cannon and Musketry."(26) The bulk of the new construction was at Fort Trumbull–named for Colonel Jonathan Trumbull, a member of Congress in 1794–which was to be provided with six 18- and 24-pounders on seacoast carriages, about a third of its capacity. Across the Thames a fort of earth and sod was begun on Groton Heights, with a water battery planned, but it was left unfinished during this phase of construction.(27)

To temporary engineer Charles Vincent were entrusted the initial defenses of New York City, one of the most important ports and certainly one of the most difficult to defend. The Congressional committee wanted to erect works on the tip of Manhattan Island, on Governors Island in the harbor, and at Paulus Hook across the Hudson; New York authorities, following Von Steuben's survey, concluded quite accurately that the harbor could best be defended at the Narrows, by fortifying two key points, one in Brooklyn and one on Staten Island. In order to liquidate part of its debt to the federal governments New York undertook to fortify the Narrows as a state project, appropriating $75,000 for the purpose. Vincent concentrated on the inner harbor, and Knox reported that "Works have accordingly been contemplated for Governors, Bedloes, and Oyster Islands and ... it is expected that fifty heavy Cannon and Mortars may be placed there for use this Autumn."(28) The citizens of New York contributed their own labor to erect works on the Battery at the tip of Manhattan and on Governors Island, the site of a colonial fort. The refurbished work on Governors Island was named Fort Jay, after the Chief Justice, and an infantry company of Wayne's Legion, fitting out at West Point, was diverted from the frontier to provide Fort Jay's first garrison. The Paulus Hook plan was abandoned, probably because it would have involved negotiations with New Jersey, and instead batteries were erected on both Bedlow's (as then usually spelled) and Oyster (later Ellis) Islands in the bay. Over the next year and a half federal expenditures were only about $17,500, or less than a quarter of New York's appropriation for the Narrows, and Secretary Knox admitted that only a bare beginning had been made in fortifying the great port.(29) (As part of the New York project, Vincent undertook repairs to Forts Putnam and Clinton at West Point; these forts had long guarded the middle reaches of the Hudson, but they were too far inland to be considered seacoast defenses, and no further reference will be made to these forts at West Point.)

The defenses of the Delaware River were of particular interest to the Congressional committee in 1794, for an enemy vessel sailing up the Delaware would threaten the capital at Philadelphia. The plan, then, called for refurbishing the fort on Mud Island, just below Philadelphia, to take 48 guns, and Secretary Knox agreed, remembering the valiant delaying action against a British fleet in 1777 by the works known as Fort Mud, or "the Mud Fort." The temporary engineer, Pierre Charles L'Enfant, began repairing the old fort, and on 15 April 1795 Pennsylvania ceded the land to the United States; at the time of the cession the fort was renamed Fort Mifflin in honor of Governor Thomas Mifflin, a wartime Quartermaster General. By early 1796 the large sum of $25,000 had been expended in repairs to Fort Mifflin and in constructing a large pier on a nearby sand bar as the foundation for a water battery. L'Enfant also made preliminary surveys at Wilmington, farther down the Delaware, but could not come to terms with the governor as to the best location and scope of the work. Knox had never favored a Wilmington site, preferring a battery farther down the river for purely warning purposes, and in the end the Wilmington project was abandoned.(30)

The arrangements for planning what might be called collectively the defenses of Chesapeake Bay were unduly cumbersome. The defenses of Norfolk, at the entrance to the bay, and Baltimore, near the head, were assigned to J.J. Ulrich Rivardi, as he signed himself, while Annapolis and Alexandria–the latter just below the new Federal City on the Potomac–were entrusted to John Vermonnet. Under this division of responsibility, each engineer had to negotiate with the authorities of two states. Vermonnet

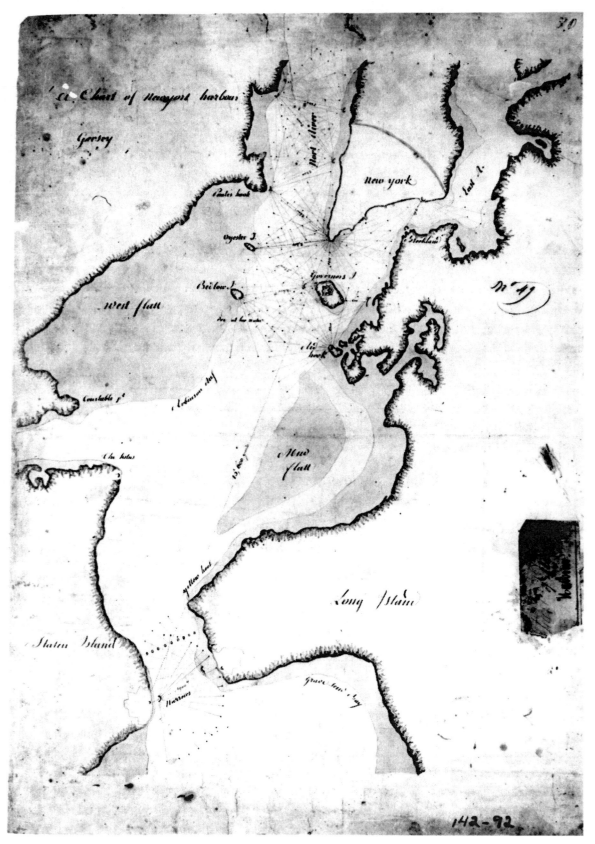

Engineering Chart of New York Harbor, Showing Fort Jay on Governors Island and Batteries on
Oyster (Ellis) and Bedlow's Islands, ca. 1799
Page 19

spent some $6,000 on surveys and preliminary construction at both Annapolis and Alexandria, but he reported poor soil conditions at Annapolis and various difficulties at Alexandria, and both sites were temporarily abandoned.(31)

Baltimore was quite a different matter. Before the end of 1793 the Maryland legislature had authorized the governor to allow the federal government to erect a fort or any similar work on the site of a wartime battery on Whetstone Point on the Patapsco River in the outer harbor. The quality of the soil at Whetstone Point proved excellent, but meager appropriations forced Rivardi to limit himself to rebuilding the existing work, which consisted of an upper and lower battery and a poorly-designed redoubt of star pattern. While Rivardi was away at Norfolk, much of the construction was performed by volunteer citizen labor, including a company of militia artillery. The excellent cooperation and progress unloosened Congressional purse-strings, and by the end of 1795 over $12,000 had been spent at what was called Whetstone Fort.(32) (During the second phase of construction in 1798 the fort was renamed to honor the then Secretary of War, and was to achieve lasting fame as Fort McHenry.)

Plans for the defense of Norfolk called for 24 guns in the immediate vicinity of the town, with apparently no thought of trying to deny access to Hampton Roads and the James River. Rivardi accordingly proceeded only to defend the mouth of the Elizabeth River, by repairing small works on each side of the river. Fort Nelson, on the west bank, had been built prior to 1779 to protect Norfolk, Portsmouth, and the Gosport navy yard; its counterpart on the Norfolk side, Fort Norfolk, was an older colonial work. Secretary Knox was in favor of fortifying Craney Island, a strategic location in the mouth of the Elizabeth River, but this would have added $15,000 to the estimate, and Knox left office shortly thereafter without pursuing the Craney Island site.(33)

The long and difficult coastline of North Carolina presented many problems, including land acquisition, to temporary engineer Nicholas Martinon. In a burst of enthusiasm, the North Carolina legislature in July 1794 had ceded to the United States certain public lands on Beacon Island in Ocracoke Inlet, on the headland of Cape Hatteras, and on the Cape Fear River below Wilmington. The latter cession, however, included only a portion of the land under an existing colonial fort, and well over a decade was required to clear the full title. Martinon decided to begin at Ocracoke Inlet, the remote and exposed entrance to Pamlico Sound, but the distances were so great along the outer banks south of Cape Hatteras that this area consumed all his time, and by the end of 1794 he had finished planning only for Ocracoke. As it turned out, these efforts were wasted, for the projected fort on Beacon Island was soon abandoned as being too exposed to the sea as well as too far–a good 90 miles–from the nearest inhabitants. Martinon then turned to the defense of the Cape Fear River below Wilmington, utilizing the ruins of old Fort Johnston on the right bank at Smithville; begun during the governorship of Gabriel Johnston, the fort had been completed in 1764 and destroyed by local patriots in 1775. During 1795 Martinon rebuilt the old fort, which retained the name of Fort Johnston, but federal title to the land remained cloudy.(34)

Charleston was the most important seaport in the South, and the Congressional report of 1794 recommended defenses second in scope only to New York City. Three sets of redoubts and batteries were envisioned at Charleston, and as an afterthought another battery was planned to the north, at Georgetown on Winyah Bay. Paul Hyacinthe Perreault, the temporary engineer for both South Carolina and Georgia, surveyed the Georgetown site, but because of its unhealthy location and a disagreement with the owner as to the value of the land, the project was shortly abandoned. In Charleston Harbor the proposed sites belonged to the state, which was reluctant to cede them to the United States, but had no objection to federally-financed repairs. Three forts of the colonial and Revolutionary War periods were well situated, but in need of massive repairs. These were Fort Johnson—not to be con-

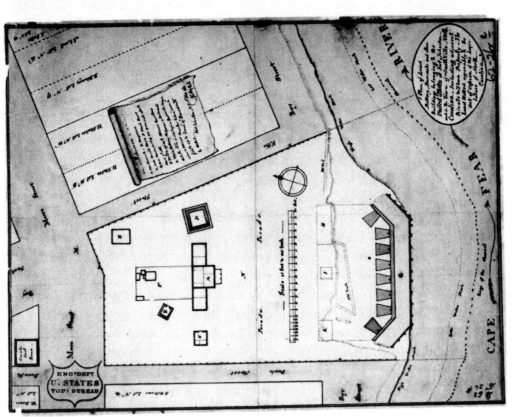

Two often-confused seacoast fortifications

Fort Johnston, below Wilmington, North Carolina

Fort Johnson, Charleston, South Carolina

fused with Fort Johnston in North Carolina—on James Island; Fort Moultrie, on Sullivan's Island at the harbor entrance; and Fort Pinckney, locally called Castle Pinckney, on an island off the city's Battery near its seaward tip. By the end of 1795 Fort Johnson had been repaired, and foundations laid for new works at Fort Moultrie and Fort Pinckney, but after the expenditure of about $20,000 work was suspended, apparently because of the continued failure of South Carolina to cede the land. In Charleston proper, meanwhile, a defensive work was thrown up by local workers, to be known appropriately as Fort Mechanic.(35)

Engineer Perreault had been so busy in South Carolina that by the end of 1794 he had submitted no plans for defenses in Georgia. Initial estimates had called only for defense of the active port of Savannah, but it was subsequently decided to erect a work at the mouth of the St. Mary's River, the boundary with Spanish East Florida. The site selected for Savannah was on Cockspur Island, near the mouth of the Savannah River, where had stood the colonial Fort George, abandoned in 1776. The new fort, constructed during 1795-96, was built of timber and earth enclosed by pickets, designed for only six guns rather than 24 as originally planned; even so, the cost ran to about $8,000. This new work was named Fort Greene, in honor of Major General Nathaniel Greene of the Continental Army, who had died near Savannah in 1786. Construction on the St. Mary's River, where since 1790 there had been a small fort known as Fort St. Tammany, was inhibited by loudly-expressed fears by Governor Quesada of East Florida that the proposed new construction would be directed against Spanish use of the boundary river. In the end only a small battery of timber and earth was thrown up in late 1795 on Point Petre, east of the settlement of St. Mary's, and during this phase it was not given a specific name. (36)

After Congress had voted the funds for construction of a minimum number of seacoast fortifications and of six ships of the line, it went on to reflect the national mood in other legislation. On 26 March 1794, in retaliation against the Orders in Council, Congress supported President Washington in imposing a one-month embargo, later extended to two months, on all shipping in American harbors destined for foreign ports. This embargo applied equally to France and Britain, but soon afterwards the Jeffersonian faction in Congress, capitalizing on the anti-British sentiment, supported legislation to suspend all intercourse with Britain. In the same wave of enthusiasm, Congress on 2 April voted to establish a national armory at Springfield, Massachusetts and an arsenal at Harpers Ferry, Virginia.(37) At the end of March Secretary Knox summed up all these activities in a letter to General Wayne on the frontier. The British attitude, Knox noted "has caused a general alarm throughout the United States and in consequence thereof war with Great Britain has been considered as inevitable. Our Sea Coast is ordered to be fortified … and certain other measures are under the contemplation of Congress for placing the United States in a respectable state of defence."(38)

This "respectable state of defence" was not to be achieved quite as simply as Knox's declaration made it seem. A start had been made toward some sort of seacoast defense, but during this first phase little had been accomplished beyond providing for rehabilitation of old forts protecting the major seaports; long stretches of coastline, particularly in Maine and North Carolina, remained absolutely unprotected, and no provisions had been made for denying the enemy entrance into Chesapeake Bay, which in turn gave access to the important region from Baltimore south to Norfolk. Moreover, while there was not a critical shortage of medium artillery pieces for the newly-authorized seacoast forts, there was indeed a shortage of federal troops to man them. The federal government had accepted at the outset the responsibility for garrisoning the fortifications, and it was now up to the United States to provide the necessary trained troops for that purpose.

CHAPTER II
THE CORPS OF ARTILLERISTS AND ENGINEERS
1794-1795

The Congressional report of 28 February 1794 with its provision that the seacoast fortifications would be garrisoned by troops "in the pay of the United States," could, of course, have been construed to mean local militia called into federal service for specified periods, and paid from the Treasury. Faced with its first threat to the maritime frontier, however, Congress wisely decided to provide for a full-time body of artillerymen to garrison the forts. It was thought at first that a handful of artillery officers of the legion could take charge of the project, but as spring arrived and Anthony Wayne's troops prepared to take the field, it was clear that no artillerists could be spared. Moreover, quite a different type of training would be required for the use of heavy guns against long-range targets, and to accomplish this some experienced artillery and engineer officers would have to be found.

By early April the threat to the seaboard appeared so real that Secretary Knox was obliged to scrape together such Legion recruits as were near the coast and send them "to guard the batteries, for the present, which are to be erected upon the Sea-Coast." President Washington agreed: "If the number of recruits in the Atlantic States can afford a detachment of fifty men to the southward, without too great an exposure of more important objects … that number should be sent thither. And they may be designated for Charleston or Savannah … ."(1) These recruits were marched to Charleston, where they formed the initial garrison of Fort Johnson, and at about the same time a company of infantry recruits marched down from West Point to become the first federal garrison of Fort Jay on Governors Island in New York Harbor.(2)

Impressed with the immediate need for seacoast troops, Congress moved to enact legislation on 9 May creating within the peacetime military establishment a Corps of Artillerists and Engineers. The act authorized the raising of 764 men, who were "to be incorporated into the corps of artillery now in the service" for a total of 992 men, excluding officers. The new corps was to be headed by a lieutenant colonel commandant and was to have four battalions, each commanded by a major, of four companies each. Companies were to consist of "one captain, two lieutenants, two cadets with the pay, clothing and rations of a sergeant, four sergeants, four corporals, forty-two privates, sappers and miners, and ten artificers to serve as privates, and two musicians." The new corps was not to be restricted to seacoast defense, for the act provided that the President "shall cause such proportions of the said corps to serve in the field, on the frontiers, or in the fortifications of the sea-coast, as he shall deem consistent with the public service."(3) The relationship of this new organization to the rest of the Army was nowhere spelled out, but it soon became apparent that the Corps of Artillerists and Engineers, although not part of the Legion, would be under General Wayne's command.

A significant part of this legislation was official recognition of the grade of "cadet," and the allocation of two cadets to each company of artillerists and engineers. The term "cadet" was not new, and potential officers had been assigned as cadets to companies of Harmar's First American Regiment in the 1780s,(4) but legislative recognition of the grade as denoting an officer candidate was to be the first step in the establishment, over the next eight years, of a national military academy. An indication that the new corps was to be a technical one, and that officers as well as cadets would be expected to learn their skills promptly, was a provision in the legislation requiring the Secretary of War to provide, at public expense, "the necessary books, instruments and apparatus, for the use and benefit of the said corps."

Finding suitable officers for the new corps would not be easy, and the problem of appointing field officers for the corps and its three new battalions—excluding Major Burbeck's battalion with the Legion—was deferred for the moment in favor of selecting captains who could at once begin recruiting companies. Secretary Knox, the wartime Chief of Artillery, gave the matter his personal attention, and a week after passage of the legislation wrote to General Wayne that he was seeking captains for three battalions: "suitable characters are sought for as it is hoped this corps will contribute most materially to the future military reputation of the United States. The greatest care will therefore be taken that none but proper characters are appointed."(5)

Unfortunately for Knox's good intentions, there was just not time for the Secretary to locate former junior officers of the wartime artillery. He sought nominations from members of Congress, and tried particularly to select captains from areas which were to have seacoast defenses, hoping that their companies could be recruited in the vicinities of the forts they were to man. By late August Knox had filled the 12 captaincies and 24 lieutenancies of the three new battalions, but as 11 initial appointees declined and had to be replaced, the geographical distribution was not as effective as Knox had planned. The final list was not particularly distinguished; only six of the 12 captains had served as officers in the Continental Army, and of these only two, Alexander Thompson and James Gamble, had served under Knox in the artillery.(6) The two appointees from South Carolina presented an interesting contrast: Captain Michael Kalteisen, wartime state wagonmaster-general, was 65 years old; his lieutenant, George Izard–son of a distinguished family, future general, and in 1794 studying at French military schools–was not quite 18.(7)

One of the difficulties in securing good officers was the changing international situation. In the spring of 1794 the country had reached a peak of indignation against Britain, and at that time it might have been possible to select the best former officers without question. But the creation of the Corps of Artillerists and Engineers came just too late to catch the crest of the patriotic wave. During the summer, for several reasons, the tension began to dissipate. The Federalist administration knew that war with Britain would ruin Alexander Hamilton's economic program, and was relieved when Britain modified the Orders in Council, allowing American ships to resume for a time the thriving trade with the British West Indies. American shipowners were mollified when the Crown made prompt payment for American cargos previously confiscated. And finally the French, retaliating against Britain by seizing American vessels headed for British ports, attracted to themselves much of the indignation hitherto directed against Britain. With no immediate threat of British invasion, the warlike spirit along the seaboard began to die out, and pressure to recruit soldiers for the new seacoast fortifications likewise abated.

In his final report to Congress on the seacoast defenses, Henry Knox urged that the gains of 1794 not be lost. "A Question may be raised," he wrote, "whether a time of peace and general prosperity is not the proper time for a nation to perfect its system of defence … and if so whether permanent fortifications should not now be decided upon." He admitted that construction would be suspended generally during the winter, but felt that most of the defenses could be completed during 1795. And he made a strong plea for the retention of the temporary engineers who had begun construction of the fortifications. "Some of them," he urged, "are Men of great science and the continuance of their services could not fail to be permanently advantageous to a nation possessing so extensive and so exposed a Sea Coast as the United States. The benefits also to be derived from their operating as Preceptors to the Corps of Artillerists and Engineers would amply compensate the expenses of their salaries."(8) Congress was inclined to agree, and resolved on 4 December that the seacoast-defense construction program should be continued, authorizing the President "to give preference, in point of time, to the completion of such of the said fortifications as he may think advisable."(9) No appropriation accompanied this resolution, however, and its net effect was to pass most of the responsibility for construction of fortifications to the President and the Secretary of War.

But Henry Knox, often called the Father of the American Artillery, had reached the end of his public career. He had been Secretary of War for almost a decade, and it was apparent to his associates that he was tired and had lost interest in his work. Pleading personal business in Maine, he had been absent from Philadelphia most of the summer of 1794–while Anthony Wayne and the Legion marched to Fallen Timbers and a whiskey "rebellion" came to a head in western Pennsylvania. At the end of the year Knox resigned as head of the War Department, and retired to private life.

Timothy Pickering as Secretary of War

Knox's resignation sent President Washington back to his list of wartime officers for a successor, but he had culled that list thoroughly in 1792, when he had selected Anthony Wayne to command the legion, and he knew that no wartime officers of Knox's stature were available.(10) He turned, then, to the group of lesser-known men who had rendered outstanding service in administrative rather than command positions. Undoubtedly Washington was seeking a strong administrator with a military background, but with the increasing political factionalism of his second term, he was also looking for a man of solid Federalist persuasion. With these qualifications in mind, there was no reason to look beyond Timothy Pickering of Massachusetts. The native of the port of Salem was then in the fiftieth year of a very active public life. A colonel of militia at the outbreak of the Revolution, Pickering had served successively in the important posts of Adjutant General of the Continental Army (1777-78), member of the Board of War (1778-80), and Quartermaster General (1780-85). Why he was not promoted to general officer rank in the latter position, in which he succeeded Nathaniel Greene, is difficult to justify; possibly his outspoken bluntness did not endear him to some members of Congress. But Pickering was a late bloomer, and the end of the war was only the beginning of his public service. After leaving the Army he settled in Pennsylvania, and was employed several times by the administration as commissioner to various Indian nations, the most recent instance being an abortive attempt to come to terms with the tribes of the Northwest Territory in the summer of 1793.(11)

Taking over Knox's office on 2 January 1795, Pickering was to serve as Secretary of War for little over a year before being called to succeed Edmund Randolph as Secretary of State. During this short tenure Pickering displayed considerably more energy than his portly predecessor, and in many ways more administrative talent; perhaps surprisingly, he adopted a less cautious and more warlike attitude than Knox, both toward the Indian threat and the international complications. It is of particular importance to this work that Pickering, long after he left the War Department, was consulted by and did favors for many officers of the Army, particularly those of the Corps of Artillerists and Engineers who were appointed during Pickering's year as Secretary of War.(12)

One of the first problems facing the new Secretary in January 1795 was to find qualified field officers–a lieutenant colonel commandant and four majors–for the Corps of Artillerists and Engineers. Here, obviously, Pickering benefited from Knox's earlier searches, but as the ultimate selections were not made until Pickering had been in office for two months, he must bear the responsibility. In retrospect, it might have been wise to have found qualified majors to speed the organization of the new companies into battalions, and later to have promoted the most effective of these majors. In theory, the early selection of an energetic, technically qualified, and prestigious commander for the entire corps would have been ideal, but the hard fact was that no such individual was available.

The officer first in consideration for the command of any new artillery unit, based on seniority and total service, would have been the Major Commandant of Artillery of the Legion. By American standards, Henry Burbeck was a qualified artillerist, and he knew enough basic field engineering to construct such modest forts as the Legion needed on the frontier. And Burbeck was from Massachusetts, which would have appealed to both Knox and Pickering. But Burbeck had been far from the seat of government since 1790, first on the East Florida frontier, where he had shown little diplomacy in his dealings with Governor Quesada, and then with the Legion for the Fallen Timbers campaign.(13) And it is doubtful that Burbeck, or any native American, had the degree of engineering knowledge being sought in the man who was to head the new technical corps. So Burbeck was not considered for the top position in 1795, and retained command of the battalion, essentially *field* artillery, that had been formed in 1786.

If native-born expertise was lacking, there were always European applicants. Immediately at hand, in fact, were the French "temporary engineers" whom Knox had employed to plan and supervise the construction of the first seacoast defenses; experienced former officers or engineers of artillery, most of them were quite available for extended military service. From the record, based on results achieved and energy displayed during 1754, it would seem that Rochefontaine, Rivardi, and Vincent had been the most effective, in about that order, and so it appeared to Secretary Pickering. Without perhaps giving much thought to the qualifications of these engineers to command American officers and men, Pickering on 26 February issued commissions and appointments to the first two, naming Stephen Rochefontaine as lieutenant colonel commandant and J.J. Ulrich Rivardi a major of the Corps of Artillerists and Engineers.(14)

If Charles Vincent or any other of the engineers were offered appointments— and no such record has been found—they did not accept. The search for two more majors continued, and another French-born officer was offered and accepted a commission; this was Louis Tousard, an artilleryman and a wounded veteran of distinguished service as a French volunteer with the Continental Army. This seems to have exhausted the French supply, so on 28 February the last vacant majority was conferred on Constant Freeman of Massachusetts, former captain-lieutenant of the Continental Artillery, who had been serving under Secretary Knox as a War Department agent to the federal troops in Georgia.(15) The relative seniority of the four majors was established as Burbeck, Tousard, Rivardi, and Freeman, in that order. As the old battalion of artillery was absorbed into the new corps, Burbeck's title of major commandant lapsed automatically.

The new commander of the Corps of Artillerists and Engineers, Lieutenant Colonel Commandant(16) Stephen Rochefontaine, was just 40 at the time of his appointment. Born Etienne Nicholas Marie Bechet, he acquired the title of Sieur de Rochefontaine about the time he was commissioned a lieutenant of engineers in the Royal Army in 1775, and under this name was one of many young French engineers to volunteer for service in America after the signing of the Franco-American alliance. Arriving in America in May 1778 by way of Santo Domingo, Rochefontaine promptly applied for appointment as major of engineers in the Continental Army. The Board of War—one of whose members was Colonel Timothy Pickering—recommended Rochefontaine to Congress, but thought that a captaincy would be adequate. On 18 September 1778 "Mons. Bechet de Roche Fontaine" was appointed captain in the Corps of Engineers under General Duportail, with rank from 15 May.(17) Rochefontaine's services during the war were generally excellent, particularly at Yorktown, and after Cornwallis's surrender Rochefontaine was one of only two officers for whom General Duportail recommended brevet promotions. General Washington agreed, and on 16 November Captain Rochefontaine received the brevet of major. (Captain Pierre Charles L'Enfant of the same corps was not so honored, and wrote directly to Washington to complain.) Rochefontaine returned to France in late 1783, and was appointed a captain of provincial troops; in 1792 he was named adjutant general of the army in Santo Domingo—in view of the revolutionary fervor of the time, he was known there as Bechet. After the execution of Louis XVI in January 1793, Rochefontaine left French service and returned to the United States, resuming the seignorial "de Rochefontaine" prior to his appointment as temporary engineer for the New England fortifications.(18)

Regrettably little is known of John Jacob Ulrich Rivardi prior to his appointment. Washington later wrote that Major Rivardi "is a Swiss, and was sometime in the Service of Russia."(19) Other clues as to his Swiss origin are letters from Rivardi in 1793 and 1799 bemoaning bitterly the assimilation of Switzerland into the French Republic.(20) When and why Rivardi came to America can only be conjectured; no one of that name is listed as an officer of the Continental Army, nor as an officer of Rochambeau's expeditionary force.(21) It is probable that Rivardi simply emigrated to the United States with his wife,(22) and that his Russian or other military services came to the attention of Henry Knox; he was living in Pennsylvania when Knox offered him the appointment as temporary engineer in 1794. Rivardi's work on the defenses of Baltimore and Norfolk met with general approval, and this apparently led to his appointment as major of artillerists and engineers in 1795.

The other foreign-born major was not primarily an engineer, but a former artillery officer of distinguished record. Anne Louis de Tousard, born in Paris in 1749, was commissioned on graduation from the artillery school at Strasbourg in 1769. During the next eight years he saw service in both artillery and engineers, for during this period in France there was a strong movement to combine the two fields. Tousard was among those recruited by Benjamin Franklin and Silas Deane for General du Coudray's group of artillerists and ordnance specialists, which arrived in America in early 1777. Congress declined to grant Tousard as high a rank as he felt entitled to, and he served as a volunteer, first as an aide-de-camp to Lafayette and then as an artillery officer without formal commission. In August 1778, at Newport, Rhode Island, he was instrumental in capturing a British field piece, but his right arm was so severely wounded that it had to be amputated. In October Congress commended the gallantry of "Monsieur Tousard," awarding him the brevet of lieutenant colonel and granting him a pension of 30 dollars a month for life. Temporarily disabled, Tousard returned to France in 1779, and a year later was reappointed in the French Army as a major. In 1784 he was transferred, as a lieutenant colonel, to Santo Domingo, and in 1788 married the widow of a wealthy planter. Then the French Revolution reached Santo Domingo, and in 1792 Tousard and his regimental commander were arrested for counter-revolutionary sentiments and returned to France for trial. Tousard wrote a pamphlet in his defense, which was published in Philadelphia in 1793 as *Justification of Lewis Tousard Addressed to the National Convention of France*. Released through the intervention of the American minister in 1793, Tousard sailed for the United States to rejoin his family, who had fled Santo Domingo after his arrest. He bought a hundred-acre farm near Wilmington, Delaware, and began the life of a gentleman farmer, but his wife became ill and died in July 1794. Shortly afterward Tousard came to the attention of Henry Knox as a trained artillerist, and on 26 February 1795, just short of his 46th birthday, he was appointed to the Corps of Artillerists and Engineers. At about the same time he was married again, to a lady from Delaware.(23)

Constant Freeman, the last of the field officers appointed in 1795, was born in Boston in 1757. Near the end of 1776 he was appointed lieutenant of an independent artillery corps, which took part in the retreat from Fort Ticonderoga and was later incorporated into the 3d Continental Artillery. Promoted to captain-lieutenant in 1778, Freeman served faithfully in that grade until discharged in June 1783. After the war he worked in a Boston bank, but in 1786 accepted the captaincy of an infantry company raised in Massachusetts in connection with Shays's Rebellion. His company was disbanded at the end of the emergency, and Freeman became a clerk in the state treasurer's office in Boston. He applied to Henry Knox for more interesting work, and in 1789 began a four-year stint as a senior clerk in the War Department. Offered a captaincy in the newly-authorized 2d Infantry in 1791, he declined, apparently assuming that the regiment would be disbanded after St. Clair's campaign. In August 1793 Knox appointed Freeman as War Department agent in South Carolina and Georgia, where he spent most of his time in liaison between Georgia authorities and the federal troops in that state. In the summer of 1794 his younger brother Nehemiah, 25, was appointed lieutenant in the Corps of Artillerists and Engineers, and Constant sought a similar appointment. In view of his wartime service and his more recent knowledge of War Department problems, he was selected to be the junior major of the new corps, just after his 38th birthday. Various War Department duties kept Freeman in Georgia and South Carolina until the spring of 1797, so that he was not to take part in the initial organizational pains of his new corps.(24)

Henry Knox's plan of selecting officers for the corps on a geographical basis had been sound, but it broke down when several captains and a third of the lieutenants declined appointments. In Knox's plan the 1st Battalion was to remain with the Legion as field artillery, at least for the time being; the 2d Battalion was to garrison the seacoast fortifications of New England, the 3d Battalion the forts from New York through Maryland, and the 4th Battalion those from Virginia through Georgia. But by the time all vacancies had been filled, including promotion of two veteran lieutenants from Burbeck's battalion and the appointment as lieutenants of several outstanding noncommissioned officers of the Legion, the idea of assigning officers to their home states was impracticable. The records indicate that Secretary Pickering then fell back on the early wartime system, inherited from the British Army, whereby companies were assigned within the corps based on the relative rank of their captains. This was a cherished method of preserving seniority, and had worked well when regiments raised in one geographic area maintained their integrity over the years; applied to companies raised from Maine to Georgia, for service at widely-separated locations, it was to prove a cumbersome and inappropriate system. Under this method—excluding Burbeck's 1st Battalion on the frontier—the company raised by the senior captain became the 1st Company of the 2d Battalion (Tousard's), the second-ranking captain had the 1st Company of the 3d Battalion (Rivardi's), and so on, with the junior captain commanding the 4th Company of the 4th Battalion (Freeman's). The same system was applied initially in assigning lieutenants to companies, but the importance of their recruiting in their home areas took precedence and assignment of subalterns by seniority was soon abandoned. The detailed organization of the Corps of Artillerists and Engineers in mid-1795 is shown in Appendix A.(35)

Initial Garrisons for the Seacoast Forts

The gradual relaxation of the state of near-hostilities with Great Britain that began during the summer of 1794 not only curbed the enthusiasm of prospective recruits, but also brought a slowdown in construction of even the most rudimentary seacoast defenses. The result was that relatively few of the fortifications were garrisoned by federal troops during this first phase, roughly 1794-1797, of the First System construction.

Throughout New England, where construction or repair of seven defensive sites—excluding Boston—was under way, the garrisoning of the fortifications was left entirely to local militia units throughout 1794 and most of 1795. The four captains appointed from New England—Frederick Frye, William Littlefield, Decius Wadsworth, and Donald G. Mitchell—were at least partly successful in recruiting companies from their home states, but there is no record that they were directed to establish garrisons during this period at any of the defenses from Portland to New London.

New York was a different story. This important port, which had endured British occupation for so long during the war, was determined to have a federal garrison on Governors Island, and it was for this reason that an infantry company of the Legion had been posted there in 1794. It was probably the influence of New York's senior representative in the federal government, Secretary of the Treasury Alexander Hamilton, who was temporarily heading the War Department during Henry Knox's prolonged absence during the summer and fall, that kept the infantrymen at the post, soon to be known as Fort Jay, until they were relieved in early 1795 by a newly-recruited company of artillerists and engineers commanded by Captain Alexander Thompson of New York. From that time forward the fort on Governors Island was continuously manned by federal troops.(26)

"Fort Mud" in the Delaware, shortly to be called Fort Mifflin, was in comparatively good condition in 1794, and with Congress sitting in Philadelphia, it was clear that the defense of that city would have a certain priority. Fragmentary records available indicate that Captain James Gamble of the new federal corps was ordered to recruit his company in and around Philadelphia, and to provide a garrison for the fort on Mud Island as soon as possible. Captain Gamble's first post was to be his last, for after organizing his company and assuming command of the garrison of Fort Mifflin, he became ill during the summer of 1795 and died on 20 August, on sick leave at his home in nearby Lancaster County. (27) Baltimore likewise had a garrison by late 1794, recruited by Captain James Bruff for the newly-repaired fort at Whetstone Point. Bruff had been a major in the Maryland militia when appointed to the Corps of Artillerists and Engineers, and for the next year or so he continued to look to his state executive for guidance.

In several letters to Governor John H. Stone, Captain Bruff left a good description of some of the problems facing the commander of a harbor defense fort at the end of the 18th century. There being no federal naval establishment, Bruff took it upon himself to act as a sort of Port Captain; he drew the governor's attention to the fact that at the moment the port of Baltimore had no health officer, and recommended that his attached surgeon's mate, Richard Griffith, act in that capacity. Bruff advised the governor that Secretary Knox had authorized him to communicate with the governor "respecting regulations necessary to be established at this Fort for the Defense, Health, and safety of the Town and Harbor," and with commendable initiative submitted to the state executive his proposed regulations for the conduct of vessels entering and leaving the port.(28) The captain was particularly anxious for authority to search outbound vessels, for deserters from his company at Fort Whetstone were being signed on as seamen of departing ships, both American and foreign. By April 1795 he advised the governor that of his original garrison of 101 men, 28 had deserted: "Several of these are known to be taken off by Sailors - others have been seen in Sailors shops at their rendezvous and never since heard of."(29)

The twin fortifications on the Elizabeth River at Norfolk, Fort Nelson and Fort Norfolk, were probably partially garrisoned during 1794 and early 1795, for Fort Norfolk was used as a recruiting rendezvous by Captain Richard S. Blackburn, who was raising his company in the area. Two of Blackburn's lieutenants found early graves there, for according to a later recapitulation of officers of artillerists and engineers, Lieutenant William L. Grayson "died Norfolk 1794" and Lieutenant Carey M. Carter was "killed Norfolk 1794."(30)

Fort Johnston, on the Cape Fear River in North Carolina, was not garrisoned by federal troops during this period. Repairs had not gotten started until well into 1795, and the officers appointed from North Carolina— Captain Griffith J. McRee and his two lieutenants—were ordered to West Point prior to mid-1795, as will be discussed below.

In Charleston Harbor, Fort Johnson was one of the first fortifications to be garrisoned by federal troops, possibly as early as June 1794, when a detachment of 50 Legion recruits was diverted there for defense of the city. They may have come under state control momentarily, until the appointment of Michael Kalteisen of Charleston as captain of artillerists and engineers in July. Kalteisen, 65 when appointed, took command of the garrison of Fort Johnson during the summer of 1794 and held it continuously until his death, still a captain, in 1807.(31)

No federal garrison was established in Savannah during this first phase; no Georgia captain had accepted appointment, and Fort Greene was not to be completed until 1796. There were several companies of federal troops in Georgia, but their mission was to guard the Spanish and Creek frontiers. Despite a brief flurry of activity at Point Petre, no coastal defenses worthy of the name were erected at the mouth of the St. Mary's River, and only the tiny infantry garrison at Fort St. Tammany could be considered as guarding the entrance to the river, the international boundary.

Thus came to a halt the construction and manning of seacoast fortifications against attack by Great Britain, the initial impulse of the First System of coastal defenses. The next phase of that system would begin in 1798, directed against a different enemy. In the interim the senior officers of the Corps of Artillerists and Engineers, with headquarters at West Point, would make an effort to educate their officers and cadets in the intricacies of the new technical corps of the Army.

Secretary Pickering Assembles the Corps

The Act of 9 May 1794 had given the President wide latitude in the employment of the companies of the Corps of Artillerists and Engineers, even authorizing their use on the frontiers if need be, and had not specified a location for the headquarters of the corps. Both Washington and Knox, however, realized the absolute necessity of training the officers, cadets, and soldiers of the proposed corps in the theory and practice of seacoast defense, a science that had no real roots in America. West Point on the Hudson River was selected for the assembling of those companies of recruits not being assigned immediately to fortifications; that wartime post had a large supply of military stores left from the war, and was a customary fitting-out point for newly-raised companies. In this instance, West Point also had the advantage of having two wartime river-defense forts, Putnam and Clinton, overlooking the Hudson, which could be used for training. At the beginning of 1795, with the threat of British attack dead for the moment, there was some uncertainty both in Congress and in the administration as to whether to continue the seacoast defense program. When Congress asked the new Secretary of War for his opinion, Pickering replied that in the unsettled state of international affairs "it would seem highly inexpedient and unsafe to depend on a permanent force short of our present military establishment."(32) The House agreed, and on 28 January a committee recommended a further appropriation of not to exceed $50,000 for continuing the construction and repair of the more important defenses.(33)

The strongest objection came from the Commander-in-Chief of the Legion, who thought that the recruits of the Corps of Artillerists and Engineers would be better employed on the active frontier than on a relatively unthreatened seaboard. General Wayne was desperate for reinforcements to offset the expiring enlistments of his veterans of Fallen Timbers, and during the late winter of 1795 he made a strong appeal to Secretary Pickering to send the artillerists to join the Legion in the Northwest Territory. There was much in favor of Wayne's plea, and financially it must have tempted Pickering, but the Secretary was determined to adhere to the original Washington-Knox plan. He pointed out to General Wayne that the new officers and men were generally "perfect strangers to their service," and that it was absolutely necessary to initiate a program of instruction for the nation's first scientific military organization. Pickering then announced his decision to assemble the bulk of the corps at West Point—some companies had already arrived—where "the little instruction they will now receive from the foreign officers, whose educations have been wholly military, will, it is expected, fit them for service, after the present year."(34)

Having made this important decision, Pickering seems to have had second thoughts. Two days later he wrote again to General Wayne; perhaps in an attempt to soften his refusal of Wayne's request for replacements, Pickering now volunteered quite a different ultimate mission for at least part of the new corps. "If we are so fortunate," Pickering wrote, "as to get possession of the posts now retained by the British, the corps of artillerists and engineers will furnish a very large proportion of their garrisons: and the collecting of the body of the corps at West Point, of which I have already informed you, was with a special reference to this service."(35)

One can only speculate as to the reasons for Pickering's change of mind as to the proper eventual employment of the artillerists and engineers. To use seacoast-defense troops for manning posts on the northwest frontier would be to waste whatever technical training they might receive at West Point. There could be little justification for instructing the new corps in fortifications engineering and heavy artillery gunnery techniques, only to march the companies off to such posts as Michilimackinac, Detroit, Niagara, and Oswego, where the British garrisons they would replace—if and when the British finally surrendered those posts as agreed in the Treaty of Paris of 1783—consisted of infantrymen and a few field gunners. This watering down of Pickering's original strong decision for a school of instruction at West Point unquestionably led to some of the problems that were shortly to plague the Corps of Artillerists and Engineers. Nevertheless, regardless of the ultimate employment of the corps, the Secretary's plan for instruction by the "foreign officers"—an unfortunate term for officers properly commissioned in the United States Army—was set in motion.

Nothing had been done at West Point in the way of instruction, of course, until the appointment of the three field officers of foreign origin, effective 26 February 1795, and even then it was some time before all these officers were present for duty at West Point. Lieutenant Colonel Commandant Stephen Rochefontaine and Major J.J. Ulrich Rivardi were still fully occupied in completing the fortifications for which they had originally been hired as temporary engineers, so that it was the artilleryman, Major Louis Tousard, who first arrived at West Point, drawing supplies from the quartermaster stores there on 24 April.(36) During May the first attempts were made to organize the companies of recruits present and arriving, and by the end of the month the officers and men had been formed into a detachment rendering weekly returns. The return for 25 May showed as present for duty the first three of the cadets authorized by the Act of 9 May 1794; these were Philip Landais, James Triplett, and Philip Rodrigue. (37) On 14 June the troops present were formed into a provisional battalion, with Major Tousard as both battalion and post commander.

Before the end of June Major Rivardi reported for duty from Fort Whetstone, bringing with him instructions from Secretary Pickering authorizing the prompt formation of the four battalions envisioned by Congress. This battalion organization meant little prior to 1798, however. Of the three battalion commanders on the seaboard, Major Tousard commanded the full garrison at West Point and Major Rivardi acted as second-in-command; Major Freeman, nominally commander of the 4th Battalion, was in Georgia and never served at West Point. Some of the captains had reported directly to the fortifications in their home states, but in theory their companies were "represented" in the battalions at West Point. According to Secretary Pickering's instructions, each battalion was to have a distinguishing color; including Burbeck's battalion with the Legion, these colors in order were to be red, green, blue, and white. The uniform of the new corps had not been specified in the Act of 9 May 1794, and so it remained that of the old Battalion of Artillery, now its 1st Battalion: blue coats with scarlet lining and lapels, yellow buttons, a cocked hat with yellow trim, black cockade and six-inch feathers of black with red tops. Rank was designated by epaulettes: lieutenants one gold epaulette, with a single row of bullion, on the left shoulder; captains, with two rows of bullion, on the right shoulder; majors, epaulettes on both shoulders with a single row of bullion. Corporals carried a yellow worsted epaulette on the right shoulder, sergeants on both shoulders.(38) The lieutenant colonel commandant, not provided for, presumably wore two epaulettes with two rows of bullion. Later in 1795 Secretary Pickering directed that, for the artillerists and engineers, the cocked hat be replaced by what he called helmets or "horseman's caps."(39)

The companies at West Point began to take shape during the summer. The 16 sergeants of each battalion were called together to elect one of their number—since all had about the same short length of service—as battalion sergeant major. Drill, or "exercise," was to be conducted strictly in accordance with the "Blue Book," Steuben's Regulations for the Order and Discipline of the Troops of the United States, first published commercially in 1779. By the end of August new barracks had been completed, and the troops of the three skeleton battalions moved from their temporary camp into more permanent quarters. Recruiting efforts continued, and at the end of the summer many of the officers returned to their home states to try to enlist more men. Organization and training fell off considerably during this phase, as Major Rivardi reported to the Secretary of War: "There is not a Single Captain of the 3d Battalion here, & only two lieutenants, both entirely ignorant of the Service. I am obliged to attend every where my self ... ."(40)

Colonel Rochefontaine visited West Point briefly at least twice during the latter months of 1795, but was unable to remain long with his new command. He was still occupied with the New England fortifications, and in October, at Secretary Pickering's direction, he had travelled south to seek a suitable site for a government arsenal in the Maryland-Virginia area, subsequently established at Harpers Ferry. Rochefontaine was at West Point on 7 November for the ceremony of the acceptance of a new national color, bearing 15 stars and 15 stripes, just received from the War Department. Then he was off again to make final arrangements for completion of construction of the fortifications before the onset of winter, and it was not until after the first of the new year that he was able to return to his command at West Point on a relatively permanent basis.(41)

At the end of 1795 the Corps of Artillerists and Engineers, after a year and a half of official life, was in better shape than the Legion, but was still considerably below its authorized strength. Of the 992 men authorized for the four battalions, War Department returns in December showed 731 on hand, but they were widely scattered. The 1st Battalion, of course, was not concerned with seacoast defense; of the three new battalions, the equivalent of about one full battalion was involved in manning the new defenses in New York City, Philadelphia, Baltimore, and Charleston. At West Point, the absence of a full complement of enlisted men was not critical to the plan of establishing a school of instruction, but at the end of the year only about half of the assigned officers were on hand, and of the 32 cadets authorized the new corps, only three had reported to West Point. There was, however, a military band; it was apparently Major Tousard's decision to combine the two musicians of each company, fifers and drummers, into a single garrison band, and by the end of the year it had reached 20 members.(42)

CHAPTER III
PROFESSIONAL INSTRUCTION BEGUN—AND REJECTED
1796-1797

Timothy Pickering was appointed Secretary of State in August of 1795, but for the next five months, until his successor was chosen, he continued also to head the War Department. Despite his increased duties in Washington's cabinet, there is no indication that Pickering in any way neglected his War Department duties, and his reports to Congress during the period of his dual tenure were clear, pragmatic, and honest. As War Secretary he was respected and appreciated by officers of the Army, from General Wayne down, and even after he moved completely to the State Department he continued for over a year to be a sort of secretary emeritus for the War Department. He was always interested, in particular, in what was to him the entering wedge of professionalism in the Army, the Corps of Artillerists and Engineers. As his official valedictory as Secretary of War, Pickering drafted for Congress during January 1796 a paper he titled "Objects of the Military Establishment of the United States." His thoughts covered the range of military problems, beginning with frontier defense, and concluded with his ideas about the new technical corps and the necessity for the inauguration of formal military instruction. "The corps of artillerists and engineers," he wrote, "appears to be an important establishment. To become skilful in either branch of their profession, will require long attention, study, and practice; and because they can now acquire the knowledge of these arts advantageously only from the foreign officers, who have been appointed with a special reference to this object, it will be important to keep the corps together for the present ... . Its principal station [West Point] may then become a school for the purpose ... ."(1)

The primary agent for carrying out Pickering's ideas, Lieutenant Colonel Commandant Rochefontaine, reported to West Point on 10 January and assumed active command of the corps and the garrison. As commanding officer, as well as the senior of the "foreign officers," Rochefontaine would be responsible for the quality of the technical instruction, for the details of which he could look to three foreign-born subordinates. Major Rivardi was fully qualified to instruct in engineering, particularly in the art of fortifications construction. Major Tousard was a trained and experienced artilleryman with some engineering background. And as a "geographical engineer and draughtsman," Timothy Pickering had located and sent up to West Point a French engineer residing in Philadelphia, one Joseph Warin. However, as commanding officer of the corps and garrison, Colonel Rochefontaine was also responsible for general military training, and for the order and discipline of that part of the corps under his immediate command. In this latter responsibility lay the seeds of future difficulties.

The Institution of Classroom Instruction

Early in February Colonel Rochefontaine opened the long-awaited formal instruction in fortification and gunnery. He had arranged to have one barracks fitted out as officers' quarters, with provision of a "study room" for classes. The program began on 10 February, and Rochefontaine's order of that date was explicit and informative:

> The officers are requested to attend in the study room every day, in the morning, between the hours of 11 and 12 o'clock, and from 4 to 5 in the afternoon, to receive the first lectures on the theoretical part of fortification. The morning meeting will be spent in explaining the different principles of fortification and copying the author (Mr. Muller).(2) In the afternoon the officers will draw the plans relative to the explanation given in the morning. The officers will be furnished in the room with pen, inks and paper in

the morning, and the books from which the study is originated. In the afternoon they will be provided with paper, pencils, ruler, and mathematical instruments for drawing. Mr. [Warin], temporary engineer, will attend the evening sitting and will explain the principles of drawing. The officers may meet an hour sooner if they please for their own information ... . (3)

All indications are that Colonel Rochefontaine attacked the program of instruction with enthusiasm and energy. He was alert for new texts and instruments that might facilitate the classroom work. He heard through Charles Vincent, the temporary engineer in New York, that James Madison, the minister to France, had located a new book on cannon foundry in Europe, and reportedly had sent a copy to Philadelphia; unfortunately, Vincent added, the volume had apparently gone astray. Rochefontaine at once wrote to Timothy Pickering, asking his assistance in locating the work and sending it to West Point in order to "forward the science of Gunnery.(4)

Despite Rochefontaine's efforts and example, the classroom instruction ran into difficulties almost from the start. During February, according to the returns, seven captains, 16 lieutenants, and two cadets—the third was on furlough—should have been available to attend classes. This would have been a respectable class, but in fact the sessions were plagued with absenteeism of high order. Of course there were always administrative duties to be performed, and perhaps battalion adjutants and certain other duty officers were excused, but many other officers seem to have evaded the lectures, for later reports indicate that attendance was very light during this period. Mr. Warin lectured on both fortification theory and drawing, but to a mere handful of officers. Major Rivardi recorded that Colonel Rochefontaine himself attended class faithfully—and on one occasion was the only officer present.

Attendance at scheduled instruction was, of course, a military duty, and it was Colonel Rochefontaine's responsibility to enforce his orders. But in matters of discipline Rochefontaine seems to have been both inexperienced and weak. A long-time staff officer and technical expert, he was not accustomed to command of troops, and certainly not to command of the individualistic and egalitarian American officers of the new corps. Major Tousard, on the other hand, was a stronger character with command and battlefield experience, and it is clear that he hinted to some of the officers that he would make a better commander than his countryman. Rochefontaine felt this, and soon became convinced that all the officers except Major Rivardi were hostile to him, and that Tousard was fanning the flames. Little over a week after classes began, Rochefontaine wrote plaintively to Pickering that the officers were planning to draft a letter to the new Secretary of War, James McHenry, complaining of Rochefontaine's policies and recommending that Tousard be given the command. "Major Tousard," he wrote, "has kept in his bosom an unquenchable Jealousy for the preference bestowed by the President of the U.S. upon me, over him; the officers, since their arrival, have been told over and over, that it had been an unjust and undeserved injury to him."(5) Rochefontaine complained also that his adjutant, paymaster, and quartermaster considered themselves independent of him; they had been in the habit of corresponding directly with the War Department, or with General Wayne's headquarters at Greeneville in the Northwest Territory, and they were not inclined to route this correspondence through their new commander.

The next difficulty involved Joseph Warin, the temporary engineer who seems to have conducted most of the instruction. After less than three weeks of this duty, Warin reported sick, and Colonel Rochefontaine gave him permission to go to Philadelphia to consult his own doctor. In light of subsequent events, it is doubtful that Warin's health was the problem; while he may have been affronted by the lack of attendance at his instruction, the fact is that he had received a confidential mission from the French minister in Philadelphia. Clearly Rochefontaine did not expect to see Warin again, for he wrote to Pickering asking him to recommend to Secretary McHenry that a certain Mr. Finiel, "an Assistant Engineer at present useless in Philadelphia," be sent to West Point.(6)

Joseph Warin, meanwhile, had been chosen by the French minister to join General Victor Collot of the French army, recently arrived in Philadelphia from the West Indies, in a little peacetime reconnaissance—"spying" would be too harsh—of the Ohio and Mississippi valleys. On 24 March Warin wrote to Pickering, who had hired him, resigning his appointment as temporary engineer,(7) and shortly thereafter he and Collot left Philadelphia for the western country. The Collot-Warin mission, greatly exaggerated as to its objectives, soon became public knowledge, and the troops on the Ohio were warned to be on the alert for the pair, who were described as trying "to gain a knowledge of our posts in the Western country, and to encourage and stimulate the people in that quarter to secede from the union, and form a political and seperate [sic] connexion with a foreign power."(8) Warin was described as speaking English "tolerably," which may have affected his lectures at West Point.

This Collot-Warin mission resulted in some beautiful and accurate maps and plans of rivers, settlements, and old fortifications along the Ohio and Mississippi; it was a cartographic triumph for Warin, but of probably no other great significance, and for him it proved fatal. After getting successfully past Fort Massac on the lower Ohio, despite a period of detention by the American commandant, the party headed down the Mississippi. Warin was subsequently wounded in an attack by two Indians, and died on the lower river. (9)

The Warin-incident is mentioned here only because of its effect on the instructional program at West Point. The loss of Warin himself was not serious, for Timothy Pickering located the engineer Finiel at Philadelphia and sent him off to West Point, where he arrived on 28 March. It would also be an exaggeration to say that Warin's "defection" caused an immediate anti-French reaction at West Point. Nevertheless the feeling grew that Colonel Rochefontaine had somehow had a hand in Warin's western activities, and at West Point this feeling added fuel to the rising resentment of a majority of the officers.

In retrospect, it appears that this feeling against Rochefontaine was simply a pretext to cover the resentment of many officers at being forced to attend classes. Between Warin's departure and Finiel's arrival, instruction had simply consisted of readings from and discussion of Steuben's Blue Book, led by the adjutant, Lieutenant Lovell; the officers and cadets assuredly found it more agreeable, and more immediately useful, to receive instruction in organization and basic tactics than to listen to lectures in engineering drawing and fortifications theory, delivered in a French accent. The fact was that very few of the newly-appointed officers and cadets had the educational or practical background for the theoretical instruction they were expected to assimilate. Moreover, most of the officers had sought commissions in 1794 with the idea of fighting Britain; they were not really interested in becoming engineers. They particularly resented having to attend classes, for which they seemed to blame Colonel Rochefontaine rather than Secretary Pickering and his successor. Within a week of Mr. Finiel's resuming the classroom lectures, things began to come to a boil. The adjutant resigned his post abruptly on 7 April, and a day or two later the officers' barracks, which contained the hated classroom, was destroyed in a sudden fire. Rochefontaine wrote to Pickering of this "great misfortune," but gave no hint of arson. (10) There is, nevertheless, a strong suspicion that the fire was deliberately set; Alexander Hamilton, when Inspector General, wrote that the fire was thought to have been the work of the officers who had been assembled at West Point "for instruction in the arts and sciences, as provided for by law."(11)

On 21 April a rather nasty little affair took place that illustrated all too clearly the relationship between Colonel Rochefontaine and most of his officers. The only account is Rochefontaine's own, but it rings true; he reported the events to Pickering and to Hamilton, seeking legal advice from the latter. In brief, Rochefontaine had let himself be provoked into a duel with one of his lieutenants. Convinced that Major Tousard had poisoned the officers' minds against him, and that Captain Decius Wadsworth was Tousard's principal supporter, Rochefontaine was overly quick, perhaps, to believe that Lieutenant William Wilson of Wadsworth's company had called out provoking words to him one evening. Encountering Wilson, Rochefontaine accused him of insulting language; the lieutenant denied the charge, whereupon Rochefontaine struck him on the shoulder with the hilt of his sword. The colonel realized he had been "imprudent," and at once offered to give satisfaction. Wilson called his servant to bring his sword, but admitted to Rochefontaine that he did not know how to use it. The colonel then proposed that to avoid the formality of a duel, the matter be settled by a "rencounter," each principal to have two loaded pistols and a sword. Rochefontaine described the hair-raising sequel:

> The first fire went off almost at the same time on both sides—my second Pistol went off unaware and I remained against my antagonist who had yet a loaded pistol against me. He came up to me within three steps and missed fire. It is a general rule in such occasions to lose the chance when the pistol has not gone off, yet my adversary cocked up and missed his fire a second time. In order to prevent his firing a third time, I fell on him to try to prevent him from cocking his piece, but he did it notwithstanding, and his pistol missed fire again, the muzzle touching my breast. The two witnesses came up then and separated us. My noble adversary enraged at not assassinating me on the spot, was furiously asking powder of his second, to kill said he that *Son of a Bitch*. This was his noble expression on that occasion.(12)

Colonel Rochefontaine thought that the affair, however distressing, was at an end, but two days later he received a written challenge from Lieutenant Wilson. Relying on his superior knowledge of the European duelling code, the colonel declared the matter settled, only to learn that Wilson was pushing the affair on behalf of a group of officers, who declared that if Rochefontaine would not fight again, they would publish to the world an account of his "infamous" conduct. This latter threat was subsequently modified to provide for a letter of accusation to the Secretary of War; clearly the dissident officers were determined to be rid of their commander.

But even while the feud simmered, Colonel Rochefontaine remained determined to continue the classroom instruction, the burned barracks notwithstanding. On 28 April, the day he wrote Hamilton about the duel, Rochefontaine established a board of four captains to survey the post facilities, including rooms in private quarters, to find a new classroom. During the next few weeks Rochefontaine supervised the construction of a parapet for artillery practice, and he and Major Rivardi constructed a wooden model of a bastioned fort for instruction in the theory of fortification.(13) As far as Rochefontaine was concerned, he would carry on as before unless notified to the contrary by the new Secretary of War.

James McHenry to the War Department

Since Timothy Pickering had moved to the State Department in the late summer of 1795, President Washington had been seeking a successor to relieve Pickering of his War Department duties. In the increasing factionalism that marked Washington's second term, it was important to him to have another staunch Federalist at the head of the War Department, and this consideration was perhaps paramount in his eventual selection of James McHenry. The Irish born former surgeon of the Continental Army was only 42 when he assumed the war secretaryship on 27 January 1796. He had become one of General Washington's secretaries in mid-1778, and in 1781 had been appointed a staff major. Since the war he had served two terms in Congress from Maryland, and was a member of the Maryland state senate when he was selected— reputedly the fourth choice—as Secretary of War.

Secretary McHenry took office during a military slump. Anthony Wayne's victorious campaign of Fallen Timbers had for the moment removed the Indian menace to the northwestern frontier, and Britain's conciliatory position now virtually removed the threat of an attack on the Atlantic seaboard. One of McHenry's first decisions, then, had to be the size and organization of the Army to recommend to Congress. The Legion was being praised in all quarters for its disciplined valor during 1794, but it was clear by early 1796 that its particular organization would not be adaptable to peacetime. As for the Corps of Artillerists and Engineers, its future was in question; a year and a half after its creation, that promising organization seemed to have produced little except controversy.

Three months in office, Secretary McHenry had to make a decision involving the leadership of the Corps of Artillerists and Engineers, and the continuance of the professional training that both Washington and Pickering had thought so necessary. He had just received from West Point a long list of charges, none of them particularly serious, against Colonel Rochefontaine, drawn up by Captain Decius Wadsworth. Just why Wadsworth felt so strongly against Rochefontaine and the classroom instruction is a mystery, for of all the American officers in the new corps, Wadsworth was the most experienced in practical, if not theoretical, engineering; a Connecticut inventor of local note, he had been and would in the future be associated with Eli Whitney in the production of small arms.(14) But in 1796 Wadsworth was Rochefontaine's official accuser, and he was in fact pitting his own military career against that of the administration's choice as commander of the corps.

McHenry read the charges against Rochefontaine, and may have felt that while none of the allegations had much significant individually, taken together they formed a picture—if they were proven—of a man whose qualifications for command might be questioned. Timothy Pickering in the State Department, had McHenry consulted him, probably would have advised quashing the charges, and this may well have been McHenry's first thought. But Rochefontaine knew that the charges had been preferred, and he wrote to McHenry demanding, as was his legal right, that a court of inquiry be held to clear his name. The Secretary wisely put the entire matter in the proper channels. Major General Wayne happened to be in Philadelphia on extended leave after long months on the frontier, and McHenry, in the name of the President, directed the Commander-in-Chief of the Legion to convene a court of inquiry at West Point, to be formed of "unprejudiced and the most enlightened Officers."15

A Turbulent Court of Inquiry

General Wayne realized that the court should be headed by an officer senior to Rochefontaine, but to have sent to Greeneville or Georgia for one of the four lieutenant colonels commandant of the Legion would have taken weeks. Fortunately there were several veteran officers of the Legion on the seaboard, on leave or recruiting duty, and General Wayne selected four, under the presidency of Major William Kersey, to constitute the court, including one to act as judge advocate.(16)

The members of the court arrived at West Point by 22 May, and on that date Colonel Rochefontaine properly suspended himself from command. Major Tousard had carefully arranged to be absent on a tour of inspection of the seacoast defenses, so Major Rivardi assumed command of the garrison. His wife chose this day to produce an heir, so that Rivardi's first garrison order had a domestic touch: "Mrs. J.J.U. Rivardi, on the occasion of the birth of a son, requests that the garrison prisoners be released. Major Rivardi so orders."(17)

The court of inquiry met briefly on 23 May, and then continuously on weekdays until 8 June. The judge advocate conducted the proceedings, but Captain Wadsworth arranged the testimony of the officers hostile to Rochefontaine, and seems to have cross-examined two—Major Rivardi and the French-born Lieutenant Peter Dransy—who generally supported their commander. This was not, of course, a court-martial, but simply a preliminary investigation, similar to a modern grand jury hearing. The charges, divided into 23 specifications, covered three general areas: (1) misuse of government property, specifically blankets, stationery, and firewood; (2) ineffective administration, alleging failure to keep the hospital warm enough and lack of energy in pursuing deserters; and (3) lack of effectiveness in the conduct of the program of instruction in the "Art of Gunnery and the Science of Fortification" for the officers and cadets. Eight officers and the civilian military storekeeper testified; Colonel Rochefontaine objected strenuously to his "rencounter" adversary, Lieutenant Wilson, being allowed to testify, but was overruled by the judge advocate.(18)

Much of the testimony, by modern standards, seems trivial. The bulk of the allegations concerned minor decisions by Colonel Rochefontaine which seem to have been entirely within his right as the post commander. Of more substance were the charges concerning the conduct of instruction. Major Rivardi, whose testimony was generally favorable to Rochefontaine, brought out the rampant absenteeism among the officers who should have been attending class, but he had to admit that very little gunnery instruction had been presented, and then only the "practical part"; even so, the mortars and howitzers had been fired very seldom during gunnery practice. And Rivardi had to admit what the other officers charged, that Colonel Rochefontaine was not very adept in the tactical exercises prescribed in the Blue Book.

Early in the proceedings, Rochefontaine convinced himself that the members of the court were hostile to him, and during the first week of testimony he wrote Pickering that "it is painful to me to observe that four officers who have been sent here by General Wayne to investigate the charges against me, are showing great partiality to my adversaries."(19) He had planned a lengthy defense statement, but the judge advocate disallowed it on the grounds that such was not customary in a court of inquiry. This information Rochefontaine at once communicated to Pickering, adding that "Capt Wadsworth whom I spoke to you favorably of, & D. Mitchell, whom I have seen you had a good opinion of, are openly my bitterest enemies and are going, I am told, to Philadelphia."(20) Midway in the inquiry Major Tousard returned to West Point and assumed command of the garrison from Rivardi, and now Rochefontaine isolated his real enemy. Captains Wadsworth and Mitchell, he saw, were only agents for that evil genius, his countryman Major Tousard. "My Friend T——d," he wrote bitterly to Pickering, "is ready to burst with satisfaction, in the delirium of his heart, he has destroyed what ever I had done to establish a little order, and to remove the horrid disorder which had taken birth under him."(21)

The court adjourned on 8 June, and Major Kersey and the other members departed at once for Philadelphia to report their general findings to Secretary McHenry. Colonel Rochefontaine received a copy of the summary of testimony—without recommendations—as prescribed by the Articles of War; this he copied and sent to Timothy Pickering, together with a lengthy defense of his own actions. At the same time he sent copies of his defense to Secretary McHenry and to General Wayne, who was about to return to Greeneville. Within two weeks both Pickering and McHenry replied: Pickering, after reading the summary of testimony, told Rochefontaine that he did not think any of the more serious charges had been sustained; McHenry simply noted that "I have received your defense ... & shall take an early opportunity to lay the same before the President - In the mean while you will be pleased to resume your comm[an]d."(22) This last injunction made it fairly clear that McHenry was going to make a favorable recommendation to the President, and Rochefontaine received it as evidence that he had been vindicated.

When the officers had forwarded their charges to the Secretary of War, they must have known that at least some of them were risking their own futures. And when it became evident that Colonel Rochefontaine was not to be removed from command, several officers were left in highly exposed positions. On 6 June, even before the court adjourned, Lieutenant Wilson was ordered to Fort Jay in New York Harbor; it is fair to conclude that he was being removed from Rochefontaine's immediate command for the good of all concerned.(23) But if Wilson accepted defeat and transfer quietly, not so Captain Decius Wadsworth. Learning of Rochefontaine's letter of defense, and assessing correctly that Rochefontaine had named him as a ringleader, Wadsworth wrote to Secretary McHenry for a copy of the letter. McHenry wisely declined, in a letter that was a model of both tact and evasiveness. Purporting to sympathize with Wadsworth's having to "bear with the neglects and sometimes rude ignorance of superior rank," the Secretary advised Wadsworth not to press for a copy of the letter. "It is a writing," McHenry wrote, "composed when the Colonel's sensibilities were high, and … it contains nothing which has produced any change in the good opinion I had formed of your understanding and honor."(24)

On the face of it this was a friendly and encouraging letter, but Wadsworth was not deceived. McHenry was still new at the War Department, and he was almost sure to follow Pickering's precedents, which in turn represented the President's wishes. The War Department was not willing to lose the services of the trained foreign-born officers at this point, no matter how abrasive they might be, or how inept in certain aspects of command simply because a few undisciplined American officers resented having to attend classes. Captain Wadsworth sensed this, for even before he had McHenry's reply, he announced to Colonel Rochefontaine that he intended to resign his commission. Rochefontaine passed this information on to Pickering, adding that "I must own that I am pleased with the prospect of being rid of him."(25) Nothing in McHenry's reply to Wadsworth changed the latter's mind; he submitted his resignation as an officer of the Army, and it was accepted as of 19 July.(26)

But Decius Wadsworth had a final parting shot. Upon departing West Point for civil life, he drew up a letter outlining the whole of the Wilson-Rochefontaine affair, including the interesting claim that Wadsworth himself had challenged Rochefontaine to an affair of honor. This letter, to his discredit, he sent to the *New York Minerva*, and that newspaper printed it on 30 July. A copy of the *Minerva* soon found its way to West Point, where it reopened wounds that badly needed healing. Wadsworth's letter was a malicious washing of the Army's dirty linen, but it made such pointed allegations as to Rochefontaine's personal courage that the Frenchman could not let it pass unchallenged. Rochefontaine was ill-advised enough to pen a reply to Wadsworth for public consumption in the *Minerva*; it was a sad and bombastic effort, full of references to the European dueling code, and expressing eagerness to meet Wadsworth in mortal combat at any time. Picked up and reprinted by newspapers in other cities, Rochefontaine's effort to reestablish his honor and dignity probably had a contrary effect.(27)

The Occupation of the Frontier Posts

With the court of inquiry over, interest at West Point turned to the question of which companies might be directed, on short notice, to provide garrisons for some of the British-held frontier posts soon to be surrendered. If more than one company were ordered to the Canadian frontier, then there was a likelihood that one of the majors might be sent for overall command. Major Tousard, who had maintained a discreet silence since his return to West Point, had no wish to be exiled to the frontier. He had hinted to Colonel Rochefontaine some weeks earlier that he was angling for reappointment in the colonial service of the French Army, or so Rochefontaine understood; when Tousard had departed in early May to inspect the seacoast fortifications, Rochefontaine did not really expect to see him again, and was unpleasantly surprised when Tousard reappeared curing the court of inquiry. Rochefontaine at once wrote Pickering: "Tousard is here to my great surprise for I received … a letter from Hyspaniola, informing me that he was expected there—to command as I informed you. His plan has been deranged I suppose … ." He added that Tousard now hoped to prevail upon Secretary McHenry "not to move him to the Westward, and to push on Major Rivardi, although it is impossible for him [Rivardi] to leave his family in the circumstances they are in."(28)

There is little room for doubt that Major Tousard had hoped to succeed Rochefontaine in command of the corps and the garrison of West Point, but at the same time he had hedged his bet by persuading Secretary McHenry that not he but Major Rivardi should be ordered to the frontier if the need arose. Of the two majors, Rivardi was the more experienced engineer, while Tousard was basically a field artilleryman with more background in light artillery than in seacoast defenses. But no sooner had Tousard returned to West Point at the end of May than he told Rivardi flatly that it was all arranged, that Tousard would remain at West Point while Rivardi would "have very soon an order for marching. "(29) Rivardi wrote twice to Secretary McHenry to ask that he be allowed to stay at West Point at least until his wife and new baby were able to travel, but received no reply.

The marching orders came during the summer of 1796, as the Army at long last began the takeover of the British frontier posts. The Legion was to be responsible for garrisoning the posts within the Northwest Territory, and General Wayne's troops, including Major Burbeck's artillerists and engineers, made ready to accept the transfer of Michilimackinac, Detroit, and several minor posts. Providing garrisons for Oswego and Niagara on the New York frontier was left to the Corps of Artillerists and Engineers, for the legion was far under strength, and with the need to maintain a line of supply posts from the Ohio to Detroit in mind, General Wayne insisted that some of Rochefontaine's men share the burden. This diversion of artillerists from the seacoast was not a problem in 1796—two years later there would be quite a different situation. In any event, to provide garrisons for Oswego and Niagara would require only two companies from West Point.

In mid-June Captain James Bruff's company and a detachment of McRee's company were assigned the frontier garrison duty. Captain Bruff himself may have volunteered, for he had only recently arrived at West Point from Fort Whetstone, had taken no part in the court of inquiry, and perhaps wanted no part of the intrigue at the headquarters post. Bruff's command marched north to Albany with a "train of artillery" of unspecified size, turned westward along the Mohawk, and during July moved toward Fort Oswego. According to one source,(30) Lieutenant Theophilus Elmer and a detachment went ahead and accepted the turn-over of Fort Oswego on 16 July. Bruff's main body paused at Oswego and Lieutenant John McClallen, who was senior to Elmer, took command. Captain Bruff then led his own company on to Fort Niagara, and assumed the command of that post from the British garrison on 11 August.(31)

Colonel Rochefontaine had assured Timothy Pickering that once his court of inquiry was over, he intended to resume the instruction in fortification and gunnery. However, with the need to garrison Oswego and Niagara, and with five officers and two of the three cadets on furlough, it does not appear from the record that any classroom instruction was carried out during the summer. Major Rivardi received his orders, not to Oswego or Niagara, but to far-off Michilimackinac, to command that isolated garrison; Secretary McHenry did agree that Rivardi could remain at West Point until his family was able to travel.(32) Despite his impending assignment, Rivardi seemed reconciled to leaving West Point, perhaps because his support of Colonel Rochefontaine was beginning to falter. He wrote Pickering in early August to suggest that the Secretary of State try to persuade Rochefontaine to modify the "air of severity which he assumes with the officers"; Rivardi felt unable to give such advice himself—as he put it, "I allready found it was not allways wellcome." (33)

Major Tousard requested six months' furlough at the beginning of September, to take care of personal affairs in Hispaniola. To Rochefontaine he announced bluntly that if the furlough were not granted, he would resign— which must have tempted Rochefontaine sorely. Nevertheless, Rochefontaine recommended approval to Secretary McHenry, not only to show his magnanimity to his foe but also, as he admitted to Pickering, because West Point would be "well rid of" Tousard for a while. (34) Apparently the furlough was granted, despite the shortage of officers, for Tousard did not resign and there is no mention of him at West Point for many months.

About the middle of September Major Rivardi and his family departed West Point for Michilimackinac, taking the stage through Albany to Oswego, by lake vessel to Niagara, and then by another boat across Lake Erie to Detroit. Arriving at Detroit on 18 November, after a nine-week trip, Rivardi learned that the Michilimackinac command had been assigned to Major Burbeck, and that he would be retained at Detroit in command of a handful of artillerymen from the Legion. While Rivardi was spared the long trip to the isolation of Michilimackinac, he missed the double rations that would have accrued to him as a post commander. (35)

The Army Reorganization of 1796

During the first half of 1796 Congress had been concerned as to the future size and composition of the Army in the light of the dwindling threats both to the northwest frontier and to the seaboard. As Timothy Pickering left the War Department he had drawn up for Congress a paper on "Objects of the Military Establishment of the United States," in which he listed six goals to be met, most of them involving occupation of the former British posts and establishing other posts for preserving the peace in the northwest, the southwest, and on the Creek frontier in Georgia. Pickering's sixth object was not very compelling: "To garrison the most important fortifications on the sea coast. The smaller ones in time of peace may be taken care of, each by an individual, such as an invalid, or other poor citizen, at a very small expense." (36) His successor's recommendations for the seacoast defenses were hardly stronger. McHenry, after consulting with General Wayne in Philadelphia, furnished Congress with a list of the most necessary garrisons, stretching from Michilimackinac to the Georgia frontiers. For these garrisons McHenry recommended a minimum of 34 companies, but of these only four were noted as "in the fortifications on the sea coast." (37) Congress debated the necessity for appropriations for continued construction and maintenance of the coastal forts, but soon bogged down in sectional differences; New York wanted such a large share of the proposed appropriation that the other states objected, and in the end no money at all was voted for fortifications in 1796.(38)

On 30 May Congress enacted the Army Reorganization Act,(39) to take effect on 1 November 1796. The Legion as such would be abolished, and replaced by four separate numbered infantry regiments, two companies of light dragoons, and existing Corps of Artillerists and Engineers. Much was made of the financial savings to be effected, but in fact the legislation would have little impact upon the officers and men in service. The authorized strength of the Army would be reduced 35 per cent, to 3,359 officers and men, but as the earlier ceiling had never been reached, only a handful of captains and junior majors would become excess to requirements and subject to "derangement." The Corps of Artillerists and Engineers would continue at its authorized strength of 58 officers, 32 cadets, and 992 men in four battalions—but now it would make up almost one-third of the entire Army.(40)

The publication of the details of the new organization prompted young Cadet Philip Landais at West Point to better his situation. By early summer Landais must have assumed that the classroom instruction, by which route [he] was to be commissioned at some unspecified future date, was suspended more or less indefinitely, and he wrote to the Secretary of War asking that he be appointed a lieutenant at once. Getting no satisfaction from Secretary McHenry, Landais exercised that blithe disregard for military channels that seemed to characterize the Corps of Artillerists and Engineers—he wrote directly to President Washington. Washington, of course, referred the letter to McHenry, noting that he recalled something about filling vacancies in the corps before Congress adjourned. He seemed favorable to the idea of commissioning cadets, but pointed out that if there were other cadets to be considered, Landais should not be favored over the others.(41) McHenry "reminded the President that the impending reduction of infantry strength might require offering appointments in the Artillerists and Engineers to some excess infantry officers, in lieu of their being deranged. He counseled delay in acting on Landais's application, and the President agreed; he asked McHenry to prepare a plan for taking care of excess officers, at which time Landais and the other cadets would be considered.(42)

The Army reorganization, to be effective as of 1 November, began with a directive from the Secretary of War on 27 August. The only immediate effect on the Corps of Artillerists and Engineers was the gaining of three lieutenants, all from the 2d Sublegion, who would be excess to the new organization. Andrew Marschalk had been the junior captain of the 2d Sublegion, but was willing to move his epaulette back to the left shoulder in order to remain in the service; Howell Cobb and Joseph Campbell transferred in grade, but with a loss of two years' seniority.(43) The transfer of these officers still left a shortage of nine lieutenants of Artillerists and Engineers. In December Secretary McHenry advised the President that all excess officers of the Legion who desired retention had been accommodated, and received permission to open the Corps of Artillerists and Engineers to new appointments. The first new lieutenant came from the ranks of the dragoons of the Legion, being reduced to two companies. Most of the excess troopers were converted to artillerymen and assigned to Major Rivardi's detachment at Detroit, but Sergeant Richard Whiley sought a commission, and in November presented himself at the War Department with a letter of recommendation from General Wayne himself. "I have often been a witness," Wayne wrote, "of the good Conduct & bravery of Mr Whiley, when a Sergeant of Dragoons - & wished for an Opportunity to promote him ... . Should there be a vacancy in the Corps of Artillerists & Engineers it is the Corps he would prefer."(44) Appointments from the ranks were rare in the 1790s, and would become rarer in the decades ahead, particularly as the grade of cadet had been created specifically for officer candidates. But Sergeant Whiley's timing was perfect and his credentials impeccable, and without hesitation Secretary McHenry issued him a lieutenant's commission.(45)

Then came the turn of the three cadets. The date of 19 December 1796 should retain a certain significance, for as of that date were commissioned the first products of a planned officer-candidate program. Philip Landais had stimulated the process with his appeal to the President, and it is by no means sure that he would have been commissioned so soon otherwise, for the cadets had been exposed to very little classroom instruction at West Point. Nevertheless, with eight vacancies yet unfilled, Landais, Philip Rodrigue, and James Triplett were formally appointed lieutenants in the Corps of Artillerists and Engineers—and for the moment the supply of qualified cadets was exhausted.(46)

1797—The Calm Before the Storm

With the end of 1796 came a change in the command of the Army, as the veteran Major General Anthony Wayne died unexpectedly on 15 December at Presque' Isle, Pennsylvania, while inspecting possible sites for new posts. His bitter rival, Brigadier General James Wilkinson, the only other general officer then serving, succeeded to the implied command, although he was never designated other than "senior officer" of the Army. The "Western Army," the old Legion, was considerably affected by the change in command, for there had been distinct Wayne and Wilkinson cliques as early as 1793, and now of course the Wilkinson adherents would be riding high. Major Burbeck's 1st Battalion of artillerists and engineers was hardly affected, however, for at the end of 1796 those companies were garrisoning Michilimackinac and Detroit, as well as the faraway Georgia frontier, while the bulk of the frontier troops were beginning to push down the Mississippi. So isolated was the garrison at Michilimackinac during the winter that General Wilkinson's order prescribing a 30-day mourning period for General Wayne, issued at Philadelphia on 31 December, did not reach Major Burbeck at Michilimackinac until late May.(47)

The other three battalions of Artillerists and Engineers were in almost a state of limbo at the beginning of 1797. With the Indian threat largely removed, many eyes in Philadelphia were turning toward the Spanish possessions on the lower Mississippi, and scant attention was paid to the seacoast fortifications and the troops that were to man them. Congress' sole concern during 1797 was whether the existing works might deteriorate if money were not appropriated for maintenance. A committee report of 10 February noted that there were garrisons only at Fort Jay, Fort Mifflin, Fort Whetstone, Fort Norfolk, Fort Johnston, and Fort Johnson, and from the records kept at West Point it is evident that Fort Norfolk and Fort Johnston had only a few soldiers as caretakers.(48) The committee was satisfied that the garrisoned forts had been kept in generally good repair, but some money would be needed to complete certain buildings and defensive works. As for the ungarrisoned sites—Portland, Portsmouth, Gloucester, Salem, Marblehead, Newport, New London, Savannah, and Point Petre—the committee proposed that $3,500 a year be appropriated for the pay of caretakers and for certain basic repairs. One change which affected the Artillerists and Engineers as much as the rest of the Army was the inauguration of John Adams on 4 March, the first transfer of Executive power under the Constitution. It may have reflected the general feeling of the Army that, at West Point, Colonel Rochefontaine seemed to view the occasion primarily as the catastrophe of Washington's retirement. His general order of 3 March did not mention the new President by name, but dwelt at length on the virtues of the outgoing Chief Magistrate. The order concluded, nevertheless, with the exhortation that the following day be marked with the "joy & festivity usual on political occasions," including special 16-gun salutes and an extra issue of a gill of spirits to each noncommissioned officer and private.(49) The inauguration of John Adams brought subtle changes in the relationship between the Executive and the military establishment. While the new President was of course of the Federalist faction, he lacked Washington's tremendous prestige, and his familiarity with military matters. In compensation, perhaps, Adams would be more inclined than his predecessor to give a hard look at legislation affecting the military establishment and matters of national defense. Yet Adams was no pacifist, as he would prove beyond question the following year.

In the last years of the 18th century the great single factor dividing the Federalists and the Democratic-Republicans, as Jefferson's partisans were being called, was their respective attitudes toward republican France. The terms of Jay's Treaty with Great Britain had effectively healed for at least a decade the incipient breach in Anglo-American relations, but the treaty was most unfavorably received in France, whose political leaders took the view that any nation not an enemy of Frances' enemies must then be an enemy of France. The American minister to France since 1794, James Monroe, was a Jeffersonian strongly sympathetic to the ideals of the French Revolution, and he made it clear that he sided with France in condemning Jay's Treaty; for this undiplomatic attitude Monroe had been recalled by President Washington and replaced by Charles Cotesworth Pinckney, a staunch Federalist. By the time the new envoy arrived in France, the ruling Directory had adopted an intransigent position; it refused to receive Pinckney, and effectively suspended diplomatic relations. At the same time the Directory authorized French naval vessels and privateers to seize American vessels thought to be trading with Britain, and attempted, through such bumbling emissaries as Citizen Genet, to influence the election of 1796 in favor of the Jeffersonians. President Adams was later shocked to learn that just two days before his inauguration, the Directory had issued a decree violating the Franco-American commercial treaty of 1778—which had stressed the principle that free ships carry free goods—by authorizing its warships to force into French ports all neutral vessels carrying British goods. To the Federalists, who had decried for years what they saw as the pagan excesses of the French Revolution, the Directory's new policy seemed to justify an American resort to war.(50)

The events of the so-called Quasi-War with France, as they relate to the seacoast defenses and the Artillerists and Engineers, are related in the following chapter. As early as June of 1797, however, the Federalist faction in Congress favored strengthening the coastal defenses and augmenting the force required to garrison them. Called upon for his opinion, Secretary of War McHenry—the new President had retained all of Washington's cabinet— replied in general terms that about $200,000 should be provided for seacoast defense.(51) The more warlike Federalist members of Congress wanted a larger sum, and proposed to increase the artillery establishment, while the Jeffersonians scoffed at the idea of war with France, pointed out that nothing had been accomplished by the fortifications hastily constructed in 1794 and 1795, and reminded the Federalists that Washington's outgoing administration had felt no alarm, having appropriated on 3 March the modest sum of not to exceed $24,000 for all coastal defenses.(52) It was noted that little over $100,000 could be devoted to defensive measures out of current revenue; if the figure went higher, taxes would have to be imposed. As for manning the forts, one member felt that the militia would be adequate; "the laborious part of artillery," he announced, could be taught in a few days." Another member was "of opinion that the men we had were sufficient, though he allowed it was necessary that time should be given for artillerists to learn their duty."(53) In the end the matter was referred to Secretary McHenry for more information, which effectively killed any increase in seacoast troops for that session.

It was probably coincidence, but ten days after the mention in Congress that artillerists should be given time to learn their duties, Colonel Rochefontaine resumed the formal classes of instruction at West Point. This time he made no attempt to teach the captains, but instead placed them in the role of instructors. Initially there were only five pupils, all newly appointed lieutenants; less emphasis was placed on lectures and more on practical sessions, to be held every other day at the strange hour of five o'clock in the afternoon. According to orders of 26 June, "the Captains will take turn to Instruct the Gentlemen in the exercises of the field Pieces, Howitzers, Mortars, Seacoast pieces, &c."(54) No "foreign officers" were involved in instruction, which had been the primary reason for their appointments, and it must have been an embarrassment to them that this new flurry of activity was directed against possible war with their native land; within a year this fact would receive considerable attention. Temporary engineer Finiel may have been involved in instruction, however, for as late as December the storekeeper issued mahogany rulers, india ink, paint brushes, and quantities of gambodge and indigo, which argues that engineering drawing of some sort being taught.(55)

Despite tentative Congressional interest, the end of 1797 found the seacoast defense and the Artillerists and Engineers at a new nadir. Four fortifications had single-company garrisons, generally understrength, and two others had caretakers. Many officers were on furlough, some for extended periods. Colonel Rochefontaine remained at his post, and Major Tousard, returned from a long leave, was inspecting the works at Fort Mifflin and the defenses of Newport. Major Burbeck was still commanding at Michilimackinac, while Major Rivardi, after the better part of a year at Detroit, had received orders from General Wilkinson—not transmitted through Colonel Rochefontaine—to take command at Fort Niagara.(56) The third of the four majors was also far from the seacoast. Constant Freeman, on leave in Philadelphia to get married in mid-1797, was available when General Wilkinson was reinforcing the garrisons on the lower Ohio and Mississippi; the General placed Major Freeman in charge of a detachment, mostly of recruits, marching to the westward, and by December of 1797 Freeman's men had reached Pittsburgh. Major Freeman himself, acting as General Wilkinson's agent, would proceed down the Mississippi to Natchez early the following year.(57)

If the coastal fortifications were barely manned, and most of the field officers of Artillerists and Engineers pursuing duties far removed from seacoast defense, the situation was little better at the headquarters of the corps. As 1797 came to an end, the garrison at West Point had so dwindled that the garrison guard was reduced to one sergeant, one corporal, and five privates.(58)

CHAPTER IV
REORGANIZATION FOR THE QUASI-WAR
1798-1799

If 1797 had been a quiet year for the Army and for the Corps of Artillerists and Engineers in particular, 1798 was to bring more excitement and turbulence than had been experienced since the end of the Revolutionary War.

The French Directory's refusal to receive Minister Pinckney did not at first discourage President Adams, who decided to try again with a special mission consisting of Pinckney, then in Holland, John Marshall, and Elbridge Gerry—the latter a Jeffersonian to insure a bipartisan effort. The mission was received unofficially by Talleyrand, the new foreign minister, in October 1797, but not until the beginning of 1798 were the Americans able to present their grievances over the loss of shipping. By March the mission had been subjected to petty humiliations, with hints that a bribe would be necessary to begin negotiations. Gerry, the Jeffersonian, thought that he could eventually negotiate with Talleyrand, but Pinckney and Marshall left France in furious disgust; their reports and dispatches were subsequently published and known as the famous XYZ Affair.(1) Alexander Hamilton, in legal practice in New York, was electrified by the events in France, and in mid-March wrote to Secretary of State Pickering that "I look upon the Question before the Public as nothing less than whether we shall maintain our Independence ... ." He proposed measures to be advocated by Federalist leaders, including arming of American merchant vessels, rapid completion of frigates under construction, and, if relations with France worsened, construction of ten ships of the line. Hamilton also recommended increasing the Regular Army to 20,000 men and providing for a "provisional" army of 30,000, excluding militia, as well as the "efficacious fortification" of the major seaports.(2)

Congress had already taken steps to ascertain the exact status of the neglected coast defenses, and Secretary of War McHenry forwarded a report at the end of February. About a third of the June 1797 appropriation of $115,000 had been spent, the bulk on Fort Mifflin in the Delaware, which "seemed entitled to particular attention ... to afford essential protection to an important commercial city" which also happened to be the seat of government. As concerned garrisons, McHenry thought that militia could not perform this function unless it were called into long-term federal service; he felt also that troops on the western frontiers could not be transferred to the seaboard without endangering the national security, particularly in the southwest. The Secretary recommended that the seaboard fortifications should be generally improved, and this defence of our country rendered respectable, and, also, that the army should be proportionally augmented."(3)

McHenry might well have reported his recent steps to strengthen the seacoast garrisons. Of the 16 companies of Artillerists and Engineers, eight were now manning forts from Newport to St. Mary's; in addition to the existing garrisons in the ports of New York, Philadelphia, Baltimore, and Charleston, McHenry had hurriedly provided for a company each at Fort Norfolk and at Point Petre on the St. Mary's, and had sent two companies to Newport, both to garrison Fort Washington on Goat Island and to assist in the construction, under the supervision of Major Louis Tousard, of a new work on Brenton's Point. Of the remaining eight companies, two were at West Point under Colonel Rochefontaine; three were on the Canadian frontier under Majors Burbeck and Rivardi; and three were with General Wilkinson's "Western Army" from Fort Massac on the lower Ohio to Natchez on the lower Mississippi, where Major Freeman was temporarily stationed.(4)

Before Congress could take action on Secretary McHenry's proposals for raising additional troops for seacoast defense, there arose for the second—and last—time the problem of the commanding officer of the existing Corps of Artillerists and Engineers.

The Dismissal of Stephen Rochefontaine

One of the minor mysteries of the history of the early Army has been the abrupt disappearance from the rolls of Lieutenant Colonel Commandant Stephen Rochefontaine. The destruction of the War Department records in 1800 has in general resulted in the stark notation, in biographical registers of the Army, that Rochefontaine was "dismissed 7 May 1793."(5) The full story, which can be pieced together from scattered references in the papers of Timothy Pickering, is not particularly creditable to the Adams administration.

The basic problem in early 1798 was that Rochefontaine had been born and educated in that country with which the United States seemed about to go to war. In the atmosphere of anxiety and suspicion that was shortly to produce the Alien Act, the administration was concerned that the troops for the defense of the seacoast were under the command of an alien, notwithstanding that he had been an officer of the United States Army for over three years. This may have been a legitimate concern, but it can hardly have justified subsequent events, which moved with a speed and a disregard for the rights of the accused that must have disturbed the consciences of those involved.

The proceedings were triggered by a year-old report by the accountant of the War Department, dated March 1797, which alleged certain financial irregularities on Rochefontaine's part in the use of government horses and soldier teamsters. It seemed a minor charge, which if pursued and supported might have required Rochefontaine to reimburse the Treasury a few dollars.(6) But nothing was done in the matter for nearly a year, when the charges were suddenly dusted off and forwarded to Rochefontaine for his information at the end of January 1793. As might have been expected, Rochefontaine demanded a court of inquiry—and from that point events moved rapidly. On 19 February Secretary McHenry ordered a court to convene at West Point on 1 March, under the presidency of Major Thomas H. Cushing, acting Adjutant and Inspector of the Army; two infantry lieutenants, with a third as judge advocate, completed the court. The court sat from 4-7 March, the principal government witnesses being War Department accountant William Simmons and the military storekeeper at West Point, George Fleming; the only witness on Rochefontaine's behalf seems to have been Lieutenant Peter Dransy of the garrison. Colonel Rochefontaine admitted having been issued three public horses in late 1795, and having received money for the hiring-out of these horses and Soldier teamsters; he claimed that he had done this because Fleming had advised him that no forage money was available, and in fact Rochefontaine seems to have paid forage costs from his "profit." He claimed that this was accepted practice, and that Major Tousard, when in command, had done the same with one horse. But after a year or more Fleming, for reasons not explained, had suddenly turned on Rochefontaine, not only demanding repayment of monies received from the hire of the horses, but also accusing the colonel of misappropriation of public funds. And there, seemingly, the matter had rested for another year.

The court adjourned on 7 March and Major Cushing carried the record to Philadelphia. On 12 March Rochefontaine forwarded to Secretary McHenry his "Observations Upon the Charges Exhibited Against Me, by William Simmons Esquire, Accountant of the War Department," a document presumably lost in the fire of 1800. According to McHenry, in this paper Rochefontaine "does not deny the facts charged, but endeavors to shew, that the Public sustained no injury." On 6 April McHenry forwarded the proceedings of the court and "other documents" to President Adams, with the curious advice that "Lieut Col Stephen Rochefontaine … therefore is subject to a Trial by a Court Martial, the assembling of which, in the present situation of the military of the United States, would be detrimental to the Service, inconvenient and expensive; or he may at the pleasure of the President, be removed from his command, and his Commission recalled."(7)

Probably reluctant to cashier Rochefontaine without a court-martial—it is hoped that he did not share McHenry's specious reasoning that a trial would be "inconvenient and expensive"—John Adams took the unusual step of referring the whole affair to both the Secretaries of State and the Treasury for advice. Wolcott of the Treasury replied at once and briefly. He agreed with the court of inquiry that Rochefontaine was guilty, and he thought that storekeeper Fleming had also been negligent in accounting for public property and funds; he also felt that perhaps Major Tousard—another Frenchman—should be investigated on similar charges.(8) Timothy Pickering, hitherto Rochefontaine's strongest supporter, made no move this time to protect him. Pickering, a wartime Quartermaster General, understood the proper and improper use of government property, and his own reputation for personal and public probity was high; he considered that Rochefontaine and Fleming had conducted themselves improperly, although the sums involved were not large, and that both "ought to be dismissed from the service of the United States, to check, by this example of severity, a practice capable of producing very pernicious effects." These were admirable sentiments, but Pickering greatly weakened his judicial position in a postscript referring to the defense testimony of Lieutenant Peter Dransy. "Lieut Dransy," he pointed out, "however is a *Frenchman*; and political considerations may soon require the dismission of him and others of his countrymen from the service of the U. States.(9)

Rochefontaine had by this time seen the handwriting on the wall, and in a letter to Pickering at the end of April made it clear that he had little hope of retaining his commission. "I conceive," he wrote, "that the Executive of the U. States must wish that I had never [been] appointed to the command of this Corps. Nothing could summount the jealousy, ill will and stupid animosity of some [of the officers], and it is in general very difficult to impress upon the generality, the idea that a man born upon another hemisphere can be qualified to step forth and command over them."(10) This was the heart of the matter, but Rochefontaine did not pursue the obvious. He admitted that he was tired of the situation, and hinted that he would be happy to resign if he could be offered employment "which would save me from idleness"; he suggested such areas as construction of fortifications, organization of an arsenal, or construction of gun carriages. Three days later, in a follow-up note, he stated that he was not offering to resign simply because the United States was hostile to his native land; he admitted that he had enemies in the United States, but this did not alter his warm sentiments toward his adopted country.(11) Understandably, Rochefontaine did not wish to surrender his commission until he had an offer of civil employment in hand. But there was to be no offer of employment, and as Rochefontaine did not submit his resignation, President Adams took the unusual and probably illegal step of dismissing Stephen Rochefontaine from the service of the United States, without trial, effective 7 May. (No action was taken against Major Tousard or Lieutenant Dransy at this time, and none was ever taken against Fleming.)

With Rochefontaine's dismissal, the command of the Corps of Artillerists and Engineers passed by seniority to Major Henry Burbeck at Michilimackinac; perhaps by oversight, no action was taken for many months to promote Burbeck and confirm him in command. Nor was any action taken to transfer any major to West Point, so that with Rochefontaine's departure the command of that garrison devolved upon the senior officer present, Captain George Ingersoll, who "made himself responsible for the public property in and about the late Commandant's Quarters."(12) Stephen Rochefontaine quietly departed West Point as soon as he learned of his dismissal, and settled temporarily at Newburgh, just to the north on the Hudson. He disappears from the record for a few years, but in 1804 he was living in New York City, carried in the city directory as a merchant. He died on 30 January 1814, during the second war with Britain, at the age of 58.(13) Although clearly he had not been the best possible choice for the command of the Corps of Artillerists and Engineers, Rochefontaine was to some extent the victim of events and prejudices beyond his control, and one cannot but feel that, in the end, he received rather shabby treatment at the hands of both his native-born contemporaries and the government of his adopted country.

An Augmentation of Artillerists and Engineers

Congress, meanwhile, had been considering seriously the recommendation of Secretary McHenry that additional artillerymen be raised to garrison both existing and proposed seacoast defenses. It was the crisis of 1794 all over again, with a different enemy, and Congress moved with belated alacrity to strengthen the defenses before the unprotected coastal towns should be assaulted by the maritime forces of the French Directory. Secretary McHenry was requested to list the most pressing military needs, and on 9 April he forwarded several specific recommendations, the most important of which concerned naval vessels—the War Department remained in charge of naval matters until the end of the month, when Congress established a Navy Department. The Secretary also recommended an immediate augmentation of the land forces by one regiment each of infantry, artillery, and cavalry; "the artillery is considered as indispensable," he urged. He suggested, too, that if an additional regiment of infantry were raised, its recruits should be trained partly as marines, so that they could serve aboard ship or in the coastal fortifications as the need arose.(14)

The most immediate reaction to McHenry's recommendations, and the one pertinent to this work, came on 27 April, when Congress enacted legislation authorizing what it termed "an additional *regiment* [italics added] of artillerists and engineers."(15) The organization of the new regiment was to be the same as that of the existing corps, except that initially it would have three battalions instead of four. The regiment would be enlisted for five years, as opposed to three for the existing corps, but it was to be a part of the permanent establishment "for the time being," which led to the conclusion that the new troops were being raised only for the duration of the emergency. As with existing corps, the President could employ the new troops at his discretion, and the similar provision for books, instruments, and apparatus appeared to authorize continuation of the technical instruction that the officers of the older corps had so resented.

James McHenry felt that such instruction was badly needed, and, of course, so did Secretary of State Pickering. McHenry travelled to New York in June to explore the defense needs of that port, and while there conferred with Alexander Hamilton and with a former major commandant of the old battalion of artillery, John Doughty, who had left the service in early 1791. Returning to Philadelphia armed with their views, McHenry addressed to the House Committee on Defence a long report outlining the deficiencies and needs of the old and new units of Artillerists and Engineers, and making some important general recommendations. Certain portions of this document require quotation at some length:

> The act (of 1794) providing for ... a corps of artillerists and engineers, and the act to provide an additional regiment of the same, both enjoin the procurement, at the public expense, of all necessary books, instruments, and apparatus, for the benefit of the said respective regiments.
>
> The Secretary, without designing to derogate from the merits of the officers appointed to the corps ... feels it his duty to suggest, that other, and supplementary means of instruction ... appear to be absolute-

ly indispensable to enable them to acquire a due degree of knowledge in the objects of their corps ... .

The knowledge of certain arts and sciences is absolutely necessary to the artillerist and engineer; such as arithmetic, geometry, mechanics, hydraulics, and designing. [Here McHenry gave specific examples of why mastery of each of these subjects was necessary.]

It is therefore submitted, whether provision ought not to be made for the employment of three or four teachers of the enumerated sciences to be attached generally to the two corps of artillerists and engineers, and obligated to give instructions and lessons ... .

The employment of teachers would give the intended effect to the provision of the laws, for the appointment of two cadets to each company. It was supposed, that these cadets would form a nursery, from which qualified officers might be drawn to fill vacancies, &c., but ... without proper masters to teach them the sciences, necessary to the engineer and artillerists, this nursery can produce no valuable plants.

It is also submitted ... to augment the pay of cadets to nine dollars per month, with two rations. This would excite their emulation, give them a consideration above sergeants, and enable them to appear in a more respectable dress.

[The Secretary then went into the problem of the many different types and calibers of artillery on hand and being procured.]

It is important that ... an *inspector of artillery* be appointed, to see that all regulations appertaining to the ordnance department be executed and observed with exactitude ... . I cannot conceive any appointment more necessary to our military undertakings, and infant navy, than an *inspector of artillery* ... .(10)

At the end of May, with agitation against France reaching a crescendo, Congress passed enabling legislation for what came to be called the Provisional Army. This Act of 28 May generally provided for raising additional regiments of infantry and new regiments of cavalry, for appointing general officers and staff officers, and for selecting a lieutenant general to command the entire Army, existing and Provisional. Space does not permit adequate treatment of the Provisional Army in this work, and only such portions of the military legislation and other records as concerns the artillerists and engineers will be covered in any detail here. The Provisional Army was generally raised on the seaboard and did not impinge upon the operations of the peacetime establishment, the "Western Army" of General Wilkinson, except at the top level. Former President Washington, in retirement at Mount Vernon, agreed to accept the rank of lieutenant general and nominal command of the entire Army, but in practice the day-to-day planning and operations of the provisional force, which never reached its authorized strength, were conducted with great energy by Major General Alexander Hamilton, appointed with great reluctance by President Adams as Inspector General, second-in-command to Washington, and immediate commander of the Northern Department.(17)

Although Lieutenant General Washington did not plan to join his command until an actual declaration of war or a French invasion, he had many ideas as to its proper organization, most of which he discussed in detail with Secretary McHenry and General Hamilton. One of Washington's early views was that the senior officer of artillerists and engineers should, in addition to his command functions, be a member of the "General Staff" of the military commander-in-chief .(18) "The Inspector General, Quartermaster General, Adjutant General, and Officer commanding the Corps of Artiller-

Henry Knox
Secretary of War, 1785-1794

Timothy Pickering
Secretary of War, 1795-1796

James McHenry
Secretary of War 1796-1800

Personalities of the
First System of Seacoast Fortifications
1794-1800

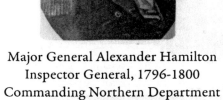

Major General Alexander Hamilton
Inspector General, 1796-1800
Commanding Northern Department

Major General
Charles Cotesworth Pinckney
Commanding Southern Department
1789-1800

Brigadier General
James Wilkenson
Commanding Western Army
1798-1800
Senior Officer of the Army
1796-1798, 1800-1812

Lieutenant Colonel Commandant
Henry Burbeck
1st Regiment of
Artillerists and Engineers

Lieutenant Colonel
Louis Tousard
2nd Regiment of
Artillerists and Engineers

ists and Engineers," he wrote McHenry, "ought to be men of the most respectable characters, and of first rate abilities; because … scarcely any movement can take place without their knowledge." A few paragraphs later he noted that "so essential and Scientific a part of the Army as the Corps of Artillerists and Engineers should have an able and respectable Officer at their head, without which it would soon sink into ignorance and disrepute."(19) Whether or not Washington had kept abreast of the story of Stephen Rochefontaine since leaving the Presidency, he had put his finger on the basic problem that had plagued the artillerists and engineers since their creation—the lack of a strong, qualified, and prestigious Commander. It was probably not by error that Washington, referring to important positions in the Army, mentioned that of "General of the Corps of Artillerest [sic] and Engineers."(20) The corps and the new regiment together would make a fitting command for a brigadier general—if a qualified officer could be found.

In July Congress shed its earlier inhibitions and voted a direct property tax by which to finance the anticipated war.(21) This hurdle surmounted, the legislators passed additional acts, including several relating to artillerists and engineers. On 16 July the pay of cadets was raised to ten dollars a month, and authority was granted to hire four teachers of the arts and sciences, at 50 dollars a month, to instruct the officers and cadets. The same act authorized the appointment of an Inspector of Artillery, to be taken from the artillerists and engineers, with pay of 30 dollars a month in addition to his regular pay. The latter two items of legislation were important and overdue; it remained only to find qualified individuals. There seemed no great hurry regarding the four teachers, however, for there was at West Point awaiting instruction that summer a single cadet, Joseph Cross, who was kept busy acting as judge advocate for the small garrison.(22)

Congress had done its part, and it was now up to the administration to select the senior officers for both units of artillerists and engineers. The original corps now lacked a commander, and the new regiment would need a regimental and three battalion commanders. General Washington still thought in terms of an overall commander for both units, and urged Secretary McHenry to consider Edward Rutledge, chief of artillery of the South Carolina militia, noting that "I know of none except General Knox who would command the Corps of Artillery more respectably."(23) Henry Knox himself was far too senior for such a command; in fact, having been offered a major generalcy in the Provisional Army junior to Alexander Hamilton and Charles Cotesworth Pinckney, Knox declined with some justice to serve at all. The search for senior artillerists was not entirely an open competition; not only were native-born Americans desired, but they should be of the Federalist persuasion—no Jeffersonians need apply for commissions in 1798.(24) McHenry, apparently with Hamilton's backing, was all for turning to Prussia or Austria for trained artillerists and engineers, but the Lieutenant General swiftly vetoed such an idea. "No Foreigner will be admitted as a member of my family [i.e., personal staff]," Washington wrote Hamilton, "while I retain my present ideas; nor do I think they ought to be in any situation where they can come at secrets, and betray a trust."(25) American secrets must have seemed particularly vulnerable in this year that saw the enactment of the Alien and Sedition Acts.

The search for qualified artillerists and engineers continued throughout 1798, underlining how completely deficient the country was in technically-trained officers. Congress did not provide for a general officer of artillerists and engineers, and Washington was doubtful that Edward Rutledge would accept the grade of lieutenant colonel commandant; there is no record that Rutledge was offered a command. The only other name the former President could think of was the Swiss-born Major Rivardi: "[He] is, I am told, a Scientific character and a man of experience … . He is gentlemanly in his appearance, and by those who know him better than I do, is said to be a man of abilities and information."(26) This lukewarm reference failed to excite either McHenry or Hamilton, who was performing much of the Army's day-to-day administration, and Rivardi was not seriously considered for promotion. The selections of the three majors for the new regiment, none very inspired choices, were made in the early fall. Adam Hoops and Benjamin Brooks were wartime Maryland infantry officers; Daniel Jackson of Massachusetts had at least served in the 3d Continental Artillery during the war. Major Hoops was a friend of General Hamilton, and by mid-October was assisting Hamilton at his New York City headquarters and nominally acting as artillery commander for New York Harbor.(27) Major Jackson's initial assignment was the command of the fortifications in and around Boston; Major Brooks remained unassigned during 1798. But none of these men had the background or prestige for the command of the new regiment, and the search continued. At the end of the year Hamilton wrote McHenry: "I believe on the whole you can do nothing better than appoint Tousard, who I understand is next in rank after Burbeck, to the command of the Regiment and Major Hoops to the Inspector-ship [of Artillery]. [Tousard's] fidelity will be best secured by giving him a fair and equal chance, and shewing him that he is not suspected. I shall be very much mistaken, if he does not prove to merit confidence." But Secretary McHenry would not hear of Tousard; there would be "no end of complain-ings and heartburning" were a foreigner placed at the head of the new regiment.(28) At last, after the turn of the year, the appointment went to John Doughty, onetime (1787-1791) major commandant of artillery, whose rank as lieutenant colonel commandant was set back to 1 June 1798.

Meanwhile the command of the older corps, vacated so abruptly by Stephen Rochefontaine in May 1798, remained unfilled at the end of the year. President Adams tentatively nominated Jonathan Dayton, Jr., of New Jersey for the post, but Dayton, who had been an infantry captain during the war, was unacceptable to the Senate. Finally, in February 1799, the administration took the easy and honest way out by promoting the senior major, Henry Burbeck, to lieutenant colonel commandant, with date of rank set back to Rochefontaine's dismissal. Burbeck, at Michilimackinac, first learned of his promotion about 24 April in a letter from General Wilkinson, but for the moment remained at his faraway post.(29) Burbeck's former battalion command, with promotion to major, went to the senior captain of the old corps, Mahlon Ford.

The position of Inspector of Artillery, created at McHenry's urging by the Act of 16 July 1798, also remained unfilled at the end of the year. The only qualified candidate was Major Louis Tousard, who had been inspecting the fortifications along the middle Atlantic, with particular attention to Fort Mifflin, during much of the year. But Tousard, although awarded the brevet of lieutenant colonel in the Continental Army, was still a Frenchman, and in 1798 President Adams was not inclined to draw attention to the fact that the Army had a Frenchman superintending the defenses against France. Ironi-cally, no one seems to have objected to Tousard's doing the work of the position, but almost two years would have to pass before Tousard could officially be appointed Inspector of Artillery.

Reorganization for Defense of the Seacoast

With two regimental-size units of artillerists and engineers now authorized, and the second be-ing raised, a reorganization of the seacoast defense structure was needed. Inspector General Hamilton took the initiative, and in mid-December 1798 drafted a letter to the Secretary of War, for General Washington's signature, outlining a plan for stationing the seven battalions. Hamilton proposed that one battalion remain with Wilkinson's "Western Army," and that four battalions be used for seacoast garrisons, with one company at Boston, two at Newport, two at New York (plus one at West Point), two at Fort Mifflin, one at Baltimore, two at Norfolk, one on the Cape Fear River, two at Charleston, one at Savannah, and one at the mouth of the St. Mary's River. Presumably, although not so stated, other existing defenses, such as Portland and New London, would be sub-posts garrisoned by detachments from the companies listed. The remaining two battalions were to be "reserved for the army in the field," implying their employment as field artillery. The majors were to be distributed proportionally to the assigned companies. Hamilton also proposed that the two reserve battalions establish a course of instruction at some central location, to which could be sent successive groups of officers and noncommissioned officers from the seacoast garrisons, whenever their services on the coast could be spared.(30)

Hamilton prepared on the same day a second letter to Secretary McHenry, again for General Washington's signature, giving in great detail his recommendations on many aspects of the Provisional Army, which in his view applied as well to the pre-1788 peace establishment. The Secretary of War added a few ideas of his own, changed Hamilton's wording here and there, and forwarded the long and important paper to President Adams, recommending appropriate legislation by Congress. The President transmitted the report to both houses on 31 December, without comment other than to recommend consideration. Many of the recommendations were incorporated into legislation in 1799, but the entire report is a valuable document in the history of the emerging Army.(31) (Certain portions pertaining to the artillerists and engineers are reproduced as Appendix B.)

Much of early 1799 was devoted to recruiting the old and new companies of artillerists and engineers up to strength. There were several officer vacancies in the older corps, caused by death or resignation; two captains of the 1st Battalion died in succession commanding the garrison at Natchez, for example—John Peirce in 1798 and George Demlar in March 1799.(32) Vacancies were filled during the year by promotion of officers strictly by seniority, without regard to battalion; while this was the fairest method, it required lieutenants being promoted to travel considerable distances, from the frontier to the seacoast or the reverse, to assume command of the companies to which they were being assigned.

Officers for the new regiment were appointed throughout 1798, although all dates of rank were set back to 1 or 7 June. Among the 12 new captains was Decius Wadsworth, late of the old corps, who apparently felt it was safe to return to the Army now that his old antagonist Stephen Rochefontaine had departed. Because of his former service, Wadsworth became the senior captain of the new regiment; ranking just behind him was William MacRea, a former infantry captain of the Legion who had been "deranged" in the forced reduction of November 1796. The 1st Battalion, nominally commanded by Major Benjamin Brooks, was marked for assignment to seacoast defenses of New York and the Delaware, although troops of the older corps were already manning those defenses. The 2d Battalion of Major Daniel Jackson was recruited in New England, and the four companies were assigned to nearby defenses: Wadsworth's to New London, Lemuel Gates's to Boston, Amos Stoddard's to Portland, and John Henry's, after a short side trip, to Newport. The 3d Battalion, on paper commanded by Major Adam Hoops but proposed by Hamilton as a reserve for the field forces being raised, was to be recruited in Virginia and the Carolinas.(33)

A brief diversion in Pennsylvania kept three companies from their seacoast stations in early 1799. In a parallel to events of five years earlier, when the British threat to the seaboard momentarily gave way to the urgency of the Whiskey Rebellion, the defense of the coast in 1799 had to give way for a time to the quelling of another insurgency, this one also in Pennsylvania. The so-called Fries Rebellion, objecting to the payment of property taxes to support the defense program, involved mostly German farmers in Bucks and Northampton counties north of Philadelphia. The Federalist administration, still sensitive to any threat to the authority of the central government, determined to repeat its decisive tactics of 1794; when in March a band of protestors, led by John Fries, stormed a jail and delivered some of their number being held by a federal marshal, President Adams issued a proclamation denouncing these acts as "treason," and called upon Governor Thomas Mifflin to send Pennsylvania militia into the disaffected area. But Mifflin was now an anti-Federalist, and partly because no further disturbances took place and partly to embarrass the administration, the governor took no action. President Adams, committed to his course, directed that both federal troops and reliable Pennsylvania militia be sent against the rebels.(35)

The senior federal officer in the immediate area happened to be newly-promoted Major Mahlon Ford of the Corps of Artillerists and Engineers, on furlough at his home in Morristown, New Jersey. After verifying that Ford was a staunch Federalist, General Hamilton sent him orders to assemble and take command of several federal companies being marched to the area.(36) The only companies immediately available were those still recruiting; they were scattered in detachments and took several days to assemble. Eventually two companies of the new regiment were assembled, under Captains John Henry and Callender Irvine, together with Captain Joseph Elliott's company of the older corps and a company of recruits of the 2d Infantry, and started off to a rendezvous at Reading, Pennsylvania.(37) Meanwhile a detachment of militia from Philadelphia under the command of William Macpherson was ordered to march to the disaffected area, and on 18 March Macpherson was appointed a brigadier general of the Provisional Army; as a federal officer he now assumed command of the entire expedition.

There is no need to recount the tragi-comic events that followed, ending with the capture of Fries and other "rebel leaders." Macpherson's militiamen thoroughly overawed and intimidated the disaffected counties, effectively converting the German immigrant populace from Federalism to Republicanism almost overnight. Macpherson's troops were accused of unnecessary harshness and even brutality; whether this charge applied to any of the relatively untrained federal troops is not specified. Fries and several others were tried and sentenced to death, but the following year were pardoned by President Adams, to the chagrin of his ultrafederalist supporters. This was the third time—after Shays's Rebellion in 1786-87 and the Whiskey Rebellion of 1792-94—that the central government had moved against dissident elements of the population; although the Fries Rebellion is the least-known of the three, it was the only one in which federal troops—as distinguished from militia in the federal service—were directly involved. As in every subsequent instance in which the Regular Army was called out to support the civil power, it had to do a job for which it was not designed or trained, and from which it gained no laurels.(38)

During the early months of 1799 both Congress and the War Department struggled to bring some degree of order to the raising and disposition of the new troops, the many and varied units of the Provisional Army as well as the scattered companies of artillerists and engineers. As a first step, in early February, the entire military force was divided into two unequal parts. General Hamilton assumed command of the Northern Department, consisting of "all the troops in garrison on the northern Lakes, in the Northwestern Territory, including both banks of the Ohio, and on the Mississippi," as well as all forces from Maryland northward. To General Pinckney went command of the Southern Department, encompassing Virginia, the Carolinas, Georgia, Kentucky, and Tennessee.(39) Hamilton continued to maintain his headquarters in New York City, while Pinckney initially set up at Shepherdstown, Virginia. Although this geographical division seems plausible, it should be remembered that the only organized and trained troops, those of Wilkinson's peacetime establishment, came under Hamilton's overall command.

Congress continued to produce military legislation as if invasion were imminent, and on 2 March authorized the President to increase the establishment again, by up to 28 regiments; most of these forces were never raised, but action was taken under this authority to raise another battalion of artillerists and engineers, which would become the fourth battalion of the new regiment.(40) The following day legislation was enacted which provided the same organization for both units, and they were known thereafter as the 1st and 2d Regiments of Artillerists and Engineers.(41)

Another provision of the Act of 3 March 1799 is of minor interest. In an excess of enthusiasm, possibly foreseeing several American armies taking the field against a Gallic invasion, Congress abolished the grade of lieutenant general held by Washington, and proclaimed that the commander of the American forces would be known thereafter as the "General of the Armies of the United States."(42)

Two sections of the new legislation were directly pertinent to the artillerists and engineers, and pointed the way to the eventual separation of the artillery and engineering functions three years later. The President was authorized to "engage and appoint, distinct from the officers of the corps of artillerists and engineers, two engineers with the rank of lieutenant-colonel"; as there were no qualified native-born Americans at this point, the authority was not used, but it was on the statute books if needed. The other provision was for the much-needed position of Inspector of Fortifications. Such an official could be selected either from among the officers of artillerists and engineers, or from civil life; in the latter case he would be "entitled to the rank of major." Again, for various reasons, this appointive authority was not exercised for over two years.

Completing and Manning the Second-Phase Defenses

The war scare that reached its peak in 1799 brought greatly increased appropriations for construction and repair of the seacoast fortifications. Secretary of War McHenry had requested the enormous sum of $1,000,000 in 1798, although he admitted that a lesser sum would suffice if a navy were authorized and quickly constructed. The House debated at some length the whole approach to seacoast defense, divided generally as to whether Congress should specify the exact sites to be fortified, or whether the President and his advisors should determine how to expend the overall appropriation. Several members questioned the possibility of defending the long coastline at all, feeling that patrol vessels should be employed and that fortifications should be provided only for the larger cities. In view of the emergency, however, and considering what had already been done during the First Phase of construction four years earlier, it was decided to let the Executive decide on the details of the defensive system, and on 3 May 1798 the House appropriated the sum of $250,000 for seacoast fortifications generally.(43)

With no Congressional guidelines as to sites to be defended, Secretary McHenry—supported and sometimes prodded by Inspector General Hamilton—drew up his own priority list of the most important and vulnerable areas, with the temporary national capital continuing to claim the largest outlay. As McHenry was to summarize expenditures late the following year, the Congressional appropriation, together with monies remaining from 1797, was expended in 1798 and part of 1799 as follows:(44)

	1798	1799
Portland, Maine District	$1,200	$4,264
Portsmouth, New Hampshire	1,000	——
Salem, Massachusetts	——	2,000
Marblehead, Massachusetts	——	6,000
Newport, Rhode Island	5,900	50,000
New London, Connecticut	——	7,520
New York City	30,117	30,116
Philadelphia (The Delaware)	51,365	43,503
Baltimore, Maryland	18,023	4,469
Norfolk, Virginia	——	402

Cape Fear River, North Carolina	——	5,333
Charleston, South Carolina	4,206	11,500
St. Mary's River, Georgia	═══	2,000
	$111,811	$167,107

It will be noted that no federal funds were expended for Boston Harbor; as Massachusetts still declined to cede the necessary sites, fortifications there remained a state responsibility. For New York City, the expenditures were for the forts in the inner harbor only; the state retained responsibility for the fortifications being erected at the Narrows.

Very little was done to provide augmented federal garrisons for any of the defenses until 1799, when the old and new units of artillerists and engineers were recruited to near strength and redesignated as the 1st and 2d Regiments. Although some of the First Phase forts had been manned more or less continuously by federal troops since 1794, the additional troops raised in 1798-99 were superimposed upon the original garrisons in some instances, and formed new garrisons in others. And in 1799, for the first time, some battalion or "district" organization was provided for the supervision of companies manning two or more defenses. The unmanned defenses of New England were given priority for garrisons during the Second Phase, although federal troops were not available until mid-1799. All seacoast defense from Maryland north came under the department commanded by Alexander Hamilton, and the energetic Inspector General took detailed steps to organize them, giving emphasis to the New England fortifications. He assigned the immediate direction of the New England defenses to Major Daniel Jackson, nominal commander of the 2d Battalion of the 2d Regiment, and in May 1799 ordered that "all the garrison posts within the vicinity of the sea board in the States of Connecticut, Rhode Island, Massachusetts, including the Province of Maine, and New Hampshire be placed under the command of Major Jackson, his general Station will be at or near New Port, Rhode Island."(45) In turn, Major Jackson issued a battalion order on 4 June assuming responsibility for garrisons of varying sizes at nine locations—Portland, Portsmouth, Newburyport, Cape Ann, Marblehead, Salem, Boston, Newport, and New London.(46)

The town of Portland itself raised $2,000 to put Fort Sumner in condition for a garrison, being raised in the vicinity by Captain Amos Stoddard of Jackson's battalion, and by late September 1798 it appears that Stoddard's men were manning the defenses. The following summer, however, most of these troops were marched to add to the garrison of "Rhode Island Harbor."(47) It is probable that Stoddard's company provided a detachment for Fort William and Mary at Portsmouth early in 1799, but whether this detachment remained when Stoddard's men left for Newport is not recorded.

The defenses of the Massachusetts coast north of Boston were provided from within the resources of Major Jackson's battalion. Only a handful of men could have been allocated to Newburyport—apparently added to the War Department list by Jackson—and to Fort Point at Gloucester on Cape Ann. At Salem the local militia had repaired and manned Fort William, possibly reinforced by a federal detachment from Boston in 1799. At the end of October 1798, at the direction of Secretary of War McHenry, Fort William was redesignated Fort Pickering, in honor of McHenry's predecessor then Secretary of State.(48) The post at Marblehead, Fort Sewell, remained ungarrisoned until 1799, when it was repaired and manned by a small detachment from Boston.

In Boston itself the state had made limited repairs to Castle William on Castle Island on the south side of the inner harbor, and the fort served as a rendezvous for recruits of the artillerists and engineers. Despite lack of federal status, Castle William was garrisoned by the company of Captain Lemuel Gates, and for the first half of 1799 it was also the headquarters of the battalion and district commander, Major Daniel Jackson.

Newport, Rhode Island, commanding the entrance to Narragansett Bay, was considered the most important coastal site in New England, and was the only one with a federal garrison throughout 1798. Two companies of the old Corps of Artillerists and Engineers were posted in Newport; Captain William Littlefield's was at Fort Wolcott—formerly Fort Washington—on Goat Island, while Captain Joseph Elliott's was returned simply as "Rhode Island." Late in 1798 Captain John Henry's company of the new regiment was recruited for station in Newport, but early in 1799 both Elliott's company and Henry's recruits were marched to Pennsylvania to assist in putting down the Fries Rebellion. To strengthen the Newport defenses, Major Louis Tousard was directed to construct a new work on Brenton's Point to take one company and mount 12 guns, while a separate battery of about the same size was designed for North Point. The latter work was never completed, but was nevertheless declared ready for a garrison and was named Fort Greene, after General Nathanael Greene. The work on Brenton's Point was not completed during 1799, but it also was considered ready to be manned and was christened Fort Adams, in honor of the President. The first garrison was provided by Captain Henry's company, which returned from Pennsylvania just in time for the dedicatory ceremony on 4 July. Major Tousard had erected an elaborate temporary arch at the entrance to the main battery, on which was inscribed "FORT ADAMS: The Rock on Which the Storm Will Beat," and after the naming of the fort its battery fired a 13-gun salute, returned by the guns of Fort Wolcott on Goat Island.(49) Major Daniel Jackson at once moved his district headquarters from Boston to Fort Adams.

The two works at New London, Connecticut, guarding the mouth of the Thames River, were garrisoned on a part-time basis by local militia companies until late 1798, when Captain Decius Wadsworth, returning to service after a two-year absence, recruited a company locally for the 2d Regiment. Federal funds for New London during the Second Phase went primarily to Fort Trumbull, which was garrisoned by Wadsworth's company. Fort Griswold on Groton Heights across the river received some money for repairs, but was manned by no more than a caretaking detachment at this time.(50)

The stretch of the Atlantic coast from New York City south to include Maryland was also in General Hamilton's department. Its major fortifications had been garrisoned since the First Phase by companies of the older corps, but in early 1799 newly-recruited companies of the 2d Regiment also took stations in the area. Near the end of the year, in an attempt to divide artillery troops and responsibilities equitably, General Hamilton announced that his command would include the entire 2d Regiment of Artillerists and Engineers, but only that battalion or the 1st Regiment serving with Wilkinson. The remainder of the 1st Regiment theoretically went to Pinckney's Southern Department, along the seacoast from Virginia through Georgia.(51) But it is doubtful from surviving records that this division was actually effected prior to the disbandment of the Provisional Army in June 1800, and it is clear that throughout 1799 companies of both regiments were manning the fortifications of the middle Atlantic coast.

In New York Harbor a considerable amount of construction was accomplished during the Second Phase, both by the federal and state governments. As New York still declined to cede the necessary land, all work in the harbor was a joint venture; Ebenezer Stevens, a wartime lieutenant colonel of artillery, represented both the state, as a committee head, and the federal government, as War Department agent for fortifications. Stevens in turn selected Joseph Francois Mangin, another French-born engineer, to succeed Charles Vincent, and in 1798 placed Mangin in direct charge of completing Fort Jay on Governors Island. In October the state legislature appropriated $150,000 for defense of New York City, and Governor Jay asked General Hamilton, in his capacity both as a citizen of New York and a "national officer," to give his attention to the project; Hamilton agreed, and delegated Major

Adam Hoops of the artillerists and engineers as "commandant of New York harbor."(52) The governor proposed to spend the state money both in the inner harbor and in planning defenses at the Narrows, which remained a state project. The federal defenses were limited to works on Governors, Bedlow's, and Ellis (or Oyster) Islands, although plans were drawn up also for a work just off the Battery at the tip on Manhattan Island. During most of 1798 the federal garrison in the harbor consisted of the company of Captain Frederick Frye of the Corps of Artillerists and Engineers, stationed at Fort Jay; Frye's men were badly clothed for the winter, and those who were not incapacitated by dysentery showed a distressing tendency to desert. By the end of 1798 small garrisons had been established on Bedlow's and Ellis Islands, and on the latter 12 guns—state property—had been mounted in the uncompleted work.(53) Early in 1799 Stevens strongly recommended that the United States purchase Ellis Island, which was privately owned, and that New York cede its jurisdiction, as well as that of Governors and Bedlow's Islands, to the United States, but this action was not taken until 1800. By the summer of 1799 Frye's men at Fort Jay were joined by the new company of the 2d Regiment commanded by Captain Walter L. Cochrane.(54)

Fort Mifflin on Mud Island in the Delaware, ceded to the federal government in 1795, had been continuously garrisoned by artillerists and engineers since that time. Major Louis Tousard devoted much of 1798 to repairs and new construction at Fort Mifflin, under the generous Congressional appropriation, before being transferred to Newport. Something about Fort Mifflin had proved unhealthy to its garrison commanders from the start: the first, Captain James Gamble, died in 1795; his successor, Captain Donald G. Mitchell, died in August of 1798. By June 1799 two companies of the 1st Regiment, McClallen's and Massey's, were reported at or in the vicinity of Fort Mifflin, McClallen's simply reported as "Philadelphia." The Fort Mifflin jinx on commanders was apparently still working, for Captain Ebenezer Massey died there on 3 September.(55)

In late 1798 the fort at Whetstone Point in Baltimore, garrisoned by artillerists and engineers since 1795, was renamed Fort McHenry in honor of the Secretary of War, a citizen of the city. Major Tousard had been directed to supervise improvements to the First-Phase works, within the roughly $20,000 appropriated by Congress in 1797-98; Tousard regarded the amount as insufficient and local authorities agreed, for it was decided that a local committee would raise an additional $11,000 by popular subscription and complete an improvement program according to Tousard's specifications.(56) During 1798 the fort was garrisoned by Captain Staats Morris's company of artillerists and engineers; by June of 1799 the garrison was reinforced by Captain James Bruff's company of the same—now 1st—regiment. Bruff, transferred from Fort Niagara, had commanded at Whetstone Point four years earlier; being senior to Morris, Bruff resumed command of the garrison. (57)

South of Maryland the seacoast fortifications came under the overall command of Major General Charles Cotesworth Pinckney's Southern Department. In theory Pinckney had at his disposal three battalions of the Corps—later 1st Regiment—of Artillerists and Engineers, but in fact the companies of that regiment were widely scattered by 1799, as were the field officers, and only Major Constant Freeman, returning from the Natchez area, and five or six of the 12 companies were available for seacoast-defense duties.

At Norfolk the twin works of Fort Norfolk and Fort Nelson, facing each other across the Elizabeth River, had been relatively neglected since the First Phase. From the 1797 appropriation, however, $3,000 was expended in basic repairs, and a single company, Captain Richard S. Blackburn's, provided a garrison for both forts throughout 1799.(58)

The plan to erect a work at Ocracoke Inlet having proved infeasible, the only defense on the rugged North Carolina coast was Fort Johnston, some 28 miles below Wilmington on the Cape Fear River.

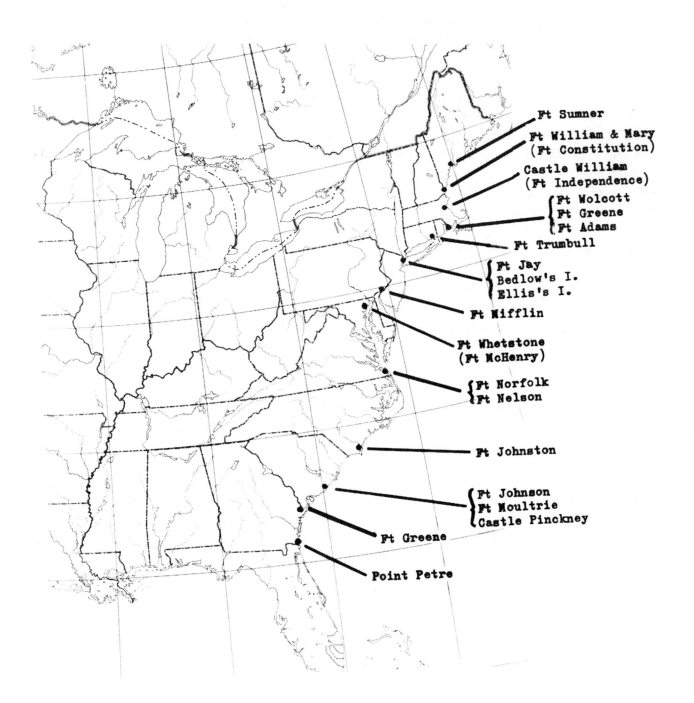

Ft Sumner

Ft William & Mary
(Ft Constitution)

Castle William
(Ft Independence)

Ft Wolcott
Ft Greene
Ft Adams

Ft Trumbull

Ft Jay
Bedlow's I.
Ellis's I.

Ft Mifflin

Ft Whetstone
(Ft McHenry)

Ft Norfolk
Ft Nelson

Ft Johnston

Ft Johnson
Ft Moultrie
Castle Pinckney

Ft Greene

Point Petre

PRINCIPAL SEACOAST FORTIFICATIONS
OF THE FIRST SYSTEM
1794-1801

The first federal garrison at Fort Johnston was assigned in 1797, a small detachment under a sergeant transferred from West Point to "the command of N. Carolina."(59) North Carolina having failed to cede the entire area of the fort because of title difficulties, little work was done on the defenses, and at the end of 1799 the garrison was small enough to be commanded by a lieutenant, Patrick C. Harris of the 2d Regiment.(60)

Three works in the harbor of Charleston—Fort Johnson on James Island, Fort Moultrie on Sullivan's Island, and Castle Pinckney on tiny Shute's Folly—had been repaired during the First Phase, but only Fort Johnson had been garrisoned by Federal troops. Captain Michael Kalteisen's company of artillerists and engineers had manned the fort since 1794, but not until November 1797 did his senior lieutenant, George Izard, return from an extensive military education in France to take up his commission. In latter 1798 Major Constant Freeman returned from Natchez and was assigned by General Pinckney to the overall command of the harbor defenses, being augmented by a company of the 2d Regiment raised by Captain Francis K. Huger of Charleston.(61) To accommodate Huger's company, Lieutenant Izard was assigned to repair and fortify Castle Pinckney. In late 1799, however, Izard was promoted to captain and assigned as aide-de-camp to General Hamilton in New York City, traveling north in January 1800. Coincidentally, a few months later Captain Huger was selected as aide-de-camp to Brigadier General James Wilkinson.(62)

In Georgia the First-Phase construction of Fort Greene on Cockspur Island—not to be confused with Fort Greene in Rhode Island—had received appropriations of over $8,000, but it did not receive a federal garrison and was not included in Second-Phase estimates. Instead, attention was devoted to the defense of the mouth of the St. Mary's River, the boundary with Spanish East Florida. The frontier post of Fort St. Tammany, established by then-Captain Henry Burbeck in 1790, was too far inland for coastal defense, and in 1797 a small fort was erected at Point Petre, east of the town of St. Mary's; it was not named, and the defenses here were usually referred to simply as "St. Mary's." Captain Abimael Y. Nicoll's company of the Corps of Artillerists and Engineers, at Fort St. Tammany in 1796, occupied the new works and remained there through 1799.(63)

It will be noted that during 1798 and 1799 there was no overall direction of the artillerists and engineers, nor was there an active commander for either regiment. Henry Burbeck, eventually promoted lieutenant colonel commandant of the 1st Regiment to succeed Stephen Rochefontaine, remained at Michilimackinac until November 1799, when he was ordered to Detroit. Directed by General Wilkinson to take station on the seacoast, it was not until July of 1800 that Colonel Burbeck reported to the new Federal City of Washington.(64) The nominal commander of the 2d Regiment, Lieutenant Colonel Commandant John Doughty, spent most of his time in New York City; overshadowed by the energetic Major Adam Hoops, Doughty appears in the record occasionally as a sort of artillery advisor to General Hamilton.

No organizational or stationing lists of the two regiments of artillerists and engineers during this period survived the War Department fire of November 1800. The nominal organization of the battalions of both regiments, together with the stations of the companies and the field officers, as far as can be reconstructed from fragmentary sources, is shown in Appendix C.(65)

CHAPTER V
TURBULENCE OF A CHANGE OF ADMINISTRATION
1800-1801

During 1799 President Adams, who had been one of the most warlike members of his administration the year before, gave increasing evidence that his attitude had changed, and that he had every intention of averting war with France. His successful negotiations with Talleyrand were received with chagrin if not hostility by Hamilton, Pickering, and other members of the pro-war faction, and by the end of the year it was clear that the Federalists faced an irremediable schism. Hamilton, the active head of a Provisional Army for which there seemed less and less likelihood of employment, was still sustained by the tremendous prestige of the titular head of that Army, General Washington, and could usually count on Washington's support in his differences with the President and the peace faction. This satisfactory state of affairs came to an abrupt end on 14 December, when, after a brief illness, George Washington died at Mount Vernon.

Unquestionably Hamilton knew that the death of Washington, to whom alone he owed his seniority, weakened badly his own position and the future of the Provisional Army. As he wrote General Pinckney, "perhaps no friend of [Washington] has more cause to lament on personal account than, myself."(1) But his nominal position was unimpaired, and by virtue of seniority, although without any specific confirmation by Congress or the Executive, Major General Alexander Hamilton assumed command of the United States Army.

Long-Range Planning for a Dwindling Army

Hamilton had devoted much of the latter half of 1799 to two major projects. The first was a sincere effort to reorganize the United States Army into a more effective and better-trained force for the years ahead; the second was a less praiseworthy plan to lead a major part of that army down the Mississippi, to dispossess Spain of her North American colonies, and possibly even to try to eject that power from the western hemisphere. The latter project, which has no place in this work, died a natural death when the paper troops of the Provisional Army failed to match Hamilton's needs, and particularly when President Adams made it clear that he wanted peace with France and most certainly no war with Spain.(2)

But in his capacity as Inspector General, Hamilton worked prodigiously, delegating very little, at the task of improving the organization and administration of the Army. Several of his projects concerned directly or indirectly the artillerists and engineers, none more than Hamilton's plan for a national military academy, a true professional school. The subject was not new, for Washington and others had discussed the matter in general terms during the war, and in 1794 legislation had provided for cadets and for their instruction. But in November 1799, writing to Secretary of War McHenry on "such measures for the improvement of our military system as may require legislative sanction," the Inspector General developed a detailed plan worth quoting in some detail:

> One which I have always thought of primary importance, is a military academy. This object has repeatedly engaged the favorable attention of the administration, and some steps toward it have been taken. But these, as yet, are very inadequate ... .
>
> Since it is agreed that we are not to keep on foot numerous forces ... military science in its various branches ought to be cultivated ... so that there may always exist a sufficient body of it ready to be imparted and diffused, and a competent number of persons qualified to act as instructors to the ad-

ditional troops which events may successively require to be raised ... .

To avoid great evils, [the government] must either have a respectable force prepared for service or the means of preparing such a force with expedition. The latter, most agreeable to the genius of our government and nation, is the object of a military academy.

I propose that this academy shall consist of five schools— one to be called "The Fundamental School"; another, "The School of Engineers and Artillerists"; another, "The School of Cavalry"; another; "The School of Infantry"; and a fifth, "The School of the Navy"... . (3)

Hamilton went on to spell out in great detail his ideas as to the composition and curriculum of these five schools. For the "Fundamental School," for example, he proposed a director, four professors of mathematics, one professor of natural philosophy, and one drawing master. He thought that this basic school should teach arithmetic, algebra, geometry, the laws of motion, mechanics, geography, topography, surveying, and the design of structures and landscapes. His ideas as to who should attend which schools were clear:

The cadets of the army, and young persons who are destined for military and naval service, ought to study for two years in the Fundamental School; and if destined for the corps of engineers and artillerists, or for the navy, two years more in the appropriate school ... .

In addition to these, detachments of officer and noncommissioned officers of the army ought to attend the academy in rotation, for the purposes of instruction and exercise [i.e., drill] ... .

It would be a wise addition to the system if the government would always have such a number of sergeants, in addition to those belonging to the regiments of the establishment, as would suffice with them for an army of 50,000 men.(4)

The comprehensive plan that Hamilton was proposing here—in far greater detail than extracted above—was basically the system of service academies and branch schools eventually adopted, the latter three-quarters of a century later. There were also proposals throughout the plan, such as the concept of a cadre of noncommissioned officers for a 50,000-man army, which foreshadowed the "expansible army" plan of Secretary of War John C. Calhoun two decades later. Hamilton knew, of course, that his plan would meet great opposition for many reasons, one of them being the obvious cost of the establishments he proposed, and just before Washington's death he submitted his proposals to the Commander-in-Chief of the Provisional Army. In what was apparently the last letter he ever wrote, Washington replied on 12 December, but in none-too-strong terms:

The Establishment of an Institution of this kind ... has ever been considered by me as an Object of primary importance to this country;—and while I was in the Chair of Government I omitted no proper opportunity of recommending it ... to the attention of the legislature:—But I never undertook to go into a *detail* of the organization of such an Academy; leaving this task to others, whose pursuits in the paths of Science, and attention to the Arrangements of such Institutions, had better qualified them for the execution of it.

For the same reason I must now decline making any observations on the details of your plan ... .

I sincerely hope that the subject will meet with due attention, and that the reasons for its establishment

... will prevail upon the Legislature to place it upon a permanent and respectable footing. (5)

Hamilton's year-end report to the Secretary of War included many other recommendations, most of them sound and several inspired—and none likely to be accepted either by Congress or by an administration now committed to returning to a peacetime establishment. One of Hamilton's more interesting recommendations was that the artillerists and the engineers should be separated, on the ground that European experience had shown that the art of fortification and the service of artillery, as he put it, were essentially distinct functions. He actually proposed a three-way division of the artillerists and engineers: the existing two regiments, he suggested, should be reorganized as a regiment of foot artillerists, a regiment of horse artillerists, and a corps of engineers, the latter to consist of officers and cadets only. But the corps of engineers should be formed by new appointments, not by transferring officers from the existing regiments; Hamilton was careful not to say so, but the inference was plain that there were few if any qualified engineers in the existing establishment.(6)

Within two months of Washington's death, however, the knell began to sound for the Provisional Army. Congress first prohibited further enlistments in the additional regiments of infantry and troops of dragoons, and on 11 March the Adjutant General in New York issued an order suspending the recruiting service for those arms.(7) During March and April Congress debated whether or not to retain any of the additional troops authorized in 1798 and 1799. The Federalists, in the majority for the last session, determined to retain both regiments of artillerists and engineers, even in the absence of an immediate threat to the seacoast, and on 14 May 1800 Congress directed that all other additional troops be discharged by 15 June, leaving only

> The General Staff, and other Staff,
> The Engineers [authorized in 1799 but never appointed],
> Inspector of Artillery,
> Inspector of Fortifications,
> 2 Regiments of Artillerists & Engineers,
> Of dragoons—2 troops; and the first 4 Regiments of Infantry.(8)

Except for the virtual doubling of the artillerists and engineers, the Army was to be returned to its peacetime strength of late 1796. Only one brigadier general was authorized, and the office of Inspector General was discontinued. Even had the President and the so-called Moderate Federalists not desired to be rid of Alexander Hamilton, it is doubtful that Hamilton would have agreed to remain at the head of the small and scattered peacetime force. At the end of February he had counselled his aide-de-camp, Captain George Izard, to exchange the Army for a diplomatic appointment, noting rather bitterly that "It is very certain that the military Career in this country offers too few inducements ... ."(9)

Most of the troops of the Provisional Army were disbanded by 15 June, although it was about 1 July before Major General Hamilton issued a final general order of appreciation to those who, like himself, were being discharged. On 2 July Hamilton wrote a brief note to Secretary McHenry: "From the terms of the act disbanding the additional army and correspondence with the Department of War, I consider our military operations ceased."(10)

The Reorganization of 1800

Although Hamilton was unaware of the fact when he wrote his note, James McHenry was no longer Secretary of War. President Adams had felt for some time that he and the holdovers from Washington's cabinet were out of tune, and in May the President asked for the resignations of both Secretary of State Pickering and Secretary of War McHenry; both complied, McHenry asking that his own departure be effective 1 June. McHenry had not been a strong Secretary, nor particularly talented, but his problems in 1798-99 had been compounded by the necessity of maintaining the fiction that he was the administrative military superior of both George Washington and Alexander Hamilton. McHenry's immediate successors provided no improvement. The President asked Secretary of the Navy Benjamin Stoddert to oversee the War Department *ad interim*, and later in June persuaded Senator Samuel Dexter of Massachusetts, a 39-year-old lawyer, to take the post of Secretary of War. (It is of passing interest to note that of the first six Secretaries of War, from 1785 to 1813, all except McHenry were from Massachusetts.)

As the only general officer now authorized, Brigadier General James Wilkinson resumed the command of the Army without formal designation. It was essentially the 1796 organization, with the addition of the second regiment of artillerists and engineers; the senior officers of that regiment, however, did not remain in service. Major Benjamin Brooks had died in January 1800, and with General Hamilton's departure, Lieutenant Colonel Commandant John Doughty and Major Adam Hoops both submitted their resignations. President Adams's son-in-law, Lieutenant Colonel William S. Smith, who had been commanding a regiment of the Provisional Army, announced his willingness to assume command of the 2d Regiment of Artillerists and Engineers. But McHenry, before leaving office, had recommended the promotion of Major Louis Tousard of the 1st Regiment; Tousard was back in favor as Franco-American relations healed, and technically he was best qualified for the position. The President queried both McHenry and Hamilton as to Smith's fitness, and both intimated that he was a fine officer entirely unacquainted with artillery or engineer duties. Satisfied, Adams then appointed Tousard to the vacant command, with promotion to lieutenant colonel commandant.(11)

Tousard's promotion and transfer left a vacant majority in the 1st Regiment, which was shortly filled by the promotion of Moses Porter of Burbeck's old battalion on the frontier. The two vacant majorities in the 2d Regiment went to the two senior captains, Decius Wadsworth and William MacRea. (12)

The disbandment of the Provisional Army had the effect of removing from the top of the peacetime establishment not only an energetic commanding general, but also the beginnings of a functioning central staff. Secretary of War Samuel Dexter established his office in the new capital of Washington City during the summer of 1800, but General Wilkinson set up no fixed headquarters at this time, preferring to devote his efforts to supervising the far-flung elements of the Army on the Ohio and the Mississippi. To replace both the Inspector General and the Adjutant General, as far as their purely administrative functions were concerned, Major Thomas H. Cushing of the 1st Infantry was ordered from the lower Mississippi to Washington City. In the position of "Major and Inspector," as he signed himself, Cushing conducted the administration of the Army single-handedly. He assisted and advised Secretary Dexter in military matters, often through the Chief Clerk of the War Department, John Newman, and also carried out the directives he received by mail from General Wilkinson at irregular intervals.(13)

The only other resident military advisor to the Secretary of war was the senior officer of artillerists and engineers, Lieutenant Colonel Commandant Henry Burbeck. Arriving from Detroit in early July, Burbeck took up a position known unofficially as "Chief of Artillery," but he had no command except within his own regiment; his duties were essentially those of a staff officer: "They relate solely to the Ordnance Department of which he is head, and it was for this duty and not as a military commander, that he was posted here."(14) This was not entirely accurate, as there was no Ordnance Department authorized during this period, but it appears that Colonel Burbeck was in charge of procurement of guns, carriages, and ammunition for the seacoast fortifications, and probably for the frontier artillery companies as well. In the fall of 1800, however, when General Wilkinson, after a brief stay in the capital, departed for Pittsburgh and the western posts on an indefinite tour of inspection, Colonel Burbeck was placed in command of all the posts on the Atlantic seaboard, with his headquarters in Washington; he was authorized direct communication with the Secretary of War, and given authority to convene general courts-martial.(15)

Before leaving Washington, General Wilkinson issued instructions designed to reestablish the military chain-of-command and to revitalize the district organization of the seacoast defenses. Colonel Tousard was assigned to duty at the new "laboratory" on the Schuylkill near Philadelphia, detached from the 2d Regiment in the capacity, still unofficial, of Inspector of Artillery; he also carried out the functions of Inspector of Fortifications, an office authorized by Congress but as yet unfilled. Major Daniel Jackson continued in command of the garrisons in Boston and to the northeast; Major William MacRea was assigned the command of the defenses of Newport, as well as the garrison of Fort Trumbull at New London; and Major Decius Wadsworth received the command of the defenses of New York Harbor and the post of West Point. In the 1st Regiment, Major J.J. Ulrich Rivardi was transferred back to the seaboard from Fort Niagara, but received only the immediate command of Fort Mifflin's two-company garrison; Major Mahlon Ford was assigned the command of the garrisons on the coast of North Carolina and "in the Chesapeake"; Major Constant Freeman continued at Charleston to command the seacoast defenses of South Carolina and Georgia. Although a company of Major Mose Porter's battalion garrisoned Fort McHenry at Baltimore, Major Porter himself was assigned to Fort Niagara on the Canadian frontier, and the company at Fort McHenry was directed to report directly to Colonel Burbeck in Washington.(16)

On 8 November there occurred the historically-disastrous fire in the newly-established War Department in Washington. Secretary Dexter reported that all the papers of his office were destroyed,(17) and it appears that the fire consumed not only Dexter's current work, but also the bulk of the records of his predecessors back to Henry Knox. It is because of this catastrophe that the story of the War Department and the Army prior to November 1800 must be reconstructed from orderly books and personal correspondence, together with such documents as were subsequently collected and published in the *American State Papers.*(18)

From the elections of November 1800 until the results were fully known in February 1801, politics dominated the new national capital. It was clear to all that if the Federalist candidates, Adams and Pinckney, failed to carry the election, the Army was in for a severe reduction. In mid-December the House debated the proper strength of the artillerists and engineers; Republican members demanded at least the withdrawal of authority for the fourth battalion of the 2d Regiment, which had not been raised. Federalists argued that the artillerists and engineers were defensive in nature, had not been directly connected with the controversial Provisional Army and ought to be kept at full strength in peacetime. New England Republicans, in particular, countered that seacoast defense should be a militia responsibility, one boasting that "in Massachusetts alone, there were forty companies of [militia] artillerists and engineers, well equipped and well disciplined, ready, at a moment's notice ... ."(19) In the end the nationalist view prevailed by a small margin, and the 2d Regiment retained the authority to complete its fourth battalion.

The last months of the Adams administration were increasingly chaotic, particularly after it was evident that the Federalists had lost the election and the only question was which foe, Jefferson or Burr, would be President. On 31 December Adams nominated Samuel Dexter to be Secretary of the Treasury, but no successor in the War Department was named. Dexter continued to oversee the War

Department to some extent, and as late as 10 February Major Cushing, the Inspector, was addressing letters to Dexter as War Secretary. At last Representative Roger Griswold of Connecticut was designated to serve as Secretary of War during the last few weeks of the administration; he was nominated on 13 February, according to one source, but the nomination was apparently not acted upon by the Senate, and Major Cushing addressed no letters to Griswold during this period.(20) But John Adams, though embittered by the schism within his own faction, for which he blamed Hamilton and Pickering particularly, had not yet struck his tent as Chief Executive. Right up to his last day in office Adams signed legislation and commissions that represented hard-won Federalist victories. Well-known is the minor appointment that led to the pivotal Marbury v. Madison decision of the Supreme Court; less familiar are Adams's successful efforts to fill the vacancies in the officer corps of the Army before he left office. On 16 February the President signed commissions for scores of new officers from lieutenant to major; not all eventually accepted and served, but at least on paper the Army had almost its full complement of officers before the Jeffersonians took over, including the controversial fourth battalion of the 2d Regiment of Artillerists and Engineers.

Perhaps because it was raised during his administration, John Adams had always taken an interest in the 2d Regiment, and as early as mid-1799 he had sought advice as to a qualified American-born engineer whom he could appoint to high rank in the regiment. Unlike Hamilton, Adams had viewed Louis Tousard with disfavor during the French crisis, and although by mid-1800 he was willing to let Tousard take nominal command of the 2d Regiment, he continued his search for qualified native Americans. The search took on added importance when, for some months at the end of 1800, it appeared that Congress might establish the missing battalion, at reduced strength, as a military academy, for in that event the prospective battalion commander could become director of the academy.

Soon after the controversial battalion had been authorized in March of 1799, Secretary McHenry had proposed two candidates for its command. Both came from Massachusetts: John Lillie had served as an artillery captain and as an aide-de-camp to General Knox; Jonathan Williams had not seen military service. President Adams knew and liked Lillie, whose postwar business ventures had been unfortunate; he also thought the name of Jonathan Williams was familiar. He queried McHenry: "I wish to know whether the Jonathan Williams, you mention, is the gentleman who lived in France when I was there, and is now in [Philadelphia]. If it is the same, although I have not known much of his military character, his other qualifications are respectable."(21)

It *was* the same Jonathan Williams, and his overall intellectual qualifications were respectable indeed. To begin with Williams was the grand-nephew of Benjamin Franklin, and in many ways Franklin's intellectual heir. Born in 1750, educated before and after the war at Harvard College, Williams had twice accompanied Franklin to Europe, acting as his official secretary in Paris. While Franklin was back in America, Williams became the American commercial agent at the French port of Nantes, where he made an intensive study of the medieval fortifications at Nantes and Angers, later broadened to include the general art of fortification and military science in general. Returning to the United States in 1785, Williams became a judge of common pleas in Philadelphia, and an active member of the American Philosophical Society, founded by his great-uncle. In 1799 he became Counsellor of the Society, and was one of six members of a committee "to collect information respecting the past and present state of this country"—his colleagues on the committee included Thomas Jefferson and General James Wilkinson.(22)

Opposition in Congress to filling the missing battalion forced the President to defer his appointments for a year and a half. But after the favorable vote in December 1800, Adams nominated Jonathan Williams to be junior major of the 2d Regiment of Artillerists and Engineers, effective 16 February, and John Lillie to be a captain of the same regiment. Lillie's appointment passed unnoticed, but that of Williams excited favorable comment, and there was a feeling in the upper echelons that the Army was fortunate in securing the services of such a gentleman of intellect and talent. (23)

Despite the appointments of 16 February, which went far toward filling up the officer corps according to Federalist standards, a sense of anxiety hung over the officers, the great majority of whom were Federalists, at the prospect of a rival administration. On 6 February, when the Presidency was still contested, Major Cushing noted in an official letter to Major Constant Freeman in Charleston that "if Mr._____ is President we may hold up our heads a little longer, but should Mr._____ succeed we shall most probably go to the right about." Three weeks later Cushing wrote hastily to General Wilkinson at Pittsburgh, urging him to return to Washington at once: "It is understood on all sides that an entire new Administration is to be formed & that many other alterations are to take place.... In short every body & every thing here are so much out of tune that I wish with all my heart that the period was arrived for transferring the public functions."(24)

President Jefferson and Secretary Dearborn

The inauguration of Thomas Jefferson as President of the United States on 4 March 1801 marked a distinct break in the 17-year history of the United States Army. While the wily and flexible Brigadier General James Wilkinson expected to get along with Jefferson as well as he had with Washington and Adams, other officers less highly placed had some basis for their trepidation. Those who had kept abreast of the political ideologies of the period knew that the incoming Democratic-Republicans, who now controlled both houses of Congress,(25) were committed to financial retrenchment even more than the opposition Federalists, and committed also to a decentralization of federal authority which included reliance on the state militias instead of a standing army. It would be nearly a year, however, before the Army and the infant Navy felt the full impact of legislation to this end.

After the contested election within his own faction, President Jefferson at first moved quite slowly. He seemed in no great hurry to grasp the Executive authority, and took several months to complete his cabinet appointments. He had difficulty in finding a suitable Secretary of the Navy, for there seemed little future in assuming an office that promised to be almost self-liquidating; indeed, for some months in the spring and summer of 1801 the Navy functions were supervised, as they had been for the first decade under the Constitution, by the head of the War Department. For the latter position the new President had early found his choice, and one of the first of his appointees to enter actively upon his duties was the new Secretary of War, Henry Dearborn of Massachusetts.

Secretary Dearborn was just over 50 years old when he took over the War Department on 9 March 1801. Like his predecessor James McHenry, Dearborn had been trained as a physician and entered practice in New Hampshire in 1772; unlike McHenry, Dearborn abandoned medicine in 1775 for a combatant role in the Revolutionary War. He served from first to last with considerable distinction, and left service in March 1783 as lieutenant colonel of the 1st New Hampshire Regiment. Settling in the Maine District, Dearborn rose to be major general of Massachusetts militia, and in 1790 was appointed United States Marshal for the District of Maine. He then veered in the antifederalist direction; he ran successfully for Congress as a Republican and served in Philadelphia from 1793-1797, but these were Federalist years and Dearborn's record was undistinguished. His excellent war record and his Republican leaning brought his appointment as Secretary of War, an office he would hold throughout both terms of Jefferson's administration.(26)

When Dearborn took office the Army he was to supervise was in a state of almost suspended animation. The disbandment of Hamilton's Provisional Army the year before had deprived the remaining peace establishment of strong leadership and adequate staff management. General Wilkinson, the only general officer, spent most of this time inspecting the widely scattered garrisons on a frontier that extended from Fort Niagara, New York, to Fort Fayette at Pittsburgh, down the Ohio to Fort Massac, and then north to the lakes and south on the Mississippi to the Spanish frontier. During this period the busiest and perhaps administratively the most important officer of the Amy was Major Thomas H. Cushing, the Inspector, a strong Wilkinson adherent since the days of the Wayne-Wilkinson feud. Despite his title, Cushing was primarily an adjutant general, acting as an executive officer both to General Wilkinson on the frontier and to the Secretary of War in the new capital. Cushing was not considered a member of the War Department, but maintained a separate temporary office; he was an advisor to the Secretary on military administration, and a liaison officer between the Secretary and General Wilkinson. In the War Department itself the Secretary was assisted by a Chief Clerk, initially John Newman and later Joshua Wingate, Jr., and exercised direct supervision over the Paymaster of the Army, Caleb Swan; the Quartermaster, John Wilkins, Jr., at Pittsburgh; and the Superintendent of Military Stores, William Irvine, in Philadelphia.

Within two weeks of assuming office, Henry Dearborn made it plain to the Army that fiscal economy would be the order of the day, and he made it equally clear that among the first projects to undergo financial retrenchment would be the seacoast fortifications. On 18 March he wrote to Colonel Tousard, then at Newport, that "it is with the approbation of the President of the United States, that I now direct a suspension of all expenditures of public money as far as relates to fortifications in the Harbour of Rhode Island... ."(27) He then directed Tousard to report to Washington to discuss his future functions as Inspector of Artillery.

Another of the Secretary's economies was the use of troop labor instead of contract laborers. He wrote to Captain Staats Morris, commanding at Fort McHenry, directing that construction, although contracted to a civilian superintendent, be performed whenever practicable by soldiers and artificers of Morris's company. Shortly afterward Dearborn wrote sharply to Major Rivardi, now commanding at Fort Mifflin, admonishing him for employing workmen for emergency repairs to damages caused by a sudden rising of the Delaware; necessary work, Dearborn directed, would be done by the troops, "making them the usual allowance for extra service, viz. one gill of Spirits and ten cents extra per day." As the repairs were almost completed when Major Rivardi received the Secretary's letter, he made the mistake of allowing the workmen to finish the job. This brought down Dearborn's full wrath; he wrote sarcastically that he "had flattered myself that officers in the service of the United States, had at least acquired the habit of obeying orders, and am not a little disappointed in finding myself mistaken in so essential a point."(28)

It was evident very quickly that Henry Dearborn was not going to be friendly to the few foreign-born officers remaining in the Army. Unlike Timothy Pickering, who had sought French-trained artillerists and engineers, and even unlike James McHenry, who had tolerated them, Secretary Dearborn seemed to find it demeaning that the Army should have need of this talent. His correspondence indicates that he resented the very presence of Colonel Tousard and Major Rivardi—and to a lesser extent the younger Lieutenant Peter Dransy—in the officer corps, although he did not hesitate to employ their services on technical projects.

Among these technical projects in 1801 were two that required considerable education and experience; these were the engineering aspects of fortifications design, and the ordnance function of inspecting and proving cannon and small arms before acceptance by the War Department. Fortifications design had occupied the foreign-born officers since the beginning of First-Phase construction, but inspecting and proving cannon was a time-consuming activity which should have been accomplished by others. The testing and acceptance of small arms was considered a function of the Inspector of the Army—although in 1801 that title was something of a misnomer—and on several occasions Major Cushing was called away from his administrative duties to pass on new muskets before the government would pay the contractor. Occasionally Colonel Burbeck, the so-called Chief of Artillerists, had to go with the superintendent of the new Harpers Ferry arsenal to inspect and accept small arms manufactured in the Maryland-Virginia area.(29) A more appropriate small-arms inspector was found in Major Decius Wadsworth of the 2d Regiment, commanding at Fort Jay; Secretary Dearborn either knew or learned that Wadsworth was an inventor and gunsmith himself, a onetime associate of Eli Whitney, and in the early summer of 1801 Major Wadsworth was pulled away from his artillery duties to act as inspector of contract small arms at Hartford, Connecticut.(30)

The proving and acceptance of cannon was a more complex business, one in which few officers except Colonel Tousard and possibly Colonel Burbeck were qualified. Tousard, at the time of his promotion to succeed John Doughty as lieutenant colonel commandant, had been advised that he was also to be Inspector of Artillery, but the appointment seems never to have been formalized, and Tousard probably assumed that it lapsed with the change of administrations. In early April 1801, however, Secretary Dearborn wrote to Tousard that no cannon cast for public use would be accepted by the government unless Tousard had certified them as Inspector of Artillery.(31) Tousard may have queried the authenticity of his appointment, for ten days later the Secretary drew up a formal certificate of appointment dated back to 26 May 1800, together with a list of detailed duties of the position. One of the duties was to make an annual return to the War Department of all ordnance belonging to the United States, with its location and condition—a duty earlier assigned to Colonel Burbeck as Chief of Artillerists. Tousard was also to be responsible for inspecting and proving all ordnance and other articles for the artillery, both that produced by civilian contract and that manufactured in government arsenals or armories, and for providing models of gun carriages and other artillery accessories to prospective contractors. As most of the foundries for casting ordnance, as Dearborn pointed out, were in Pennsylvania, New Jersey, New York, and Rhode Island, Tousard was advised to make his permanent headquarters at West Point.(32) Dearborn's detailed instructions to Tousard contained several paragraphs on the relationship of the Inspector of Artillery to the military school to be established at West Point. To understand these references, it will be necessary to break chronology at this point and to review the events which led in 1801 to the establishment of what would become officially, the following year, the United States Military Academy.

The Creation of a Military School

Several desultory attempts had been made during the Revolutionary War to establish military schools of one sort or another; a few regimental schools were briefly in operation, and when Congress authorized the so-called Corps of Invalids in 1777, its duties included acting as "a military school for young gentlemen previous to their being appointed to marching regiments.(33) But these efforts were abandoned in the face of more pressing military requirements, as well as lack of funds, and the new republic struck out on its own in 1783 without any central system for the schooling of its future military officers. Not until the war scare of 1794 did Congress provide for any sort of federal military educational program, and the details and fate of the system of classroom instruction established at West Point in 1796 by Stephen Rochefontaine have been covered earlier in this work. Despite other sources of friction, the basic failure to found an academy in 1796-98 lay in the fact that no American officers were qualified to instruct in engineering and gunnery—and at the same time they were unwilling to accept instruction from foreigners who were qualified.

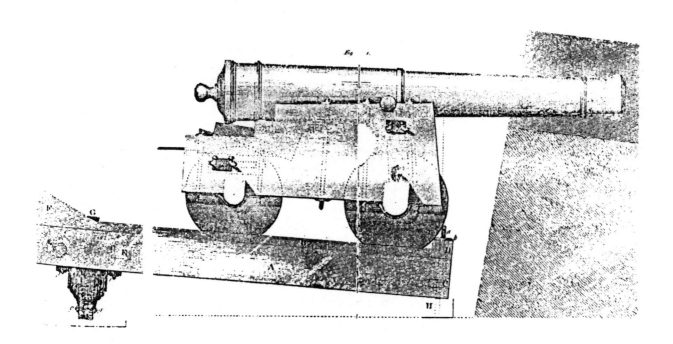

24-pounder Gun on Travelling Carriage
18-pounder Gun on Truck Carriage, mounted on
Pivoted Chassis or "Wheeling Frame"
Seacoast Cannon of the First System, from Tousard, American Artillerist's Companion

A considerable impetus toward the creation of a formal military academy came from Alexander Hamilton's detailed plan at the end of 1799 discussed in the previous chapter. But Hamilton's plan was far in advance of its time, and far beyond the needs of the nation at the end of the 18th century; at a time when the existing colleges of the country were little more than junior high schools by modern standards, Hamilton was proposing the curriculum of a first-class European military college. Hamilton's entire plan would have been prohibitively expensive as peaceful prospects returned in 1800, but Secretary McHenry forwarded an estimate of $39,000 for a combination fundamental school and school for artillerists and engineers, and Harrison Gray Otis introduced a bill in the House for such a school. But the impending elections of 1800 took precedence, and the bill was deferred to December at the earliest.(34)

President Adams showed increasing interest in the idea of a military academy, and realized that the success or failure of such an institution would depend to a large extent upon its head; what was needed, Adams felt, was a director of national or even international reputation. In June 1799 the President wrote Secretary McHenry about the possibility of attracting Benjamin Thompson, the expatriate Royalist from Massachusetts who was widely known in Europe under the imperial title, conferred by the Elector of Bavaria, of Count Rumford. Through Rufus King, the minister in London, Adams offered Rumford the dual position of Inspector of Artillery and director of the proposed military school. But Rumford was fully engaged with the incorporation of what became the Royal Institution in London, and declined the American offer.(35)

Meanwhile the two senior officers of artillerists and engineers had submitted, independently, their own ideas for schools for officers of their arm. The first had been drafted in 1798 by Louis Tousard, and presented to Secretary McHenry under the title "Formation of a School of Artillerists and Engineers"; as regards a curriculum, Tousard's study was even more detailed than Hamilton's. Implicit in Tousard's proposal was the thought that the best man to head the proposed school was Louis Tousard—which may well have been true. But McHenry remembered the Rochefontaine affair; he was aware of President Adams's aversion to foreign-born officers in high places, and to a degree he shared it. There is no evidence that McHenry took any specific action to convert Tousard's ideas into legislation.(36)

The other in-service proposal for a military school came in the early fall of 1800, submitted by Henry Burbeck as Chief of Artillerists. According to his sole biographer, Colonel Burbeck sent to Secretary of War Samuel Dexter, on 23 September, a list of recommendations for the better organization of the artillerists and engineers, urging in particular a "MILITARY SCHOOL, for instructing the arts of gunnery, fortification, pyrotechny, and everything relative to the art of war; and that there be taken from the line of artillerists and engineers one field officer and four captains well versed in science, especially in mathmatics and natural philosophy, to be employed in superintending the laboratory and instructing the officers of the line and the cadets ... . (37) Burbeck's proposal was more modest in scope than either Tousard's or Hamilton's; he put considerable emphasis on the laboratory being established at Frankford, outside Philadelphia, to be manned by a company of artillerists and engineers, and he seems to have envisioned the military school as being based there. Significantly, Burbeck also proposed that "there be formed a small corps of engineers ... separate from the artillerists," which exactly anticipated the legislation of 1802.(38)

Secretary of War Dexter, during his brief tenure, took his duties seriously, and in reviewing military legislation still in force found that he was charged with providing the necessary books and apparatus for schooling officers and cadets of artillerists and engineers. On 16 July 1800 he wrote to the President at his Quincy home, outlining a plan for bringing the number of authorized cadets up to strength and for appointing the engineers and teachers already authorized. Adams was interested, and replied to Dexter at length; he was ready, he wrote, to appoint the whole number of cadets authorized, 64, as soon as suitable candidates presented themselves. As to engineers and teachers, he asked Dexter to recommend suitable persons, but thought that one engineer and two teachers would suffice for a start. As a teacher he suggested Captain William A. Barron, newly appointed to the 2d Regiment of Artillerists and Engineers. He also mentioned a French engineer in New York, Bureaux de Pusy, as a possibility, but added, "I have an invincible aversion to the appointment of foreigners, if it can be avoided. It mortifies the honest pride of our officers, and damps their ardor and ambition."(39)

Of the two names brought forward by the President, William Amherst Barron was a Harvard classmate of the President's son, John Quincy Adams, and a skilled mathematics tutor; his appointment to the 2d Regiment had been made with the idea that he might conduct mathmatics instruction, at least within the regiment. Bureaux de Pusy had been associated for several years with another Frenchman, Jean Foncin, in designing fortifications for the Narrows below New York Harbor—for the state, not the federal government. Secretary Dexter, in investigating De Pusy, encountered Foncin's name, and on 4 August recommended to the President that teaching appointments be offered to Barron, De Pusy, and Foncin. The President replied decisively: "I will not object to the appointment of Mr. Foncin as one of the three. But I shall not appoint him first as long as Barron lives. If you can find another American mathematician better than Barron, it is well, if not, we will appoint him first teacher."(40) But Adams's interest waned in the bitterness of the 1800 election, and in the end neither Frenchman received an appointment.

As the President had noted, the existing laws in 1800 provided for 64 cadets, two for each company of artillerists and engineers. The term "service" cadet became current about 1802-1805 to distinguish those serving with companies from the "academy" cadets who were ordered to West Point for formal instruction; strictly speaking, the three cadets commissioned in 1796—Landais, Triplett, and Rodrigue—had been service cadets. The first service cadet to become an academy cadet was Joseph Gardner Swift of Massachusetts. Young Swift had first encountered the Army when his father, a physician, became a temporary surgeon in the Provisional Army, and during this time the young man had visited Captain Amos Stoddard's company of artillerists and engineers, camped in Massachusetts en route from Portland to Newport. The officers introduced Swift to the subjects of artillery and fortification, lent him a copy of Muller's treatise—which he found hard going—and encouraged him to become a cadet in their regiment. Dr. Swift applied to the Secretary of War for a cadetship for his son, then 16, and the following spring, in one of his last official acts, Secretary McHenry forwarded to Joseph Swift a cadet warrant, dated 12 May 1800, with orders to report to Colonel Tousard of the 2d Regiment at Newport. Probably at his request, Cadet Swift was attached to Stoddard's company at Fort Wolcott, where he served as a junior officer under Tousard and Lieutenant Dransy, and in the fall was attached to Captain John Henry's company, which was completing the construction of Fort Adams. Well before he became an academy cadet, Swift had gained considerable practical knowledge in fortifications design and construction.(41)

During the early weeks of 1801, as his administration neared its end, President Adams moved, as he had promised Secretary Dexter, to appoint at least two teachers for the academy. His first choice as teacher of mathematics, Captain William A. Barron, was still recruiting his company of the 2d Regiment, and had already been notified to superintend repairs to the fortification in Portsmouth, so Barron's appointment had to be deferred.(42) The first official appointment, therefore, went to George Baron—note the confusing similarity of names—a civilian who had been an instructor at the Royal Military Academy at Woolwich, England.(43)

Prior to the end of Adams's administration about a dozen cadets were serving with companies of artillerists and engineers. On 3 March, just as he left office, President Adams appointed nine new cadets; together with Joseph G. Swift, these would become the first academy cadets. They included the appropriately-named Henry Burbeck Jackson, son of Major Daniel Jackson of the 2d Regiment; Samuel and William Gates, sons of Captain Lemuel Gates of the 2d Regiment; Joseph Proveau Proveaux, son of a wartime captain from South Carolina; Joseph Biddle Wilkinson, son of the General, and four noncommissioned officers: Sergeant Simon Magruder Levy, 4th Infantry; Sergeant Major Josiah Taylor, 1st Infantry; and Sergeant Major Ambrose Porter and Sergeant Silas Clark of the 2d Artillerists and Engineers.(44) None of these cadets, however, was as yet ordered to West Point for instruction.

The incoming Secretary of War, Henry Dearborn, took up where Adams and Dexter had left off, and at that point it appeared that the officer to be in charge of the new academy would be Louis Tousard. When Dearborn delivered to Colonel Tousard on 14 April his overdue certificate of appointment as Inspector of Artillery, with the implication that Tousard would take station at West Point, the Secretary also assigned him some general functions in connection with the academy. "When you shall not be otherwise necessarily employed," Dearborn wrote, "… you will give all the assistance in your power in the instruction of such officers and cadets, as may be at West Point, for the purpose of learning their duty. Such Ordnance materials and apparatus, as may be necessary for experiments in Gunnery may at all times, be used under your direction, or such other person, as may be particularly appointed, as a Teacher to the officers and cadets at that Post." Dearborn added that "the commanding officer of the post will be directed to give you all the aid you may require."(45)

It can be inferred from Dearborn's instructions that while Tousard was to have certain supervisory authority at West Point, he was not to be considered the post commander. Later authorities see in this arrangement the roots of the subsequent struggles for command between line and technical officers, particularly that in 1803, but in fact the division of responsibility seems to have been based partly on good administration and partly on economy. In theory Tousard, as Inspector of Artillery, would report directly to the Secretary of War, while the post commander, in common with all other post commanders, would report routinely through a district commander to the Inspector of the Army in Washington, acting for General Wilkinson. The economy lay in the fact that a post commander drew double rations, commuted to cash; a captain commanding would draw six rations, while a lieutenant colonel commandant, if designated post commander, would be entitled to the princely sum of the value of ten rations daily. Colonel Tousard assumed, or pretended to assume, that he would have command of the post, but the troop commander at West Point, Lieutenant Robert W. Osborn of the 2d Regiment, received his own instructions from the Secretary of War. "It is in contemplation to establish a Military school at West Point," Dearborn wrote in mid-April, "and also to consider that place as the permanent residence of the Inspector[s] of Artillery and Fortifications, the latter is not appointed, the former, Colonel Tousard will probably take up his residence there … will be the Senior Officer, and will have the command of the Troops, so far as he may find it convenient for the duties of his office." Nonetheless, Dearborn concluded, as Tousard would be absent much of the time, the actual post commander would draw the double rations.(46) The Secretary left the issuance of orders concerning Tousard to General Wilkinson, then at Pittsburgh. Wilkinson was apparently unaware of Dearborn's decision and prepared to assign Tousard as post commander at West Point, but Major Cushing, the Inspector, knew the facts and explained the matter to the General in a tone quite prejudicial to Tousard:

> The Colonel in several conversations pressed the Secretary for the command of West Point which would secure to him the double rations of a Lieut Colonel as Commandant of a post. But the Secretary [told] him that so long as he held the Office of Inspector of Artillery he must content himself with

the emoluments & devote his whole time to the duties of that office. That West Point was assigned to him as a convenient spot for his permanent Quarters [as] Inspector of Artillery subject to the orders of the Secretary of War. But that the command of posts must be in Officers acting in the regular line of duty & subject to his (the Secretary's) orders through the Commanding General only.... The Colonel I presume very carefully concealed from you this decision of the Secretary ... .(47)

The affair was of no great importance, but by his insistence on the point Tousard alienated the important Inspector of the Army and presumably both Secretary Dearborn and General Wilkinson. He would miss the support of these men the following year.

It seems to have been Henry Dearborn's decision that both the Inspector of Artillery and the as-yet-undesignated Inspector of Fortifications should reside at West Point and have some connection with the military academy. In early May he approached President Jefferson, who had barely settled into his duties, about going ahead with the plans of the Adams administration for the school and also for Jefferson's wishes as to an Inspector of Fortifications. The new President was not an expert in military affairs, but he appreciated the need for some sort of scientific schooling for the Army officers which would free the Army from reliance on foreign experts. He was also prepared to advance the interests of his fellow member of the American Philosophical Society, Major Jonathan Williams, and to take advantage of Williams's theoretical knowledge of fortifications by naming him Inspector of Fortifications. Dearborn transmitted the President's wishes to General Wilkinson. "The President having decided in favor of the immediate establishment of a Military School at West Point," Dearborn wrote, "and also on the appointment of Major Jonathan Williams as Inspector of Fortifications, it becomes necessary for the Major to be at West Point as soon as possible, for the purpose of directing the necessary arrangements at that place for the commencement of the school ... ."(48) As Major Williams was temporarily at Fort Niagara preparing to repair the works, the Secretary asked Wilkinson to send Williams back to Washington.

Dearborn seems to have envisioned an initial group of no more than 25 cadets for the school, and directed the military storekeeper at West Point to prepare quarters for that number. In addition, four houses would be required, for the Inspector of Artillery, the Inspector of Fortifications, the Teacher of Mathematics (Mr. Baron), and for use as a school house. Barracks for a company of artillerists and engineers were already available, Dearborn noted, but quarters would be needed for the captain commanding the post and his subalterns, an adjutant, and a surgeon.(49) The detachment under lieutenant Osborn was being augmented by recruits enlisted by Captain John Lillie of the 2d Regiment, one of President Adams's last appointees; Captain Lillie arrived in June and assumed command of the post from Lieutenant Osborn.

By mid-July Secretary Dearborn was ready to get the academy under way, and instructed Major Cushing to order cadets to West Point. Just how many cadets were in service in 1801 is not known; there were at least 12 and probably nearer 20. On 20 July Major Cushing wrote to Colonel Burbeck, asking him to issue orders "that all the Cadets in service, except Joseph B. Wilkinson, be sent to West Point by the first of September ... ."(50) The slowness of the mails and of transportation generally made compliance with that reporting date impracticable. Cadet Joseph G. Swift at Newport received his orders about 1 October; he took the packet to New York, spent a day or two in visiting friends at Fort Jay, and reported to West Point about 12 October.(51)

There was considerable activity at West Point during the fall of 1801, but it was not very encouraging. First there was bad feeling between Captain Lillie and his predecessor, Lieutenant Osborn, which culminated in a sharp confrontation on 22 September. Osborn reportedly accused Lillie of misappropriation of government property; Lillie flew into a rage, suffered an attack of apoplexy, and dropped dead.(52) (Lillie left a large family, and as a means of providing some financial relief, Secretary Dearborn issued a cadet warrant to "a son of the late Captain Lillie, now at West Point, [to be] immediately entered in the Military School at that post."(53) Dearborn was probably unaware of the ages of the children, for John Lillie, Jr., who accepted the warrant, was 10 years old; despite his youth, he was admitted to the academy and drew pay and emoluments for four years.(54)

The other major problem in the fall of 1801 was almost a repetition of the troubles of 1796. As in the earlier instance, it seems to have stemmed from the popular belief that an officer, once commissioned, should not be required to attend schooling of any kind—an idea that lingered in some quarters until well after the Civil War. In mid-October the sole teacher, George Baron, complained directly to Secretary Dearborn; as Dearborn notified Major Cushing, "I have the unexpected and unpleasant intelligence that some subalterns, who were ordered to West Point for the purpose, refuse to attend and receive the instruction offered them by the wisdom of the Government. Its important and useful designs must not be permitted to be frustrated in this manner; the instruction ... is necessary for an Officer, and those who will continue to refuse it, must be considered unfit for service."(55) Cushing at once wrote to Colonel Burbeck, on the basis that "as Senior Officer of Artillery and Commandant of the district comprehending West Point," Burbeck should take the necessary action.(56) Burbeck conferred with the Secretary, and a few weeks later Dearborn directed that the three offending lieutenants be transferred from West Point. The Secretary then picked two highly-regarded officers of the 2d Regiment, lieutenants Stephen Worrell and James Wilson—the latter the son of Justice Wilson of the Supreme Court—and ordered them to West Point specifically to attend the academy. All went well for a few weeks, and then Worrell assumed command of Lillie's old company; with this responsibility, he felt obliged to drop out of his classes. Dearborn learned of this and wrote to urge the lieutenant to resume his studies; two weeks later he took action to remove Worrell from administrative duties, directing that "lieut. Worrell is to be considered as attached to the Military School and subject to the orders of the superintendent."(57)

This was not the first time that the Secretary had referred to the "superintendent" of the academy, but in fact no such superintendent had been officially appointed. Colonel Tousard, the Inspector of Artillery, had been entrusted with certain supervisory functions, but his duties took him away from West Point frequently, and it was clear that he could not devote adequate time to the academy. He wrote to Dearborn to this effect in November,(58) and this letter probably made up the Secretary's mind. Dearborn, like former President Adams, disliked having foreign-born officers in senior positions, and although Tousard was without much question best qualified to supervise instruction in engineering and gunnery, the Secretary decided to bypass him. He consulted the President, Jefferson agreed, and on 14 December the direction of the military academy was conferred upon Major Jonathan Williams. But the primary title was not yet Superintendent, for as Dearborn wrote Williams, "The President is pleased to appoint and you are hereby appointed Inspector of Fortifications, under the Act of Congress of March 3, 1799. You will ... repair to West Point in the State of New York, and take upon yourself the superintendence of the Military School at that post, until you shall receive further instructions."(59) Thus Williams, like Tousard, became Inspector first, and Superintendent ex officio. (It is curious that Dearborn did not inform Williams of his appointment as Inspector of Fortifications until seven months after he had advised General Wilkinson that Williams would be so appointed.)

In the last weeks of 1801 there was another unpleasant flurry at West Point. It had begun in October when George Baron, the sole teacher, complained to the Secretary of War of improper conduct and lack of respect on the part of Cadet Joseph G. Swift. Dearborn at once wrote Swift, directing him to "make proper concessions to Mr. Baron, and attend to your duty under his direction [or] you will be dismissed from the service." Swift replied contritely, and there the matter rested for about a month. (60) But at the end of November Swift changed his mind. The main problem seems to have been his refusal to lodge and mess with other cadets in a building operated by Baron, preferring to mess with the lieutenants who were about to be transferred for their unwillingness to attend instruction. Supported by these officers, Cadet Swift notified Secretary Dearborn that he could not be reconciled with Mr. Baron, to which the Secretary replied angrily that the subject was closed, and that Swift would "make the Concessions required and take up your Lodgings with the other Cadets or quit the service."(61) But now Swift sought and received support from all the officers at the post, for having been connected with Army officers for over two years, and being by far the senior by date of appointment, he considered himself somewhat superior to the ten or 11 other cadets at the school.(62) What followed is unclear, but in mid-December Lieutenant Osborn, whose transfer had not yet taken place, preferred charges with the Secretary of War against Mr. Baron, alleging immoral conduct. At this juncture Major Williams arrived to superintend the academy, and the Secretary forwarded to him a copy of Osborn's charges. "If the charges can be substantiated," Dearborn wrote. "Mr. Baron is assuredly a most unfit man for his station, if they cannot, he ought to have an opportunity of clearing his character ... ."(63) The rest can only be inferred from fragmentary records. Major Williams conducted a preliminary investigation, seemingly found substantiation of Osborn's charges, and so advised the Secretary. Dearborn offered Baron the opportunity to resign, but Baron declined and insisted on a court of inquiry. A court was convened in New York, from the results of which Secretary Dearborn concluded that Baron had "conducted himself in a manner unbecoming his station and improper in a man." In the face of the findings Baron now offered to resign, but the Secretary was now hostile, and wrote to Major Williams that Baron was dismissed from the service of the United States.(64)

It must be remembered that the military school at West Point, as has been described here, antedates by some months the formal legislative authority for a national military academy, enacted in March of 1802. The school itself, however, clearly dates from 1801. By the end of that year the future Superintendent, Major Jonathan Williams, was present for duty— and the first duly-appointed teacher, George Baron, was in the process of being dismissed. The military academy, as it was formally established the following March, was in many ways a bipartisan effort. Officially it was a creation of the Jeffersonians, but its roots were clearly Federalist.

CHAPTER VI
REDUCTION OF THE ARMY AND SEPARATION OF ARTILLERISTS AND ENGINEERS
1802

On 8 December 1801 President Jefferson delivered his first Annual Message to Congress, setting the tone for the following year and, indeed, for much of his first- term. There were few references to the Army, but those few reflected the President's great desire for fiscal economy at all levels of government. It was his expectation, he said, that "a sensible and at the same time a salutary reduction may take place in our habitual expenditures. For this purpose those of the civil Government, the Army, and the Navy will need revisal." He noted that the Secretary of War had prepared a list of the minimum number of troops required to man the necessary posts, and that this number was "considerably short of the present military establishment"; no particular use could be proposed for the "surplus." As Jefferson pointed out, even the existing military establishment would be inadequate in the event of invasion; but as there was no possibility of maintaining a peacetime force large enough to repel an invasion, reliance would continue to be placed on the militia. He hoped, therefore, that future sessions of Congress would address the problem of improving the militia of the several states. As to the seacoast fortifications, the President was frankly at a loss for a recommendation. "While some of them," he thought, "are on a scale sufficiently proportioned to the advantage of their position, to the efficacy of their protection, and the importance of the points within it, others are so extensive, will cost so much in their first erection, so much in their maintenance, and require such a force to garrison them as to make it questionable what is best now to be done." The Chief Executive concluded that he would have an estimate of current and projected costs of seacoast defense laid before Congress, so that the legislative branch could make the decision.(1)

The information promised Congress was prepared by Secretary of War Henry Dearborn, with little or no assistance from General Wilkinson or Colonel Burbeck. The administration of the Army, in fact, was almost entirely in the hands of the Secretary at this period, particularly with General Wilkinson inspecting the western garrisons, but after six or eight months in office Dearborn was finally beginning to relax his rigid personal control, at least to the extent of allowing the Inspector and the regimental commanders to pass on such trivial matters as granting furloughs and approving discharges for soldiers. But in matters of policy, such as the optimum size of the Army, or the number of companies of artillerists needed to garrison the seacoast defenses, there is no indication that the Secretary asked for or accepted any recommendations from officers whose titles implied a certain responsibility for such matters.

One of the difficulties was that the senior officers of artillerists and engineers, in particular, were not necessarily doing what their titles indicated. Colonel Burbeck, the nominal Chief of Artillerists, was concerned with the command of all troops on the seaboard, infantry included, in the absence of General Wilkinson. Colonel Tousard, the Inspector of Artillery, did in fact inspect and prove newly-cast cannon, but his primary function, for which he was well qualified, was construction and repair of fortifications. Yet this latter function had in theory been given to Major Jonathan Williams, whose title was Inspector of Fortifications—but who was now expected to devote most of his time and energies to the new military school at West Point. Nevertheless, it was to Major Williams that Secretary Dearborn turned for a return of the state of the seacoast fortifications, on which to base his report to Congress.(2)

To what extent the Secretary of War considered the changing international situation is not apparent, nor is it clear how much the President let international events affect his economy program. Although John Adams's determined stand in 1799 had removed the immediate threat of war with France, and the disbandment of the Provisional Army in mid-1800 had eliminated another possible source of discord, in fact the international scene was not as quiet as it had appeared at the time of the elections of 1800. Within weeks of Jefferson's inauguration a new French threat had appeared, this time to the Caribbean and the mouth of the Mississippi.

The vast and ill-defined region known as Louisiana had been a pawn of European diplomacy since the Seven Years' War. Settled at great effort by French explorers and administrators, France's title to Louisiana had passed by cession to Spain in 1762, partly as compensation for the Spanish ally's loss of the Floridas to Britain. Such a cession was acceptable in the days of the monarchy and the Family Compact, but by the early 1790s the new French Republic took a different view: Louisiana represented a valuable asset to be recovered, preferably by force, and Citizen Genet in 1793 carried vague plans to attack Louisiana from the United States, with the help of American adventurers like George Rogers Clark. But President Washington had spiked any such ideas, and France turned to diplomatic measures. By secret treaties in October 1800 and March 1801, First Consul Bonaparte arranged for the retrocession of Louisiana from Spain to France.

Unofficial rumors of this retrocession had reached the United States as early as May 1801, but President Jefferson, in the absence of official confirmation, made no mention of the matter in his December message to Congress.(3) But while Louisiana in the hands of an inept Spain was one thing, the region in the control of an expanding Revolutionary France was quite another. The United States would face a very real threat from that area if, as expected, the retrocession proved a fact. But the Jefferson administration was committed to economy and to a reduction of the Army, and indeed such a reduction had been set in motion in Congressional committee before the end of 1801; all that remained was to insure that the reduced Army was stationed in the most effective manner to counter a possible threat from the southwest.

The President and Secretary Dearborn had already decided that the Army should be reduced to 20 companies of artillerists and 20 companies of infantry for 1802, and they made the further decision to hold to this reduction despite the French threat. At the end of the year Dearborn forwarded to Congress his proposed stationing plan for 1802, which upon examination showed a severe reduction in the coastal garrisons, as well as in those on the northwest frontier, in order to begin a buildup of strength—relatively speaking—on the lower Mississippi:(4)

| | Companies | |
	Arty	Inf
Michilimackinac, Northwest Territory	1	1
Detroit, Northwest Territory	1	4
Fort Niagara, New York	1	1
Fort Wayne, Northwest Territory		1
Pittsburgh and the upper Ohio		1
Fort Knox, Vincennes, Indiana Territory		1
Fort Massac, on the lower Ohio		1
South West Point, &c., Tennessee	1	2
Chickasaw Bluffs on the Mississippi		1
Fort Adams on the Mississippi near Spanish boundary	1	4
Fort [Stoddert] on the Mobile River		1
Fort Wilkinson, Georgia, on the Creek frontier		3
Fort Greene, Savannah, Georgia	1	
Fort Moultrie &c., Charleston, South Carolina	1	
Fort Johnston, North Carolina	1	

Fort Norfolk and Fort Nelson, Virginia	1
Fort McHenry, Baltimore, Maryland	1
Fort Mifflin and arsenal near Philadelphia	2
Fort Jay, New York	1
West Point, New York	1
Fort Trumbull, Connecticut	1
Fort Wolcott, Rhode Island	1
Fort Independence, Boston, Massachusetts	2
& Springfield arsenal, Massachusetts	
Fort Constitution, N.H., and Fort Sumner, Maine	1
	20 20

From the above listing, it will be seen that only 11 of the proposed 20 companies of artillerists were to be assigned to seacoast fortifications. In January 1802 Congress began open debate on the administration proposal for reducing and reorganizing the Army. In brief, Jefferson and Dearborn were recommending that the military peacetime establishment be set at two regiments of infantry and a single regiment of artillerists, together with a separate but very small Corps of Engineers, consisting only of officers and cadets, which would in itself constitute the new military academy. The total authorized strength of the Army would be reduced from 4,436 to 3,287 officers and men; the enlisted strength was already below the proposed ceiling, but some officers would have to be "deranged." Although the number of regiments was to be cut in half, the strength reduction was less drastic; the single regiment of artillerists would have 20 companies, as opposed to the old two-regiment total of 32, and in the infantry, with ten instead of eight companies and with more privates per company, the two new regiments would have about the strength of three of the old. In Dearborn's proposal, initiated earlier by Hamilton, the grade of colonel would be revived for regimental commanders.

Initially the House wanted to abolish the grade of brigadier general, some members on the grounds of economy, based on the small size of the proposed Army, and others because they did not trust James Wilkinson. Bayard of Delaware then proposed to reject the grade of colonel, and to add an equivalent number of majors, but here his colleagues balked. And when the Senate made known that it would not agree to abolishing the general, the House fell into line, with Bayard objecting that the office was a "perfect sinecure." John Rutledge of South Carolina opposed the great reduction in the artillery, hoping it "would have been retained to keep in order the forts already built," for there were four forts in Charleston harbor and he was unwilling to see them fall into decay. In the end the House passed Dearborn's bill with minor revisions, by a vote of 77-12, and sent it to the Senate.(5)

As bits and pieces of the House debate were reported, officers of the Army reacted in different ways. Those who wished to remain in service, particularly those without private means, were alarmed at the possibility of derangement; those who had already considered resigning now decided to wait and be deranged, so as to qualify for severance pay of one month's pay for each year of service. There turned out to be a considerable number of officers, subalterns and a few captains, in this latter category, and it soon became apparent that not many officers would have to be deranged involuntarily except in the field grades. Major Cushing, the Inspector, acted as a clearing house for rumors and requests; several officers who desired derangement wrote directly to Cushing instead of General Wilkinson or Secretary Dearborn. Cushing's reply in January to Captain Staats Morris of the 1st Regiment was probably typical: "[I]f any diminution of Artillery should be made your wish to retire under the bountiful provisions of your Country … shall be made known to the Secretary of War, who will doubtless arrange as you desire, but you will allow me to add, that it will be a circumstance of regret to the Officers who may be doomed to continue in service, that you should retire from it."(6)

Cushing's reference to the officers "doomed to continue in service" seems a little strong, as the option of resignation was always open. Cushing himself was suffering from overwork, and he viewed the pending abolition of several staff offices—not including his own—with some trepidation. He wrote urgently to General Wilkinson that the bill had passed the House and was in the Senate; he wished the General were in Washington to argue against the "cutting off" of the "General Staff," although he saw little hope of the bill's being favorably amended. As for himself, Major Cushing was determined to rejoin the 1st Infantry rather than "to drudge here for so scanty a pittance as 1400 Dolls per Annum—I look toward the lakes."(7)

The Act of 16 March 1802

The legislation that passed the Senate and was signed by President Jefferson on 16 March was the severest reduction in the size of the Army since the disbandment of the Continental Army in 1784—discounting, of course, the temporary Provisional Army. The 29 sections of the act were distilled in the first section, which provided that "the military peace establishment of the United States from and after the first of June next, shall be composed of one regiment of artillerists and two regiments of infantry, with such officers, military agents, and engineers, as are hereinafter mentioned."(8)

The command of the Army remained unchanged, although the brigadier general was not specifically designated as Commanding General. The grade of colonel was restored, for the first time since midway in the Revolutionary War, for the three regimental commanders, and the grade of lieutenant colonel commandant was abolished. Each of the two infantry regiments was assigned a colonel, a lieutenant colonel, and a major; the wartime distinction between first and second lieutenants was revived, and each of the expanded companies was authorized a captain, a first lieutenant, a second lieutenant, and an ensign. The single regiment of artillerists was to have a colonel, a lieutenant colonel, and four majors, and was to be formed into five battalions. Each company of artillerists would have a captain, a first lieutenant, a second lieutenant, and two cadets.

The staff functions for the reduced establishment were spelled out in exact detail. All that was left was "one adjutant and inspector of the army, to be taken from the line of field officers; one paymaster of the army, seven paymasters, and two assistants … to be taken from the line of commissioned officers, who, in addition to their other duties, shall have charge of the clothing of the troops; three military agents and such number of assistant military agents … not exceeding one to each military post … taken from the line; two surgeons, twenty-five surgeons' mates, to be attached to garrisons or posts, and not to corps." That was the total staff structure of the Army. Replacing the single Quartermaster General, Secretary Dearborn had substituted three widely-separated Military Agents: Peter Gansevoort in Albany for the Northern Department, William Linnard in Philadelphia for the Middle Department, and Abraham D. Abrahams in Savannah for the Southern Department—although these "departments" did not exist for any other functions of the Army. To accomplish the field work, subaltern officers at each post would be appointed assistant military agents, and would receive eight dollars a month above their line pay. Similarly, assistants to the Paymaster of the Army, Caleb Swan, would be line officers appointed on a district basis, who would not only pay the troops but would also receive and issue uniforms, procured and forwarded by the Superintendent of Military Stores, William Irvine, in Philadelphia.

Finally, the system of regimental surgeons and surgeons' mates was abandoned, and the medical establishment reduced to two surgeons—one each for the northwest and southwest frontiers—and one or more surgeons' mates at each post. The net effect of the new staff organization was to decentralize functions and to eliminate centralized direction, with the result that the Secretary of War would have to communicate directly with many more subordinates than formerly. To assist him the Secretary would continue to rely on Major Cushing, whose new title of Adjutant and Inspector reflected his duties more accurately. (Not because of his staff position, but because of his seniority in the line, Cushing would be promoted to lieutenant colonel of the 2d Infantry during the reorganization of March-June 1802.)

The reorganization of the infantry regiments was primarily a matter of deciding which field officers to retain. The new 1st Infantry, north of the Ohio, was a consolidation of the old 1st and 2d regiments; the new 2d Infantry, on the southwest and southern frontiers, was made up of the former 3d and 4th regiments. Space does not permit a discussion of the politico-military maneuverings by which infantry field officers were selected for either retention or derangement, but for purposes of future reference it should be noted that, when the smoke had cleared, those retained in the new 1st Infantry were Colonel John F. Hamtramck, Lieutenant Colonel Thomas Hunt, and Major Zebulon Pike (father of the later explorer); in the 2d Infantry, Colonel Thomas Butler, Lieutenant Colonel Thomas H. Cushing (detached as Adjutant and Inspector), and Major Jacob Kingsbury.

The problem was similar in combining the two regiments of artillerists and engineers into a regiment of artillerists and a tiny corps of engineers. One of the two lieutenant colonels commandant would become colonel of the new regiment; the other would not be offered the option of stepping down to the lesser grade of lieutenant colonel, but would be deranged. The choice was obvious: Henry Burbeck, native-born as well as senior, was promoted to colonel of the Regiment of Artillerists; Louis Tousard, still damned by his French birth, was summarily deranged. Tousard seems to have salvaged some pride by making formal application for derangement, for Secretary Dearborn wrote him that "In compliance with your request of yesterday, ... You Sir with many other Officers who have grown old in the service of their Country will have permission to retire from service on the last day of April. ..."(9)

The lieutenant colonelcy of the new regiment was not offered to the senior major, because that officer happened to be J.J. Ulrich Rivardi. Highly qualified and unassuming, Rivardi was nevertheless foreign-born, and his reward was notification that he, like Tousard, could "retire" from the service. With a clear conscience, Dearborn then proffered the lieutenant colonelcy to the senior major being retained, Constant Freeman. The junior major, Jonathan Williams, was transferred to head the new Corps of Engineers. This left five majors for four vacancies, and the derangement fell on Mahlon Ford; this was probably a difficult decision, as Ford had been in service since 1784, but he was considered a die-hard Federalist, and in fact his military effectiveness seems to have fallen off after his promotion to major.(10) The four majors retained, who together with Lieutenant Colonel Freeman would nominally command battalions of the Regiment of Artillerists, were Daniel Jackson, Decius Wadsworth, Moses Porter, and William MacRea.

Each of the officers being deranged received a politely vague letter from the Secretary of War; field officers received handwritten letters, company officers printed certificates. To soften the blow, each deranged officer received a cash settlement of one month's pay for each full year of service, and in the cases of the older officers this was construed as including service during the Revolutionary War.(11) In some cases the derangement process resulted in clearing out dead wood; a few captains and lieutenants with growing reputations for drunkenness, particularly those on the lower Mississippi, were eliminated without recourse to courts martial. But several officers had to be deranged, for one reason or another, who could ill be spared, and prominent among these were Tousard and Rivardi. Both would have been highly qualified for the Corps of Engineers, and in view of the lean years that were to mark this new corps, it is possible that the summary elimination of the "foreign" officers was later regretted. Both Tousard and Rivardi returned to the French West Indies, and Rivardi is recorded as having died in Martinique in January 1808. Tousard served briefly in LeClerc's ill-fated expedition to Santo Domingo and subsequently returned to France, but in 1805 he was appointed to the French consulate in New Orleans, and later served as vice-consul in Philadelphia. During these years back in the United States Tousard published a work he had begun at Washington's urging in 1795, a two-volume set he called *The American Artillerist's Companion*, to which he later added a volume of plates drawn by himself; this rather interesting work enjoyed considerable vogue, particularly in the militia, for the first three decades of the 19th century. Dismissed from his consular post at the Bourbon restoration, Tousard returned to France and died in Paris in 1817, at the age of 68.(12)

The Corps of Engineers and the Military Academy

The legislation for the military peacetime establishment of 1802 was initially a severe blow to the morale and effectiveness of the Army. One immediate effect of the reorganization was to remove from the new Regiment of Artillerists, by derangement or transfer, almost every officer of any scientific attainment, with the possible exception of Colonel Burbeck. But in the long view, with the creation of the Corps of Engineers and the Military Academy, the legislation proved to be a considerable step in the direction of the scientific education and training of officers in the two fields most in need of educated officers, the seacoast artillery and the engineers. In the matter of seacoast fortifications, the new Corps of Engineers was to bring new vitality and new methods to the field of military architecture.

The wording of the legislation providing for a corps of engineers and a military academy was vague and imprecise. According to the Act of 16 March, the Corps of Engineers was the Military Academy. It was also a staff-type department, entirely separate from the line of the Army; its senior officer was to be, not exactly a major, but an engineer with the rank, pay, and emoluments of a major—a subtle distinction that was soon ignored. The initial ceiling of 20 officers and cadets would seem to indicate very modest hopes for the new corps and school, but it should be remembered that the legislation also provided two cadets for each company of artillerists, or 40 cadets from that arm. Whether it was planned from the start that the cadets of artillerists would receive instruction at West Point is not evident, but it soon became apparent that they were eligible. And for the first time the problem of command at West Point seemed to be clarified, for the principal engineer, with the rank of major, was to have the superintendence of the military academy.

Prior to the legislation of 16 March Major Jonathan Williams, as Inspector of Fortifications, had held the nominal superintendence of the academy. Not until 13 April, however, did Secretary Dearborn announce the first three appointments to the Corps of Engineers; these, by transfer from the old artillerists and engineers, were Major Williams, Captain William A. Barron, and Lieutenant Peter A. Dransy. In May Lieutenant James Wilson was similarly transferred, and the Secretary made the first appointment to the corps from civil life by proffering a captaincy to Jared Mansfield, a 43-year-old Yale graduate who was considered one of the most original mathematicians in the country. The only one of the five to decline appointment was Lieutenant Dransy, a thoroughly experienced young officer of seven years' service who had acted as principal assistant to Colonel Tousard in the construction of the fortifications at Newport. Dransy was of French birth, and may have been discouraged by the treatment accorded to other foreign-born officers during his service; for whatever reasons, Dransy did not accept appointment, and as the regiment of Artillerists was full, he was considered deranged and left the service.(13)

The return of the Army for 19 December 1801 showed nine cadets, names not listed, as attached to the military academy. On 24 December the underage John Lillie, Jr., received his warrant, and on 22 February Cadet Ambrose Porter resigned; Walker K. Armistead, appointed in 1801, did not report until the following summer. As of 16 March 1802, then, it appears that nine cadets were present for duty at West Point: Joseph G. Swift, Simon M. Levy, Henry B. Jackson, Samuel Gates, William Gates, Joseph P. Proveaux, Josiah Taylor, Silas Clark, and John Lillie, Jr. Of this number, only the first six were to complete the course of instruction and "graduate."(14)

As the academy got under way in April or early May of 1802, its only faculty member was Captain Barron. Major Williams was on leave, Captain Mansfield had not reported for duty, and Lieutenant Wilson had been detailed to act as judge advocate for a court-martial at Fort Mifflin— the office of Judge Advocate of the Army having been abolished and its incumbent deranged only weeks earlier.(15) Details such as Wilson's were to plague the Army for the next six years; legislation having abolished many of the necessary staff positions, those functions had to be performed by detailing officers who were not necessary qualified and who had other and often more important duties elsewhere.

The tiny Corps of Cadets, as it would come to be called, was in a state of flux throughout most of 1802. Probably at the requests of their fathers, officers of the Regiment of Artillerists, Secretary Dearborn granted furloughs during June and July to Henry Jackson and Samuel and William Gates. Walker K. Armistead reported during the summer, as did John Livingston, a new appointee. Livingston was specifically appointed as a cadet of artillerists, the first from that regiment since the reorganization. Then on 28 July Secretary Dearborn notified Major Williams that Cadets Swift, Levy, and Armistead were transferred to the Corps of Engineers, an indication that a distinction would be made between cadets of engineers and those of artillerists.(16) According to the new law, the number of officers and cadets of the Corps of Engineers was limited to 20, so that as more officers were appointed, the number of authorized cadets would necessarily decrease.

The Act of 16 March provided that officers of the Corps of Engineers would initially be appointed in the grades of major and below, but that they could be promoted on merit, and without regard to rank and seniority. On 8 July President Jefferson exercised this prerogative, on Secretary Dearborn's, recommendation, by promoting Jonathan Williams, the principal Engineer, to the grade of lieutenant colonel. To fill Williams's vacant majority the Secretary did not recommend the promotion of either Captains Barron or Mansfield, but instead approved a request by "Major Decius Wadsworth of the Regiment of Artillerists to be transferred in grade to the Corps of Engineers; the transfer was effected as of 8 July, and Major Wadsworth, who thus became the second-ranking officer of Engineers, was directed to report to West Point.(17)

Lieutenant Colonel Williams, almost as soon as he was confirmed in his superintendence of the academy, drew up a list of books and instruments needed for instruction and forwarded it to the Secretary of War. Dearborn showed the list to President Jefferson, and the President made comments in the margin; it appears that the rigorous Republican economy was to be waived in this instance. Colonel Williams was directed to procure what he could in New York or Philadelphia, "in addition to those you propose to spare from your own Library, which you will please to make a Bill of," and to prepare a separate list of items for which it would be necessary to send to Europe. Without any of his usual exhortations about economy, Dearborn simply added that "the Bill will be paid."(18)

But having established the Military Academy as an integral part of the Corps of Engineers, Secretary Dearborn kept interfering in its embryonic operations. He had already ordered Lieutenant James Wilson to Fort Mifflin as a judge advocate, and in August he directed Major Wadsworth, who had just joined the Corps, to travel to Fort Nelson, at Norfolk, to "act in the character of an Engineer in repairing the works, buildings, barracks &c … ."(19) This could, of course, be considered proper engineer duty, but it was trivial compared to the need to establish a strong engineering school at West Point; assignments such as these were to fritter away the talents of the bare handful of partly-qualified engineer officers for several years. The Secretary did try to find additional civilian engineers for appointment to the new Corps, but without much success. One transfer within the Army, however, turned out to be highly successful. On 12 October the Secretary announced that 2d Lieutenant Alexander Macomb, Jr., of the 2d Infantry, son of a prosperous New York merchant and originally an officer of dragoons of the Provisional Army, was transferred to the Corps of Engineers, with promotion to 1st lieutenant. (20) Before young Macomb, then 20 years old, lay a brilliant career which would carry him not only to the head of the Corps of Engineers but to the head of the entire Army.

Except for the fortunate acquisition of Lieutenant Macomb, the only other source of new officers for the Engineers seemed to be the cadets undergoing instruction at the academy. On the same day that Macomb was transferred, Secretary Dearborn addressed a letter to Cadets Joseph G. Swift and Simon M. Levy, advising them that the President had been pleased to appoint them 2d lieutenants in the Corps of Engineers. This action was in effect the "graduation" of the "Class of 1802" at West Point; because Swift had been senior as a service cadet to Levy, his name appeared first, and thus he became, at the age of 18 years and 10 months, the first "graduate" of the United States Military Academy, only seven months after the official establishment of the institution.(21) Within ten years Swift would become Chief Engineer, but this can hardly be attributed to his education at the academy; rather, he had learned the science of fortifications engineering at the hands of Louis Tousard and Peter Dransy in the very practical way of constructing works for the defenses of Narragansett Bay. Another future Chief Engineer began his military education at the end of 1802. On 4 November the Secretary of War tendered an appointment as an academy cadet to Joseph Gilbert Totten, the 16-year-old nephew and ward of the newly-appointed Captain Jared Mansfield of the faculty. Totten's early years in the Army were something less than outstanding, but he persisted in his chosen field and in the decades before the Civil War he would become one of the best-known of all American engineers, and a world-renowned authority on seacoast fortifications.(22)

The Corps of Engineers considered itself from the beginning as a unique and special organization, a part of the Army and yet separate.(23) By definition it was not part of the line of the Army, and yet at the beginning it was not really a staff department, with its chief at the seat of government; indeed, the very concept of central staff departments had been virtually destroyed by the Act of 16 March 1802. The Corps of Engineers had no troops, being limited initially to 20 officers and cadets, and the relationship of engineer officers to line officers was ill-defined and soon to be the subject of controversy. One of the earliest indications of the self-assumed independent status of the Corps of Engineers came in late 1802, when Colonel Williams, as Chief Engineer and commander of the corps, submitted to the Secretary of War a proposal for a special dress uniform for his officers. Dearborn hastily approved the sample submitted, although he told Williams that his junior officers might find the proposed uniform unduly expensive. A few months later, however, Dearborn took a closer look at the details of the Engineer uniform, and discovered that Williams had designed for his corps a completely different system of designating the grades of the officers. The Secretary drew the line at such exclusiveness, and wrote Williams that in the Corps of Engineers "the distinction by Epauletts shall in future be the same established in the army of the United States."(24)

Organization of the Regiment of Artillerists

Two days after the passage of the Act of 16 March, Secretary Dearborn drew up a proposed stationing list for the companies of infantry and artillerists that would make up the line of the Army. General Wilkinson being absent on the western frontier, Dearborn forwarded the listing to Lieutenant Colonel Cushing, now known as the Adjutant and Inspector of the Army, for necessary action. Cushing in turn passed the proposed postings for the companies of the Regiment of Artillerists to Colonel Burbeck, the regimental commander, who must have been in some doubt as to the Secretary's exact intentions. Under the new organization the Regiment of Artillerists was to consist of five four-company battalions, to be commanded by Lieutenant Colonel Constant Freeman and Majors Daniel Jackson, Decius Wadsworth, Moses Porter, and William MacRea. In line with the planned de-emphasis on seacoast defenses in early 1802, initial proposals called for three battalions for seacoast defense and two for frontier duty; of the latter, one would serve with the 1st Infantry north of the Ohio, the other with the 2d Infantry on the lower Mississippi and in western Georgia and Tennessee. The list as drawn up by Secretary Dearborn on 18 March purported to provide for all 20 companies of artillerists, but in fact only 19 were accounted for, and any sort of battalion organization was ignored. As Colonel Burbeck received it, the proposed plan was as follows:

> Fort Independence and Portsmouth: Two companies, to be formed from those of Stoddard, Gates, Dunham, and Henry (deranged)
>
> Newport and Fort Trumbull: Two companies, to be formed from those of Stillé, Beall, and Steele (deranged)
>
> Fort Jay and West Point: Two companies, to be formed from those of Ingersoll, Frye (deranged), Izard, and Tallman
>
> South West Point, Tennessee: One company, to be formed from Read's company and the disbanded dragoons
>
> Fort McHenry and Fort Norfolk: Two companies, to be formed from those of Nicoll, Nehemiah Freeman, and Muhlenberg
>
> North and South Carolina & Georgia: Three companies, to be formed from those of Blackburn, Bruff, Kalteisen, McClallen, and Robeson
>
> Fort Adams and the Chickasaw Bluffs: Two companies, to be formed from those of Meminger (deranged), Livingston, and Cooper
>
> Niagara, Detroit & Michilimackinac: Three companies, to be formed from those of Thompson, Elmer, and Morris (all deranged), and Sterrett.(25)

It might be noted that not only does the list provide for 19 instead of 20 companies, but shows 21 active captains—12 retained from the old 1st Regiment and nine from the old 2d. This embarrassment was relieved by arbitrarily reducing the junior captain, Peter Tallman, to 1st lieutenant, with the understanding that he would receive the first vacant captaincy. Tallman did not have to wait long, for Major Decius Wadsworth was transferred to the Corps of Engineers on 8 July, and was succeeded by the senior captain, George Ingersoll; Tallman then received Ingersoll's captaincy, probably before he had even moved his epaulette back to the left shoulder. Although the new organization provided for a

1st and a 2d lieutenant in each company, all lieutenants in service on 16 March were considered as 1st lieutenants; new appointments after that date were in the lower grade. During the summer and early fall of 1802, before changes of station required by Secretary Dearborn's new plan began to be effected, the seacoast fortifications remained manned at a modestly respectable level. (Appendix D shows the companies of artillerists assigned to each seacoast fortification, as well as those stationed at frontier posts.)

Major Daniel Jackson, with headquarters in Boston, commanded the battalion and district extending from Portland to Newport. Fort Sumner in Portland, however, remained garrisoned only through the initiative of Captain Amos Stoddard, whose home was in Portland. Stoddard's company was assigned to the newly-renamed Fort Constitution at Portsmouth, and in May Stoddard wrote to Colonel Burbeck that quarters were limited at Fort Constitution, proposing that he divide his company between Fort Constitution and Fort Sumner, taking his own station at the Maine post. But Burbeck was absent and the letter sent to Secretary Dearborn, who met Stoddard only halfway: Stoddard might post a lieutenant and up to 33 men in Portland, and Stoddard himself might spend a third of his time there—asking permission before each move from General Wilkinson or Colonel Burbeck—but Stoddard's permanent headquarters would remain at Fort Constitution.(26) The Secretary, who passed Portsmouth going to and from his home in the Maine District, had already decided that the fortifications in Portsmouth harbor needed repairs and improvement, and in mid-1801 had ordered Captain William A. Barron to proceed there for that purpose. Barron was directed to build a magazine, erect stone platforms for six 24 pounders and two 12-pounders, and to mount those guns as soon as they arrived.(27) It was apparently at this time, as Barron completed his work in late 1801, that the name of the fortification was changed from Fort William and Mary—sometimes Fort Hancock—to Fort Constitution.

In Boston the work on Castle Island, known for a century as Castle William, was in 1800 or 1801 renamed Fort Independence. It was still garrisoned in 1802 by two companies, those of Captains Lemuel Gates and Nehemiah Freeman, and was also Major Jackson's battalion and district headquarters. At the beginning of 1802 there had been some discussion as to erecting a work on Governor's Island in Boston harbor, but in March Secretary Dearborn had advised Major Jackson that the federal government, at least, would for the present undertake no new construction.(28) It was expected that the garrison of Fort Independence would provide at least caretaking detachments for the small forts at Salem and possibly Marblehead; however, as Secretary Dearborn's new plan for the seacoast defenses allotted only one company of artillerists to Boston harbor, it seemed that either Gates's or Freeman's company would soon receive marching orders.

The activity that had once characterized Newport and Narragansett Bay while Louis Tousard was Inspector of Artillery evaporated under the new administration. Captain Lloyd Beall's company garrisoned Fort Wolcott on Goat Island and was responsible for detachments at the other forts in the harbor, but all work was suspended on Fort Adams on Brenton's Point. Even the name of Tousard's creation was appropriated, and for the next several years the name "Fort Adams" usually referred to General Wilkinson's old headquarters post at Loftus Heights on the lower Mississippi.

The remaining New England seacoast fortification was Fort Trumbull at New London, garrisoned by the company of Captain James Stille. As New London was closer by water to New York than to Boston, and probably to divide up the companies more equitably, Fort Trumbull came under the supervision of the battalion-district with headquarters at Fort Jay on Governors Island. Major George Ingersoll, newly-promoted on the transfer of Major Decius Wadsworth to the Corps of Engineers, succeeded to Wadsworth's district command, which included Fort Trumbull, West Point, and New

York Harbor.

The fortifications in New York harbor were extensive, if incomplete. The state of New York still retained responsibility for construction of works at the Narrows between Brooklyn and Staten Island, which in 1802 were still in the design and land-acquisition stage. There were defensive works on Governors, Bedlow's, and Ellis's Islands in the inner harbor, and these had been a federal responsibility from the start, but in 1802, during the reorganization of the artillerists, it appears that all federal troops were quartered on Governors Island. The only company planned for retention in the harbor was that of Captain John W. Livingston at Fort Jay.

Why a garrison from the Regiment of Artillerists was maintained at West Point, except from force of habit, is unclear. Fifty miles up the Hudson, whose entrance was theoretically blocked by the harbor island works, West Point could be classified neither as a seacoast fortification nor as a frontier post. In fact, the garrison at West Point now served primarily to support the new Military Academy and the headquarters of the Corps of Engineers, a function not entirely to the taste of the company of artillerists. The post commander was Captain George Izard, newly-returned from a year's leave of absence in Europe following his service as aide-decamp to Alexander Hamilton. As both Captain Izard and Lieutenant Colonel Jonathan Williams of the Engineers were European-educated in military matters, it might have been expected that either perfect harmony or considerable friction would exist between the two officers. Unfortunately for both, it was to be the friction which prevailed.

The section of the Atlantic coast from Pennsylvania through Virginia was not under the supervision of a battalion-district commander, for two of the majors of artillerists were still assigned to the frontier—Moses Porter at Fort Niagara and William MacRea at South West Point in Tennessee—and whenever problems arose the garrisons in Pennsylvania, Maryland, and Virginia were supervised directly by Colonel Burbeck in Washington.

Fort Mifflin on Mud Island, in the Delaware, guarding the river approaches to Philadelphia, had been the most sensitive location on the seaboard as long as Congress sat at Philadelphia; this is clear both from the size of the garrison and the amounts of the annual appropriations through 1800. The movement of the seat of government to Washington meant a loss of emphasis on Fort Mifflin, although without a corresponding interest in fortifying the Potomac approaches to the new capital. In the late summer of 1802 Fort Mifflin was still garrisoned by two companies, those of Captains James Bruff and Henry M. Muhlenberg, and according to Secretary Dearborn's plan, two companies were to remain there. If the French threat materialized at the mouth of the Mississippi, however, it was almost certain that the Fort Mifflin garrison would be halved.

Fort McHenry at Baltimore was fairly well situated to defend that city against direct attack, but by its location near the head of upper Chesapeake Bay it made no contribution to the defense of the new capital against waterborne attack. The fort was manned by Captain John McClallen's full-strength company, and no change was planned. Fort McHenry being the post nearest Washington, certain pay and supply functions for all the seaboard posts were carried out from there, and McClallen's company was levied upon from time to time to furnish soldiers to assist Colonel Burbeck and Lieutenant Colonel Cushing, the Adjutant and Inspector of the Army, in their administrative duties.

Of the twin forts at Norfolk, facing each other across the Elizabeth River, Captain Richard S. Blackburn's company garrisoned Fort Nelson and provided a caretaking detachment at Fort Norfolk. Secretary Dearborn's original plans had called for continued work on Fort Norfolk, but he changed his mind in mid-1802, and it was to Fort Nelson that he dispatched Major Wadsworth of the Engineers in August, with orders to repair the works and barracks. Dearborn was strong on the virtues of troop labor, and he expected much from the eight soldiers of each company of artillerists enlisted as "artificers." Blackburn's company had not exploited its artificers, in Dearborn's view, and he wrote a sharp-note to the assistant military agent reminding him that "it is of very little use to attach Artificers to each Company of Artillery, if [they cannot] repair Carriages for so many Cannon as may be necessary for the purpose of firing salutes," adding pointedly, "especially when each officer in the [Regiment of Artillerists] has been heretofore contemplated as an Engineer."(29)

The posts in North and South Carolina, and on the Georgia seaboard only, came under the supervision of Lieutenant Colonel Constant Freeman at Charleston. Secretary Dearborn's stationing plan provided only three companies for the three states, and as Charleston was the most important city, both economically and politically, as well as a first-class port, the largest concentration of troops, relatively speaking, stayed there. Thus the post of Fort Johnston in North Carolina, still uncompleted, was allocated only a lieutenant and about 27 men, just enough to keep the post in an active status, from the two-company garrison in Charleston.

The three fortifications in Charleston harbor in 1802 were in varying states of construction and repair. Fort Johnson on James Island had been repaired continuously since the First Phase and had been manned since 1794 by the company of Captain Michael Kalteisen. Fort Moultrie on Sullivan's Island had been refurbished in 1798-99, and in 1802 was garrisoned by Captain Jonathan Robeson's company. Castle Pinckney, on the island known as Shute's Folly, had been repaired and garrisoned during the crisis of 1798-1800, but in the summer of 1802 Secretary Dearborn authorized the use of the barracks of Castle Pinckney as a marine hospital.(30)

The southernmost seacoast fortification garrisoned in any strength in 1802 was Fort Greene at Savannah. On Cockspur Island, commanding the mouth of the Savannah River, Fort Greene was still uncompleted, but was manned by the company of Captain Abimael Y. Nicoll. Nicoll had received medical training in his early years, and as Fort Greene had no surgeon's mate in the summer of 1802, Secretary Dearborn authorized Nicoll to perform the duties of surgeon's mate as well as commanding officer, an unusual arrangement that allowed the captain to draw an extra $30 a month for his medical services.(31) There is no record of a garrison at the small fort at Point Petre in 1802, but there was probably a caretaking detachment from Nicoll's company. Although General Wilkinson two years earlier had referred to "Fort Washington, St. Marys River, Georgia," there were too many other forts honoring the late President and the name was apparently dropped within a year.(32)

Before the end of 1802 a few changes in the seacoast garrisons were ordered, the first of many that would take place the following year. At the end of September the Secretary of War directed that Captain Amos Stoddard's company, garrisoning both Fort Constitution at Portsmouth and Fort Sumner at Portland, move by water to Philadelphia and then overland to Pittsburgh to await further orders as to its eventual destination. To replace Stoddard's men at Portsmouth, Captain Lemuel Gates's company was directed to move from Fort Independence in Boston to Fort Constitution; nothing was said about providing a small garrison for Fort Sumner. Gates's departure left the Boston defenses garrisoned only by the company of Captain Nehemiah Freeman at Fort Independence.(33) At about the same time Secretary Dearborn advised Military Agent Abraham D. Abrahams at Savannah that he was considering withdrawing the entire garrison of Fort Greene on Cockspur Island, not only to free the troops there for service in the southwest, but also because the fort was proving to be in annual danger of hurricane-force winds.(34) No action was taken at Fort Greene, however, during the rest of 1802.

A word should be said at this point about the effect of the new administrative structure on the support of the seacoast fortifications. As previously mentioned, the Act of 16 March 1802 had abolished the so-called Quartermaster's Department, a quasi-military group headed by John Wilkins, Jr.; Wilkins and several assistants were summarily discharged as of 30 April.(35) To replace them Secretary Dearborn appointed three autonomous Military Agents who reported directly to his office; these were to supervise supply matters in what Dearborn designated as the Northern, Middle, and Southern Departments, but these geographical divisions were misleading. The so-called Northern Department, under Peter Gansevoort, Jr., at Albany, actually provided supplies and furnished necessary funds for the post on the northwestern frontier, garrisoned by the 1st Infantry and three companies of artillerists, *plus* the post of West Point. The Middle Department of William Linnard at Philadelphia was charged with the support of all seacoast garrisons from Maine through Virginia, as well as the posts on the lower Mississippi, supplied by way of Pittsburgh and the Ohio River. The Southern Department, headed by Abraham D. Abrahams in Savannah, initially supplied the seacoast garrisons in the Carolinas and Georgia, as well as the posts on the Creek frontier in western Georgia. Instead of issuing supplies and providing funds through the regimental structure, issue was made directly to posts, to line officers at each post who had been designated as assistant military agents. Although this system could be made to work, and did for a year or so, it tended to exclude the military command structure from involvement in supply operations.

Thus the far-flung companies of the Regiment of Artillerists received their supplies from all three Military Agents, and Colonel Burbeck in Washington had no knowledge of or interest in the supply problems of those companies, six at this time, stationed north of the Ohio or on the Mississippi. For the seacoast garrisons the system was workable; the garrisons under Lieutenant Colonel Freeman were supported by Agent Abrahams in Savannah, while those to the north, the posts supervised by Majors Jackson and Ingersoll, were the responsibility of the capable Agent Linnard at Philadelphia. The single exception, for reasons not explained, was West Point; command of the company of artillerists at that post came under Major Ingersoll at Fort Jay, but the supply and pay support came from Agent Gansevoort at Albany, who was otherwise charged with the northwest frontier. In the relatively static situation of 1802, thanks to three energetic Agents, the system appeared successful. But in succeeding years, as will be seen, the almost constant movement of companies from seaboard to frontier, and from north to south of the Ohio, was to put an intolerable strain on a system not centralized in Washington and oriented to geographical posts rather than to regiments and battalions.

A final if minor administrative change took place in the Army's structure before the end of 1802. General Wilkinson decided that the office of the Adjutant and Inspector of the Army should be established outside Washington, and in August Lieutenant Colonel Cushing began negotiations to rent a building in Frederick Town, Maryland, for his use. Why the Secretary of War was willing to let his military advisor move out of Washington is not apparent, unless because of the scarcity of office space in the new capital. Although mail went from Frederick to Washington three times a week, there would now be a one-day separation between the War Department and what became effectively the Headquarters of the Army.(36)

CHAPTER VII
ARTILLERISTS, ENGINEERS, AND LOUISIANA
1803-1805

Although President Jefferson had by mid-1802 verified Spain's cession to France of the Province of Louisiana, he treated this knowledge calmly in his Annual Message of 15 December. "The cession," he wrote, "… which took place in the course of the late war, will, if carried into effect, make a change in the aspect of our foreign relations … ." No increase would be necessary in the American military establishment, the President felt, but "considering that our regular troops are employed for local purposes, and that the militia is our general reliance for great and sudden emergencies, Congress might wish to review the effectiveness of the militia."(1)

Nevertheless, at the beginning of 1803 there was concern in Washington about possible French expansion northward from New Orleans. On 11 January the President nominated James Monroe as envoy extraordinary to the French Republic, to sound out First Consul Bonaparte about mutual arrangements for the port of New Orleans, but the events that would lead to the unexpected purchase of all of Louisiana were not known for many months. Meanwhile the officers and men of the Regiment of Artillerists began to receive marching orders with increasing frequency. Captain Amos Stoddard's company, having reached Pittsburgh as directed earlier, was ordered to proceed down the Ohio and then up the Mississippi; Stoddard was told to reconnoiter a site for a post near the mouth of the Illinois River.(2) In mid-March Captain William L. Cooper, already at Fort Pickering on the Chickasaw Bluffs, was ordered to move his company south to Fort Adams in the Mississippi Territory; he would be relieved at Fort Pickering by a detachment of the 1st Infantry from Fort Massac on the lower Ohio. (3) At the same time Major William MacRea, commanding the post of South West Point in Tennessee, was alerted to move a company of artillerists and one of infantry to Fort Adams.(4) And the Atlantic defenses were further reduced by orders for Captain Henry M. Muhlenberg to move his company from Fort Mifflin to Pittsburgh, with an implied eventual destination of Fort Adams.(5)

Secretary Dearborn was determined not only to build up the troop strength on the southwestern frontier, but also to provide improved fortifications along the old Spanish colonial boundary. To this end he ordered Major Decius Wadsworth of the Corps of Engineers, then supervising repairs of Fort Nelson at Norfolk, to proceed to Fort Adams to construct a temporary defensive work and to begin planning a permanent fortification.(6) Notifying General Wilkinson of this action, Secretary Dearborn went on to advise Wilkinson that the international situation seemed less ominous:

> … although we have the most explicit assurances of the friendly disposition of the French and Spanish Courts, and have good reason to believe that all differences relating to the navigation &c of the Mississippi will be amicably adjusted, it is thought advisable to make some preparation for a different state of things. [The American right of deposit at New Orleans had been suspended by the Spanish Intendant in late 1802.] … it appears that no troops are to accompany General Victor and the civil officers who are to take possession of Louisiana, that Spain is to continue to garrison the Country, until the St. Domingo business is settled, that the troops which were destined for New Orleans are to go to the West Indies [Leclerc's expedition] … . The President is authorized to callout and employ if necessary Eighty thousand Militia in the recess of Congress, but no measure of that kind will be resorted to until we hear the result of Mr. Monroe's mission, unless compelled by new aggressions on the part of our neighbors, which at present are not expected.(7)

In late March the Secretary decided that in view of the build-up of artillerists on the lower Mississippi, a field officer of the regiment should be ordered there to command. Deciding to leave Major MacRea in Tennessee, Dearborn chose his old friend Major Daniel Jackson, who had been in command of the New England district virtually since his appointment in 1798. The Adjutant and Inspector notified Major Jackson of the decision, advising him that no new district commander would be appointed; Captain Nehemiah Freeman would command Fort Independence, with detachments at Salem and Marblehead, and Captain Lemuel Gates would command both Fort Constitution and Fort Sumner; both officers would report directly to Colonel Henry Burbeck in Washington.(8) But within the Army there was doubt that Major Jackson would accept his new assignment. The senior captain, Richard S. Blackburn at Fort Nelson, was very ill, and had written to the Adjutant and Inspector for sick leave. "I think it probable," Cushing replied, "you will soon have an opportunity of making a sea voyage without asking for a furlough; Major Jackson being ordered … to Fort Adams in the Mississippi Territory … it is generally believed that he will resign upon receipt of the order. Should this be the case, your promotion and orders of March will follow … ."(9)

The general belief was correct, and on 9 April Major Jackson, pleading family problems, submitted his resignation. Secretary Dearborn had no choice but to accept the resignation, but he unburdened himself to Jackson on the subject of sunshine soldiers. "I am under the painful necessity of observing," he wrote, "that it has become too common for Officers when ordered on duty to make excuses and long statements, shewing that it would be very inconvenient for them to comply with the orders instead of paying that prompt obedience, which is so essential to a military system."(10) Captain Blackburn was at once promoted to the vacant majority and ordered to proceed to Fort Adams; Lieutenant John Saunders, promoted to captain, assumed command of Blackburn's company and the Norfolk forts. In forwarding the promotion order to the ailing Blackburn, the Adjutant and Inspector expressed the hope that Blackburn might "rise to another and another Grade in the Service of your Country, before it shall please Him who Governs the universe, to transfer you to that army in which there are no vicissitudes, and which is to stand forever."(11) But Cushing's wishes availed little; Blackburn's health continued to deteriorate, and before he could take the beneficial sea voyage to Mississippi Territory, he died on 15 November.(12)

Another death had occurred earlier which affected the Regiment of Artillerists indirectly. The senior colonel of the Army, the veteran and popular John Francis Hamtramck of the 1st Infantry, died at Detroit on 11 April, and his death set off a chain of infantry promotions: Lieutenant Colonel Thomas Hunt of the 1st to colonel; Major Jacob Kingsbury of the 2d to lieutenant colonel of the 1st; and Captain Thomas Pasteur of the 1st to major of the 2d. Secretary Dearborn had felt great confidence in Colonel Hamtramck, but that confidence did not extend to his successor, Hunt, who had been commanding the two-company garrison at Michilimackinac. The Secretary did not attempt to block Hunt's promotion, but was curiously unwilling to let him assume command of the five-company garrison at Detroit.

For reasons best known to himself, Dearborn decided to entrust the command of Detroit for the time being to the Chief of Artillerists, Colonel Burbeck. The Secretary's instructions to Burbeck were vague. "The death of Col. Hamtramck," he wrote, "in addition to the loss of such an experienced and valuable officer, has so materially interfered with the arrangements of that Department as to render your presence at Detroit necessary. As soon as you can conveniently, you will therefore be pleased to repair to Detroit and take command of the Department of the Lakes… . Col. Hunt will remain at Michilimacanac [sic] until further orders."(13)

Whatever may have impelled Secretary Dearborn to remove the Chief of Artillerists from the seaboard, his decision was discussed unfavorably within the Army. Colonel Burbeck was puzzled and unhappy, and wrote privately of his displeasure to the Adjutant and Inspector. Cushing himself was equally unhappy, for if Hunt was not considered qualified to command the 1st Infantry, then the promotion should go to the next senior lieutenant colonel—who was Thomas H. Cushing.

> I am fully of your opinion [Cushing replied] that Detroit is not your proper post, and that you will have a very unpleasant Command if you go there. The Garrison consists of one Company of Artillerists & four Companies of the 1st Regiment of Infantry, and is unquestionably the proper Command for the Colonel of that Regiment.
>
> If Government has not sufficient confidence in Lieut Colonel Hunt to give him the Command of Detroit, it should not promote him... .
>
> For my own part, I should be very much mortified to see the Colonel of Artillerists sent from the Atlantic Coast to Command the first Regiment of Infantry at Detroit... .(14)

Despite their private feelings, neither Burbeck nor Cushing seems to have protested to Dearborn, as it was known that the Secretary did not encourage discussion of his orders. On 2 July Colonel Burbeck left Washington for Detroit, traveling by way of New York City, Albany, Utica, Buffalo, and then by vessel across Lake Erie. Awaiting his supervision were the posts of Detroit, Fort Wayne, and Michilimackinac—making up, as Cushing put it, "what the Honorable Secretary of War has been pleased to style the 'Department of the Lakes'... ."(15)

The Engineer Command Controversy

One of the touchiest subjects in the Army of the early 19th century was the matter of who should command a post—and draw double rations. Single company posts posed no problem, and where two or more companies were stationed together, the senior captain clearly commanded and received the commuted pay. Difficulties arose when a field officer resided at a post occupied by one or more companies, and they were exacerbated when the field officer and the senior captain were of different corps. Petty as it may seem today, the command problem was taken deadly seriously at the time, and several good officers resigned from the service on this point. Nowhere was the problem more sensitive than at West Point, where Louis Tousard's attempts to claim command in 1801 had probably contributed to his subsequent discharge.(16) By the fall of 1802 the matter was more complex, for now the Corps of Engineers, consisting only of officers and cadets, lived on a post garrisoned by a company of artillerists, that of Captain George Izard. There was no good reason to maintain a company of artillerists at West Point, except to act as support troops for the Military Academy, but according to the 1801 decision Captain Izard was the post commander, and in his view the Engineer officers and the cadets were simply tenants on *his* post. But Lieutenant Colonel Jonathan Williams, as Chief Engineer and particularly as Superintendent of the Military Academy, felt that the command belonged to him, both by virtue of his office and by right of seniority. Williams and Izard were well matched despite the 26-year difference in ages; both came from prominent families, both had received European schooling in the military art, and both were insistent on their prerogatives. Captain Izard, in fact, would have been well qualified for the Corps of Engineers, and a biographer feels that Izard was unhappy at not being selected for membership in that corps.(17) There is an implication in subsequent correspondence that Izard, as post commander, may have interfered to some extent in the instruction of the cadets.

In September 1802 Captain Izard wrote to the Adjutant and Inspector that his position as post commander was not being honored. Cushing referred the letter to Secretary Dearborn, with the comment that "I have no reason to believe that any personal ill will exists between Captain Izard & Colonel Williams [but] such a state of things may soon exist unless the rights and interests of the individuals & their Corps are … distinctly pointed out and secured … ."(18) This was good advice, and the Secretary prepared a letter which Cushing forwarded to both Izard and Williams as "a standing instruction for the Commanding Officer of Artillerists at West Point."(19) According to a later authority, Dearborn wrote that no officer or cadet of the Corps of Engineers would be subject to the orders of an officer of another corps, but to the orders of the President alone, or to the Commanding General when "in actual service," and that conversely no officer of Engineers would in any circumstances command officers or troops of another corps, except by a specific order of the President.(20) This decision has been described as unpalatable to Colonel Williams, and is the reason usually assigned for his subsequent resignation.(21)

Jonathan Williams, however, had other sources of irritation by early 1803. When he submitted a routine claim for his additional pay as Inspector of Fortifications, a position from which he had not been relieved by any official orders, he received a sharp rebuke from the Secretary of War:

> Your claim for pay as Inspector of Fortifications [is] not well founded. If ever I conveyed to you an idea of your retaining your appointment as Inspector of Fortifications after you had been placed at the head of the Corps of Engineers, it has entirely escaped my recollection.
>
> You Sir, must be convinced that it never could have been intended by the Government to establish sinecure places, and under the present circumstances your holding the Office of Inspector of Fortifications could be considered in no other light.… [F]rom there having been no pay stipulated or money appropriated for such an Officer in the law fixing the military peace establishment it would be improper in me to sanction the payment of your claim. If I am erroneous in my opinion … you have a remedy by referring your claim to Congress."(22)

Williams's assumption that he had continued to be Inspector of Fortifications seems to have been an honest error, and he must have been stung by the Secretary's tone. As late as the following April, in fact, Dearborn was directing him to inspect fortifications and payoff abrogated contracts, so the Secretary's reference to "sinecure places" must have been particularly galling. But for the moment Williams held his peace and his position.

The Chief Engineer had already inaugurated at West Point a very promising professional society intended to stimulate scientific military thinking and the exchange of new ideas in the various fields of the military art. Established on 12 November 1802, it was designated the "United States Military Philosophical Society"; its spiritual parent was the American Philosophical Society, of which Jonathan Williams was a valued member. The new society's initial membership, which convened in the "Long Room" of the small Academy building at West Point, was made up entirely of officers and cadets of the Corps of Engineers, but it is clear that Colonel Williams hoped to extend its influence throughout the Army. As he later explained the need for the Society: "It will become an immediate object to join to the institution the most respectable military and scientific characters of our country; and before all the veterans of our Revolutionary contest are gone from this world, it is hoped that the knowledge resulting from their honourable experience will be saved from oblivion, and secured among the archives of the society."(23)

At a second meeting on 29 November the membership formally adopted Williams's proposed title, and elected him president. Williams at once wrote to the President of the United States, inviting him to become Patron of the United States Military Philosophical Society. Jefferson replied on Christmas Day, accepting the honor with a few graceful comments on the importance of engineering and of science in general. By the end of 1802 it appeared that the new society was well established.(24)

The relationship between Colonel Williams and Captain Izard, the post commander, continued strained during early 1803, but relief came soon. On 20 April, as part of a general shifting of seacoast-defense troops, Secretary Dearborn alerted Captain Izard and his company for movement to the isolated post of South West Point in Tennessee. Izard may have felt that he was being transferred to facilitate Williams's command of the post, but more probably he simply viewed the prospect of frontier service as a waste of a European military education; in any event, upon receipt of movement orders Izard submitted his resignation, which the Secretary accepted with regret as of 1 June.(25) With Izard's resignation and the departure of his company, only a small detachment of artillerists—"a Sergeant's Guard," as Dearborn put it—was left at West Point, and it appeared that Colonel Williams would soon be designated post commander.

It has been represented(26) that about this time the officers of the Corps of Engineers dramatically forwarded to the President a memorial protesting the decision that Engineer officers could exercise no line command, and that when this petition was ignored they determined to resign in a body, with Colonel Williams and later Major Wadsworth actually resigning. The record indicates otherwise. While it is true that Secretary Dearborn acknowledged on 26 May the receipt of "the memorial of the Officers and Cadets," the subject of the memorial was nothing more dramatic than the poor quality of the rations being issued at West Point.(27)

Nevertheless, Colonel William's dissatisfaction was growing. If any one cause could be assigned, it might be Henry Dearborn's continual interference with the functions of the Military Academy. The Secretary was unwilling to stabilize the Corps of Engineers long enough for it to get organized and to inaugurate a proper curriculum, both educational and military, for the new school. During the Corps' first year of life, the Secretary had ordered its few officers hither and yon on relatively secondary matters. Major Decius Wadsworth, second-ranking officer, had been sent to Norfolk in 1802 to supervise construction, and in March 1803 he was ordered all the way to Fort Adams in Mississippi Territory. Lieutenant James Wilson then had to be sent from West Point to replace Wadsworth at Norfolk. And finally, in mid-April, the Secretary casually notified Colonel Williams himself to travel to Fort Johnston in North Carolina to inspect work done under an old contract and to pay off the contractor.(28)

Colonel Williams complied with Dearborn's instructions, but almost immediately upon his return from North Carolina, on 21 June, he submitted his resignation, giving as his primary reason the Engineer command decision. Dearborn accepted the resignation in the name of the President, expressing regret but making no real effort to persuade Williams to change his mind. And then Dearborn immediately directed a curious letter to Major Wadsworth at Fort Adams. No mention was made of Wadsworth's right to head the Corps of Engineers, and there was no indication that he might expect to be ordered back to West Point in the near future; instead, Dearborn went out of his way to reinforce the command principle, and to warn Wadsworth against violating it:

> Lieut. Col. Williams having this day resigned his appointment ... from a dissatisfaction with the principle originally established and heretofore practised (Viz) that no military command should be attached to any Members of the Corps of Engineers - And having observed in a letter this day received from Gen. Wilkinson, that he proposed to give you the Command of the Garrison at Fort Adams, in the absence of [Colonel Thomas Butler, 2d Infantry], I consider it my duty to inform you, you will not

consider your present Command as a precedent .... I should advise you to decline the Command, and attend merely to your duties as an Engineer .... It is the wish of the Executive that the Gentlemen [of] the Corps of Engineers should devote their time & attention exclusively to the theory & practice of their profession, by which means we may avoid the unpleasant necessity of employing Foreigners as Engineers....(29)

The next-ranking officer of Engineers was Captain William A. Barron, who was on duty at West Point, and to Barron the Secretary of War passed the "direction" of the Military Academy in the absence of Major Wadsworth. Dearborn spelled out for Barron his views on the subject of command, adding that as the principle had been in effect during the Revolutionary War, and had worked no hardship on the Engineers, "the resignation of Col. Williams was the more unexpected."(30)

Jonathan Williams's departure was not to be permanent, but with his resignation there was a vacancy at the head of the Corps of Engineers which was not to be filled officially until his return to service nearly two years later. With Major Wadsworth and Lieutenant Wilson on detached service, only six officers of Engineers remained assigned to West Point. These were Captain Barron, acting superintendent; Captain Jared Mansfield; 1st Lieutenant Alexander Macomb, newly transferred from the infantry; 2d Lieutenants Joseph G. Swift and Simon M. Levy, of the Class of 1802; and 2d Lieutenant Walker K. Armistead, who had graduated in March 1803. (The two other members of the Class of 1803, Henry Burbeck Jackson and John Livingston, graduated in April and were appointed to the Regiment of Artillerists.)

Two minor pieces of legislation affecting the Engineers were enacted in early 1803. On 28 February Congress authorized the appointment of a teacher of French and a teacher of drawing, to become part of the quasi-military faculty of the Academy. Another section of the same act authorized one artificer and 18 enlisted men for the Corps of Engineers; although not so specified, these men were to provide the support formerly rendered by Izard's artillerists. In fact, instead of enlisting new men, it appears that the Engineers simply assimilated the 15-20 men left behind by Izard's company.(31)

The Army and the Louisiana Purchase

James Monroe's efforts in Paris to secure New Orleans for the United States mushroomed into the unexpected and glittering opportunity to purchase the whole of the vast and indefinite region known as Louisiana. On 30 April 1803 the treaty for the cession of the region to the United States was signed by Bonaparte's representatives, and on 4 July—auspicious date—the news was printed in the *National Intelligencer*.(32) On 20 June President Jefferson had given instructions to Captain Meriwether Lewis of the 1st Infantry regarding exploration of the region, and for the rest of the month Secretary Dearborn's correspondence had been largely devoted to arranging for the military support of Lewis's forthcoming expedition.

Even before the documents of the Louisiana purchase reached Washington, the Secretary of War began to alert various officers as to what was about to happen and how it would affect the Army. On 10 July he wrote Major Wadsworth at Fort Adams that the United States might take possession as early as autumn; because the frontier would be moving, there would no longer be a need for extensive fortifications at Fort Adams, and a strong blockhouse would suffice for the single company to be left there. More important was a survey of what forts, both land and seacoast, might be transferred to the United States, particularly in the New Orleans area, and Dearborn urged Wadsworth to report as soon as possible on the state of the existing works in "lower Louisiana."(33)

The Secretary then turned his attention to "upper Louisiana." To Captain Amos Stoddard, whose company of artillerists was about to establish a post near the mouth of the Illinois, Dearborn sent a change of orientation:

> In consequence of the recent cession of Louisiana to the United States, it will probably become necessary ... to place an American Garrison in the Military Post on the Western Bank of the Mississippi now occupied by Spanish Troops— Your Company will probably be ordered to that Post.... You will please to take the earliest opportunity of ascertaining the present state of the Post on the Louisiana side, without giving any uneasiness to the Spanish officer. You may inform him of the Cession & the probability of our taking possession previous to the next winter.(34)

Dearborn went on to ask Stoddard for much information on the flora and fauna of the Louisiana side of the Mississippi, which was the origin of Stoddard's subsequent pioneer work on the subject.(35)

Because of the impending take-over of Louisiana, President Jefferson delivered his third Annual Message on 17 October in 1803. It was the President's theory that American coastal ports and harbors needed a fleet of gunboats to reinforce the seacoast fortifications—this subject became of more importance a few years later—and he noted with satisfaction that the "favorable and peaceful turn of affairs on the Mississippi" removed the urgency in the construction of those gunboats.(36)

At the end of October Secretary Dearborn summed up the status of the Louisiana cession and the plans for military occupation of the new territory in a letter to General Wilkinson:

> ... Congress have by law authorized the President ... to take possession of the Country thus ceded and to establish such Government ... as he may judge expedient - until Congress shall constitute some other system of Government.... Governor Claiborne [of Mississippi Territory] and yourself will be authorised to receive possession of Louisiana [and] you are hereby authorized and directed to proceed to New Orleans (in concert with Govr Claiborne) without loss of time, with Six companies of regular troops and one hundred of such of the militia of the vicinity as may voluntarily engage to join you.... The Government of the Territory will devolve upon Governor Claiborne. Captain Stoddard at Kaskaskias will receive orders from this Office to take possession of upper Louisiana ....(37)

In brief, the Congressional authority provided that the United States would take possession of Louisiana on 20 December. On that date Governor William C. C. Claiborne would assume temporarily the civil government of Louisiana, with General Wilkinson becoming the military governor of lower Louisiana and Captain Amos Stoddard at St. Louis acting temporarily as military commandant of upper Louisiana. As Congress had not authorized any augmentation of the military establishment, it was evident that troops to reinforce the garrisons on the lower Mississippi would have to come from the posts north of the Ohio and, in particular, from the Atlantic seacoast garrisons.

Activities on the Seaboard, 1803-1804

Even before the occupation of Louisiana levied additional requirements on the seacoast troops, almost all productive activity had ground to a halt in the face of that administrative nightmare of the period, a general court martial. The case was that of Colonel Thomas Butler of the 2d Infantry, charged by General Wilkinson with a variety of military crimes and misdemeanors too involved and politically-inspired to detail here, and ordered to stand trial at the headquarters at Frederick Town, Maryland, in November of 1803.(38) The Adjutant and Inspector set about the tedious business of appointing a court and notifying the far-flung members to assemble at Frederick by 20 November. Cushing knew that Colonel Henry Burbeck of the Artillerists, the next senior officer after Butler, would have to preside, despite the fact that Burbeck had only just departed Washington for Detroit and the temporary command of the "Department of the Lakes." A letter notifying Burbeck of the November court was sent to Detroit at once, and may well have been waiting for him when he arrived.(39)

Three other field officers of artillerists were warned for the court, but only lieutenant Colonel Constant Freeman was able to sit. A letter was sent *pro forma* to Major Richard S. Blackburn, deferring his orders for Fort Adams, but it was known that Blackburn was mortally ill, and he died before the court convened. Major George Ingersoll at Fort Jay was alerted to serve, but in August charges were preferred against Ingersoll by the district paymaster, Lieutenant Charles Wallstonecraft, alleging financial irregularities; instead of sitting on the Butler court, Major Ingersoll had to be ordered to Frederick Town in November for his own trial, to follow Butler's.(40) Infantry officers were equally hard to locate for the court, and by the beginning of November the Adjutant and Inspector despaired of forming a regulation court-martial; he wrote the Secretary of War for assistance:

> There is not a field Officer or Captain nearer than Niagara, not already warned for this duty except the two Capts of Engineers at West Point [and] Capt. Gates who is the only Officer at Fort Constitution, and Capt. Livingston who is the only Officer at Fort Jay, and I do not therefore see how it is possible that the Court should consist of thirteen [as] some of the Officers warned may be prevented from attending... and Col. Butlers objecting to particular Officers may make it necessary to curtail the court... . I ... suggest whether it may not be proper for you to say, that if a sufficient number of Officers do not attend to form a Court Martial of thirteen members for the trial of Colonel Butler ... the Adjutant & Inspector of the Army is authorized to form a Court Martial for this trial to consist of such Officers as do attend and are not excepted to ... .(41)

Secretary Dearborn took the responsibility of authorizing the court to proceed with less than 13 members, Colonel Burbeck returned from Detroit to act as president, and the trial began on 20 November. Space does not permit a discussion of the Butler trial, but the colonel was acquitted of most of the charges and sentenced only to be reprimanded in general orders by General Wilkinson. This was only the first phase, however, of what became a running feud between Butler and Wilkinson. Following the Butler trial, Major George Ingersoll was tried on charges of financial irregularities while commanding Fort Jay, a principal allegation being that he profited from the sale of milk to the garrison. (42) Ingersoll also was sentenced to a reprimand by General Wilkinson, and pending the General's review of his case, returned to his home in Boston. Wilkinson did not act on Ingersoll's case for many months, and Ingersoll spent most of 1804 at home awaiting further orders.

The death of Major Richard S. Blackburn was reported to the Adjutant and Inspector on 27 November. A week later it was announced to the Army that Captain James Bruff was promoted to major in Blackburn's place, and that Lieutenant Richard Whiley would assume the captaincy of Bruff's company of artillerists.(43)

The official United States occupation of Louisiana took place on 20 December 1803, and for a month or so later Secretary Dearborn waited anxiously for word from General Wilkinson as to the reaction of the Spanish garrisons to the French-imposed cession. Twice in early January he complained to Wilkinson of lack of news, but by the end of the month he concluded that all must be well. He wrote the Adjutant and Inspector on detailed arrangements for building up the troop strength in the New Orleans area, generally at the expense of the Atlantic seacoast garrisons.

> You will be pleased [he directed Cushing] to issue orders to the following effect - Lieut Col Freeman of the Artillerists should be directed [to proceed to] New Orleans, to take the immediate Command

of the Military Post of that place and the direction of the Posts in Lower Louisiana and Fort Stoddard (Stoddert] on the Mobile. It is expected that he will arrive at New Orleans in the month of April ... . Captain Stille and that part of his company at Fort Trumbull should be prepared to take passage by water to New Orleans, [calling] at Norfolk [to pick up 33 men] of Captain McClallen's Company ... . Captain Robeson should sail with his Company from Charleston for New Orleans, the first of April - The detachment [at] Fort Johnston should be transferred to Captain Kalteisen's Company ... . Captain Nicoll with his Company should sail from Savannah for New Orleans by the first of April - One Lieutenant [and 20 men] should be detached from Fort Wilkinson [Georgia] ... for Cockspur [Fort Greene] in Savannah Harbour ... .(44)

Secretary Dearborn wrote to General Wilkinson of the impending troop transfers, noting also that the newly-promoted Major James Bruff of the Artillerists would be ordered to Upper Louisiana. Dearborn proposed certain general measures for the defense of the New Orleans area, suggesting that six companies be stationed in the city and the other four as Wilkinson thought best. "A number of large Gun Boats," Dearborn added, "will I presume be ordered to be built and manned as soon as possible to be stationed near the mouth of the Mississippi and Lake Ponchartrain ... .(45)

After these proposed transfers were effected, only eight cities on the Atlantic seaboard would have federal artillery protection; single-company garrisons would remain at Portsmouth, Boston, Newport, New York, Philadelphia, Baltimore, Norfolk, and Charleston. Of the remaining 12 companies of artillerists, six would be assigned to the lower Mississippi, two to Tennessee, and four north of the Ohio. Except at New Orleans, where Lieutenant Colonel Freeman would directly supervise at least three companies, the old battalion district system was suspended; Colonel Burbeck, who had resumed his office in Washington after returning from Detroit for the Butler trial, was considered in direct command of all the Atlantic seacoast garrisons. Of the four majors, Moses Porter was still at Fort Niagara, William MacRea at South West Point, George Ingersoll at home awaiting disposition, and James Bruff under orders for St. Louis in Upper Louisiana.(46)

In the spring of 1804 General Wilkinson was ordered back to Washington to confer with the President and Secretary of War as to the best means to defend the newly-acquired territory. On the General's departure, Lieutenant Colonel Freeman was assured that he would remain in command in New Orleans— Colonel Butler, if he remained in service, would be sent to Fort Wilkinson on the Creek frontier in Georgia—and to make his command more palatable, he was authorized *triple* rations.(47) At the same time Major Decius Wadsworth, the only officer of Engineers on the lower Mississippi, was directed to book passage back to the Atlantic coast and to report to Washington to assist in the defense deliberations. Wadsworth found a vessel proceeding directly to New York, and on 25 May reported to the Secretary his arrival in that city.(48) General Wilkinson arrived in Washington in June, and by the 22d had established his headquarters with the Adjutant and Inspector at Frederick Town, Maryland. Almost at once, however, the General went off to take the waters at York Springs in Pennsylvania, despite Colonel Cushing's urgent pleas that Wilkinson return to deal with many administrative matters. Cushing wrote him to complain of the conduct of Captain Henry M. Muhlenberg at Fort McHenry, who had remained behind on various pretexts when his company departed for New Orleans. Cushing was tired of "the game Capt. Muhlenberg is playing," and urged that the officer be ordered to join his company. General Wilkinson at once directed that Muhlenberg be arrested for disobedience of orders, and Cushing wrote to Captain James Read at Fort Mifflin to detain Muhlenberg "should he be in Pennsylvania and within your reach." Old General Peter Muhlenberg in Philadelphia wrote to protest his son's arrest, but the younger Muhlenberg, who had served earlier at Fort Adams, was determined not to return to the lower Mississippi, and he resigned as of 8 October.(49)

A minor disaster struck one of the seacoast fortifications in the fall of 1804. At the end of September a great hurricane swept the Georgia coast, and Cockspur Island at the mouth of the Savannah River was raked from end to end by high waves, completely destroying the still-unfinished Fort Greene. After the departure of Nicoll's company for New Orleans, the fort had been manned by a detachment of the 2d Infantry under Ensign J.R.N. Luckett; although Luckett himself survived, a number of his men were swept away and drowned. News of the disaster reached Frederick Town on 2 October, and at General Wilkinson's direction Colonel Cushing wrote Ensign Luckett directing him to abandon the ruins of Fort Greene and to march his survivors back to Fort Wilkinson as soon as they were able to travel.(50)

Of interest to the Army in the fall of 1804 was the appointment of a new Superintendent of Military Stores, the quasi-military position charged with the storage of ordnance and other items and their issue to the troops through the Military Agents. The position had been held since mid-1800 by General William Irvine, a Revolutionary veteran who died during the summer of 1804. Secretary Dearborn recommended the appointment of the old General's son, Callender Irvine, a former captain of artillerists and engineers; President Jefferson agreed, and Irvine took office as of 24 October.(51)

At about the same time Major George Ingersoll, awaiting action on his court-martial, was restored to duty by General Wilkinson and ordered to the New Orleans area. Instead of being grateful, Ingersoll wrote the Adjutant and Inspector to protest his transfer to the frontier. Cushing was firm: "I am truly sorry that you cannot be posted more to your mind than at New Orleans– But you must be sensible that there is not a post on the Sea Coast garrisoned by more than one company, and of course there is not a field officer's command at any one of them … .(52) Major Ingersoll saw the picture, realized that there would be no commands on the seacoast for the foreseeable future, and on 1 December submitted his resignation. For the moment, his vacancy remained unfilled.

Not only were there no field officers, except Colonel Burbeck, stationed on the Atlantic coast, but by the end of 1804 the number of company officers assigned to the remaining garrisons had reached a new low. Colonel Cushing forwarded to General Wilkinson, then in Washington, a detailed listing of the officers assigned to the seacoast defenses, together with their various extra duties:

> There are at this time eight vacancies for 2d Lts … of Artillerists, and if Charles M. Taylor be dead [he was], nine … .

> The company of Capt Gates is deficient but four men, his 1st Lt (Swett) is on command at Springfield … the 2d Lt (Ritchie) is reported sick with the company at Portsmouth.

> Capt Freeman is a district paymaster, and his only Subal. (1st Lt Williams) is the [assistant] Military Agent at Fort Independence. This company has a surplus of twelve men.

> Capt Beall has 1st Lt Wollstonecraft a district Pay Master and 1st Lt Howard assistant Military Agent for Fort Wolcott. This company is deficient eight men.

> Capt Whiley [at Fort Jay] has 1st Lt [Walbach] (Adjutant of the Regiment) and 2d Lt Kimball. This company is deficient twenty five men.

> Capt Read has no officer with him at Fort Mifflin, his only Subaltern (1st Lt House) being a District pay Master and stationed at Fort McHenry. This company is deficient thirty four men.

> Capt McClallen [at Fort McHenry] and his two subalterns are already on the Recruiting Service.

Capt Saunders' 1st Lt (A.B. Armistead) is on the R Service ... his 2d Lt Livingston is the Asst. Military Agt. at Fort Nelson, this company will be complete after the ten for New Orleans are sent off.

Capt Kalteisen [Fort Johnson, S.C.] has but one Subaltern (1st lt Barnes) and he is District pay Master— This company is deficient thirty two men.(53)

Cushing made a few recommendations for transfers to equalize the size of the various companies, and suggested that there were too many paymasters for the number of troops on the seaboard. He did not belabor the obvious, that the seacoast defenses were at their lowest strength and their lowest state of efficiency since 1800.

The Engineers and the Military Academy, 1804-1805

By the end of 1803, following the resignation of Jonathan Williams, the Corps of Engineers and the tiny Military Academy began to stagnate. The promising United States Military Philosophical Society, without Williams's guidance and initiative, suspended operations. Captain William A. Barron, the senior Engineer officer at West Point in the continued absence of Major Decius Wadsworth, carried on the necessary administration and supervised the rudimentary instruction of 11 cadets. Then in January of 1804 Captain Jared Mansfield, in charge of mathematics instruction, was offered by President Jefferson the post of Surveyor General of the Northwest Territory. While Jefferson was perfectly willing to remove Mansfield from the Academy, he considered him too valuable a mathematician to be lost permanently to the Corps of Engineers; thus ensued an arrangement whereby Mansfield would retain his Engineer commission during his tenure as Surveyor General, and would be eligible for promotion as if he were on duty with the Corps. The net effect of this agreement was a permanently unfillable vacancy in the Engineers. (54)

A few weeks later 2d Lieutenant Simon Levy, who was in poor health, applied for extended leave in a warmer climate; Secretary Dearborn approved a six months' absence, suggesting that Levy spend the time at St. Mary's, Georgia.(55) The Secretary may have had in mind that Levy, while convalescing, could inspect and repair the fortifications at Point Petre at the mouth of the St. Mary's River. As a replacement for Levy, Captain Barron secured Dearborn's permission to allow 2d Lieutenant Samuel Gates of the Artillerists, who graduated on 27 March 1804, to remain at West Point as a sort of combination postgraduate student and instructor.(56)

The Corps of Engineers almost gained a distinguished name in early 1804. After Captain Meriwether Lewis's selection to head an exploring expedition, he looked for another officer to act as his second-in-command. His first choice was his old company commander in the 2d Sublegion, Captain William Clark, younger brother of George Rogers Clark, who had left the Army in 1796. Lewis wrote to Clark in 1803, stating that the President had authorized a captaincy if Clark accepted. But Clark was hard to locate, and after weeks of silence Lewis tentatively offered the position to Lieutenant Moses Hook of the 1st Infantry, who as assistant military agent at Pittsburgh had done a good job of collecting supplies and transport for Lewis. Hook wrote Secretary Dearborn for permission, and Dearborn approved. But meanwhile William Clark had finally received Lewis's letter, and at the last minute accepted the position. Then a legal difficulty arose concerning Clark's promised captaincy. There were no vacant captaincies in either regiment of infantry or in the artillerists, and unless Congress authorized a new regiment —which was hardly likely—President Jefferson was without legal authority to appoint Clark a captain. Then Captain Lewis learned that several vacancies at the top of the Corps of Engineers had not yet been filled, and calmly wrote to Secretary Dearborn requesting a captaincy in that corps for his friend Clark. But Henry Dearborn drew the line at appointing the frontier-bred, semi-literate Clark to the elite Engineers; instead, he agreed only to Clark's appointment as a 2d lieutenant in the Regiment of Artillerists. "The peculiar situation, circumstances and organization of the Corps of Engineers," Dearborn wrote Lewis," is such as would render the appointment of Mr. Clark a captain in that corps improper and consequently no appointment above that of a Lieutenant in the Corps [sic] of Artillerists could with propriety be given him, which … commission is herewith enclosed." To soften the blow, Dearborn added that "his Military Grade will have no effect on his compensation for the service in which he is engaged."(57) Thus the soon-to-be-famous name of William Clark never graced the rolls of the Corps of Engineers—and during the long expedition 2d Lieutenant William Clark was carried by the Regiment of Artillerists as assigned to Captain Josiah Dunham's company at Michilimackinac.

During the summer of 1804 Major Decius Wadsworth, after assisting General Wilkinson and Secretary Dearborn in planning the defense requirements of Louisiana, reported back to West Point for duty. As senior officer of the Corps of Engineers, he assumed command of the post and the superintendence of the Military Academy. It was to Wadsworth as superintendent that Secretary Dearborn wrote in mid-July to report that four new cadets of artillerists were being assigned to the academy. They were Auguste Chouteau, Charles Gratiot, Louis Loramier, and Pascal Vincent Bouis, and they were the first new citizens of the United States residing in the Territory of Louisiana—their fathers were traders in and around St. Louis—to be appointed to the Military Academy. All would graduate in 1806, but none was to serve long except Charles Gratiot, who would rise to Chief Engineer in 1828.(58)

Before the end of the year Major Wadsworth was dissatisfied with his position. Dissatisfaction, of course, was nothing new to Decius Wadsworth; he had been dissatisfied at West Point under Stephen Rochefontaine in 1796, and eight years later, when he was in Rochefontaine's position, he became equally dissatisfied. Determined to put the school in good running order, he found—or thought he found—the same foot-dragging and opposition to instruction that he himself had helped to encourage eight years before. A spirit of mild insubordination grew up among both officers and cadets, and Major Wadsworth was forced to convene a series of courts-martial. In December, when particularly heavy snow buried the post, he wrote Secretary Dearborn urging that the academy be moved elsewhere. As it happened, Dearborn had been considering moving the institution closer to Washington, and early in 1805 he wrote Wadsworth that Congress might provide the necessary authority at its next session.(59)

Shortly afterward, however, the Secretary decided that Major Wadsworth was not the man for the job at West Point, and decided to transfer him back to New Orleans. The record does not reflect his reasoning; Dearborn may well have felt that the defenses of New Orleans required the services of the senior officer of Engineers. But Dearborn had already learned of a strong movement within the Corps of Engineers to bring Jonathan Williams back into the service, a movement he approved, and he probably felt that the touchy Williams and the abrasive Wadsworth could not work together at the same post. For whatever reason, the Secretary notified Wadsworth in late January that he would be ordered back to New Orleans. Wadsworth was consistent; unhappy at West Point, he decided he would be just as unhappy at New Orleans, and at the end of the month he submitted his resignation, effective 15 February.(60) It was then time for Henry Dearborn and Jonathan Williams to get together. It is not clear who made the first move, but on 19 April Williams was in Washington, and may have handed the Secretary a private letter in which he solicited reappointment. Dearborn at once conferred with President Jefferson, who had almost surely been sounded out in advance, and three days later addressed to Williams an official letter notifying him that he was reappointed a lieutenant colonel in the Corps of Engineers. It was a recess appointment, but no difficulty was anticipated in the Senate, and Williams was directed "to repair to West Point, to take command of said Corps, and the direction of the

Military Academy."(61)

Lieutenant Colonel Williams returned to his old duties almost at once. The point of command over which he had ostensibly resigned two years earlier remained unchanged, but as there were no officers at West Point except those of Engineers, the problem lay dormant. The morale of the officers picked up at once with Williams's return, and was further stimulated by the news in mid-June that the President had approved several promotions. William A. Barron and the absent Jared Mansfield were promoted to major; James Wilson and Alexander Macomb were advanced to captain; and Joseph G. Swift and Walker K. Armistead became 1st lieutenants. Rather pointedly passed over was 2d Lieutenant Simon M. Levy, who had ranked between Swift and Armistead; Levy was still on extended sick leave in the South, and had twice applied for transfer to the Artillerists.(62) Dearborn's patience ran short, and he peremptorily ordered Levy back to duty at West Point. But Levy decided not to comply, and in mid-July submitted his resignation. His health failed to improve in civil life, and he died in March of 1807.(63)

With Colonel Williams when he returned to West Point came two of his sons, for on 14 May Secretary Dearborn had nominated to the President the names of Alexander John Williams and Henry Jonathan Williams to be cadets of Artillerists.(64) (Henry later withdrew; Alexander, after nearly six years in school, graduated in 1811 and was killed at Fort Erie in 1814.) The following month the Secretary solicited Williams for graduating cadets for appointment to the Artillerists, where there were several vacancies for 2d lieutenants. At the same time he stressed again that "whenever a new site for the Academy is established," he thought it would be in Washington.(65) This preoccupation with moving the Academy was to inhibit its development until after the War of 1812.

Replying to Dearborn's request for nominations for appointment to the Artillerists, Colonel Williams forwarded a formal certificate recommending Cadets William Gates and Julius F. Heileman; both were sons of officers— Captain Lemuel Gates of the Artillerists and Surgeon's Mate John F. Heileman of the medical staff—and both only 17 years old. The certificate, signed by Major Barron, attested to their proficiency in "Arithmetic, the Elements of Algebra, in the theoretical & practical Geometry, Trigonometry, and the elements of Fortification … ." Colonel Williams, however, was not satisfied that either cadet was yet fully qualified as an artillerist. "It must be remarked," he wrote Dearborn, "that the Theory and Practice of Gunnery make the most essential part of the Education of an artillerist, and of these, nothing is said in the Certificate. The Truth is that the academy has not possessed the means hitherto of making experiments in this Branch … .(66) He suggested that even if the cadets were commissioned, they be allowed to remain at the Academy until they could complete gunnery courses. Dearborn agreed with this reasoning, and both cadets remained at West Point until March of 1806, when they were commissioned.

Agreeable as the Williams-Dearborn relationship seemed to be in the summer of 1805, the Secretary continued to interfere directly in the operation of the Corps of Engineers. Passing through Portsmouth on his way to his home in Maine, Dearborn decided that Fort Constitution needed repair, and discussed the necessary work in detail with Captain Lemuel Gates. Then, instead of asking Colonel Williams to select an Engineer officer to superintend the repairs, the Secretary directed that the work would be carried out by Captain Alexander Macomb, who was to proceed to Portsmouth as soon as possible. Then, thinking it was too late in the season, Dearborn changed his mind, but Macomb had already left for Portsmouth and in the end Dearborn let him continue.(67) If nothing else emerged from this confusion, it was the fact that Alexander Macomb was an efficient and energetic young officer.

Not all the Engineers were quite as willing and energetic as Macomb as the case of Captain James Wilson testified. In January 1805 the Secretary had granted Wilson a furlough to take care of private business in the West Indies; Wilson did not return until November and at once requested a second furlough. Dearborn's reply was a model of tact. "I feel every disposition to accommodate you" he wrote Wilson, "but having contemplated an employment for you as an Engineer in the course of the next season, it would be with reluctance that I would consent to be deprived of your services. If you can make it convenient to postpone your second voyage to the West Indies until next Autumn, I will consent to your having further indulgence." But requiring Wilson to return to duty after ten months' absence, even with the promise of another furlough the following year, was not acceptable to that young officer and shortly after the beginning of 1806 he submitted his resignation.(68)

Before the end of 1805 Colonel Williams undertook to revitalize one of his favorite projects, the United States Military Philosophical Society at West Point. The officers and many of the cadets convened again with as much enthusiasm as they had shown at the end of 1802, and the stage was set for the Society to undertake a real and valuable interest in the matter of improving and developing the architectural design of American seacoast fortifications along new and different paths.

CHAPTER VIII
OLD DEFENSES AND NEW THEORIES
1806

The First System of federal seacoast defenses, with its two separate impulses of 1794 and 1798, may be said to have lasted through 1800, or perhaps through the accession of the Democratic-Republican administration in the spring of 1801. No new construction of any consequence was undertaken after 1800—excluding possibly that being supported by individual states, as in New York City and Boston—and by mid-1802, when the last of the "foreign" officers was discharged from the service of the United States, an era had closed. Whatever might be accomplished in the future in the way of construction of seacoast fortifications, it was assumed that it would be done by American-born engineers and artillerists; it was to this end, indeed, that Congress had created the Corps of Engineers.

For over three years that tiny corps had been hard put to maintain its own existence in the face of resignations, extended furloughs, and detached service. Although the law did not so specify, it seems to have been accepted after 1802 that the only source of new Engineer officers would be graduates of the Military Academy; at the end of four years of life, however, that little institution had produced only six lieutenants for the Corps of Engineers, and by the spring of 1806 two of these had resigned.(1) It was fortunate for all concerned that these first few years of the Corps of Engineers coincided with a brief period of relative peace in Europe, and that the French threat to Louisiana evaporated with the remarkably fortunate American purchase of that vast region. In the absence of a direct threat to the Atlantic and Gulf seaboards, it passed unnoticed by most that the United States had hardly achieved its proud goal of a corps of trained, native-born fortifications engineers.

The lethargy that had settled over this whole subject of seacoast fort fortifications began to lift at the beginning of 1806. Warfare in Europe had been resumed in 1805, the year of Ulm and Austerlitz, and operations on land were paralleled by increased activity at sea. Again the rights of neutral nations were ignored or threatened, and on no point was the United States more acutely sensitive. In his Annual Message of December 1805, President Jefferson devoted considerable space to the problem, and proposed certain solutions:

> "Since our last meeting the aspect of our foreign relations has considerably changed. Our coasts have been infested and our harbors watched by private armed vessels, some with illegal commissions, others with those of legal form, but committing piratical acts beyond the authority of their commissions. They have captured in the very entrance of our harbors, as well as on the high seas, not only the vessels of our friends coming to trade with us, but our own also.... These enormities appearing to be unreached by any control of their sovereigns, I found it necessary to equip a force to cruise within our own seas, to arrest all vessels of these descriptions found hovering on our coasts within the limits of the Gulf Stream and to bring the offenders in for trial as pirates.
>
> The same system of hovering on our coasts and harbors under color of seeking enemies has been also carried on by public armed ships...."(2)

Jefferson's statement about an American naval force to cruise home waters was premature, however. Beyond the force in being when he took office in 1801, which had generally done good service in the inconclusive war with Tripoli, the President proposed building six ships of the line. But resolutions to that effect died in Congress in early 1806; many Congressmen simply felt that building new warships would irritate Britain and invite retaliation by the Royal Navy.(3)

The President's message then turned to the problem of seacoast defense, and here he continued his reliance on gunboats:

> The first object is to place our seaport towns out of the danger of insult. Measures have already been taken for furnishing them with heavy cannon for the service of such land batteries as may make a part of their defense against armed vessels approaching them. In aid of these it is desirable we should have a competent number of gunboats, and the number, to be competent, must be considerable. If immediately begun, they may be in readiness for service at the opening of the next session. Whether it will be necessary to augment our land forces will be decided by occurrences probably in the course of your session.(4)

The possible necessity of increasing the size of the military establishment, cut to the bone four years earlier, added a degree of urgency to the Presidential analysis. The House at once called upon the Secretary of War for a detailed report on the status of the existing seacoast defenses, and on 13 February 1806 Secretary Dearborn forwarded the necessary information. His report was a thorough summary of the two phases of the First System, to which he added the status of the newly-acquired defenses at and below New Orleans.(5)

North of Boston, Dearborn admitted, much remained to be done. The works at Portland, Portsmouth, Cape Ann, and Salem had been relatively untouched since 1802, and many repairs were needed. In Boston Fort Independence was in good repair, the federal government having underwritten extensive work between 1800 and 1803; in fact, Dearborn noted, since 1794 the considerable sum of $186,195 had been expended on the works on Castle Island. At Newport both Fort Adams and Fort Wolcott, after a total expenditure of over $107,000, remained uncompleted, and would require substantial further sums to complete; even if they were finished, Dearborn admitted, the two forts would protect only one of the three "open and convenient passages by which Rhode Island may be approached." At New London old Fort Trumbull, dating from the Revolution, had been repaired and improved, and few further repairs would be needed.

New York Harbor continued to pose many problems, not only financial but also of dual jurisdiction. Through 1801 fortifications had been constructed and repaired on Governors, Bedlow's, and Ellis's Islands in the inner harbor, and off the Battery at the tip of Manhattan, at a cost of just over $100,000. Secretary Dearborn went into detail on the construction problems and the division of responsibility between federal and state governments:

> Engineers were employed by the Governor of the State to survey and examine the harbor, and to report the best practicable mode of defence. The report [was completed] in the year 1801. By this project, the principal works were to be at Sandy Hook.(6) The estimates, amounting to 3,968,658 dollars, were considered as a sufficient reason for rejecting the report; the debt of the State of New York (which was the limit of the sum authorized to be expended) being only $1,852,035. In January, 1805, a report was also received ... from the mayor of the city, in which the Narrows were contemplated as the principal place of defence. The estimates for completing the works amounted to 2,000,000 of dollars, and the plan of defence proposed inspired no confidence..

> Lieutenant Colonel Williams, of the corps of engineers, was, last autumn, directed to make such a survey of the harbor of New York.... [Here Dearborn went into a long discussion of harbor defense problems in general, with specific references to New York; his conclusions follow.]

> That the harbor of New York is not susceptible of such defence as ought to be relied on by perma-

nent or fixed batteries ... and, consequently, that some other system ought to be adopted. This, it is presumed, should consist of at least one regular enclosed work, capable of being defended against a sudden assault, together with such fixed batteries as may most effectually annoy ships of war on their approach to the city, and while in a situation to batter it; and also of a suitable weight of moving batteries ... mounted on travelling carriages, and placed in the city, together with a sufficient number of well constructed gun boats.... .

If the system proposed was not considered adequate, Dearborn concluded, then in his view the only solution would be "heavy ships of war, in sufficient number to meet any force which an enemy may direct against that place." Below Philadelphia, almost $65,000 had been spent on Fort Mifflin in the Delaware since 1794, most of it during the period 1798-1800, before the capital moved to Washington; although some repairs were still needed, the fortification was generally sound. Farther down the Delaware a site had been surveyed near Wilmington, but no defensive works had been erected. Within the Chesapeake Bay the situation was mixed. Fort McHenry at Baltimore, on which $95,000 had been expended since 1794, was in excellent condition and needed few if any repairs. On the other hand, defenses planned in 1795 for Annapolis and Alexandria—which now lay on two possible approaches to the new capital—had never been carried out; Alexandria, on the Potomac just below Washington, was now particularly important. Near the mouth of the Chesapeake—but not sited to defend it—the twin forts, Nelson and Norfolk, on the Elizabeth River both needed extensive improvements and repairs.

The long exposed stretch of North Carolina coast posed an almost insoluble problem. In both 1794 and 1799 works had been proposed on Beacon Island of Ocracoke Inlet, but it was decided that no work could be erected and supported at that isolated location; Dearborn now "presumed that two gun boats would more securely protect that harbor than any fixed batteries that might be erected." Up the Cape Fear River below Wilmington, some progress had been made on Fort Johnston in 1799-1800, but lack of title to all the land and difficulties with a local politician-contractor had caused suspension of work for a time. Secretary Dearborn hoped that the fortification would be completed during 1806, but thought that the aid of several gunboats would be needed to protect the river and the town of Wilmington.

The harbor of Charleston, South Carolina, was considered most important, and three fortifications—Fort Johnson, Fort Moultrie, and Castle Pinckney— had been erected on the sites of Revolutionary works. South Carolina, however, had not ceded the sites of these forts until 1805, and no recent repairs had been carried out by either state or federal government. All three works, Dearborn noted, were now nearly in ruins, having been badly damaged by a severe coastal storm in 1804.

There were no federal garrisons on the Georgia coast at the beginning of 1806. Fort Greene at Savannah had been totally destroyed, and part of its temporary infantry garrison drowned, in a sudden hurricane in 1804. As the state had ceded no other suitable site near Savannah, and as the federal government had been unable to purchase private land on reasonable terms, there were no immediate plans for defending Savannah. Farther south at St. Mary's, the small garrison had been withdrawn from the work at Point Petre, east of the town, because of Georgia's reluctance to cede the land. The Secretary thought that gunboats, backed by cannon on travelling carriages, would be the best immediate protection for the Georgia coastline.

New to Congress was the matter of the defensive works near the mouth of the Mississippi acquired by the Louisiana Purchase, in the region now known as the Territory of Orleans. Of the former French forts later garrisoned by Spanish troops, Forts St. Louis, St. Charles, and St. Philip were the most important, all in generally poor condition. Secretary Dearborn described the status of these defenses. "The town of New Orleans," he reported, "is surrounded, except the front, by a mud wall, with three redoubts in the rear, and two in front; the two latter called forts [St. Louis and St. Charles] ... . About fifty miles below the town there is an ancient fortification called St. Philip ... which require[s] considerable repairs and improvements. At the junction of Bayou St. John with lake Ponchartrain, a small ancient work remains, intended to guard the communication with New Orleans against the approach of an enemy, by way of the lake... . Gun boats will be necessary for the defence of the river and the lake, in addition to fixed batteries."

Priorities for Seacoast Defense for 1806

The new responsibility for protection of the Gulf approaches to the Territory of Orleans meant, in all probability, a revision of the priorities hitherto established for seacoast defense sites. In fact, for obvious political reasons, Congress had never listed all the coastal sites in strict order of importance for defenses, but rather had allowed the Secretary of War quietly to assign emphasis to one area or another at various times. In 1806, however, there seemed less reluctance to pinpoint the ports requiring priority of attention. The matter was discussed between Congress and the administration until spring, and not until late May did Secretary Dearborn notify the Chief Engineer of the decision—although Colonel Williams could probably have anticipated the result. The decision had been made by the President, Dearborn wrote, "that every possible exertion should be made for improving the fortifications for the protection of our Sea ports generally, and especially those of New York, Charleston S.C. and New Orleans, and that there should be no unnecessary delay in the actual commencement of such improvements as are deemed expedient ... ."(7) Just what was meant by "every possible exertion," after almost six years of comparative neglect, was not spelled out.

In New York Harbor, Colonel Williams himself was to take personal charge, not only because of the size and complexity of the harbor—perhaps the second most difficult after Narragansett Bay—but also because of the stature needed to deal with Ned York authorities, when necessary, on matters involving the split responsibilities between the inner harbor and the Narrows. Despite Secretary Dearborn's call for every possible exertion, economy remained an ever-present consideration. Thus when Mayor Dewitt Clinton offered to provide his own superintendent for construction of the works on the harbor islands, Dearborn quickly declined. Captain Richard Whiley, the commander of Fort Jay, could also act as assistant military agent, and as Colonel Williams would be "Engineer & General Superintendent"—in addition to his duties as head of the Corps of Engineers and Superintendent of the Military Academy—Dearborn saw no need for Clinton's nominee. As he wrote Captain Whiley, there "was no point in employing a civilian engineer at a rate considerably higher, than we have usually paid to the best Engineers, who have been in our service ... .(8)

Construction in the harbor of Charleston was placed under the supervision of Captain Alexander Macomb of the Engineers. Macomb was already in South Carolina, superintending the building of a small federal arsenal at Rocky Mount, and had to divide his time and efforts between there and Charleston. He had the advice and assistance in Charleston of the veteran Captain Michael Kalteisen, who had commanded Fort Johnson since 1794. Kalteisen who was about 75 years old, was now the senior captain of the Regiment of Artillerists, and on the resignation of Major George Ingersoll at the end of 1804, he had been offered promotion. But Kalteisen had observed that every major of the regiment had been ordered to the frontier, and having no wish to leave Charleston, wrote the Secretary of War indicating his wish to waive promotion and remain at Fort Johnson. The Secretary was agreeable, replying that "you will be continued in your present rank and command," and the promotion went to the next-senior captain, Abimael Y. Nicoll, who was en route to New Orleans with his company.(9) As a further assistant to Captain Macomb in Charleston, he was given the services in September of Cadet Charles Gratiot, who had been at the Military Academy for two years and was officially graduated on 30 October. But as it turned out, neither Macomb nor Kalteisen nor Gratiot could accomplish much before winter, for the ironic reason that they could find no state official able to furnish a map showing the exact boundaries of the sites ceded by South Carolina to the federal government.(10)

At New Orleans, also, little was accomplished during 1806. Because of the amount of work to be done, as well as the increasingly large concentration of troops in the New Orleans region, Secretary Dearborn transferred Abraham D. Abrahams, the Military Agent for the so-called Southern Department, from Savannah to New Orleans, authorizing him to take passage from Charleston on one of the new gunboats being sent to New Orleans.(11) But there was no officer of Engineers in New Orleans, Decius Wadsworth having resigned in early 1805 rather than return there and the Secretary having inexplicably failed to replace him. So for the rest of 1806 Dearborn contented himself with soliciting opinions from Governor Claiborne as to the defenses needed; Claiborne in turn relied on advice from General Wilkinson and probably the two resident field officers of Artillerists, Lieutenant Colonel Constant Freeman and Major Abimael Y. Nicoll. Dearborn subsequently reported to Congress that he had received many opinions on the subject, and that "the present prevailing opinion appears to be, that no system of fortifications, within our power, at or about the city, could be of any essential use for its defence … ." Beyond repairing some old works and establishing batteries at English Turn on the Mississippi below the city and at the junction of Bayou St. John with lake Ponchartrain, Dearborn thought that a "suitable number" of gunboats should provide the primary form of defense for the moment.(12)

At the end of the year, in his Annual Message of December 1806, President Jefferson reviewed the status of the seacoast defenses. Despite the seeming lack of urgency in providing defenses for New Orleans, the President continued to stress that region:

> "The possession of both banks of the Mississippi reducing to a single point the defense of that river, its waters, and the country adjacent, it becomes highly necessary to provide for that point a more adequate security. Some position above its mouth, commanding the passage of the river, should be rendered sufficiently strong to cover the armed vessels which may be stationed there for defense … .

> The gunboats … are so advanced that they will be ready for service in the ensuing spring … . As a much larger number will still be wanting to place our seaport towns and waters in that state of defense to which we are competent and they entitled, a similar appropriation for a further provision for them is recommended for the ensuing year.

> A further appropriation will also be necessary for repairing fortifications already established, and the erection of such other works as may have real effect in obstructing the approach of an enemy to our seaport towns … ."(13)

It was clear that the President continued to place strong reliance on the use of gunboats for defense of the seacoast, and here he was reflecting current naval thinking. The American gunboats, first authorized by Congress in 1803, were an outgrowth of operations in Europe, both in France and Denmark, and off Tripoli, that were not fully understood in the United States. As Howard I. Chapelle sums up, "by chance, events placed emphasis on this type, and this seemingly produced the Jeffersonian theory of employing gun vessels in place of normal naval craft."(14) By no means all naval officers were in favor of gunboats, but then few naval officers gave a high priority to seacoast defense, preferring to turn their thoughts to operations on the high seas. There is little evidence that officers of the Army were asked to comment on the use of gunboats, although old General Horatio Gates, just before his death in 1806, was reported to favor their use, and in 1807 the President queried General Wilkinson on the subject: The officers of the Corps of Engineers, as a matter of professional interest, discussed various types of gunboats from time to time, but by the fall of 1806 they were more interested in certain novel aspects of military architecture introduced by the Chief Engineer, Lieutenant Colonel Jonathan Williams.

New Theories of Seacoast Fortification

Almost immediately after he returned to the Army in 1805, Colonel Williams determined to revive his favorite project, the United States Military Philosophical Society. He applied to President Jefferson for a modest sum from appropriated funds for the day-to-day expenses of the Society, but was reminded that War Department funds could be used only as specifically appropriated.(15) Determined then to make the Society financially self-sustaining, Williams began a Society treasury by contributing six shares of stock in the Eagle Fire Insurance Company, and in May of 1806 the members stationed at West Point voted to assess themselves five dollars a year each—an assessment that proved unnecessarily large and was subsequently reduced. The membership then decided to hold meetings twice monthly "wherever the Military Academy may be established," but the few surviving records indicate that this ambitious goal was not met.

One of the meetings for which summary minutes are available was held at West Point on 6 October 1806. Although a list of those present was not included, it is probable that this meeting was attended primarily by the officers and cadets, with a few visitors from New York City. Colonel Williams presided—he was president of the Society throughout its active life—and many of the papers presented and discussed were originated or sponsored by Williams himself. Although the discussions ranged over the field of the military art, many items were directly or indirectly related to the principal function of the Corps of Engineers at the time, the design and construction of seacoast fortifications. Various members presented for the Society's archives maps and plans of harbors and their defenses and detailed descriptions of fortifications along the coasts of the United States—happily, many of these now repose in the National Archives. It was probably a visitor from New York, perhaps a civilian engineer employed by the state, who presented a plan for defending the city by proving, at least to his own satisfaction, that the only practicable site for the main batteries was at the tip of Sandy Hook, New Jersey.(16) Colonel Williams, however, was committed to a defense of New York City within the inner harbor—the "upper bay"—and the Sandy Hook plan, rejected earlier because of its expense, was not reintroduced. The members also discussed at some length a paper on the design of a heavy gunboat, almost a floating battery, undoubtedly stimulated by President Jefferson's well-known penchant for gunboats for seacoast defense.(17)

The most significant result of this 1806 meeting was a stimulation of interest in the theories and designs of the Marquis de Montalembert, the French military engineer who had died in 1800. Two specific items originating with Montalembert were introduced at the meeting; one was a description of a breech-loading gun, the other a treatise on marine batteries in general. These specifics broadened to generalities under Colonel Williams's direction, and the members of the Society were introduced to Montalembert's theories of fortification, particularly as they applied to seacoast defenses. From discussions such as this was to evolve a new and distinctive style of American military architecture and result in the eventual abandonment by American military engineers of the time-hallowed Vauban system.

The seacoast fortifications constructed during the First System, as described in earlier chapters, derived almost entirely from Vauban's designs, taken either from his own published works or those in English by John Muller.(18) They remained in vogue in the United States through 1802, primarily because no other system arose to challenge Vauban's horizontal-fortress designs. The French military engineers who had supervised most of the First System construction—Rochefontaine, Tousard, Vincent, L'Enfant, and the others—had studied military architecture prior to 1776, when Vauban was still the great example and French military doctrine admitted of no other system. But prior to the end of the 18th century a quite new system, based on very different engineering principles, made its appearance in France, although it was never to find official governmental acceptance in that country.

This new system, which was to exercise great influence on American seacoast-defense architecture, was devised by Marc Rene, Marquis de Montalembert, who was born in 1714, seven years after the death of the great Vauban. Entering the French army at eighteen, Montalembert became an engineer and served through several of the sieges of the Seven Years' War, impressed by Vauban's theories of the attack of fortified places, but less so by the latter's defensive theories. Montalembert began to challenge some of Vauban's ideas, which was heresy in the French army, and in 1761 he was appointed governor of the Ile d'Oleron in the Bay of Biscay, probably to get him and his new ideas away from Paris.(19) For the last 38 years of his life he worked on the publication and revision of an 11-volume work he called *La Fortification Perpendiculaire*, the first edition of which appeared in Paris between 1776-1778. Thus publication came too late to affect the ideas of the French engineers who were even then sailing for America—supposing that they would have been willing to open a work that challenged Vauban's theses.

Montalembert's volumes challenged the very heart of Vauban's defensive system, the bastioned trace. He made two basic points: first, that the curtain walls connecting the bastions were indefensible and virtually useless, requiring the bastions themselves and the outer works to protect them and keep the enemy at a distance; and second, that the great virtue of the bastions, the ability to pour enfilade fire across the front of the curtains, was outmoded in an era of longer-range and more accurate cannon—there were, Montalembert proposed, better uses for the improved guns than close-in defense. Montalembert's system abandoned the bastioned trace and reinstituted the tenaille trace, which was a succession of triangular redans joined at right angles to form a defensive front resembling the teeth of a saw.

It must be remembered that both Vauban and Montalembert concerned themselves primarily with the design of great frontier fortresses; seacoast fortifications were secondary, certainly to Vauban, although Montalembert gave considerable thought to coast defense in his capacity as governor of Oleron. And from the point of view of seacoast defense, Montalembert's tenaille trace was of much less importance to the future than two subsidiary aspects of his system. First, to be able to direct more firepower against the distant enemy, rather than against troops assaulting the curtains, he designed circular towers, usually three stories high, containing from 24 to 36 guns placed to exploit their maximum effective range rather than maximum traverse; at the same time he raised his caponiers—covered routes of communication between defensive works—to three stories, so that they became gun platforms rather than simply covered ways. But perhaps more important, Montalembert did not place his guns en barbette on the terrace atop the walls of the fort, but built galleries and casemates within the thick walls, so that each gun was protected inside a casemate, firing through a slit-like embrasure. The idea of casemates did not, of course, originate with Montalembert, but he rescued them from the disuse into which they had fallen in the age of bastions.(21)

The result of these various theories was a system, published in 1777, that Montalembert called "polygonal fortification," based on multi-gun towers and caponiers, with guns emplaced in bombproof casemates whose embrasures could be protected by solid shutters when not in use. Montalembert's new system made no great impression prior to his death in 1800, and was in fact never officially considered by the French army. But both the Prussian and Austrian armies, during the era of the Wars of Liberation, picked up many features of Montalembert's system, particularly the multi-tiered towers and caponiers.

Well before Prussian or Austrian interest, however, certain essential elements of Montalembert's system appeared in the United States.(21) There seems little doubt that Montalembert was introduced into America either by or through the direct agency of Jonathan Williams. Williams had been American commercial agent at Nantes, the heavily fortified coastal city not too far from the Ile d'Oleron, in the late 1770s. Whether he ever met Montalembert can only be conjectured, but as Franklin's kinsman and secretary Williams would have had the necessary entree; in his course of self-study of military architecture he almost certainly would have been exposed to the volumes of *La Fortification Perpendiculaire* as they were published. Perhaps Williams purchased the set before he returned home in 1785, or perhaps he arranged the purchase later, but it is almost certain that at least ten volumes of Montalembert's work, acclaimed as the only set in the United States, were in the library of the United States Military Philosophical Society prior to 1806.(22) It is clear that members of the Society discussed Montalembert's work on marine batteries at the meeting in October 1806; Joseph G. Swift, who attended that and most other meetings of the Society, wrote that Colonel Williams "had become pleased with the perpendicular system of defence of Montalembert ... ."(23) Of course, whether or not Jonathan Williams was responsible for the introduction of Montalembert's theories is hardly critical to the story of American seacoast fortifications, but available evidence would seem to award him the credit.

In no sense, however, were Montalembert's designs accepted *in toto* by American military engineers. As Vauban had been, so Montalembert too was concerned primarily with great frontier fortresses and fortified cities, and the tenaille trace and the three-story caponier were not necessarily applicable to the problems of seacoast defense in the United States. Possibly the most significant aspect of Montalembert's work was his use of the term "perpendicular," implying that his fortifications stood boldly upright and exchanged gunfire with the enemy, while Vauban's horizontal defensive works were designed so that enemy solid shot, in particular, might ricochet over the fortress proper without doing damage. Where a seacoast fortress had to stand up to an enemy line-of-battle ship and exchange virtually point-blank volleys, there seemed much to recommend a solidly-constructed tower several stories high, with guns in tiers protected by covered casemates. Another Montalembert feature adopted in the United States both before and after the War of 1812 was a modified form of his "polygonal trace," in which the landward sides of a seacoast fort retained rudimentary bastions and curtains while the seaward sides were rounded and built in tiers in order to bring maximum gunfire to bear on enemy vessels.

A different but similar form of military architecture that had some influence on American design of the Second System was the so-called Martello tower. It is not clear whether this structure derived from Montalembert's work or whether it was simply a local improvisation, but it followed Montalembert's theories in that it was usually three stories high, round, and provided a rudimentary casemate for each gun. The name came from the small round tower erected in the Bay of Martello, in Corsica, which was renowned for having beaten off, with a single gun, the attack of one or possibly two British warships in 1794, without sustaining serious damage. Anticlimactically, however, the tower had soon been forced to surrender when attacked by land artillery.(24) But the conclusion was drawn that a well-mounted and protected battery on land had a natural advantage over shipboard guns whose position was constantly changing, and Martello towers were erected at several points along the American seaboard during the War of 1812[1] usually by local citizens or militia as a last-minute addition to defense works nearby. Admittedly, however, a Martello tower with only one or two guns, or guns on only one tier, threw away the advantage inherent in the Montalembert system of many guns on multiple tiers, so that heavy gunfire could be concentrated simultaneously on a single enemy vessel.

The surviving minutes of the United States Military Philosophical Society are not complete enough to provide any details of the discussion by the members of Montalembert's major work, or his separate treatise on marine batteries. It does not appear that there was an immediate and total transfer of allegiance from Vauban to Montalembert by all members, nor that Colonel Williams, as Chief Engineer, attempted to impose the new system upon his officers as official doctrine. Indeed, subsequent evidence shows that the older officers of Artillerists, even those who became members of the Society and attended the meetings, tended either to ignore or to resist the new developments. As will be seen in subsequent chapters, the Second System of American seacoast fortification, undertaken beginning in 1807, would contain examples of both styles, but with more Vauban designs than those of Montalembert. Nevertheless, from the Society meeting of October 1806, Montalembert's designs became an increasingly important factor in the construction plans of the Corps of Engineers.

Artillerists in Louisiana

Beginning in 1804, the seacoast-defense mission of the Regiment of Artillerists had been forced to take a poor second place to the requirements of occupying Louisiana and keeping watch on the Spanish troops still in that region. Although a narrow but very important maritime frontier had been added to the United States in the delta below New Orleans, by no means all of the artillerists in Louisiana were concerned with the defenses of that frontier; most of the field officers, in fact, became involved either in civil administration or in the operations of the small field army that was building up under General Wilkinson on the lower Mississippi. A few pages, however, must be devoted to these artillerists during the years 1805-1806.

The senior officer of the regiment in the Territory of Orleans was Lieutenant Colonel Constant Freeman, who had arrived there in April of 1804 to assume command of all troops in the region. Freeman had been superseded briefly in late 1804 by the unexpected arrival of Colonel Thomas Butler of the 2d Infantry, who had declined to resign from the Army in the face of General Wilkinson's hostility. Butler's earlier court-martial had not made him any more amenable to Wilkinson's orders; he immediately reopened his feud with the General, who shortly arrested him and charged him with disobedience of orders and mutinous conduct.(25) Neither Colonel Burbeck nor Colonel Hunt of the 1st Infantry being available, Lieutenant Colonel Freeman was designated to preside at Butler's second court-martial. Again the court found Butler guilty of only a few of the charges, but this time sentenced him to a year's suspension from command. Before the record of trial reached General Wilkinson, who was then in St. Louis, Colonel Butler died in New Orleans in September 1805, and Freeman resumed command of the region.

In the spring of 1805 Major Moses Porter, who had commanded Fort Niagara for several years— and who had never been assigned to the seacoast defenses— was transferred with most of his command to Orleans Territory, leaving at Fort Niagara only a small garrison under Lieutenant George Armistead. Major Porter's eventual destination was the Spanish frontier, and by October he had assumed command of the garrison at Natchitoches, well up the Red River to the northwest of New Orleans.(26) During the same period Major James Bruff had arrived at St. Louis to supersede Captain Amos Stoddard as military commandant of Upper Louisiana, a title he retained even after General Wilkinson was appointed governor of the so-called Louisiana District, all the settled portion of the great purchase north of Orleans Territory. Wilkinson began to build up a troop concentration on the upper Mississippi, concentrated at the "Cantonment on the Missouri," subsequently named Camp Belle Fontaine, and brought from Washington the Adjutant and Inspector, Lieutenant Colonel Thomas H. Cushing, to command the troops at Camp Belle Fontaine while still performing his administrative functions. (27) The justification for the dual assignment was that Cushing was the senior lieutenant colonel of infantry and would sooner or later succeed Thomas Butler in command of the 1st Infantry; Butler, in fact, was already dead, but the news had not reached St. Louis.

Meanwhile Major Bruff ran afoul of General Wilkinson in the matter of civil *vs.* military authority in the Louisiana District. Bruff was one of the few antifederalists among the field officers of the Army, and has been called a "fault finder" with an "unfortunate temper";(28) for reasons of his own he decided to side with one of the President's local appointees against General Wilkinson, the civil governor in addition to his military command. At first Wilkinson ordered Bruff down the Mississippi to Fort Adams, but then changed his mind and ordered him court-martialed.(29) Tried on charges that boiled down to "seditious and mutinous conduct," Bruff was convicted and sentenced to be suspended from command and to forfeit all pay and emoluments for twelve months.(30) He returned to Washington and later testified against Wilkinson in the matter of Aaron Burr; failing to see Wilkinson removed from the head of the Army, Bruff finally resigned in mid-1807.

Meanwhile, about the beginning of March 1806, Major Porter at Natchitoches reported that Spanish forces across the Sabine River were showing signs of offensive activity. Based on this and similar reports, Secretary Dearborn directed General Wilkinson to form a little field army and move to the possibly threatened area. Wilkinson gave command of an advanced detachment to Colonel Cushing, who had just been promoted to command the 2d Infantry, vice Butler deceased, while still retaining his title of Adjutant and Inspector; Cushing would command the entire area of the Territories of Mississippi and New Orleans, with Lieutenant Colonel Freeman in immediate charge of "that Section of the District which embraces New Orleans, Placquemines, Mobile, and their out Posts."(31) The troop movements consumed several months, and General Wilkinson himself did not reach the Natchitoches area until late September. As Major Porter reported continued Spanish activity, Wilkinson considered a clash imminent, and the little army went on a crash training program. One of the General's first moves was to organize two companies of artillerists into a provisional battalion of field artillery under Major Porter, and to provide for their mobility he directed that six horses or mules would be assigned to each company. "Those animals," he directed, "are to be … attached to the Pieces and driven a mile or two daily, under the immediate attention of a commissioned officer who is to practice the Matrosses [gunners] in unlimbering & maneuvering their pieces in all practicable Ground."(32) (It was thus General Wilkinson in 1806, and not Secretary Dearborn in 1808, who made the first move toward establishing horse-drawn field artillery in the Army.)

Space does not permit further discussion of the serio-comic confrontation across the Sabine, other than to note that an agreement as to the international boundary was reached early in November, and both the Spanish and the American forces withdrew from the disputed area. Similarly left untold here must be the events of the so-called Burr Conspiracy and the activities in West Florida, both of which directly or indirectly involved elements of the Army. A summary of the Spanish-American frontier situation was contained in a letter from Secretary Dearborn to General Wilkinson in late November:

> You will please to direct the Stations of the armed vessels in the Mississippi and Lake Ponchartrain, in
> such manner as you may judge most advantageous under existing circumstances, and if your arrange-
> ments with the Spaniards will permit you to withdraw from the Frontier with some part of the Troops,

you will please to take Post at such places and dispose of the Troops in such manner as will most effectually intercept and prevent any unlawful enterprise [i.e., Burr's activities] either in New Orleans or else where ... which has for its object, directly or indirectly any hostile act on any part of the Territories of the United States or on any of the Territories of the King of Spain.(33)

Back in New Orleans, General Wilkinson gave directions for the rehabilitation of the two major fortifications of the city, Forts St. Charles and St. Louis. As there had been no officer of Engineers in the area since the departure of Decius Wadsworth in mid-1804, Wilkinson gave the responsibility to the field officers of the Regiment of Artillerists. Lieutenant Colonel Freeman was appointed general superintendent, with Major Porter to supervise the work at Fort St. Charles and Major Abimael Y. Nicoll that at Fort St. Louis. A local civilian engineer, one M. Monsuy was engaged for technical advice, "to trace the lines of the works to be erected"; there can be little doubt that the trace delineated by M. Monsuy would have had at least four bastions, after the style of the still-revered Marechal de Vauban.(34)

At the end of 1806, having noted the flurry of activity on the southwestern frontier, a committee of the House recommended that "provision ought to be made by law to fortify and defend such positions on the Mississippi, below the city of New Orleans" as the President thought appropriate.(35) The House agreed, and asked the Secretary of War to report on the relative strengths of Spanish and American forces across the frontier. Dearborn replied that estimates of Spanish strength were imprecise and had probably been exaggerated; as for American troops; 22 companies of infantry and artillerists, or just over half of the United States Army, were under General Wilkinson's immediate command in the Orleans and Mississippi Territories. The bulk of the Army and the attention of the nation having been transferred to Louisiana and the Mississippi, the pendulum of international events now began its long, slow swing to the other extreme. The beginning of 1807 was to see again a threat to the Atlantic seaboard, and this time the threat would not be dissipated by diplomacy or good fortune. The crisis that now faced the nation eventually brought full-scale war.

CHAPTER IX
ORIGINS OF THE SECOND SYSTEM
1807-1808

After a short and uneasy truce, the war between Napoleon and most of the rest of Europe broke out again in 1805, the year that saw not only the great French victories at Ulm and Austerlitz, but also the resounding victory of the Royal Navy at Trafalgar. The following year the French emperor defeated the Prussian forces at Jena and Auerstadt, and pursued them to near-annihilation. From his temporary headquarters in Berlin, Napoleon issued a decree in November 1806 establishing a blockade by which the entire Continent would be interdicted to British trade. Britain, in quick retaliation, issued Orders in Council on 7 January 1807, designed to counter the Berlin Decrees and to strike at the economic basis of the French empire. Aimed at neutral commerce, these Orders in Council affected primarily the chief neutral carrier, the United States. Basically the British edicts placed French commerce under blockade, and forbade neutral nations to trade with or between ports under French jurisdiction.

In carrying out this blockade, vessels of the victorious Royal Navy ranged far from the shores of continental Europe, and were soon hovering off the American coast with all their old-time arrogance. The wide entrance to Chesapeake Bay had already attracted British attention the previous summer, when two French vessels fleeing a superior British force took refuge in the Chesapeake and a third entered the Delaware. A British squadron shortly took station at the mouth of Chesapeake Bay, riding at anchor in Lynnhaven Inlet and sailing into the bay at will. Tenders stopped and searched merchant vessels leaving the bay, and on occasion impressed members of the crews. The citizens of Norfolk found particularly galling this flouting of American sovereignty.(1)

Both Congress and the President turned reluctantly from the immediate threat of the Burr expedition to consider the problems of coastal defense for 1807. The House asked the Executive for proposals on the subject, and for information as to the status of the coast-defense gunboats. On 10 February Jefferson sent a detailed reply to both chambers, outlining a sound general plan of defense which would "combine, first, land batteries furnished with heavy cannon and mortars ... ; second, movable artillery, which may be carried, as occasion may require, to points unprovided with fixed batteries; third, floating batteries, and fourth, gunboats which may oppose an enemy at his entrance and cooperate with the batteries for his expulsion." The President indicated that he had consulted military men on the subject, mentioning General Wilkinson, the recently-deceased Horatio Gates, and Commodore Barron and Captain Tingey of the navy; he also interjected a brief history of gunboats in Europe, claiming that the gunboat "is believed to be in use with every modern maritime nation for the purposes of defense." To protect the seacoast from "Orleans to Maine, inclusive," the President concluded that about 200 gunboats would be needed, assigned as follows:

> To the Mississippi and its neighboring waters, 40 gunboats.
>
> To Savannah and Charleston, and the harbors on each side from St. Mary's to Currituck [N.C.], 25.
>
> To the Chesapeake and its waters, 20.
>
> To the Delaware Bay and River, 15.
>
> To New York, [Long Island] Sound, and waters as far as Cape Cod, 50.
>
> To Boston and the harbors north of Cape Cod, 50.

Two sizes of gunboats were proposed: a size smaller than previously built, for close-in defense of specific harbors, and the larger size already constructed, capable of navigating the high seas and of reinforcing those ports attacked or threatened.(2) Of the 200 gunboats proposed, 73 were on hand or under construction; the additional 127 should be built half in 1807 and half in 1803, in order not to swamp shipbuilding facilities as well as to spread the expense.(3)

Despite the anger and anxiety of the citizens of Norfolk, the President was not unduly concerned in early 1807 about British depredations. A week after his gunboat message Jefferson notified Congress that American envoys in London were confident of concluding a treaty that would remove all sources of friction, while at the same time the American minister in Paris had assured him that the Berlin Decrees would not affect American commerce. Of more immediate import to the nation, the President felt, was his announcement that Aaron Burr had just surrendered to the civil authorities of the Mississippi Territory.(4)

The state of New York was concerned less with the fate of its citizen Burr than of the defenses of New York Harbor. On 20 March the legislature passed a formal resolution to Congress, requesting that adequate attention and funds be given for the protection of that great port.(5) Again, many prominent civilian engineers urged concentration on the defense of the Narrows, but Lieutenant Colonel Jonathan Williams, the Army's Chief Engineer, insisted that federal funds, at least, should be spent on the fortifications on the islands of the inner harbor. In retrospect, it probably would have been better to put all available funds, federal and state, into one site or the other. (Forty years later, another Chief Engineer admitted that, with respect to the island forts, "the destruction of the city might be going on simultaneously with the contest between the forts and the fleets.") (6)

Colonel Williams had other problems in early 1807. First he had to make an inspection trip all the way to Charleston, to assure state authorities that their large port was not being neglected. While he was gone the active command at West Point devolved upon Major William A. Barron, who had exercised the temporary command several times before. In mid-April Captain Joseph G. Swift, acting second-in-command, arrested Major Barron on the charge of consorting with prostitutes, "thereby setting an example injurious to the morals of the [cadets] and disgraceful to the institution."(7) Colonel Williams returned in late April, reviewed the charges, apparently thought them substantiated, and offered Barron the choice of resigning or facing a court-martial. Barron opted for trial; as Williams wrote Secretary of War Dearborn, "Major Barron has not accepted the offered Favour, and is of course arrested.,"(8) A court-martial was convened at Fort Jay, where Colonel Williams and other officer were making surveys, but at the last minute Barron changed his mind and submitted his resignation, which was accepted on 15 June.(9) Another vacancy was created in the Corps of Engineers and another name struck from the tiny faculty of the Military Academy.

In April Secretary Dearborn sent orders to General Wilkinson to return to Washington to testify in the trial of Aaron Burr, and to turn over command on the lower Mississippi to Colonel Thomas H. Cushing, who was both commanding officer of the 2d Infantry and Adjutant and Inspector of the Army. This anomalous situation was relieved when the President appointed Major Abimael Y. Nicoll of the Regiment of Artillerists to succeed Cushing as Adjutant and Inspector, although for the moment Major Nicoll would remain on the Mississippi under Colonel Cushing's direction. Cushing wrote to a friend that Nicoll's appointment was "a great relief to me, and I shall turn over the Office to him with great cheerfulness."(10)

HMS *Leopard* Excites the Seaboard

The British squadron that had been hovering off the entrance to Chesapeake Bay for over eight months, alarming and irritating the population of Norfolk in particular, finally pushed American forbearance to the limit. On 22 June 1807, off Hampton Roads, *HMS Leopard* stopped and searched the American naval frigate *Chesapeake*, which was not manned for action. When the *Chesapeake* refused to surrender alleged British deserters to the *Leopard*'s boarding party, the British vessel opened fire; after losing three killed and some 20 wounded, the American captain surrendered, whereupon the attackers removed four American sailors. The effect upon American public opinion was instantaneous and violent, and along the seaboard citizens called for war and began shoring up local defenses.(11)

President Jefferson remained calm, and on 2 July issued a moderate proclamation deploring the *Leopard*'s action, calling for negotiations with and reparations from the British government, and denying the British squadron the further "hospitality" of American ports. Jefferson had little expectation, of course, that the British vessels would comply completely with his interdiction, and he took tentative measures to strengthen the seacoast defenses. He asked Secretary Dearborn and Secretary of the Treasury Albert Gallatin for recommendations; Dearborn made certain immediate proposals, while Gallatin—who as head of the Revenue Cutter Service was familiar with seacoast problems—began a long-range study of the defense of the maritime frontier.

After conferring with the President, Secretary Dearborn issued several basic directives to Colonel Henry Burbeck, the Chief of Artillerists. The first was a general warning to all commanders of seacoast garrisons to get their men and materiel in the best possible order as rapidly as possible. The second went into more detail, ordering heavy mortars transferred all the way from Newport to Fort Nelson at Norfolk, directing powder and shells from Philadelphia to Norfolk, and giving specific instructions to the commander of Fort Nelson, Captain John Saunders. Fort McHenry at Baltimore was alerted and its commander told to mount cannon on ten new travelling carriages; similar instructions went to Fort Constitution at Portsmouth, rather far from the immediate threat. Colonel Burbeck was directed to begin supplying cannon on travelling carriages for the use of the militia at Norfolk, Charleston, Savannah, and New York City. Three days later Dearborn addressed a circular to the governors of the seaboard states, requiring them to have about one-sixth of their militia strengths ready for call—the total for all states being 100,000 men.(12)

Secretary Gallatin submitted his recommendations to the President on 25 July. As being developed by a civilian official, a confidant of the President, and the cabinet officer most conversant with the nation's finances, Gallatin's memorandum is of particular interest. He listed all the American seaports by their annual export tonnage, their annual payments into the Treasury, and what he considered their relative importance with respect to commerce and revenue; it was a dispassionate assessment, devoid of sectional sentiment. Gallatin's basic assumption was that "if the British Ministry is possessed of energy, and that we have no reason to doubt, we must expect an efficient fleet on our coast late this autumn, with perhaps a few thousand land forces, for the purpose of winter operations in the South. Their great object of attack will be one of four places, according to seasons and circumstances,—New York, Norfolk, Charleston (or perhaps Savannah), New Orleans." Gallatin then divided the seacoast cities and towns into two categories. Those that were already defended by forts, were difficult of enemy access, and had populations nearby to furnish militia, Gallatin thought might need only repairs, additional artillery, and augmented garrisons. But cities in the second category posed problems; they were those that, in Gallatin's view, "from either great facility of access by land or water, weakness of population, importance as compared with the means sufficient to take them, or difficulties attending the protection," would require particular attention. For these, the Secretary made specific comments:

Portland—was burnt [during the Revolution]—is quite open.

Newport [and] New York—need no comment. But the plan of defending the approaches of New York by narrowing the channel [with obstacles] at the most convenient place ... might be at once commenced by the city. I think it the only plan which will give real security. Its practicability and expense must be examined.

Washington will be an object, in order to destroy the ships and naval stores; but particularly as a stroke which would give the enemy reputation and attach disgrace to us. The Potomac may be easily defended. But an active enemy might land at Annapolis, march to the city, and re-embark before the militia could be collected to repel him. [A proscient forecast of 1814!]

Norfolk—forts and gunboats may defend the approaches by water, for the depth of water is such that a 74, injured by those near the town, could hardly repass the narrow channel below ... . But I think the great danger to be by land. The white population is weak. Three thousand men landing at Lynn Haven Bay, within eight miles from Norfolk, might certainly burn it, or take the batteries, open the way to their fleet, destroy the shipping, plunder the town. I see no remedy but a sufficient garrison, and such intrenchments as ... would give time to the militia to assemble ... .

Savannah—water shallow; but three or four million of produce sometimes deposited there, and the extreme want of white population in all the country near it might offer inducement to land a force sufficient to plunder the place. A garrison seems also the only remedy.

New Orleans, like Savannah and Norfolk, cannot be defended by its population alone. Its defences, in support of gunboats in the river and on the lake, should be strong forts at Placquemine and St. John. A garrison and forts in the city do not appear to be of any use. If an enemy lands on terra firma, he will take the town and garrison, and we must retake it from the upper country. But with a moderate force, properly distributed on water and in the forts, which command the navigation, it is the most easily defended place, of equal importance, in the United States.(13)

Gallatin's memorandum went on to include an elaborate plan, presumably called for by the President, by which American forces could attack Upper Canada and other British possessions in North America—perhaps the formal genesis of the improvised scheme that was implemented with such marked lack of success in 1812. But the seacoast-defense aspects of Gallatin's recommendations were important, and would be given full consideration in the next surge of coastal fortifications construction.

Steps Toward a Second System of Fortifications

The summer of 1807 was a period of great activity for everyone connected with the defense of the seacoast. Many agreed with Secretary Gallatin that a British fleet and landing force could be expected off the Atlantic or Gulf coasts in a matter of months, and from the Secretary of War to the junior officers of the Corps of Engineers there was a rush to accomplish as much as possible before the anticipated invasion. Secretary Dearborn penned letter after letter to Colonel Burbeck concerning the casting of cannon and construction of carriages, particularly the travelling carriages to be furnished the militia in areas not yet adequately fortified; he wrote repeatedly also to Callender Irvine, the Superintendent of Military Stores, directing that guns and ammunition in storage be moved to critical points. The firm of E.I. Du Pont de Nemours in Delaware was kept busy with contracts for high-quality gunpowder, and various private foundries were urged to speed their production of shot and shells. A note of near-desperation seems evident in Dearborn's urgent order to Irvine to conduct a search in the vicinity of Batsto Furnace in New Jersey for ammunition reported to have been buried there during the Revolution.(14)

President Jefferson was not yet ready to declare a state of crisis, feeling sure that amicable relations with Britain could be restored, and Congress took no action on seacoast fortifications pending a Presidential message. It was accepted, nevertheless, that new appropriations would be forthcoming by late fall, and Secretary Dearborn confirmed to the Chief Engineer and the Chief of Artillerists that construction and repair for the rest of 1807 would follow Gallatin's priorities—New York, Norfolk, Charleston, and New Orleans. This was a slight change over earlier priorities; Norfolk now took precedence over Newport because of the presence of the British squadron off Lynnhaven Bay.

Colonel Williams was determined to use at least a part of the next appropriations bill to introduce into any new construction the modified Montalembert system discussed at the last major meeting of the Military Philosophical Society. In effect, Williams proposed to abandon the horizontal style of Vauban, with its bastions, ditch, and glacis, in favor of Montalembert's perpendicular design, with most of the guns mounted in casemates rather than on barbette carriages. The advantages of the new system were summarized 80 years later by a senior officer of Engineers:

> Ever since the general introduction of gunpowder into warfare, the rule has been recognized that no masonry must be exposed to the fire of *land* guns; but this rule was not deemed applicable when ships, themselves much more vulnerable than stone walls, carried the guns. Moreover, the distinguishing characteristic of the line-of-battle ship of that day was her enormous concentration of fire. To reply with equal chance of success, *many* land guns were demanded; and space was lacking for them at most sites, unless advantage were taken of the facilities to pile tier above tier afforded by a masonry scarp... . To the needs of sea-coast fortifications casemates were peculiarly well adapted, and [Montalembert] had presented special designs for the purpose.(15)

Another advantage of the Montalembert casemate over earlier versions was the improved embrasure. Early embrasures, widening sharply outward, had tended to funnel enemy projectiles into the casemate; Montalembert reduced the size of the embrasure, and designed the cheeks to parallel the limits of the field of fire.(16)

The best examples of the new tower-and-casmates system to be introduced into the 1807 construction program were in New York Harbor, primarily because Colonel Williams was to take personal charge of construction there. Williams's ideas were fully incorporated into a memorandum of agreement between the state and federal governments, signed 21 July 1807, which provided a complete plan of defense for the inner harbor, the federal area of responsibility. The signed memorandum became a directive to the Chief Engineer:

> It being the Intention of the General Government, so to fortify the Harbour of New York, as will with aid of Gun Boats, afford a reasonable defence ... against ships of War, unaccompanied by any formidable Armament, such as can only be opposed by a superior Army:

> The following system [is approved and] Col. J. Williams will therefore consider the subsequent detail, as his instructions and authority for commencing and completing the contemplated works, with as little delay as circumstances will admit.

Governors Island

Fort Columbus [the new Republican name for the site of old Fort Jay] is to be completed according to the plan [which provided for a larger bastioned fort, still of the Vauban type]. A circular casemated battery ... is to be erected on the extreme westerly point, ... also a position on the Island will be chosen, so as to command the entrance of Buttermilk channel [on the Brooklyn side], and a Battery will be constructed ... .

Bedlows Island

... should be occupied by a small, but strong Redoubt, so constructed as to resist an Enemy who might land, until it can be relieved from some other point ... .

Ellis's Island

Upon this Island a Casemated Battery is to be erected on the old Foundation ... for the command of North [Hudson] River, and the Channel, in the range of a Semicircle.

New York

As soon as a proper title can be obtained, a foundation should be made round the Bastion of the Old Battery [and on it] a Casemated Battery should be constructed in such manner, that the Gun upon the right, will take the North river, while that upon the left will range along the Courtine [curtain?] of the old Battery ... .

Rhin[e]landers Wharf

At a convenient spot ... as far out into the North River, as the depth of Water will permit, a Block will be sunk of a sufficient size, to erect thereon, a twelve or fifteen gun Battery in one tier, so directed, as to prevent any Ship from lying against the Town, either near the wharves, or in the Channel... .(17)

Colonel Williams devoted most of his time and effort to the circular "castle" to be built on Governors Island, the work off the tip of Manhattan which was to be almost its twin, and the Hudson River battery near Rhinelander's Wharf, later referred to as the foot of Hubert Street. In correspondence with city officials, Williams was enthusiastic about the new design, referring to "modern improvements of marine Batteries which give double the number of Guns on the same horizontal base, and by multiplying the Tiers may give six times the number ... with a bombproof security above, render[ing] the question of Combat, a question of floating wooden Walls against impregnable Stone Walls on shore with equal ... number of Guns within the same space. It is not a very bold assertion to say, that no Ship sails the Ocean, that would engage on such terms."(18) The reconstruction of old Fort Jay had been authorized earlier, together with the expunging of the name of the Federalist former governor, but here there was no attempt to convert from the Vauban to the Montalembert design. The new Fort Columbus was to be slightly larger; two of the curtains were extended, but the four bastions remained, with a ravelin guarding the north face, and the whole surrounded by a ditch. At Norfolk the activity during the summer of 1807 was more apparent than real. Captain John Saunders, commanding Fort Nelson, kept Secretary Dearborn informed of the activities of the British squadron and the temper of the citizens, but the only fortifications activity was continuing repairs to Fort Nelson and basic touches to Fort Norfolk. A local citizen, William Tatham, corresponded regularly with President Jefferson, and it is evident from Tatham's reports that Norfolk was not placing much reliance on the two federal forts.

Tatham found the old 1795 plan for Fort Norfolk prepared by Major Rivardi and was organizing volunteer repairs to that work, but he did not consider the fort as tenable under attack and thought that repairing it was "a grave digging business." Tatham made no unfavorable comments on Fort Nelson, which had been refurbished in 1798, but thought that the first line of defense should have been at Lynnhaven Bay, with secondary works on Craney Island at the mouth of the Elizabeth River.(19) The events of 1813 were to prove Tatham quite correct.

In Charleston the newly-designated Engineer officer was Captain Alexander Macomb. Macomb seems to have underestimated the national anxiety, for in July he had calmly requested permission to visit Europe to study military developments. Secretary Dearborn snapped in reply that "under the existing circumstances of our country, neither your Patriotism as a Citizen, nor your duties as a military officer, can leave you a wish to have the favor granted."(20) Macomb saw the light, immediately buckled down to work, and by mid-August forwarded to the War Department a status report which showed that the defenses of Charleston would not soon be an ornament of the Montalembert system. In the interests of speed and economy, Macomb thought that temporary repairs could be made, with the help of the local militia, to put the harbor in a fair state of defense at little cost. He proposed to repair Fort Moultrie with traditional palmetto logs, and to erect breastworks along the beach on Sullivan's Island of palmetto logs filled with sand, to be defended by heavy guns on travelling carriages. On the site of Castle Pinckney Macomb thought that "a mud fort of considerable strength might ... operate as well as the most permanent works."(21) Although Macomb's letter was written from Fort Johnson, he made no mention of that post on James Island. It had been manned and kept in repair since 1794 by federal troops under Captain Michael Kalteisen, who had declined promotion in order to remain in Charleston. Kalteisen, the last original captain of the old Corps of Artillerists and Engineers, was 78 years old; during the fall of 1807 he caught influenza, and on 3 November he died. "His death was announced by 17 minute guns from Fort Johnson, which were answered by the same number from the Gun-Boats in the harbor," and he was buried in Charleston with full military and civil honors.(22)

The fortifications around New Orleans were still generally in poor repair, but Captain Walker K. Armistead of the Engineers was sent there during the summer of 1807 to survey the situation. Proceeding as far toward the mouth of the Mississippi as Fort St. Philip, Armistead submitted to the Chief Engineer the first comprehensive report on the works below New Orleans. Some extracts are of interest:

> English Turn is situated 12 miles below the City [on] a very commanding site ... for a Fortification, or Navy Yard, or both combined ... . [It has] a command of the river for more than two miles above and below [and] no vessel coming up the river is able to pass with the wind that brought her within cannon shot of the point ... .

> Fort St. Philip is ... distant from New Orleans 60 miles, and from Balaise 30 in a low and marshy situation, and 6 miles on either side from the sea... . I apprehend a Work entirely of Masonry would be too great a weight for this soft and plyable soil, in my Judgement a Work with Bastions would be preferable.

> Fort Bourbon is situated nearly opposite ... at present in ruins. ... I would recommend a Work different from the present [with] a flank defence in front, and defended by heavy Artillery; in the rear I would have a Breast work for Infantry.(23)

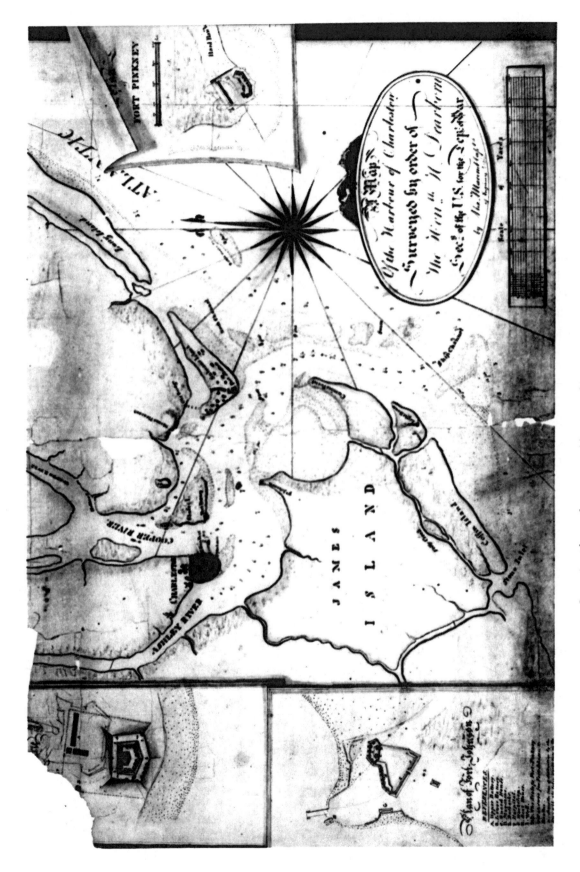

Captain Alexander Macomb's Map of Charleston Harbor
ca. 1807

The lack of progress in resolving Anglo-American differences prompted President Jefferson to deliver an early Annual Message, on 27 October. He reviewed the many infringements on American navigation in recent years, reminded Congress that he had sent a special mission to London, and detailed the *Chesapeake-Leopard* encounter from the American point of view. He reiterated the priority for seacoast defenses, including gunboats, at New York, Charleston, the Chesapeake, and New Orleans; "whether a regular army is to be raised, and to what extent must depend on the information so shortly expected.(24)

Knowing that Congress would soon call for specific information on the seacoast defense needs, Secretary Dearborn wrote to Colonel Williams in New York, asking him to come to Washington; General Wilkinson was already there in connection with the Burr trial, and Dearborn proposed that the three confer on the problems of "organizing a general system for fortifying our Ports and Harbors."(25) On 20 November, in response to the anticipated request by a House committee, the Secretary submitted a long list of ports and harbors requiring defenses, divided into two categories as to urgency, at the same time recommending how many gunboats, of the 257 on hand or under construction, should be stationed in each area. On 24 November the committee reported to the House, using Dearborn's listing verbatim:

> ... the protection desired can be best and most expeditiously afforded by means of land batteries and gun boats; ... by a judicious combination and use of these two powers, effectual protection can be given, even to our most important seaport towns, against ships of any size unaccompanied by an army. That our most important ports and harbors, and those requiring the earliest attention, and the most expensive fortifications, are New Orleans, Savannah, Charleston, S.C., Wilmington, N.C., Norfolk, Baltimore, Philadelphia, New York, New London, Newport, R.I., Boston, Salem, Newburyport, Portsmouth, N.H., and Portland.

In the less important and less urgent category the committee listed some 30 general locations along the Atlantic coast from St. Mary's, Georgia, to Passamaquoddy Bay in Maine.(26)

Congress did not accept the committee report without considerable debate. One segment of the House was in favor of immediate construction of 74-gun warships and whatever fortifications were necessary; Josiah Masters of New York expressed the strongest view. "I hope to see our coast lined with forts and batteries," Masters said on the floor, "at suitable and proper places, and our harbors filled with frigates and gunboats, and some block ships; and were it not esteemed heresy by some, I would say a few seventy-four gun ships."(27) The heresy to which Masters referred was based on the strong feeling by many members that construction of warships would invite prompt and devastating retaliation by the Royal Navy, and so the matter of 74-gun ships was not officially addressed at this session. The use of gunboats was generally favored, and additional money was almost certain to be made available, but the gunboats had their opponents. Friends of a large and effective navy sneered at the idea of tiny gunboats—and land fortifications too, in some cases–as being useless against ships of war and a possible invasion force.

Those who generally favored land fortifications and batteries were divided between those who called for stronger forts, and those who thought that more cannon should be mounted on travelling carriages and placed at many points along the exposed shoreline. A proposal that the entrance to New York Harbor should be obstructed by sinking blocks at strategic points drew horrified opposition from the New York delegation, which feared permanent damage to the port. The debate lasted for over three weeks, and the arguments in the *Annals of Congress* make fascinating if sometimes discouraging reading. In the end, however, the modest Administration recommendations prevailed—the Democratic-Republications dominated the House by 118-24 and the Senate by 26-6—and Congress voted the sum of one million dollars for gunboats and essential fortifications. At the same time, hoping to achieve by economic pressures what it was unwilling to attempt by stringent military measures, Congress passed the Embargo Act proposed by the President.(28)

The Congressional debates that had brought Jonathan Williams to Washington in late 1807 terminated before the end of the year, but Williams's presence in the capital was to be required some weeks longer. General Wilkinson's role in the Burr affair was in considerable question, and behind the Burr expedition was the larger allegation that Wilkinson was secretly in the pay of the Spanish government. Wilkinson took advantage of his presence in Washington to demand a court of enquiry to silence the widespread rumors, and in accordance with Army Regulations the Secretary of War had little choice but to comply. On 2 January a small but senior court consisting of Colonel Burbeck, Colonel Cushing, and Lieutenant Colonel Williams was directed to convene on 11 January "for the purpose of hearing such Testimony as may be produced in relation to said Genl Jas. Wilkinson's having been or now being a Pensioner to the Spanish Government, while holding a commission under the Government of the United States."(29) Space here does not permit treatment of this court of enquiry, which failed once more, for lack of evidence, to indict Wilkinson. But once again the requirements of military justice brought much other military administration to a standstill, and once again, at a time of national emergency, both the Chief of Artillerists and the Chief Engineer were diverted from their own important duties.

Engineer Planning for the New Construction Program

As long as Lieutenant Colonel Williams had to remain in Washington, he put his spare time to good use. First he reminded Secretary Dearborn that the President, under the Act of 16 March 1802, had authority to promote officers of the Corps of Engineers without strict regard to seniority and without specific grade limitation; undoubtedly he also made a case for the fact that the Chief Engineer of the Army should rank with the Chief of Artillerists and the commanders of the infantry regiments. The Secretary agreed, and on 26 January 1808 he submitted to the President a full slate of promotions within the Corps of Engineers. As approved by the Senate, to take effect 23 February, these promotions affected ten officers: to colonel, Jonathan Williams; to lieutenant colonel, the absent Jared Mansfield; to major, Alexander Macomb and Joseph G. Swift; to captain George Bomford, William McRee, and Charles Gratiot; to 1st lieutenant, Eleazer D. Wood, William Partridge, and Prentiss Willard. At the same time Joseph G. Totten, Class of 1805, who had resigned in 1806 to join his uncle, Jared Mansfield, as a surveyor, was reappointed a 2d lieutenant, losing nearly two years' seniority. Three cadets—Samuel Babcock, Daniel A.A. Buck, and Sylvanus Thayer—were appointed 2d lieutenants. Only two officers were unaffected: Walker K. Armistead remained the senior captain of the Corps; Alden Partridge, jumped by his classmate Gratiot, remained senior 1st lieutenant.(30)

While he was in Washington, Colonel Williams decided to call a meeting of the United States Military Philosophical Society. With Secretary Dearborn's approval, the meeting was held at the War Department on Saturday, 30 January. Just which members attended was not recorded, although the minutes of the meeting listed the total Society membership, which had reached 146. Among the members in January 1808 were six federal officials of cabinet rank or higher, 13 senators and representatives, 11 governors and former governors, and 12 ministers, envoys, and superior court judges; farther down the scale of prestige were 33 active Army officers, four cadets, nine Navy officers, and four officers of the Marine Corps. (The entire membership for the period 1807-1809 is shown in Appendix E.)

The presentations and discussions during this Washington meeting were of above-average interest. Most of the papers read or artifacts donated pertained to engineering or artillery, but several documents of general historical interest were given to the Society for retention.(31) William R. Davie, former minister to France, forwarded the manuscript of a manual for horse artillery written by Kosciusko, "said to have been introduced into the French armies," and Lieutenant John R. Fenwick, the Adjutant of the Marine Corps, presented a paper on the French system of horse artillery. (Fenwick would leave the Marines in 1811 to join the Army's new regiment of light artillery.) John Armstrong, the minister in Paris, forwarded a plan of the siege of Danzig and three maps of the battle of Eylau, presented by Napoleon's chief of staff, the Marshal Prince of Neufchatel—who as Alexandre Berthier had served as an engineer in America with Rochambeau. Captain Richard Whiley, commanding Fort Columbus on Governors Island, donated eight manuscript books of orders issued by Major General Anthony Wayne during his command of the legion, and Caleb Swan, Paymaster of the Army, presented notes on the formation of the Legion, its order of battle, and a description of some tactical maneuvers. Alexander Macomb of the Engineers presented the manuscript of his work on martial law and courts-martial, published the following year and adopted by the Army.

The minutes do not reflect how much unofficial discussion must have taken place concerning the new impulse given to the construction of seacoast fortifications at the end of 1807. Recorded, however, is the fact that Colonel Williams at this time gave into the Society's custody the model of a new seacoast artillery carriage based on Montalembert's design; this carriage had been discussed at an 1806 meeting, and the model had been constructed at West Point.

At this meeting, or soon thereafter, Secretary Dearborn and Colonel Williams got together to try to regularize the duties of the Corps of Engineers with respect to the new construction program and to divide responsibilities among the more senior Engineer officers. Up to this point the Secretary had handled most Engineer assignments himself, and in fact just before the Society meeting he had employed a civilian engineer, the French-born John Foncin, to replace Captain Armistead in New Orleans and allow that officer to assume larger responsibilities on the Atlantic coast. Foncin, who had done some of the planning and supervision of works in Boston and at the Narrows in New York Harbor, accepted the superintendence of such works as might be erected at or near New Orleans, at a flat compensation of five dollars per day.(32) Whether Foncin's appointment had been discussed with Colonel Williams is not clear, but shortly thereafter Secretary Dearborn instructed Williams to recommend assignment of Engineer officers to the several regions where new works or extensive repairs were planned. Williams's reply set up what might be called Engineer "districts," as the term would be used a century or more later:

> I shall proceed ... to distribute the Officers of Engineers in the most convenient way. We are but sixteen in the whole of which two (Lt Col Mansfield & Lieut [Alden] Partridge) are fixed for special duties, one being Surveyor General in the western country and the other a Professor at West Point. I have thought it best to have four fixed Points as the head Quarters of the four detachments into which I have divided my Strength ... .

> I have left New Orleans out of the question, presuming on your arrangements with Col. Foncin; and I must take an occasional view of Philadelphia [Williams's home] myself for I have no Officer to send there; its River is so long & difficult, that I suppose by resorting to obstructions as formerly it may in conjunction with Fort Mifflin be defended. - I shall this day order the commanding officers to their Posts.

Distribution of the Corps of Engineers and Assistant Engineers who may be employed for Special Purposes.

1. The River Mississippi & the Coast to be put under the Care of Mr. Foncin.

2. All the Ports in Georgia & the two Carolina's to be under the direction of Major Macomb, who is to take post in Charleston & to be assisted by Capt McRee, Capt Gratiot, and Lieut W. Partridge.

3. All the Ports in Virginia & Maryland to be under the direction of Capt Armistead who is to take post at Norfolk & be assisted by Capt Bomford & Lieut .D. Wood.

4. The River Delaware & New York Harbour will be taken charge of by Col. Williams whose station will be in the latter place, assisted by Lieuts Totten, Babcock & Buck with such Cadets as may be taken from the military academy.

5. All the Ports in Connecticut, Rhode Island, Massachusetts & New Hampshire to be under the direction of Major Swift who will take Post at Boston & be assisted by Lieuts Willard and Thayer with such Cadets as can be drawn from the military academy.(33)

In addition to the five Engineer "districts," there remained the matter of the Military Academy. The fact that only one officer, 1st Lieutenant Alden Partridge, was assigned to the faculty–together with civilians Francis de Masson, Ferdinand R. Hassler, and Christian E. Zoeller—was an index to the neglected state of the six-year-old institution. For some time it had been expected that the academy would be moved to Washington, but the years of Jefferson's administration went by without action. Early in 1808, in connection with an impending augmentation of the Army, Colonel Williams drew up a lengthy report on the condition of the school, with proposals for strengthening the faculty and the courses of instruction. Secretary Dearborn passed the report to the President substantially unchanged, and on 18 March Jefferson forwarded it to Congress with a rather lukewarm covering statement:

> The scale upon which the military academy, at West Point was originally established is becoming too limited to furnish the number of well instructed subjects, in the different branches of artillery and engineering, which the public service calls for with the enlargement of our plans of military preparation. The chief engineer having been instructed to consider the subject, and to propose an augmentation which might render the establishment commensurate with the present circumstances of our country, has made the report which I now transmit … .

> The idea suggested by him of removing the institution to this place, is also worthy of attention. Besides the advantage of placing it under the immediate eye of the Government, it may render its benefits common to the Naval Department, and will furnish opportunities of selecting, on better information, the characters most qualified to fulfill the duties which the public service may call for.(34)

Colonel Williams's report was considered by a subcommittee of the Committee on Military Affairs of the House, composed largely of members "identified with republican principles,"(35) and came to nothing. Except for certain on-paper increases in the number of authorized cadets, finally enacted in 1812, Williams's recommendations were filed without action.(36) In retrospect, it is probable that establishing the Military Academy in Washington, "under the immediate eye of the Government," would have been fatal to its apolitical role.

At the end of February, efforts to reach an agreement with Great Britain concerning American maritime rights having proved fruitless, President Jefferson forwarded to Congress a general plan for augmenting the nation's military strength. Drawn up by Henry Dearborn, the plan provided first for raising 24,000 volunteers, "enlisted to serve twelve months in any twenty-four months within the term of five years," and second for increasing the Regular Army by 6,000 men, to be organized as five additional regiments of infantry and one regiment each of light artillery, light dragoons, and riflemen. Dearborn was specific that there should be no designated Commanding General; "until a larger army shall be raised than is now proposed," he added, "it may not be advisable to have any officers above the rank of Brigadier General; of that grade it may be proper to have four or five, as soon as a suitable proportion of the troops is raised."(37) In denying the need for a General-in- Chief, the Secretary may have had in mind that such a position would have been claimed by James Wilkinson, whose status in early 1808 was cloudier than usual. On the other hand, Dearborn may have been expressing the Republican philosophy of strict civilian control, at the expense of requiring the Secretary of War to operate through four or five widely scattered military subordinates. It was by no means a new theory, but is application would be disastrous in 1812.

Congress passed and the President signed the necessary legislation on 12 April, in the form of "An act to raise for a limited time an additional military force."(38) The addition of eight regiments increased the authorized strength of the Army from 3,287 to 9,921 officers and men, but as the title of the act implied, the increase was not necessarily to be permanent; if the difficulties with Britain could be smoothed over, assuredly part or even all of the new regiments could be disbanded. Certain features of the act directly affected the pre-1808 organization, which continued to be known as the "Military Peace Establishment": two additional brigadier generals were authorized, certain changes were made in staff procedures, and the companies of the new Regiment of Light Artillery were eventually to be considered as virtually interchangeable with companies of the existing Regiment of Artillerists. In theory each of the new regiments was authorized two cadets per company, but in fact the number of service cadets ordered to report to the Military Academy never reached the pre-1802 authorization of 46, and from 1803 to the outbreak of war in 1812 the number of cadets actually at West Point declined steadily.

The organization of the Regiment of Light Artillery had several effects on the personnel and missions of the Regiment of Artillerists. The new regiment, of ten companies, was authorized a colonel, lieutenant colonel, and major, but no officer above major was appointed until the end of 1811. The majority for the Light Artillery went to Captain John Saunders of the Artillerists, who had attracted Secretary Dearborn's favorable notice in his command at Norfolk during the tense summer of 1807. Saunders had been only the sixth-ranking captain of Artillerists, but that was not a bar to appointment to a new regiment; the surprising fact is that the appointment did not go to a prominent civilian. Captain George Peter, just promoted to Kalteisen's vacancy in the Artillerists, was transferred to the Light Artillery and at once found himself senior captain of the new regiment. Captain Peter was selected in 1808 to organize and equip a company of light horse-drawn artillery, usually considered the first such in the American artillery.(39) The fate of that company, unhorsed for economy reasons the following year, is interesting, but forms no part of this work. Captain Peter resigned in June of 1809 and Major Saunders's promising career was cut short by his death in March 1810, which severed any lineal connection between the two regiments. Nevertheless, as will be related, companies of light artillery were to serve alongside companies of artillerists in seacoast fortifications even before the outbreak of the

War of 1812.

The augmentation of the Army, and particularly the increase in artillery, forced Secretary Dearborn to turn his attention to production of cannon and carriages. During the early years of his tenure scant attention had been paid to this subject, but after the *Leopard* crisis Dearborn realized the need for some sort of centralized government cannon foundry. He recommended such an establishment to Congress, and a House committee recommended that funds be appropriated "for the purpose of building a national foundry in the city of Washington, for casting ordnance."(40) Anticipating approval, Dearborn approached the only cannon founder then capable of establishing a national work, Henry Foxall of the Columbia Foundry in Georgetown. The British-born Foxall, then 50, had emigrated to the United States in 1797 and had formed a partner-ship with Robert Morris, Jr., son of the wartime financier in the management of the Eagle Iron Works in Philadelphia, which did a brisk business in general founding and cast cannon for the War Department during the era of the Provisional Army. In 1800 Foxall bought out Morris, moved to Georgetown, and established the Columbia—sometimes called Columbian—Foundry. By 1804 Foxall 's foundry received the most important contracts for cannon of all sizes; in that year, for example, the Columbia Foundry cast the brass cannon to be delivered as tribute to the Dey of Algiers.(41)

Henry Dearborn proposed to Foxall in the summer of 1807 that Foxall construct on public land at Greenleaf's Point in the District of Columbia a "large foundry and boring mill intended solely for the public use." Foxall's reply was patriotic but businesslike. He pointed out that if he built a foundry on public land, and after a year or two the need for cannon was satisfied, before he had paid for his investment, he would be unable to convert the establishment to other uses, whereas if he owned the land he could convert to foundry to, say, a flour mill. As a counterproposal, Foxall suggested a sort of leasing arrangement. He would construct a foundry on Greenleaf's Point, complete with steam engine, furnaces, and boring mill; in return for erecting and operating this foundry, Foxall asked for "the use of the same, without rent or charge, with a contract sufficient to keep it at work for two years after its completion." At the end of the two years, "should there still be a want of ordnance, I would gladly pay [the government] a rent for the use of the works … for as long a time as might be necessary to keep them in operation."(42)

Secretary Dearborn favored this plan, but for reasons not clear it was not acceptable to Congress, and for the moment the government continued to rely on private cannon foundries. Four years later a Congressional committee reported that 530 forges and furnaces were operating in the country, and that the manufacture of cannon was adequate to emergencies. Foxall's Columbia Foundry eventually reached a capacity of 300 heavy cannon and 30,000 shot a year during the War of 1812. However, the proliferation of private foundries and furnaces made standardization of bores and ammunition almost impossible, and when war came in 1812 the system was not fully adequate to the greatly expanded requirements of the Army and Navy.(43)

In August of 1807 Secretary Dearborn foresaw no lack of seacoast cannon. There were on hand 927 heavy pieces, including 498 24-pounders, 116 32-pounders, and 20 new 42-pounders, and as the Secretary could only add up a need for 692 pieces overall, he reported to Congress that the nation had a surplus of 235 heavy iron cannon.(44) But after the introduction in November 1807 of what became the Second System of fortifications construction, Dearborn interested himself increasingly in the heavier guns, persuaded by Colonel Williams that they would be needed for mounting in the several new forts being designed along the Montalembert principles. In order to take full advantage of the concentration of fire made possible by the multiple tiers of casemated guns, a heavier weight of metal than the familiar 32-pounders was desirable, and it was for this reason that a limited number of

42-pounders had been purchased. In late 1808 the Columbia Foundry produced a few experimental 50-pounders, and it was apparently from this gun that the ambiguous and over-used term "columbiad" first derived. In June 1808 the Secretary wrote to Colonel Burbeck to prepare a target mound for testing the "Columbiade"; no description of the weapon was given, nor an explanation of the term, but it seems clear from other evidence that in 1808 the new weapon was the iron 50-pounder, and that the name derived from Foxall's Columbia Foundry.(45) (A year later, as will be related in the following chapter, the term "columbiad" referred to a different cannon.)

Fortifications Construction in 1808

The Wilkinson court of enquiry adjourned in early June 1808, unable—or unwilling—to substantiate the allegations that the General was in the pay of the Spanish government. Wilkinson was ordered to take charge of recruiting the new regiments authorized by the legislation of 12 April, and shortly established his headquarters at the recruiting rendezvous already in operation at Carlisle, Pennsylvania. Colonel Williams resumed his supervision of the construction in New York Harbor; Colonel Burbeck, now that General Wilkinson was "east of the mountains," limited his command to the seacoast garrisons, acting also as supervisor of ordnance functions in the continued absence of a proper Ordnance Department. In August the new Adjutant and Inspector of the Army, Major Abimael Y. Nicoll of the Artillerists, established his office in Washington.(46)

The Engineer "districts" established by Colonel Williams soon required minor modifications, beginning at New Orleans. Secretary Dearborn had personally selected John Foncin to be Assistant Engineer in charge at New Orleans, and on that basis Colonel Williams had transferred Captain Walker K. Armistead to Norfolk. Mr. Foncin sailed for New Orleans as scheduled, but whether he arrived prior to Armistead's departure is uncertain. In any event, Foncin seems to have been very quickly disenchanted with his prospects in New Orleans, for within a matter of weeks he booked return passage to New York, ostensibly for reasons of health. Dearborn learned of Foncin's defection in early June, and at once wrote to Major William MacRea of the Artillerists—not to be confused with Captain William McRee of the Engineers—the senior artillerist in New Orleans, that because of Foncin's unexpected resignation Major MacRea would have to assume the duties of engineer in charge of fortifications construction. MacRea, the former infantryman of the Legion, was probably the least-qualified engineer of all the field officers of Artillerists, but he was perfectly willing to try his hand at engineering, and on the Secretary's authority he took over the duties. His general instructions were to complete and repair the fortifications at Placquemines, following plans drawn up by Captain Armistead, and then "to erect a battery for 8 or 10 guns at English turn, as well as a battery at the mouth of Bayou St. John's for 4 or 6 Guns."(47)

The Secretary also decided to reduce the size of the "Eastern district," comprising all of New England, which had been assigned to Major Joseph G. Swift. As the entire coastline northeast of Portland would probably have to be defended by guns on travelling carriages rather than fortifications, that region could be handled by an artillerist, and about 1 April Dearborn wrote to Major Moses Porter, then on leave in Massachusetts, assigning him responsibility for surveying the exposed coast for the best locations for beach defense guns.(48) Major Swift, who retained responsibility for the coast from Portland to New London, made some preliminary surveys of his area, and selected "Naugus Head at Salem, Black Point on the Merrimack, Kittery opposite Fort Constitution, New Hampshire, Spring Point and House Island at Portland, for new positions for defensive works." He also proposed to repair the works erected by Stephen Rochefontaine at Marblehead and Gloucester, which he found in surprisingly good condition.(49) At about this time Major Swift was advised by the Secretary that arrangements had been completed for the federal government to purchase sites on Governor's Island in Boston Harbor—at "the enormous sum of $15,000"—for the construction of a major fortification and a connected water battery, to be under Swift's supervision.(50) Major Swift prepared to survey the various ports and submit detailed plans, but was chagrined to learn from Dearborn that necessary maps and plans would be prepared in Washington.

The Second System of seacoast fortifications was the first series of forts designed and constructed entirely by American officers, most of them of the Corps of Engineers. The young Engineer officers, however, were not given an entirely free hand, for both Secretary Dearborn and Colonel Burbeck, as well as most field officers of Artillerists, were Revolutionary veterans brought up on Vauban and by no means converted to Montalembert. Major Swift confided the sequel to his Memoirs:

> On 10th May ... I received from the War Department several plans of a species of Star Fort, contrived at Washington, too small for any flank defense, and too complicated for a mere battery, unsuited to the positions for which they had been devised. The only resort left to me was to turn these plans on their centre until they might suit the sites as best they might, in Boston, Portland, and other harbors. I ... presume these plans to have emanated from some Revolutionary worthy near the War Department—probably Col. Burbeck. Evidently they were adopted in preference to the plans of us young officers who had given our opinion in favor of a more appropriate form and extent. We were indeed very young and inexperienced ....(51)

Despite his distaste for the plans forced upon him, Major Swift spent the summer of 1808 in applying the "Washington Stars," as he called them, to various New England sites. One of the more important and lasting of the new fortifications was a battery at Kittery, Maine, across Portsmouth harbor from Fort Constitution in New Hampshire; designed to "cooperate with the fire of Fort Constitution," the new work was named Fort McClary after Michael McClary, the adjutant general of the New Hampshire Militia.(52)

Construction in New York Harbor continued during 1808 under Colonel Williams's immediate supervision. In addition to Fort Columbus on Governors Island, a classic Vauban fortress, works of the "star" type were continued on Bedlows and Ellis's Islands. Colonel Williams applied the Montalembert design, however, to three locations within the harbor—on the west point of Governors Island, off the tip of Manhattan Island, and in the Hudson River off the foot of Hubert Street. There is some indication that Secretary Dearborn initially opposed the circular castle design at the latter sites, and Swift in his Memoirs implies that Colonel Williams received permission from President Jefferson,(53) but there seems no doubt that by the summer of 1808 Dearborn supported the new design, willingly or not.

Neither Fort Mifflin nor Fort McHenry required more than routine repairs, and the bulk of the activity in the middle Atlantic region took place at Norfolk and in the defenses newly authorized for the defense of Washington. Captain Walker K. Armistead, in charge of the district, devoted his attention to constructing additional batteries at Forts Norfolk and Nelson; then, at Secretary Dearborn's order, he undertook to construct an entirely new battery and redoubt at Hood's Bluff on the James River, to be known as Fort Powhatan.(54) His principal subordinate, Captain George Bomford, was in charge of constructing works at Annapolis and on the north bank of the Severn River, primarily, it would appear, to defend the capital against a landing from Chesapeake Bay. Bomford then turned his attention to erecting a major work at Warburton, Maryland, on the Potomac below Washington, which had been selected earlier in the year by Colonel Williams and Colonel Burbeck while they were serving on the Wilkinson court of enquiry.(55) The new work was initially called Fort Warburton, and that name lingered locally, but by the end of 1808 it was officially known as Fort Washington.

From his district headquarters in Charleston, Major Alexander Macomb reported periodically on progress in that harbor. In July he sailed north to Wilmington and reported on repairs to Fort Johnston; then on to Beaufort, where Captain Charles Gratiot was erecting a work. He advised Secretary Dearborn that Lieutenant William Partridge was in charge of the work being erected in Winyah Bay at Georgetown, South Carolina, and that Captain William McRee was supervising construction in Georgia. In September and October Major Macomb made an interesting inspection trip to the southern limit of his district:

> [I have completed] a most perilous journey to the southward as far as St. Marys and the Floridas on the duties of my profession. I went through the inland navigation with a Boat & six men and returned after an absence of two months with only three of my crew and they all sick. I made this voyage not only on account of its being the only means of getting at the different points in my district, but with a view of obtaining a complete knowledge of the Inland navigation and the avenues through which an enemy might assail the weaker parts of our country.

> This information I conceived essentially necessary to form a just idea of the means requisite to the defence of our southern seaboard ... .(56)

Macomb added certain comments with respect to the fortifications within his district. At Savannah he thought the site selected for the new Fort Wayne was excellent; like his colleague Major Swift, however, Macomb did not like the "Plan of the Star Fort sent with my orders," and proposed a less formal work. At Charleston he noted that Fort Mechanic was completed and the local militia claimed the right to garrison it; Fort Moultrie, when completely refurbished, would mount 30 heavy guns and take a 300-man garrison. The work at Georgetown, nearing completion, would be named Fort Winyaw—usually Winyah—after the bay, unless the Secretary preferred another name.

As construction of the Second System got fully under way, it was quickly apparent that the Regiment of Artillerists alone would be unable to provide all the necessary garrisons, unless of course all its companies were ordered from the Mississippi and elsewhere to the seaboard. It was cheaper and faster to post newly-recruited companies of Light Artillery and other arms to some of the new fortifications; in July Captain Solomon D. Townsend's light artillerymen were stationed on Ellis's Island in New York Harbor, and in October Captain Joseph Chandler's company of that regiment were ordered to newly-completed Fort Preble at Portland. (In Chandler's case, the compelling need was for troops to assist in enforcing the Embargo.) Similarly, several companies of the new Regiment of Riflemen being raised in Pennsylvania were stationed at Fort Mifflin under Lieutenant Colonel William Duane, who was better known in civil life as the editor of the Republican organ, the *Aurora*.(57)

In preparation for his annual message, planned for early November, President Jefferson asked Secretary Dearborn for the status of the seacoast fortifications. For once Dearborn was caught short, and could only forward a general statement that he had "reason to believe that in the course of the present year, the works proposed for the defence of our ports and harbors will, with but few exceptions, be nearly completed." He stressed the shortage of Engineer officers, and mentioned the failure of John Foncin at New Orleans. He would, Dearborn assured the President, have a full report within a few weeks.(58)

The President's message necessarily contained only a short general paragraph on the seacoast defenses. A few weeks later, as promised, Secretary Dearborn submitted a comprehensive status report on the defenses of the coast from the Canadian frontier in Maine to New Orleans. This valuable report, the last one prepared under Jefferson's administration, is reproduced as Appendix F.(59)

CHAPTER X
MADISON, EUSTIS, AND THE SECOND SYSTEM
1809-1810

Three weeks after Jefferson's Annual Message of November 1808 another crisis arose, the response to which was to color much of the next two years. Sources of information in Canada reported the buildup of British regular troops there, and in mid-November it appeared that some 4,000 men were being fitted out at Halifax. Their destination was reported to be New Orleans, to sail as soon as war was imminent. The same reports claimed that if the British moved against New Orleans, they were prepared to abandon Upper Canada to the Americans.(1)

Unwilling to wait until the reports could be fully verified, President Jefferson decided once again to shift the bulk of the American forces to the southward. On 2 December Secretary of War Dearborn gave orders to that effect to General Wilkinson, directing him to alert three of the new infantry regiments—3d, 5th, and 7th—and companies of light dragoons light artillery, and riflemen being recruited south of New Jersey. These troops were to be moved to the New Orleans area, where Wilkinson would assume command. In case of emergency, Wilkinson would be authorized to call for militia from the governors of Mississippi and Orleans Territories.(2) It could not, of course, be certain that the British threat was to New Orleans; there was always the possibility that a seaborne invasion force might put in without warning at any Atlantic port. To alert the tiny seacoast garrisons, Dearborn gave orders to the commanding officers from Maine to Georgia "to have their Cannon & Ammunition in good order, and fit for service on the shortest notice."(3) In light of the dispositions being made for defending New Orleans, the protection of the Atlantic seaboard would be in the hands of the companies of artillerists already manning the forts, supported by the 4th Infantry being raised in New England, about half the 6th Infantry around New York, and those companies of light artillery, dragoons, and riflemen being recruited in New Jersey and northward.

At the beginning of 1809 the organization and command of the Atlantic defenses was more chaotic than usual. Colonel Henry Burbeck, the Chief of Artillerists, should have exercised some overall supervision of the many garrisons, but in the late fall Burbeck had been sent off to Detroit once again, so that the "Department of the Lakes" could have a colonel commanding in the interim between the death of Colonel Thomas Hunt in August and the anticipated arrival, after an extended furlough, of the new colonel of the 1st Infantry, Jacob Kingsbury. With the new threat to the seacoast, of course, Colonel Burbeck had to be recalled, and on 15 February the Adjutant and Inspector, Major Nicoll, wrote Colonel Kingsbury in Connecticut to terminate his furlough and report to Detroit. At the same time Burbeck was notified that as soon as he was relieved by Kingsbury at Detroit, he would proceed to Fort McHenry at Baltimore, "where you will take up your quarters and resume the command on the sea coast."(4)

But correspondence was slow, Colonel Kingsbury was in no hurry to travel to Detroit during the winter, and it would be many months before Henry Burbeck resumed his seacoast command. During his continued absence, the command was parcelled out to several officers of other arms. The supervision of the New England garrisons, except Connecticut, was assigned to Colonel John P. Boyd of the new 4th Infantry, with headquarters in Boston. Boyd was an energetic former soldier of fortune, 44 years old; although he knew little of fortifications or artillery, he supervised the routine of the seacoast garrisons for about two years without recorded difficulty.(5) Major Joseph G. Swift of the Engineers, based at Fort Independence on Boston Harbor, was in charge of construction and repair of fortifications in the same region.

The middle reaches of the Atlantic, New York and Pennsylvania, continued under the engineering supervision of Colonel Jonathan Williams, the Chief Engineer, in New York Harbor. Williams also eased Major Swift's burden by supervising the repairs to Fort Trumbull at New London and the works being erected by Lieutenant Joseph G. Totten at New Haven.(6) At this time no line officer was appointed to exercise command over the seacoast garrisons in New York Harbor and at Fort Mifflin in the Delaware.

The garrisons in Maryland and Virginia, usually under Colonel Burbeck's immediate supervision, fell under the nominal control of Major John Saunders of the Light Artillery, who before his transfer and promotion had commanded the company of artillerists in Norfolk. Saunders remained at Fort Nelson to recruit light artillerymen, turning command of his old company over to newly promoted Captain Enoch Humphreys.(7) Also at Norfolk was Captain Walker K. Armistead of the Engineers, in charge of the Engineer district comprising Maryland and Virginia.

Temporary administrative command of the long stretch of coast from North Carolina through Georgia was given to Colonel Wade Hampton of the new Regiment of Light Dragoons. As the dragoons were being recruited over a wide area, and most of them destined for New Orleans without mounts, Hampton was free to supervise the southern defenses, of which Charleston, in his home state, was the most important. The senior officer of Engineers for the same region, the energetic Major Alexander Macomb, raised a question with Secretary Dearborn as to his status with respect to the newly-appointed colonel; Dearborn replied that Hampton would be responsible for overall defense plans, but that Macomb would receive instructions on the subject of fortifications directly from the War Department.(8)

The early months of 1809 were the last of Jefferson's administration; on 4 March James Madison was to be inaugurated as fourth President of the United States. Thomas Jefferson worked diligently right up to his last day in office, but the same was not quite true of his Secretary of War. About the first of February Henry Dearborn quietly made arrangements with Jefferson for his political future. After recommending the appointment of two additional brigadier generals, to ease somewhat the administrative duties he was quitting, Dearborn received from Jefferson a near-midnight appointment. The Army's first word of Dearborn's abrupt departure was notification by the Adjutant and Inspector to General Wilkinson in New Orleans, on 18 February, that "The Secretary has been appointed Collector of the port of Boston and yesterday morning commenced his journey to that place. Col. Wade Hampton of South Carolina and General Gansevoort of Albany have been appointed Brigadiers in the Army of the United States."(9) The capable Chief Clerk, John Smith, became Acting Secretary of War for the remaining weeks of Jefferson's term.(10)

A degree of haste seems to have characterized the selection of the two new brigadier generals, the first appointed since 1799. Both had served during the Revolutionary War, Hampton as a colonel of South Carolina militia under Thomas Sumter, and Gansevoort as colonel of the 3d New York, celebrated as the defender of Fort Schuyler in 1777. In 1802 Peter Gansevoort, Jr., was major general of New York militia, commanding the western district, when he accepted the federal appointment as Military Agent for the Northern Department; he was serving quietly in that supply position when he was unexpectedly appointed a brigadier general of the line. Hampton had not served since the war until his appointment in late 1808 as colonel of light dragoons, followed a few months later by his advancement to brigadier general. Under the new arrangement, Gansevoort would command the Northern Department and Hampton the Southern, while James Wilkinson would continue in command of the forces on the Mississippi. No Commanding General of the Army was designated; except for the undeniable fact that Wilkinson's date of rank was 17 years senior, he was now one of three equals. One of Acting

Secretary Smith's last official acts was to approve a request by Colonel Jacob Kingsbury for an extension of his furlough. Claiming poor health, Kingsbury asked to remain in Connecticut until 1 May, after which he would begin the long trip to Detroit to relieve Colonel Burbeck. On 2 March Smith granted permission, which meant that it would be summer before the Chief of Artillerists could be at his post at Fort McHenry to resume supervision of the seacoast defenses.(11)

William Eustis as Secretary of War

James Madison was inaugurated on 4 March 1809, and the following week Major Nicoll, the Adjutant and Inspector, wrote General Wilkinson: "Among the heads of Departments the following changes have taken place:-Mr. Robert Smith is appointed Secretary of State, Doctor Eustace [sic] of Boston Secretary of War and Mr. Paul Hamilton of South Carolina Secretary of the Navy."(12) Thus unfamiliar to the Army was the new Secretary of War, William Eustis of Massachusetts.

Eustis, who took office on 8 April, was in his 56th year. A graduate of Harvard College in 1772, he had studied medicine and served as an army surgeon during the war, first with Knox's artillery and then in a military hospital. He resumed medical practice after the war, but gradually abandoned it for politics, in which he was an early Massachusetts anti-Federalist; he served two terms in Congress, but was defeated in 1804. Why Eustis was selected as Madison's Secretary of War is puzzling, except that in Congress he had consistently voted the Jeffersonian way—and perhaps because by now the War Department seemed a fief of Massachusetts, five of the first six secretaries having come from that state or its Maine district.(13) William Eustis was not without administrative talent, however, and was to identify and try to correct several basic flaws in organization and procedure authored by the more militarily experienced Henry Dearborn. As history as skimmed lightly over Dearborn's many faults as war secretary, so it has generally ignored Eustis's many contributions prior to the outbreak of war in 1812.

As Secretary Eustis assumed his duties, he was disconcerted by the lack of military advice available to him. In his first official letter to General Wilkinson at the end of April, he recorded his dissatisfaction that the senior officers of the Army were so scattered that he had no one to turn to for technical advice. For this reason, he told Wilkinson, he had written to General Hampton asking him to visit Washington at his earliest convenience—probably disquieting news to Wilkinson, who wanted no other general officer to have the new Secretary's ear.(14) Eustis also found that there was no general return available for the Army under the 1808 augmentation, and he directed the Adjutant and Inspector to prepare one as of the end of April. Within three weeks of taking office, the Secretary found himself bogged down in paper work, all directed to his office by several levels of administrative officers, most operating far from Washington.

The fact was that Eustis had inherited from his predecessor a weak and defective staff organization. The promising staff that had been put together by Hamilton and McHenry in 1793-99, with an Adjutant General, Quartermaster General, and strong Inspector General, together with the useful offices of Inspector of Artillery and Inspector of Fortifications, had all been wiped away by the economy-minded Jeffersonians on 16 March 1802. Lacking a Quartermaster General, Secretary Eustis had to rely on a five-headed supply arrangement consisting of the Purveyor of Public Supplies, the Superintendent of Military Stores, and three Military Agents, all reporting directly to the Secretary. Instead of an Inspector of Fortifications, Eustis found a Chief Engineer devoting his attention to New York Harbor almost exclusively, together with a long list of "agents for fortifications" at the various ports, each of whom seemed entitled to communicate directly with the War Department. While there *was* a Chief of Artillerists, who could be employed in lieu of a non-existent Chief of Ordnance, that officer was languishing in Detroit commanding the unimportant "Department of the Lakes"—Dearborn's creation. This

Henry Dearborn
Secretary of War, 1801-1809

William Eustis
Secretary of War, 1809-1813

Brigadier General
James Wilkinson
Senior General Officer, 1800-1812

Colonel Henry Burbeck
Chief of Artillerists, 1802-1812

Personalities
of the second system of
seacoast fortification
1807-1812

Colonel Jonathan Williams
Chief Engineer, 1802-03, 1805-12

Alexander Macomb
Corps of Engineers 1802-1812

Joseph G. Swift
Corps of Engineers, 1802-1818

Joseph G. Totten
Corps of Engineers, 1805-06, 1808-64

last problem could be rectified by getting Colonel Burbeck back to the seaboard as soon as possible, and the Secretary fired off a curt letter to Colonel Kingsbury, directing him to get himself to Detroit without further delay to relieve Burbeck.(15)

In Burbeck's absence the Secretary relied to some extent on the advice of the Chief Engineer. When Colonel Williams reported on the status of construction of the new castle on Governors Island, he asked that specific types of cannon be provided. Colonel Burbeck probably would have stuck to standard calibers, but the Secretary agreed that Henry Foxall at the Columbia Foundry would cast 15 new pieces to Williams's specifications. Like his predecessor, however, Eustis was concerned with economy, and he encouraged Williams and his officers to be careful about their expenditures. He specifically asked Williams for an estimate of the cost of all the federal works in New York Harbor, and made the decision that the circular fortification off the tip of the city and that in the Hudson off Hubert Street would each consist of only one tier of casemated guns.(16)

Another cloud that appeared early on the Secretary's horizon concerned the health of the troops in the New Orleans area. As a qualified if non-practicing physician, Eustis was conversant with medical matters, and when he saw a return by Colonel Alexander Smyth of the new Regiment of Riflemen that listed a quarter of his men on the lower Mississippi as sick, he at once wrote General Wilkinson on the subject, assuring him that necessary medical supplies and hospital equipment would be sent to the area at once. Despite Eustis's seeming best efforts, the mortality of the troops around New Orleans over the next year was to become one of the scandals of Madison's first term.(17)

Relations with Great Britain appeared to take a turn for the better in the spring of 1809, for the British minister in Washington announced that the Orders in Council would be modified and reparations offered for the attack on the *Chesapeake* two years earlier—an announcement subsequently repudiated in London. Under this erroneous impression, President Madison delivered a special message to Congress on 23 May, announcing, among other items, that he was cutting back the gunboat construction program; the fortifications construction would continue, however, and would require additional appropriations.(18)

A committee of the House at once called upon Secretary Eustis for specific estimates of the cost of the seacoast-defense program. Eustis, relying on Dearborn's records, reported that only $265,000 had been spent of the $4509000 appropriated on 10 February 1809. In addition to the unexpended $185,000, he estimated that a further $750,000 would be needed during the rest of 1809, of which $340,000 would be for New York City alone; if that sum were furnished, Eustis predicted rather unwisely, the system of defense contemplated by the government could probably be completed.(19) The new Secretary had yet to learn that providing an adequate defense for New York City alone could be like trying to fill a bottomless well.

In June the Secretary wrote on administrative matters to both the new brigadier generals. To Wade Hampton, commanding the department that included Virginia, the Carolinas, Georgia, and Tennessee—with headquarters at Columbia after 1 July—Eustis stressed that the troops should be concentrated for training, and the number of posts reduced; troop labor should be made available when possible for constructing the new seacoast defenses. To Peter Gansevoort at Albany, commanding the "Northern and Eastern States," the Secretary complained that every post, detachment, and recruiting party seemed to want to report directly to the War Department, and he desired General Gansevoort to filter those under his command through his own headquarters. Noting that the district from Massachusetts north was assigned to Colonel Boyd of the 4th Infantry, the Secretary now assigned the district around New York City to Colonel Jonas Simonds, about half of whose 6th Infantry had been sent to New Orleans; Simonds would furnish necessary troop labor to Colonel Williams of the Engineers for completing the fortifications in New York Harbor.(20)

Secretary Eustis inherited from his predecessor a project to produce a larger seacoast cannon than heretofore cast, one apparently designed for use in the casemates of the circular forts, or "castles," being erected in New York Harbor. The project probably originated with Colonel Williams who was determined to have the latest and most effective weapons mounted in the new fortifications, and in mid-1808 Henry Dearborn had taken a personal interest in the casting of the new cannon at Foxall 's Columbia Foundry, which the then-Secretary referred to as "the Columbiade."(21) During 1808 Colonel Burbeck had been in charge of testing the new guns, apparently none larger at the time than 50-pounders, but before the end of the year Burbeck had been sent off to Detroit and Colonel Williams had to furnish an inspector from the officers of the Corps of Engineers. The choice fell upon Captain George Bamford at Norfolk, and Bomford came to Washington to supervise tests to be conducted at the new federal arsenal at Greenleaf's Point. The selection was a good one, for Bomford had already shown an interest in ordnance matters and would eventually find his career in this field.

Eustis's interest in ordnance matters did not extend to viewing the actual tests, and in fact when they took place the Secretary was absent, visiting the seacoast forts in New York and New England in latter July of 1809, following which he took leave of absence at his home in Massachusetts until the end of September. The day the Secretary departed for New York, Chief Clerk John Smith wrote to one A.J. Villard that Eustis had left instructions "that he wishes the Columbiad to be mounted without delay."(22)

References to the "Columbiade" in 1808 did not specify either the caliber of the bore or the weight of the projectile, but from the fact that Colonel Williams subsequently mounted new 50-pounders in his castle on Governors Island, it seems evident that the earliest references to the Columbiad applied to those weapons. Just who coined the term is not recorded; it may have been Henry Dearborn, or it may have been Henry Foxall, in whose Columbia Foundry the guns were cast.(23) Fortunately, the test report of 1809 spells out exactly what caliber weapon and what weight of shot were used, because the acting Adjutant and Inspector, Lieutenant Colonel John Whiting of the 4th Infantry—Major Nicoll was on furlough—decided to forward the test results to Secretary Eustis in Boston, and thus copied the letter into the letter book of his own office:

> I have the honor to transmit you the results of experiments made at Greenleaf's Point the 20 & 21 inst by Captain Bomford of Engineers with the Columbiade of nine inch Caliber, and carrying a Ball of *100 lbs.* [Italics added.]
>
> The Piece placed at the distance of 440 yards from a mound of clay 11 feet in thickness, faced in front by 3 inch oak plank, secured to timbers 6 inches thick. & the rear by two inch pine. Three of the shot rested upwards of 200 rods beyond the mounds. [Here was copied a chart of charges and elevations used.] Note, the powder used in these experiments with a 5 1/2 inch Eprouvette, projected a 24 lb Shot 125 yards on a horizontal plane.
>
> The ground at this Post did not admit of a greater range; as it is, the accuracy of the Engineer does him much credit. When it is considered that these heavy pieces are cast near water transportation, it may be justly viewed as an increase of the means of defence in our Seaports.
>
> As General Dearborn interested himself much in this species of Ordnance, Captain Bomford thinks it would gratify him much to know the result.(24)

Despite the apparent detail of this report—as analyzed by an infantry officer—many questions

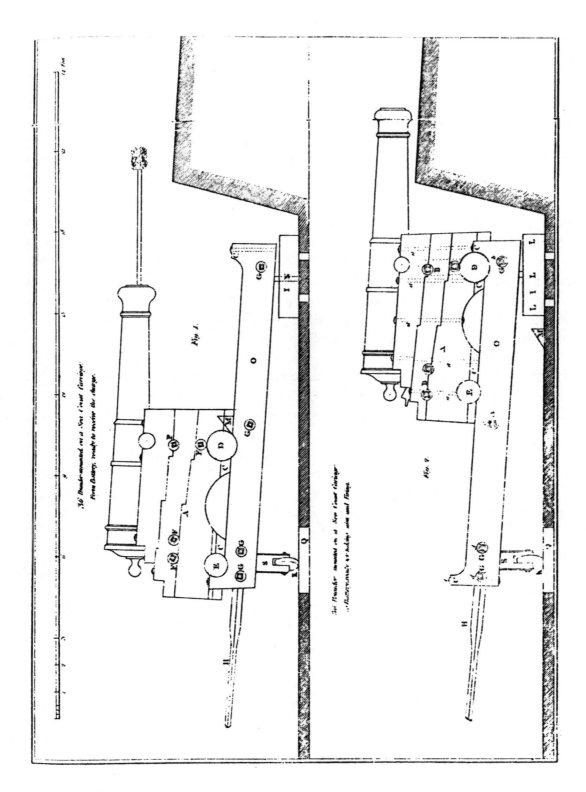

Seacoast cannon and carriage, ca. 1812. Shown is a 36-pounder, probably of French manufacture. The upper carriage is the naval truck type, mounted on a single-wheeled chassis pivoted at the front for use in a casemate. From Tousard, *American Artillerist's Companion.*

remain unanswered. While it seems clear that 100-pound solid shot was used, nothing is reported of the penetrating effect, although it can be inferred that three shot penetrated clay and plank and rolled to a stop 200 rods behind the mound. Similarly, it seems that the 9-inch tube, with a type of powder which would propel a 24-pound shot 125 yards, projected the 100-pound shot at least 440 yards "on a horizontal plane." Obviously both Bomford and Whiting were impressed by the results, but this particular version of the Columbiad was not adopted for service at this time. Less than two months later Colonel Burbeck, back on the seaboard for duty, was at Greenleaf's Point testing newly-cast cannon of the older and smaller pattern—24- and 32-pounders. Three 32 pounders out of 38 tested burst during proving; those that passed the test were forwarded to Colonel Williams in New York Harbor.(25)

Fortifications Construction in 1809

During the summer and fall of 1809 construction and repair of the seacoast defenses proceeded generally on schedule. Secretary Eustis took personal interest in viewing the progress in New York and southern New England, and Colonel Burbeck, on his return from Detroit at the end of July, visited the New England posts to inspect the armament and carriages, particularly the three-wheeled seacoast carriage that bore his name.(26) Construction activity in New England continued until early October, when Major Swift of the Engineers declared the season closed and his mission completed. By mid-November Swift had completed a report to the Secretary of War which indicated considerable progress in new construction.(27)

In the harbor of Portland, to reinforce the outdated Fort Sumner, two new works had been erected. Fort Preble, on Spring Point on the west side of the main channel, was a mixture of stone, brick, and sod capable of mounting 15 guns, including two 50-pounder Columbiads. On House Island, 3/4 of a mile away, was Fort Scammell, built of similar materials; mounting 15 guns and a 10-inch mortar, the new fort commanded White Head and Broad Sound passages into the harbor. (Fort Preble was named for Commodore Edward Preble, who died in Portland in 1807; Fort Scammell honored Colonel Alexander Scammell, mortally wounded at Yorktown.) At Kittery Point in Maine, across Portsmouth harbor from Fort Constitution, had been erected Fort McClary, a large elliptical battery of stone, brick, and sod enclosed with palisades, mounting 10 guns.

Fort Constitution had been extensively rebuilt as an enclosed work primarily of stone, with brick parapets and stone ramparts; built to accommodate 150 men, it mounted 37 guns and could take 10 more. There had been a brief setback at Fort Constitution during the 4th of July salute in 1809; as reported by the commander, Captain John DeB. Walbach, a corporal had placed a slow match too near an ammunition chest on the rampart, and the resulting explosion killed the corporal and seven other men and wounded several spectators. Captain Walbach had at once notified Major Swift, who came to Portsmouth to direct the necessary repairs to a shattered barracks and magazine.(28)

Minor additions only had been made to the batteries on Plumb Island in Newburyport harbor and at the head of Gloucester harbor; both had been furnished with 18-pounders on Burbeck carriages. Similar minor repairs and additions were made to Fort Pickering in Salem harbor and Fort Sewall at the entrance to the harbor of Marblehead; Fort Sewall, however, mounted eight guns, with room for 12 more.

Boston Harbor was the site of considerable construction at this early stage of the Second System. Fort Independence on Castle Island had received continuous repairs since its initial refurbishing in 1794; by 1809 it mounted 39 guns and could take 11 more, with facilities for a garrison of 400 men. The major effort at this time went to Governor's Island in the upper harbor, on which was erected a star fort of stone, brick, and sod, mounting 12 guns. The new fort was named Fort Warren, after Dr.

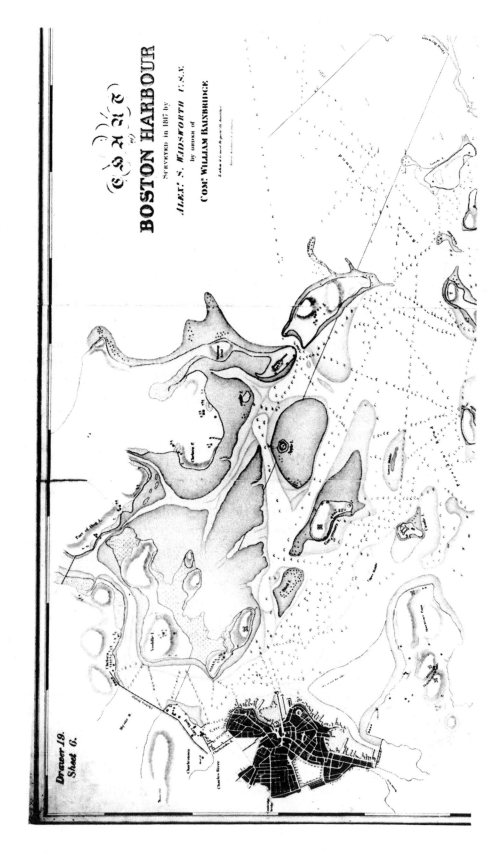

Boston Harbor at the Completion of Second System Construction

Fort Independence on Castle Island and Fort Warren on Governor's Island, defending the main entrance into the inner harbor.

Joseph Warren, killed at Bunker Hill. Water batteries were constructed on the south point and the west head of Governor's Island, each designed for 13 or 14 guns. An eight-gun battery was erected at the navy yard at Charlestown Point, the junction of the Charles and Mystic Rivers, and nearby a large brick magazine was erected for joint army-navy use.

South of Boston, an old enclosed fort in Plymouth harbor had been repaired with stone and sod. In the harbor of New Bedford a small enclosed fort was built on Eldridge Point; designed to take seven guns, it remained unnamed during this period.

Most of the defenses of Newport and Narragansett Bay, built by Louis Tousard during the First System, were falling into disrepair. The exceptions, as reported by Major Swift, were Fort Wolcott on Goat Island and Fort Adams at Brenton's Point, both of which were extended to take additional guns. Swift reported that quarters at all the Newport posts would accommodate 400 troops.

Lieutenant Joseph G. Totten reported the progress on the fortifications in Connecticut at the end of November.(29) At New Haven a small fort for six guns was erected well within the harbor; Totten's suggestion that the fort be named for General David Wooster, killed in 1777, was approved. Not reported by Totten in 1809 was Fort Hale, named for Nathan Hale, which had been started in 1808 at the eastern entrance to New Haven harbor; originally funded by local subscription, Fort Hale was subsequently garrisoned by federal troops. At New London, Totten reported extensive repairs to Fort Trumbull to enable that work to take 25 guns, of which 12 had been mounted.

In New York Harbor, as Colonel Williams notified the district commander, Colonel Jonas Simonds in early August, Fort Columbus was nearly completed; the Vauban-type work with four bastions and a ravelin, was designed for 104 guns of the heaviest types, of which 50-odd had been mounted by year's end. On the west tip of Governors Island the circular castle was also nearing completion, and near the end of the year Colonel Williams described its status:

> The Castle on the Point of Governors Island has eleven French 36's mounted & fifteen more have long been expected to arrive from the Columbian Foundry. These 26 may be ready for action as soon as they can be mounted.— Although it would be prudent to avoid putting Guns in the second tier until the arches are dry yet upon an emergency, 16 thirty two pounders might be placed there immediately. The force of this Castle when compleated may be considered at least 52 heavy Guns under a Bombproof cover & 48 on the terrasse above making 100 Guns, if it were necessary, 26 more might be put in the third tier of embrazures intended to serve as windows to the Barracks under the Arches.(30)

The other works in New York Harbor were in varying stages of completion. On Ellis's Island the enclosed masonry battery was ready to take 20 guns, and before the end of the year eight had been mounted. The work on Bedlow's (or Bedloe's) Island was progressing more slowly; it was to take 40 guns, but by the end of 1809 only its mortar battery was ready to receive its ordnance. The battery in the Hudson off Hubert Street, with only one tier authorized for completion, was ready to take 16 guns of the heaviest types. Off the point of the city's Battery, however, construction had just begun on a circular tower similar to the one on Governors Island. Colonel Williams summed up the capabilities of the New York defenses: "... the ordnance of this Harbour may be actually taken to be one hundred & sixty six Guns, so far as the Fortifications are ready & the ordnance that may be mounted when finished will be three hundred and four guns & ten Mortars without taking into account the State works at the Narrows which are now ready to receive upwards of eighty Guns."(31) Williams made a point of reminding his correspondents that the mounting of Guns does not belong to the Engineer Department, unless (according to the 63d article of war) the President of the United States were specially to order it; but this would be ordering me to take command of the Artillery whose duty it is."(32) (Wil-

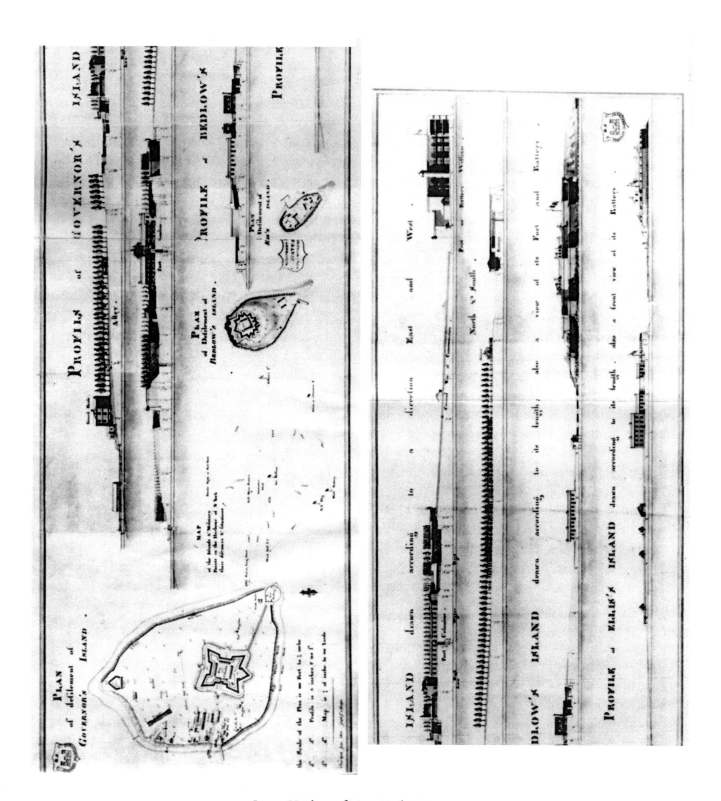

Inner Harbor of New York City, 1813
Plans and Cross-Section elevations of the Second System Works on Governors Island, Bedlow's Island, and
Ellis's Island. Drawn by Joseph Mangin.
Page 143

liams had every hope that this latter eventually would came to pass.)

Although Fort Mifflin in the Delaware was under Colonel Williams's direct supervision, he made no report concerning that work. Kept in generally continuous repair since a major effort in 1793, Fort Mifflin was thought to require no further construction or major repairs at this time. A bastioned work of masonry, it was designed to take 60 guns, of which 29 had been mounted, and included a water battery of eight guns, already mounted.

A report of progress in Maryland and Delaware was submitted by Captain George Bomford on 1 December. The work at Warburton, on the Potomac in Maryland, was now officially called Fort Washington. It was an enclosed work of masonry with a semi-elliptical face and circular flanks on the side facing the Potomac; it was designed as a two-company post and 15 guns had been mounted. Nearby, commanding Fort Washington, was a masonry tower for another company and six "18 lb Columbiads"—an unusual designation—which had not been mounted by the end of 1809. Under construction at Annapolis was Fort Madison, designed for a single company and 11 heavy guns, of which two 50-pounders had been mounted. At nearby Windmill Point a circular battery of masonry was under construction; designed for 11 guns, eight had already been mounted.(33)

Captain Bomford made no report on Fort McHenry at Baltimore. Like Fort Mifflin, the work at Whetstone Point had been garrisoned and kept in repair continuously since 1794, and required no major repair effort during the Second System. An enclosed pentagon of masonry with five bastions, it was designed for two companies and 40 guns; by the end of 1809, for reasons not indicated, only ten of these guns were mounted, but ten more were in place in a water battery.(34)

The defenses of Norfolk continued to receive attention, although by now many experts felt that the works, situated on both sides of the Elizabeth River west of the town, were badly sited; they gave no protection against a hostile force in Lynnhaven Bay, and were less than useless for denying entrance into the Chesapeake itself. By the end of 1809 Fort Nelson, an enclosed work of brick and earth supported by half bastions to take two companies and 40 guns, had 33 guns mounted. Fort Norfolk on the east bank, an enclosed masonry fort for two companies and 30 guns had only ten guns mounted. (35)

Fort Johnston on the Cape Fear River in North Carolina was far behind schedule. Not until December of 1809 did the state legislature finally cede the site to the United States—an earlier cession had been withdrawn because of title difficulties—and up to that time there had been difficulties with civilian contractors. At the end of the year only four of the 12 guns had been mounted, and Secretary Eustis decided to send Major Swift, whose work in New England was finished, to take charge of construction at Fort Johnston in 1810; in violation of regulations concerning Engineer officers, Swift was appointed post commander. He was also to keep his eye on the completion of a small enclosed work at Beaufort,(36) mounting five guns; either in 1809 or early 1810 this post was named Fort Hampton for the department commander.(37) (General Hampton, however, was transferred from the Southern Department at the end of the year, to relieve General Wilkinson in New Orleans so that Wilkinson could return to Washington to face another court of enquiry.(38)

Major Alexander Macomb, acting as Engineer for the Southern Department, had devoted most of his attention to the defenses of Charleston. By November 1809, however, Secretary Eustis was concerned with the mounting expenditures in Charleston, and wrote Major Macomb to cut back his program. He pointed out that the original estimate of $55,000 for Charleston had already been exceeded by $15,000, and directed Macomb to confine his attention entirely to Castle Pinckney. This work was similar in design to the Montalembert-inspired castles in New York Harbor, and had been planned for two tiers of casemated guns, but now Secretary Eustis told Major Macomb to complete the work in one tier only, "or at the height to which it may have been already carried."(39) The other works in the harbor were of conventional design. Fort Johnson, an enclosed work with masonry bastions and exterior batteries, would now hold two companies; of 40 guns planned, only 26 had been mounted by the end of 1809. Fort Moultrie, the refurbished Revolutionary War fort at the entrance to the harbor, was of similar design, but only seven of its 30 guns had been mounted. Fort Mechanic within the city was being considered a state fort, to be garrisoned by militia; the federal contribution to its armament seems to have been limited to guns on travelling carriages. Farther south at Beaufort a small enclosed work, as yet unnamed, awaited completion.(40)

In Georgia very little progress had been made since the destruction of Fort Greene in the hurricane of late 1804. Designs had been completed for a fort at Five Fathom Hole in the Savannah River about three miles below Savannah, and a battery of masonry for eight guns had been erected on marshy ground by the end of 1809; unfinished, it had been named Fort Jackson after former governor James Jackson, who died as a U.S. senator in 1806. Projected works in Savannah proper, and at St. Mary's on the East Florida boundary, were still held in abeyance pending cession of title to the land.(41)

In and below New Orleans Major William MacRea of the Artillerists, acting as the supervising engineer, had made satisfactory progress at Fort St. John and at English Turn. Secretary Eustis promised MacRea that an officer of Engineers would soon relieve him, and when General Hampton was ordered to New Orleans in late 1809 he asked for the services of Captain Charles Gratiot of Major Macomb's district, particularly as Gratiot came from the Louisiana region and spoke fluent French. Macomb and Eustis agreed, but the Secretary subsequently wrote Major MacRea that no Engineer officer would relieve him after all—which seems to indicate that Captain Gratiot was to be General Hampton's personal engineer advisor.(42) In any event, Major MacRea could take credit for all fortifications work since Captain Walker K. Armistead's departure, for John Foncin had not stayed in New Orleans long enough to make any substantial contribution. By the end of 1809 Fort St. Charles, in New Orleans proper, and Fort St. John, at the passage into Lake Ponchartrain, were substantially completed, the former mounting 19 guns, the latter only six. Below the city the unnamed fort at English Turn, an enclosed work with two bastions and a masonry battery with nine guns, was almost finished. Secretary Eustis urged MacRea to devote the bulk of his attention to Fort St. Philip, at Placquemines near the mouth of the Mississippi, which was being refurbished as an enclosed work of masonry and wood to take 20 guns.(43)

President Madison delivered his first Annual Message to Congress on 29 November 1809. He now reported officially that the British government had refused to ratify the concessions made by its minister in Washington—since replaced— and reminded Congress that he had reinstated the embargo by Executive proclamation on 9 August. The President's references to military affairs were brief; he noted that the defenses of New York, in particular, were not completed, and promised that the Secretary of War would furnish Congress a detailed report on the status of all seacoast fortifications.(44) Secretary Eustis was already laboring on that report, which he completed on 19 December.(45)

The Military Philosophical Society Meets in New York

The end of 1809 saw the last "occasional" meeting of the United States Military Philosophical Society for which minutes have survived, held at the City Hall in New York on 28 December. The host was Mayor DeWitt Clinton, whose interest in military engineering was doubtless stimulated by his appreciation of the problems of defending his city against naval attack. The meeting was attended by a large number of visitors, who withdrew at the end of the open session to allow the voting members to conduct a business meeting. Colonel Jonathan Williams, in the chair, addressed the meeting on a broad spectrum of subjects, many of them concerned with the progress of the Napoleonic wars. Contrasting the efficiency of the French armies to the disorganized condition of many of the American state militias, Williams stressed the motto of the Society, *Scientia in Bello Pax,* which he translated as "Science in war is the guarantee of peace." Following the formal address, Colonel Williams acknowledged recent acquisitions by the Society and the activities of some of its widely-scattered members:

> Major Zebulon Pike [the younger] has asked permission to dedicate his travels and discoveries of the sources of the Mississippi and the Arkensaw to this Society ... .
>
> Our Recording Secretary [Francis de Masson], who is at the same time professor of the art of an engineer in the military academy, has presented the Society with a manuscript copy of his lectures as far as they have been delivered. This work, when completed, will be a transmission of all that is known in Europe on this subject into our own language ... .
>
> Our member, Major [Amos] Stoddard, who commands the forts in this harbor [since early December], has notified his intention to publish a history and description of Louisiana ... as [it was] when it was delivered to us. [This important work appeared in 1812 as *Sketches, Historical and Descriptive, of Louisiana* .]
>
> Our constitution provides that the President of the United States shall be its patron. The consent of the *then* president was obtained before the clause was inserted, and I have the pleasure to announce to you that the *present* chief magistrate has not only accepted the same office, but has in the most obliging terms testified his high sense of the usefulness of our institution, and his disposition to afford us his paternal protection.(46)

At the following business meeting, the Treasurer reported that the six shares of stock in the Eagle Fire Insurance Company, contributed by Colonel Williams, yielded an income of $54 a year. Three works published by the Society since the Washington meeting were announced: Alexander Macomb's *A Treatise on Martial Law and Courts-Martial,* published in Charleston earlier in the year and distributed by the War Department as an official reference work; an anonymous *Short Essay on the Military Constitution of Nations,* published in New York in 1809 "by direction of the Society"; and Colonel Williams's translation of Tadeuz Kosciuszko's *Manoeuvres of Horse Artillery,* also published in New York in 1803. The Society continued to acknowledge its debt to its parent American Philosophical Society, in which Colonel Williams had been elected a counsellor in 1809 and to which Professor Ferdinand R. Hassler of the Military Academy was elected to membership the same year. Professor Hassler secured for the American Philosophical Society a set of official French weights and measures, and that Society's library received a copy of Williams's translation of Kosciuszko and bound copies of earlier minutes of meetings of the Military Philosophical Society.(47)

There had been a gain of 71 members since the Washington meeting of early 1808, bringing the total membership to 217, and by all indications the Military Philosophical Society was firmly established and on its way to a long and respected life. In fact, however, this occasional meeting in New York City was to be the last such gathering, and even the stated meetings at West Point became less and less frequent. As the number of cadets at the Military Academy fell off because of uncertainty as to the future location of the school—there was no graduating class in 1810—and as the officers of the Corps of Engineers scattered to their districts to supervise construction of fortifications, it became more and more difficult to assemble the necessary quorum of 20 members. Despite its bright promise as a harbinger of professionalism in the Army, the United States Military Philosophical Society was not to survive the outbreak of the War of 1812.(48)

Secretary Eustis Attempts Organizational Reforms

William Eustis has been assessed by historians as one of the weakest Secretaries of War prior to the reorganization of that office by John C. Calhoun after 1817. Yet the record shows clearly that Eustis recognized most of the organizational defects in his office and in the Army inherited from his predecessor and tried to do something about them. The year 1810 was the high point of the Secretary's efforts at reform; it was also the year in which, because of partisan politics and the uncertainties of the international situation, Congress was least willing to tackle the problems.

As reflected in his correspondence with senior officers of the Army as well as with the House committee on military affairs, Eustis felt that the Army generally lacked adequate representation at the seat of government. There was no designated Commanding General to whom the Secretary could turn for advice, and no qualified officers at the head of ordnance and quartermaster functions. The ordnance responsibilities in 1810 were badly fragmented. Actual procurement of weapons, including seacoast cannon, carriages and ammunition, was in theory a duty of the Purveyor of Public Supplies, Tench Coxe, but Coxe had no ordnance background and needed someone to spell out for him the desired specifications. That function was supplied on an *ad hoc* basis by the Chief of Artillerists, Colonel Burbeck, whenever that officer happened to be in the Washington area. The proving of weapons and their acceptance from the contractors had also been assigned to Burbeck although this responsibility could be delegated by him or assigned elsewhere by the Secretary. Once ordnance items were accepted by the government, they were either forwarded to the appropriate location or placed in storage; in either event the responsibility was that of the Superintendent of Military Stores, Callender Irvine, who exercised loose control over military storekeepers at certain posts like West Point which had since the Revolutionary Wart been designated as depots for military stores. Gunpowder was also produced under contract, the largest powder supplier being E.I. DuPont de Nemours in Delaware. Trying to bring some order to the ammunition program, Secretary Eustis had decided at the end of 1809 to place one officer at a central ammunition "laboratory." Learning of young Captain George Bomford's interest in ordnance matters, the Secretary directed Colonel Williams "to order Capt. Bomford to proceed to the Laboratory at N. York for the purpose of fixing ammunition; first for the Ordnance at the Post,- & afterwards as he shall be directed."(49) From this beginning, Bomford would remain on Ordnance service for almost 40 years.

Quartermaster functions were in almost complete disarray in early 1810. Although the Act of 16 March 1802 had provided for three Military Agents, the authors of the legislation augmenting the Army on 12 April 1808 had harked back to the 1799 example and provided for two brigade and eight regimental quartermasters for the new troops—but not for the "peacetime" regiments of 1802. Secretary Eustis approved of the regimental and brigade—or department—quartermasters, but complained to Congress that

> ... no provision is made for the appointment of an officer whose duty it should be to have charge of, and be responsible for, the property appertaining to that department, to regulate and superintend the distribution of supplies, *and to whom all subordinate officers should be accountable.*

> In want of such an officer, the Secretary of War has been obliged to perform the duties of Quartermaster General. Under the military peace establishment, these duties were laborious. Since raising the

additional military force, they have necessarily increased, until ... the Secretary of War cannot continue to discharge them, either satisfactorily to himself, or with justice to the public.

It is, therefore, respectfully suggested, that the President be authorized by law to appoint a Quarter-master General [and necessary assistants] ... .

In time of peace, the proposed system ... would instruct the officers in a branch of service acknowledged by military men to be of first importance.(50)

Not for over two years, however, would Congress get around to considering and eventually accepting Eustis's proposal.

The Secretary next determined to terminate the arrangement, authorized by President Jefferson, which allowed Jared Mansfield to serve as Surveyor General of the "Western Territory" while retaining his commission—now a lieutenant colonelcy—in the Corps of Engineers. He wrote Mansfield, stressing in particular the shortage of instructors for the Military Academy and "the importance of that Institution to the public interest,"(51) and directing him to relinquish his civil post and report to the War Department. "Should a compliance with this order be incompatible with your views," Eustis added, "you will perceive the necessity of relinquishing your commission in that Corps for the purpose of enabling the Executive to avail itself of the services of some other person."(52) Mansfield took the latter course: preferring to retain his position as Surveyor General, he resigned his Engineer commission in July.(53)

Eustis's next project was to try to regularize the chain of command of the seacoast defenses, but it was a slow process. The problem was two-fold: too few field officers of Artillerists were on the seaboard, and too many field officers of the 1808 augmentation had to be given commands commensurate with their rank. Thus in late 1809 the bulk of New England came under Colonel Boyd of the 4th Infantry; the New York City area under Colonel Simonds of the 6th Infantry; the Philadelphia region under Lieutenant Colonel William Jane of the Regiment of Riflemen; and the Charleston area under Lieutenant Colonel John Smith of the 3d Infantry. While none of these officers was causing any major problems, there was a strong need for qualified officers of Artillerists to exercise technical supervision and to provide direct command in those harbors garrisoned by more than one company.

The Secretary began reassigning senior officers of the Regiment of Artillerists before the end of 1809. Major Amos Stoddard, returning from the lower Mississippi, was in Washington in November, and on the 24th Secretary Eustis directed Stoddard to "repair to New York, take his Quarters at Fort Columbus, and take Command for the present of the Troops stationed in the different works in the Harbour of New York."(54) Major Stoddard's status was not entirely independent, however, for Colonel Williams considered that harbor as his own domain, and Colonel Burbeck visited the area periodically; still, as far as the troops were concerned, Stoddard commanded the entire installation.

The situation at Boston was similar. With Fort Warren on Governor's Island nearing completion, two companies of artillerists would be needed and a field officer would be desirable. About the first of the year Secretary Eustis directed Major Moses Porter, who was selecting defensive sites along the Maine coast, to report to Fort Independence; Colonel Boyd, the district commander, was notified that Porter would have "the immediate command of the Artillery in the Harbour of Boston, & the Superintendence of mounting the Ordnance."(55)

The only other harbors with multi-company garrisons were Norfolk, Charleston, and New Orleans. Norfolk had been commanded by Major John Saunders, now of the Light Artillery, but Saunders died unexpectedly on 15 March; gradually, without any specific order, the fortifications at Norfolk came under the district command of Colonel Edward Pasteur of the 3d Infantry, who established his headquarters at the newly-completed Fort Powhatan at Hood's Bluff on the James River. Charleston was in the district commanded by Lieutenant Colonel John Smith, an officer whose intermittent service went back to the old First American Regiment. The commander of Fort Johnson, Captain Addison B. Armistead, protested Smith's interjection into his chain of command, but the Adjutant and Inspector, on the Secretary's orders, advised Armistead that "Lieut Col Smith has the general command of the Troops in the States of So. Carolina and Georgia, at the same time he is considered as the immediate Commanding Officer in the harbor of Charleston ... ."(56) In and below New Orleans, Major William MacRea, in addition to his temporary duties as an engineer, was considered the commander of the seacoast defenses as far south as Fort St. Philip. This now left only two field officers of the Regiment of Artillerists not concerned with seacoast fortifications: Lieutenant Colonel Constant Freeman, in command of the frontier district based at Fort Claiborne at Natchitoches, and Major Abiael Y. Nicoll, the Adjutant and Inspector of the Army.

In the Spring of 1810 Secretary Eustis turned his attention to the Military Academy. Late the previous year Colonel Williams and other Engineer officers had drawn up detailed recommendations for improvements in the school, and at the beginning of 1810 Congress, considering possible legislation, called on the Secretary of War for a report of the status of the Academy and the Corps of Engineers. Eustis replied on 5 January that there were 16 officers in the Corps of Engineers, plus an artificer and 18 privates; the faculty of the Academy, excluding officers, consisted of two professors and one acting professor; and there were four cadets of Engineers and 43 of Artillerists.(57) The Corps of Engineers was still limited by law to 20 officers and cadets; thus with 16 officers there could be only four cadets of Engineers, so that all others were carried as artillerists, and from time to time one or two of them would be transferred to the Engineers as vacancies occurred in the four spaces.

Congress debated the proposed changes in March and April. Generally, the proposals called for an increase in the Corps of Engineers, more faculty members for the Academy with assimilated military rank, and movement of the school from West Point to a location near Washington.(58) Secretary Eustis favored all the proposed changes, but does not appear to have pushed them very strongly; he called Colonel Williams to Washington in early April to argue on behalf of his proposals, but to no avail. Partisan politics intruded in 1810, and for reasons having little to do with its merits, the Engineer bill failed to pass.(59)

Perhaps to compensate for the failure of the bill, Secretary Eustis drew up in mid-May a list of regulations for the Military Academy and forwarded it, with a covering letter, to Colonel Williams. It is almost certain that Eustis meant well and thought he was tightening the administration of the Academy and the Army, but his letter contained a bombshell:

> After the Cadets shall have completed their Academical Education, it is intended that they shall be attached to Companies and perform Duty *as Soldiers in the Line*, in order to their becoming Candidates for promotion to Commisions. By Courtesy, Cadets are generally allowed to Quarter and Mess with the Officers of the Company to which they are attached ... .(60)

The enclosed regulations did not yet provide for this proposed post-graduation demotion, but were concerned with such matters as entrance requirements, leaves of absence, and eligibility for graduation. For the first time the Superintendent was to establish a single uniform for all cadets, without regard to "their respective Corps." And it was provided that "Interior Regulations shall be made by the Superintendent for the time being, provided that no existing Regulations be altered or counteracted without special order of the Commandant of the Corps of Engineers"—which was curious, because the law provided that the Chief Engineer was also the Superintendent. Finally, the Secretary referred to an annual vacation from 15 December-15 March, "while the Academy remains at West Point."

This reiteration of the possibility that the Academy would eventually move from West Point caused some problems, but it was the statement in the covering letter, that graduated cadets would be sent off to do duty as line soldiers, that really upset the officer and cadets. After all, a young man could become a soldier simply by taking a dollar from a recruiting sergeant, and a graduated cadet was not likely to appreciate the prospect of serving as a soldier indefinitely while—as he had seen in 1808 and 1809—other young men were offered lieutenancies and even captaincies directly from civil life. Within a matter of days after the Secretary's letter arrived at West Point, four cadets resigned.(61) Colonel Williams hastened to write Eustis in late May, protesting the proposal, and Eustis backed off. The Secretary replied that he still felt it would be proper for graduated cadets to serve in the ranks until vacancies occurred, when they could be promoted—not appointed—to commissioned rank. But Eustis was not adamant; he wrote that if Williams had serious objections, they would be considered before the plan was codified in Army Regulations.(62) In the end the Secretary realized that he had been hasty, and the idea was quietly dropped.

The Military Academy was slowly wasting away in 1810 for lack of cadets and an adequate faculty, but it is difficult to blame William Eustis for this situation. If the Secretary was opposed to the Academy in principle, as some historians have argued, he did not commit such opposition to paper. His expressed view was that the Madison administration was fully behind the school, and that an indifferent Congress was the villain—a view that receives considerable support from the record. Even though Congress had failed to pass the Engineer and Military Academy bill in 1810, Secretary Eustis was ready and willing to try again. Writing to Colonel Williams near the end of the year, Eustis was still confident a bill would pass:

> The subject of the Military Academy will be recommended to the consideration of Congress by the President. An extension of the establishment to embrace a branch of the present, or the institution of another academy at the seat of Government will be recomended. The President and I may add, the whole executive, coincide most entirely in the opinion I have ever entertained of the usefulness and importance of this branch of instruction, and from the favorable opinions I have observed in the members of the Legislature, I entertain strong hopes that adequate provision will be made ... .(63)

New York Harbor: A New Fort and a New Commander

The second half of 1810 saw two changes in command along the Atlantic seaboard. The first was not unexpected, and was indeed overdue. Lieutenant Colonel Constant Freeman, having spent over six years on the southwest frontier, most recently at the isolated post of Fort Claiborne at Natchitoches, returned to the Atlantic coast on furlough, visiting his wife's family, with the expectation that he would be reassigned to seacoast-defense duty. At about the same time Colonel Pasteur at Fort Powhatan decided to leave the service, and Secretary Eustis decided to replace him with Freeman. Major Nicoll wrote to Freeman in October, directing him to relieve Pasteur in command of the district and also to assume direct command of the defenses of Norfolk. Freeman was to occupy quarters at either Fort Norfolk or Fort Nelson, as convenient, and to supervise the district extending from Fort Powhatan on the James south to Fort Hampton at Beaufort, North Carolina. Shortly thereafter the post of Fort Johnston on the Cape Fear River, commanded by Major Swift of the Engineers, was assigned to Colonel Freeman's district.(64)

The second change in command was unexpected and less easy to justify. Having taken steps to establish Colonel Burbeck at Fort McHenry as overall commander of the seacoast defenses, and to install field officers of Artillerists in command of harbors with multi-company garrisons, Secretary Eustis made a complete about-face in mid-1810. Despite the fact that Major Stoddard had been named commander of the garrisons in New York Harbor only some six months earlier, the Secretary decided to place the Chief of Artillerists himself in command of the defenses of that important port. To that end Eustis wrote to Burbeck on 12 June, announcing his new assignment:

> You will immediately repair to New York, take your Quarters at Fort Columbus, and assume command of the Works and Troops in the Harbour of New York.
>
> Your first object will be to direct the labour of the Troops to the completing the Fortifications ... and to use your utmost exertions to have the Works completed, the Cannon mounted, & every necessary preparation made to fit them for action: to have the Officers and men not on fatigue trained to the use of the Guns ... .
>
> As it is determined that the Works shall be completed in the course of the present Working Season, you will consult Col. Williams and give him every possible aid in effecting it.(65)

The Secretary then wrote to Colonel Williams on the subject, noting simply that from "confidence in the attention and industry of Col. Burbeck and in his experience in the Ordnance Department, as well as his conversance with all the practical operations relating to Works, I have ordered him to take the command in the Harbour of New York," adding in general terms his confidence that the Chief Engineer would cooperate fully with the new commander.(66)

In the same letter, however, Eustis made some mild criticism of the expense of the works being completed in New York Harbor, and a week later he wrote more bluntly. Many of the magazines being built in the area were too large, he felt, and some were located too near the batteries they were to serve. He had also heard, but affected not to believe, a report that Williams had departed from his instructions by raising the battery in the Hudson off Hubert Street to a second tier. Finally, pointing out that this would be the last working season on the fortifications, Eustis advised Williams not to make any arrangements for housing his family in the city.(67)

Colonel Williams was stung by the criticism, and by the implication that Colonel Burbeck was coming to New York to rectify Williams's errors. He was also probably irked that the command of "his" harbor was being given to an experienced officer, considerably senior to him, whom he could hardly expect to manipulate. Williams's reply to the Secretary was correct but cool:

> In my orders of July 1807 ... there is no limitation respecting funds, and it became my duty to make the required plans adequate to the intended object of defence, rather than to confine them within narrow & ineffectual limits. I have had no control in the pecuniary part of the execution, rather than designating the worksmanship and requisite materials ... . You will perceive by examining the orders, that I have [omitted] the proposed Works on Butter-milk Channel and on Ellis's Island ... .
>
> I hope I may without the appearance of vain boasting call your attention to the date of those orders, & remind you that although three years have not yet elapsed, these works are, some of them finished, and others so far advanced as to afford a reasonable prospect that this harbour will in less than six months show a force of 300 Guns on Forts calculated to endure for ages, plan'd and (hitherto) executed by me ... . (68)

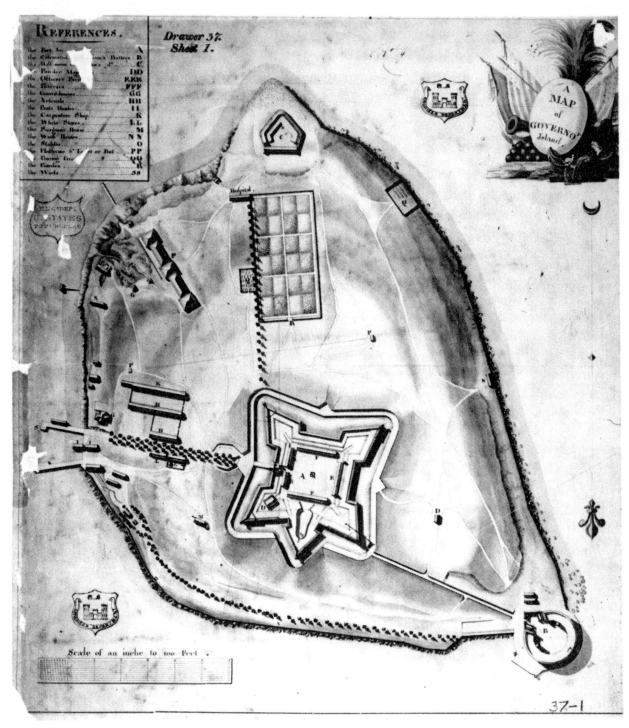

Governors Island, New York Harbor--A Blend of Two Defensive Theories
Fort Columbus (center) and South Battery (top) of the Vauban pattern; Castle Williams (lower right) based
on the Montalembert design. Ca. 1813

Secretary Eustis, perhaps because of the "(hitherto)", read into Williams's letter an impending request to be relieved from superintendence of the New York fortifications. Eustis replied, probably unnecessarily, that the War Department held to a strict policy that "all works should be completed by the officer who commenced them"; if such a policy had ever been enunciated, it had been violated more often than not. But the Secretary knew what really rankled the Chief Engineer, and he added: "Should Col Burbeck, or any other Officer, so far mistake his own authority as to interpose or interfere in any respect with the proper duties or authority of the Engineer, he will be held responsible."(69)

For the moment this mollifying tone averted a crisis. Although it was clear to all concerned that there was now one colonel too many in New York Harbor, it does not appear that there ensued any personal friction between Burbeck and Williams—a tribute more to Burbeck's easy-going personality, in all likelihood, than to Williams's acute sensitivity. The two officers cooperated well, and the last months of 1810 saw several favorable developments. One of the most significant for the long term was the willingness of the state of New York to begin negotiations with the federal government to cede the land and the state-built fortifications at the Narrows between Staten Island and Brooklyn. The terms and conditions proposed by the legislature, forwarded, to the War Department by Governor Daniel D. Tompkins, were restrictive, and it appeared that negotiations would be lengthy. Secretary Eustis advised Colonel Williams that the final decision would be delayed, and in fact the state cession was not completed until after the outbreak of war in 1812.(70) Another development in New York Harbor was a personal triumph for Jonathan Williams, and his monument to posterity. By mid-November the circular castle on the west tip of Governors Island, designed after Montalembert's general theories as Williams's significant contribution to American military architecture, was completed. Colonel Burbeck prepared to assign a garrison, and a few days later the new work was christened with some fanfare:

Orders Fort Columbus 24 November 1810

In future the Stone Tower on this Island (by the approbation of the Secretary of War) will bear the name of Castle Williams, in honor of the commandant of the United States corps of Engineers, who designed and erected it. And on Monday next, at 12 O'clock, a national salute of seventeen 42 pounders will be fired from the lower battery of Castle Williams, in commemoration of the 25 of November 1783, the day on which the British troops evacuated the city of New York.

Henry Burbeck, Colonel, Commndg Harbor N. York(71)

The naming of the new fortification in his honor pleased Colonel Williams immensely, and went a long way to mollify his irritation at not being senior officer in the harbor. Two days after the great salute, Williams wrote Secretary Eustis: "I take the earliest opportunity of expressing my gratitude for the high honour conferred upon me by adding my name to the Castle I erected... . Be assured Sir, that I shall make it a Study of the remaining portion of my life to deserve the confidence of the Government, and nothing can at any time give me greater Satisfaction than to know that I have added a mite to the defence of our happy Country."(72) This euphoric glow was to last less than two years, but Castle Williams on Governors Island was to prove its builder's boast that the forts he had constructed would "endure for ages." A century and a half after his death, Castle Williams still stood like a rock in New York Harbor, never challenged by enemy guns, but an enduring monument to the architectural design and construction techniques of Jonathan Williams, president of the United States Military Philosophical Society, counsellor of the American Philosophical Society, and first Chief Engineer of the United States Army.

CHAPTER XI
TO THE EVE OF WAR
1811-1812

The military objectives for 1811 were set, as was now customary, by the President's annual message to Congress in December 1810. Long-range plans still depended upon the reaction of the British government to the American demands for reparations for the *Chesapeake* incident and for assurances as to the rights of American and other neutral vessels in time of war. As President Madison expressed it, "In the midst of uncertainties necessarily connected with the great interests of the United States, prudence requires a continuance of our defensive and precautionary arrangements." He reported that the seacoast fortifications were generally completed and their armament in place, but admitted that certain defenses, notably those in New York Harbor, needed further time and money. The manufacture of cannon and small arms, in both government-owned and private facilities, was progressing well. The Military Academy, however, needed attention, and President Madison stressed the importance of that institution with a degree of understanding that his predecessor had not shown:

> The Corps of Engineers, with the Military Academy, are entitled to the early attention of Congress. The buildings at the seat fixed by law for the present Academy are so far in decay as not to afford the necessary accommodations. But a revision of the law is recommended,[for] providing professorships for all the necessary branches of military instruction, and by the establishment of an additional academy at the seat of Government or elsewhere.... these schools of the more scientific operations [are an] indispensable part of every adequate system. Even among nations whose large standing armies and frequent wars afford every other opportunity of instruction these establishments are found to be indispensable.... In no other way, probably, can a provision of equal efficacy for the public defence be made at so little expense or more consistently with the public liberty....(1)

The House at once appointed committees to consider various aspects of the President's message, and the committee charged with land forces and fortifications asked Secretary of War Eustis for a report on the status of the seacoast defenses and recommendations as to appropriations required during 1811. The Secretary's reply on 8 January indicated that New York and Charleston still required the most money and effort, but for 1811 the third priority would go to Newport rather than New Orleans. About $83,000 was needed in New York Harbor, of which some $56,000 would go toward completion of the castle off the tip of Manhattan to two tiers for 56 guns; about $19,000 was required to complete the work on Bedloe's Island, and a modest $8,000 or so would put the finishing touches to Castle Williams on Governors Island. For South Carolina and Georgia the Secretary asked for $55,000, the bulk to go to Charleston. For the harbor of Newport and the entrance to Narragansett Bay, one of the most difficult of all regions to defend, Eustis asked only $10,000; while this sum was clearly inadequate, it seemed large by comparison with the $12,000 that the Secretary felt would provide necessary repairs for all the remaining coastal forts. Eustis reported, nevertheless, that nearly $30,000 remained unexpended from former appropriations.(2)

Engineer Organization and Activities in 1811

In February Secretary Eustis finally proposed to the President that the vacant lieutenant colonelcy in the Corps of Engineers, created by the resignation of Jared Mansfield seven months earlier, be filled by the promotion of the senior major, Alexander Macomb. Madison approved, the Senate consented, and on 6 March Eustis notified Macomb of his promotion, at the age of not quite 29, to be second-in-command of the Corps. Macomb's advancement set off the usual chain reaction: Walker K. Armistead was promoted to major, Alden Partridge to captain, and Joseph G. Totten to 1st lieutenant; the vacant 2d lieutenancy was filled by the appointment of Cadet Alexander J. Williams, a son of the Chief Engineer.(3)

Lieutenant Colonel Macomb continued to act as Engineer for the district comprising the Carolinas and Georgia, devoting most of his efforts to Charleston. Captain William McRee assisted in Charleston, while Major Joseph G. Swift was back at Fort Johnston on the Cape Fear River, acting as both supervising engineer and commanding officer. Most of Macomb's attention was now given to the reconstruction of Castle Pinckney, conceived of as a smaller version of Castle Williams. At the beginning of the year Macomb had reported that the brick work was completed and efforts concentrating on the gun platforms, to be constructed of planking; because of a recent destructive fire in Charleston, wood was difficult to procure. Anticipating completion of Castle Pinckney, Secretary Eustis directed the Superintendent of Military Stores to ship to Charleston 25 24-pounders recently inspected by Colonel Burbeck; why larger guns were not being provided is not clear.(4) Eustis also decided that Fort Mechanic in Charleston proper was of no long-term value, writing Macomb that knowledgeable civilians had advised him that the expansion of the city below the fort would soon make that work useless.(5) When Colonel Macomb left Charleston during the summer he reported that Fort Moultrie had been completely enclosed, but still lacked outer works; Fort Johnson had been rebuilt according to plan; and Castle Pinckney was "in a great state of fowardness."(6)

In New York City progress was hampered by the necessity of ordering Colonel Williams to Washington to sit on a board of officers investigating General Wilkinson's charges against the fiery Captain Winfield Scott of the Light Artillery.(7) As Colonel Burbeck was assigned to the board also, the command of the harbor garrisons reverted to Major Amos Stoddard, while to supervise construction Captain George Bomford had to be pulled away from his ordnance duties in the New York arsenal known as "the Laboratory." Bomford tried for a while to handle both duties, but at the end of March Secretary Eustis directed him to turn over the Laboratory to Cadet William Cutbush from the Academy:

> ... you will take your quarters at Fort Columbus, and give directions for uncovering the walls of the Battery at West Head [of Manhattan], have them carried up to the proper height for one tier of Guns, and the battery completed .... After this shall have been commenced, you will likewise direct and superintend the finishing of Castle Williams. The Iron railing will be put up; the flooring laid over the second story ... the gate way of plain stone work, with a plain arch over the gate with a table of inscription for the words Castle Williams, with the month & year in which it was completed— an Eagle over the centre and no other ornamental work.(8)

Captain Bomford carried out these duties promptly, and less than two months later Eustis wrote him to proceed to the works on Bedlow's Island.(9) Despite the higher priority assigned to Newport for 1811, no officer of Engineers was assigned there after Major Swift's transfer to North Carolina. Secretary Eustis decided that since most of the remaining work involved constructing carriages and mounting guns, it could be entrusted to an officer of Artillerists. Major Moses Porter, commanding in Boston Harbor, was directed to spend some time in Newport, as he had done the previous year, and Captain James House, newly-arrived commander of Fort Wolcott, was designated as assistant military agent for the harbor and given $500 for material for carriages. Late in March the Secretary directed Major Porter to visit Fort Trumbull at New London; the seacoast carriages there were in a poor state of repair, and Eustis hoped that Porter's artificers could rebuild them as soon as they could be spared from Newport.(10) By mid-May the Secretary realized that Porter was spreading his meager resources too thinly, and told him to concentrate on Newport; he could decide whether to give priority to Fort Wolcott or Fort Adams.(11)

Meanwhile another Engineer function, the operation of the Military Academy, was suffering. When Colonel Williams completed his duties on the board of officers in Washington, he was notified by the Secretary to proceed to West Point, his presence being "peculiarly desirable in the present state of the Academy."(12) This "present state" was not spelled out, but Eustis was referring to an increasing discontent among the officers at having to instruct cadets, particularly those not of the Corps of Engineers. Colonel Williams returned to West Point to assess the situation, and seems to have agreed with his officers; he reported to the Secretary on 27 May in a letter which showed a certain lack of leadership as well as a profound pessimism regarding the future of the Military Academy:

> I found at West Point, exclusive of the Engineers, one professor of the French Language and five artillery Cadets. The Engineers are pursuing the Instruction to be derived from the professor, and such Library as they have; and the artillery Cadets having generally gone through the ordinary mathematical studies are in a situation to be instructed in the same manner. It is not to be presumed that any greater extent can be given to the military academy while its means are in the present confined state, nor ... untill Congress shall appoint proper professors, and form a Body of Scholars.

> The Officers of the Corps of Engineers have ... signified their "Opinion that the Law did not oblige them to become Tutors to any other branch of the army, the words being that the Corps of Engineers shall constitute the academy." ... This I state as the substance of *their* avowed Opinion, upon which I make no comment. The expectation that Congress would pass such Laws as have been several times recommended by successive Presidents, has hitherto induced my officers not to agitate any questions of this sort; but now that all hopes have vanished, they have come to a determination not to take charge of the Instruction of any Cadet not belonging to the Corps... .

> From this representation ... you will probably conclude to distribute [the cadets] among the Garrisons, which is in my opinion the best stations they can have untill you think proper to give them Commissions. I have sent Cadet H.J. Williams, my younger son, to Dartmouth College.(13)

This abject assessment of the Academy struck no responsive chord with the Secretary of War. Had William Eustis been opposed to the idea of a military academy, as often charged, this letter from the Chief Engineer would have been adequate ammunition for recommending the closing of the school; opponents of the Academy would have been interested indeed to learn that Colonel Williams— without any War Department authority—had withdrawn his own son from the Academy and sent him to a civilian college. But Eustis by no means favored closing the school, even temporarily, and the asperity of his reply must have surprised Williams:

> To disperse the Cadets by attaching them to companies at the present time and under the present circumstances of the Academy appears to be inexpedient. Let them remain and receive such instruction as is provided. Without exam[ining] the position taken by the Officers of the Corps of Engineers it is to be regretted that under existing circumstances a disposition is discovered to avoid the performance of any duties (whether they are strictly required by law or not) which can possibly be applicable to the small number of Cadets present at the Academy... .(14)

Weakening his firm reply here, Secretary Eustis two weeks later wrote to an applicant for a cadetship that "in the present state of that institution it is not judged expedient to add to its number. "(15) Historians have used that note to assume that Eustis was trying to destroy the Academy by appointing no cadets, but the phrase "present state" would seem to derive directly from the uncertainties surrounding the school—its future location, whether additional branches or campuses might be established, and whether in fact Congress would even take up the Engineer-Academy bill again in 1811. (As it turned out, the bill was not passed until the very eve of war in 1812.) Secretary Eustis's position was expressed clearly to Senator Samuel Smith of Maryland at the end of the summer:" Until Congress shall provide either at West Point or at some other place quarters for the accommodation of the military academy, it is not considered justified to increase the number of students ... ."(16) It is difficult to argue that logic.

So the Academy remained in operation during 1811, with Colonel Williams in charge, assisted by Major Walker K. Armistead, for much of the year. Captain Charles Gratiot, after service with General Hampton in New Orleans, was assigned to West Point, and Captain Alden Partridge was given a furlough to pursue civilian studies. Lieutenant Sylvanus Thayer was assigned to assist Captain Bomford in New York Harbor, and was replaced at West Point by Lieutenant Eleazer D. Wood. Although no cadets had been graduated in 1810, 19 had been commissioned on 1 March 1811—two months before Colonel Williams's pessimistic assessment—including Williams's elder son Alexander, who had spent nearly six years at the school. The Academy was by no means in a healthy condition, but in mid-1811 it was far from dead.(17)

Tactical and Administrative Diversions

In retrospect, 1811 was a critical year in which every effort should have been made, in view of the imminence of war with Britain, to complete the seacoast defenses and to finish recruiting the 1808 additional Military Force. But in addition to Congressional partisanship and general inactivity, 1811 turned out to be a year of many diversions from the Army's primary missions.

The first diversion took place in West Florida, in the region claimed by both Spain and the United States, by the latter as part of the Louisiana Purchase. American settlers in the Baton Rouge district rebelled against the Spanish administration in 1810, whereupon some of General Hampton's troops were sent to take possession of the disputed area; the region thus seized was incorporated into Mississippi Territory and what became the state of Louisiana in 1812. An attempt in early 1811 to seize the region of East Florida, without firm sanction from Washington, was eventually unsuccessful.(18) Although neither of these diversions directly affected the seacoast defenses, both required men and money that could have been used elsewhere; the East Florida adventure, in particular, diverted men and weapons to the St. Mary's River at the expense of the rest of the Atlantic coast.(19)

Of less historical interest, but even greater diversions of the Army's officer strength, were the general courts-martial held during 1811, which involved almost every senior officer and brought organization and training nearly to a standstill. The largest and most time-consuming of the trials involved, as usual, Brigadier General James Wilkinson. Wilkinson, who had been embroiled in legal controversies almost continuously for over a decade, was to be tried on eight-charges—"being a pensioner of Spain, treasonable projects for the dismemberment of the United States, conspiracy with Aaron Burr, conniving at treasonable designs, conspiring against a friendly nation, disobedience of orders, neglect of duty, misapplication and waste of public funds."(20) One of the specifications alleged that Wilkinson had been responsible for the very high mortality rate among his troops on the lower Mississippi in 1808 and 1809, a most serious charge in the eyes of physician William Eustis. The Wilkinson trial and another general court-martial were to convene at Frederick Town, Maryland, at the beginning of September; a third court was to assemble soon afterward in the Mississippi Territory. For the two courts in Frederick Town all four field officers of the Corps of Engineers— Colonel Williams, Lieutenant Colonel Macomb, and Majors Swift and Armistead—and four of the six field officers of the Regiment of Artillerists—Colonel Burbeck, Lieutenant Colonel Freeman, and Majors Porter and Stoddard— were assigned as members. Wilkinson's trial, for the first time, was presided over by an officer of equal rank, Brigadier General Peter Gansevoort. In addition to the members, many other officers would be required as witnesses at the several trials, and it was apparent that the seacoast defenses would be neglected by both Engineers and Artillerists for most of the remainder of 1811.(21)

The other major diversion of 1811 was the outbreak of Indian activity in Indiana Territory, "where Governor William Henry Harrison was concerned about the Shawnee chief Tecumseh and his brother Tenskwatawa, the "Shawnee Prophet." Harrison called upon President Madison for federal troops to reinforce his territorial militia, and with the President's consent Secretary Eustis decided to send Harrison the 4th Infantry under Colonel John P. Boyd. Stationed in New England to recruit and to reinforce the small seacoast-defense garrisons, the regiment had already been alerted for movement to the lower Mississippi; five companies were withdrawn from the Boston area, one from Fort McClary at Portsmouth, and two, with a company of riflemen, from Newport. Boyd and his command were ordered to proceed down the Ohio and up the Wabash to join Governor Harrison, and from July through the end of 1811 the 4th Infantry occupied much of the time and energies of the Army's ill-organized supply system.(22) The effort was justified, for Colonel Boyd and his men performed effectively at the Battle of Tippecanoe on 7 November, and Boyd returned to Washington in mid-December to find himself something of a military hero.(23)

The Seacoast Garrisons at the End of 1811

In August, as the senior officers began the journey to Frederick Town, seconds-in-command took over the seacoast defenses. In the absence of both Colonel Boyd and Major Porter the defenses of Boston were the responsibility of Captain Nehemiah Freeman of Fort Independence, who was also district paymaster, while in Newport the command devolved upon Major Abraham Eustis, the senior officer of light Artillery and the Secretary's nephew. In New York, with Colonel Burbeck and Major Stoddard gone and the veteran Captain Richard Whiley having resigned at the end of June, the several harbor garrisons came under the temporary command of Captain Moses Swett, whose company manned Fort Columbus. And so it went along the seaboard; even at Point Petre, built up in connection with the East Florida enterprise, the garrison was temporarily commanded by Major Jacint Laval of the Light Dragoons.(24)

The absence of the senior officers of Engineers and Artillerists threw a particularly heavy burden on the Secretary of War. Details of fortification construction and repair, mounting of cannon, contracting for ammunition, and many other aspects of engineering and ordnance had to be assumed by Eustis himself during the last months of 1811. During August and September, as examples, the Secretary wrote to Du Pont de Nemours on a contract for 20,000 pounds of cannon powder, to the assistant military agent at Fort McHenry on the subjects of gun carriages and cannon wadding, to Major MacRea at New Orleans reporting the shipment of 24-pounders for the battery—known as Fort St. Leon—at English Turn, and to the Superintendent of Military Stores to assure him, who should have known, that 30,000 pounds of gunpowder remained on hand at Fort Constitution.(25)

In November the Secretary recommended to the President the appointment of John Rogers Fenwick, late captain in the Marine Corps, to be lieutenant colonel and senior officer of the Regiment of Light Artillery, which was confirmed as of 2 December.(26) General Gansevoort, however, felt strongly that the appointment should have gone to Major Moses Porter of the Artillerists, a veteran of the Revolutionary War and of 25 years' continuous service in the Regular Army. In reply to Gansevoort's remonstrance, Secretary Eustis replied with some surprise that he thought highly of Major Porter, "and had an intimation been given that he would relinquish his present rank & command for a higher grade in the Light Artillery," Porter would have been selected.(27) The Secretary was quite sincere and his point was sound. In 1811 a clear distinction was still made between the Military Peace Establishment of 1802 and the Additional Militia force of 1808; the former was relatively permanent, while the latter could well be disbanded if and when relations with Britain improved. Eustis was probably correct in doubting that Porter would give up his permanent majority for a temporary lieutenant colonelcy, which might subject him to future disbandment. General Gansevoort's strong recommendation of Moses Porter would be remembered several months later.

On 5 November President Madison delivered his eagerly-awaited Annual Message, making it plain that he entertained little hope of Britain's revoking the Orders in Council. While the President was not yet ready to call for war, he discussed "ominous indications" and outlined steps he had taken for the "general security." He mentioned the seacoast forts, the gunboats, and the militia, and recommended that Congress make adequate provision "for filling the ranks and prolonging the enlistments of the regular troops." He announced that the manufacture of cannon and small arms was proceeding as planned, and that adequate stocks were on hand for emergencies; he felt, nevertheless, that Congress should authorize an augmentation of such stocks.(28) Congress took the presidential admonition seriously, and for the next six weeks a committee undertook an independent investigation of the American munitions industry as of the end of 1811. The report presented to the House on 16 December was optimistic in the extreme:

> The flourishing state of the foundries throughout the United States ... demonstrate the great resources of this republic. What nation can boast of more or better iron than the United States? Our foundries ... have arrived at perfection. Upon the best authority, we state the furnaces, forges, and bloomeries ... to be five hundred and thirty. The art of boring cannon ... is so well understood, that an inspector of our artillery has declared to the World *"he never was compelled to reject a gun on account of a defect in the bore,"* though he examined *"upwards of two thousand cannon of different calibers."*
>
> It is notorious that we may have lead, from the mines of our country, to any amount. Of sulphur we have a considerable stock in store. Each of the States can furnish an extensive catalogue of powder mills; their number in the United States amounts to two hundred and seven.... . Notwithstanding ... under the present aspect of affairs, it is proper a further provision of all the munitions of war be forthwith made.(29)

At the request of the House, the Secretary of War submitted two reports on the status of the seacoast defenses during December of 1811. On 3 December Eustis advised that the fortifications project agreed upon in 1808—the Second System—was so near completion that the unexpended appropriations still on hand would be sufficient. But he noted that events since 1808 had pointed up certain shortcomings in the 1808 plan; for fully effective defense of the maritime frontier, Eustis felt, certain existing fortifications should be expanded, while a few additional works were required in some areas. The harbors of New York and Newport, in the Secretary's opinion, needed additional defensive works—to the extent of one million dollars.(30) Such was the temper of the times, as a rupture with Britain drew ever nearer, that this startling figure was accepted almost without demur.

Eustis's second letter to the committee, a week later, contained a complete description of each existing seacoast defense work, from the largest masonry fort to the smallest timber-and-sod battery. (See Appendix G) And for the first time the Secretary added to the description of each work the number of troops required to garrison it under wartime conditions. His figures were based on a factor of 13 men per gun, which was probably sound for small four- and six-gun forts, but which seems considerably inflated for the larger defenses. For Fort Constitution, for example, which had barracks for two companies, Eustis's formula proposed 468 men; for Fort Wolcott in Newport, with barracks for one company, the recommended garrison was 594 men. Perhaps the most unrealistic estimate was for Castle Williams; the fort mounted 78 guns in two tiers, and would eventually take more, but it is difficult to visualize 1,034 men crowded into that circular fortification. The total number of artillerists required from Maine to New Orleans by this estimate came to 12,610—a strength which had not been reached by the entire Army since 1800.(31) This total, of course, was based on 970 guns mounted, or ready to be mounted, from northeastern Maine to the mouth of the Mississippi; Eustis used the term "heavy guns," which usually meant 24-pounders and larger, but in some areas, particularly along the Maine coast northeast of Portland, the totals included some 18- and even 12-pounders mounted on travelling carriages.

The end of 1811 also brought the end of the Wilkinson court-martial, adjourned on 31 December. (32) For lack of legally sound evidence of Wilkinson's derelictions, the court was forced to acquit him of all charges. The record of trial was forwarded to the President in January for approval; Wilkinson's defense statement alone filled over 600 pages, and other documents and testimony were in proportion. Madison complained to his old chief Jefferson of the size of the task, noting that "a month has not yet carried me thro' the whole."(33) On 14 February the President returned the record to the War Department: "… although I have observed in those proceedings, with regret, that there are instances in the conduct of the court as well as of the officer on trial, which are evidently and justly objectionable, his acquittal of the several charges … is approved and his sword is accordingly ordered to be restored."(34) James Wilkinson once again resumed his position as the senior general officer of the Army—a position in which he would very shortly be superseded.

The Army Augmentation of Early 1812

The President's message had made it clear that war with Britain was strongly probable, if not inevitable, but he intended to allow several months for further communication with London. The more warlike factions in Congress were less inclined to wait, and determined to raise additional troops for the Army over and above the 1808 ceiling, which had not yet been reached. On 11 January 1812 Congress passed "An Act to raise an additional Military Force," which contained several interesting features:

> *Be it enacted* … there be immediately raised, ten regiments of infantry, two regiments of artillery, and one regiment of light dragoons, to be enlisted for a term of five years, unless sooner discharged.

> SEC. 2. … a regiment of infantry … shall form two battalions, each of nine companies. A regiment of artillery shall consist of … two battalions, each of ten companies. The regiment of cavalry shall consist of … two battalions, each of six companies.

> SEC. 3. … to each regiment raised under this act, whether of infantry, artillery, or light dragoons, there shall be appointed one colonel, two lieutenant colonels, two majors, two adjutants, one quartermaster, one paymaster, one surgeon, two surgeon's mates, two sergeant majors, two quartermaster sergeants, and two senior musicians… .

SEC. 4. ... there shall be appointed two major generals ... and five brigadier generals [, and] one adjutant general and one inspector general, each with the rank, pay and emoluments of a brigadier general ... .(35)

For reasons somehow derivative of the American character at this period, the Administration and Congress were unwilling to appoint a single Commanding General of the Army. Two major generals, theoretically equal in rank, were provided to command the northern and southern subdivisions of the Army, each to report directly to the Secretary of War. The brigadier generals of the line, of whom eight were now authorized, would command districts under one of the two major generals. The provision of a separate adjutant general and inspector general was long overdue; the functions of these two officers were entirely separate, if they were to be effective, and the size of the Army now being authorized—24 regiments of the several arms—would be beyond the administrative talents of a single adjutant and inspector. The major staff reforms so long sought by Secretary Eustis, however, still remained to be authorized.

The creation of two additional regiments of artillery brought numbering problems. It was intended that the old Regiment of Artillerists should become the 1st Regiment of Artillery, so the newly-authorized regiments were designated the 2d and 3d. However, the senior regiment was on the Military Peace Establishment of 1802, not normally subject to post-emergency disbandment, and it clung to that distinction; through the war that began in 1812, the 1st Artillery companies submitted their returns under the old designation of "regiment of Artillerists."(36) Although not specifically noted, it would appear that the three regiments were designed primarily for seacoast defense, leaving the field artillery role to the Regiment of Light Artillery, but as the months went by the missions assigned to the various companies of the four regiments tended to be based on immediate need, whether for seacoast duty or assignment to forces in the field.

Not until 12 March did the Senate act on the President's appointments to the top positions in the augmented force. For many reasons James Wilkinson was not considered for higher rank in 1812, and neither Wade Hampton nor Peter Gansevoort was thought to have enough political strength for a major generalcy. The important point was to unite both New England and the Southern states behind a Republican call for war, and so each region should be awarded a major general. Republicans in New England were still in the minority, particularly those of the appropriate age, and the Administration could find no better prospect for the major general to command the northern department than former Secretary of War Henry Dearborn, now 61 and Collector of the Port of Boston. Dearborn accepted, his date of rank was set back to 27 January, and he was requested to establish his headquarters in or near Albany.(37) Not until late April was the second major general selected: Thomas Pinckney of South Carolina, also 61, was well-known nationally as the negotiator of the Treaty of San Lorenzo with Spain in 1795, but he had seen no military service since the Revolution. Pinckney's southern department would include the states of Virginia, the Carolinas, and Georgia; his date of rank of 27 March made him junior to Henry Dearborn by two months.(38)

Two other senior appointments were approved by the Senate on 12 March. The Regiment of Light Artillery finally received a colonel, and a veteran artilleryman an overdue promotion, when Major Moses Porter of the Artillerists was appointed to head the Light Artillery. For the moment, however, Colonel Porter remained on seacoast duty, as Secretary Eustis directed him to retain direct command of Boston Harbor and to supervise the fortifications from Fort Trumbull at New London to Cape Ann, Massachusetts, as well as to "correspond with officers commanding posts on the Sea Board in N. Hampshire and Maine."(39) To command one of the two new regiments of artillery, the Administration rather pointedly bypassed lieutenant Colonel Constant Freeman of the Artillerists, a New Englander, in favor of former captain George Izard of South Carolina, whose earlier career has been detailed in these pages. Despite his having been out of service for nine years, Izard's European military education and social background were still impressive; his appointment unquestionably had some political and geographical overtones. Izard accepted the colonelcy of the 2d Artillery, still entirely on paper, and for several months was the only assigned field officer.(40) For the moment the command of the new 3d Artillery remained unfilled.

During March and April three of the newly-authorized brigadier generals of the line were selected, again with political and geographical considerations paramount. Joseph Bloomfield, the governor of New Jersey, and James Winchester of Tennessee were appointed as of 27 March. Both had served during the Revolution and later as militia generals; both had seen more recent active service, Bloomfield during the Whiskey Rebellion and Winchester against the Indians in Tennessee. On 8 April Governor William Hull of Michigan Territory, a highly-regarded veteran of the Revolutionary War and governor of the territory since 1805, was appointed brigadier general for command on the northwest frontier. The average age of the three new generals was 59.

The legislation of 11 January, by providing for an Adjutant General and an Inspector General, was the entering wedge of Secretary Eustis's campaign for a proper staff for the Army. On 28 March the President signed legislation which reestablished the Quartermaster's Department, authorizing a Quartermaster General with rank of brigadier general, four deputies, and as many assistant deputies as needed. The act also provided for a Commissary General of Purchases, with necessary deputies, to replace the old Purveyor of Public Supplies. Authorized also, under the Quartermaster General were necessary wagon-masters, forage-masters, and four so-called "conductors of artillery" for ordnance duties.(41) At the end of March President Madison began to fill the new staff positions, again hoping to use the appointments to encourage support of the impending war in dissident areas. The office of Adjutant General was offered to William North, who had served in that capacity in 1799-1800, but North, a Massachusetts Federalist, declined the position. The post of Quartermaster General was accepted by Morgan Lewis of New York, and the position of principal deputy was assigned to the explorer, Lieutenant Colonel Zebulon M. Pike of the 4th Infantry. The President could find no takers for the post of Commissary General of Purchases, and eventually the position went to Callender Irvine, whose old office of Superintendent of Military Stores was abolished. Tench Coxe, whose office of Purveyor of Public Supplies had been abolished also, was offered only the post of deputy in the Purchase Department; he declined, and retired from government service.(42)

The Corps of Engineers on the Eve of War

The expansion of the Army in early 1812 created considerable turbulence, as officers of the old regiments were appointed to higher grades in the new regiments or to newly-authorized staff positions. The Corps of Engineers was not affected initially, but its senior officers became aware that there were higher positions in the augmented Army to which they might aspire, at least for the duration of the imminent war, and in the two months or so before war was finally declared there were several instances of active seeking of these positions. Colonel Jonathan Williams, the Chief Engineer, had every hope of becoming a general officer sooner or later, and at the beginning of April he calmly proposed to Secretary Eustis an arrangement which would free him from the active administration of his corps:

> Lt Col Macomb is preparing to take up his permanent Residence at West Point ... . My intention is
> (if you do not direct otherwise) to let him take the efficient Command of the Corps of Engineers in

all its detail, giving at the same time such a superintending eye to whatever is going on in [New York Harbor] when-ever my duties call me another way; while Captain Bomford takes upon himself as he did last year the detailed operations here. I have ordered all Engineers not expressly employed to repair to West Point & take orders from Lt Col Macomb. I shall find ample employment in the inspection of all the works ... between Newport & Norfolk inclusive....(43)

In effect, Williams was proposing to turn over the actual command of the Corps of Engineers, including the Military Academy, to Alexander Macomb, while Williams—retaining the colonelcy—would be free to accept whatever higher position might be offered.(44) What Secretary Eustis thought of this proposal is not recorded, for before receiving Williams's letter he had already written to the Chief Engineer concerning the eventual need for Engineer officers to be assigned to armies in the field, and had noted that he had in mind for Lieutenant Colonel Macomb the assignment of "field engineer" in General Dearborn's Northern Department.(45) Colonel Williams abandoned his plan to turn over all administration to Macomb, but with reluctance; he replied to the Secretary that he was alerting Macomb to be ready to report to the "northern army," but that meanwhile Macomb would "take post at West Point and establish a system of practice for Field Fortifications."(46) Eustis then directed Williams to select an Engineer to report to General Hull's new army on the northwest frontier; Williams chose the senior 1st lieutenant of the Corps, William Partridge, and alerted him for movement to Detroit.(47)

Perhaps to bolster his hopes for the command of New York Harbor, Colonel Williams arranged for a dramatic demonstration of the worth of his prized project, Castle Williams. The naval frigates *President* and *Essex*, under Commodore John Rodgers, were anchored off the quarantine station in New York Harbor, and Williams got the Commodore to agree to attack Castle Williams with the two vessels' 24-pounders as a test of the "resisting Power" of the new fortification. The test took place on 14 April, and Williams forwarded to Secretary Eustis an article from the *New York Gazette* of the following day:

> As they (the frigates *President* & *Essex*) passed they fired seven shots at Castle Williams for the purpose of trying its strength. Five Balls hit the Castle, & two struck the Rocks forming the Foundation ... much less injury was done than was anticipated. Three 24 pound Balls entered one of the Embrazures of the lower Tier [this would have been remarkable gunnery, but see below], knocked off a small part of the ornamental edges. One of the Balls hit one of the mounted Cannon of the Castle ... one Ball struck the Embrazure of the second Tier ... and one was a point blank Shot on the solid part or the Castle which penetrated only 3 inches & did no injury to the Wall. The Walls of Castle Williams are nine feet thick and we may conclude from this experiment upon them while yet in a green state that no apprehension need be formed of their being Battered down.

To this laudatory account the jubilant Williams, who had been inside his castle during the test, added a few corrections. The range of the bombardment had been about 400 yards, "less than point blank distance"; only one shot had entered the embrasure, the other two being buried in the stones forming the sides and top. The cannon struck by a ball was considered capable of remaining in action. The shot that struck the solid wall penetrated just one-third of its diameter, and "fell dead at the Bottom of the Wall"; this ball Colonel Williams later carried out to the *President* and presented to Commodore Rodgers.(48)

No reply to this exultant letter has been found, probably because Secretary Eustis was mired in administration. William North's non-acceptance of the office of Adjutant General left that important position unfilled during the period of raising new regiments and appointing new officers. Major Nicoll, whose position of Adjutant and Inspector no longer existed, stayed at his old desk, but considered that he was concerned with the pre-1812 regiments exclusively: "My duties being unconnected with the New Army," he replied to a routine query, "I can give you no information whatever respecting it."(49) At last, at the end of April, Secretary Eustis seized upon the most promising officer who happened to pass through Washington, and so Lieutenant Colonel Alexander Macomb—whom Colonel Williams wanted at West Point and the Secretary had planned to send to Dearborn's army—was appointed to "perfom the duties of Adjutant General until further orders."(50) Had Macomb been offered the brigadier generalcy now authorized for that position, he might well have remained permanently in Washington; at the age of 30, however, Macomb could hardly expect a two-grade advancement, and he soon set his sights on a more active position.

At the end of April Congress finally passed a bill for a slight increase in the Corps of Engineers and better organization of the Military Academy. The effect on the Corps itself was modest, providing an increase of seven officers and creating an enlisted force of 112 men, to be known as "a company of bombardiers, sappers and miners." The provisions for the Military Academy were, in the long run, of considerable importance:

> SEC. 2.... the military academy shall consist of the corps of engineers, and the following professors, in addition to the teachers of the French language and drawing already provided, viz: one professor of natural and experimental philosophy ... one professor of mathematics ... one professor of engineering in all its branches ... each of the foregoing professors to have an assistant professor ... taken from the most prominent characters of the officers or cadets ... *Provided*, that nothing herein contained shall entitle the academical staff, as such: to any command in the army separate from the academy.

> SEC. 3.... the cadets ... whether of artillery, cavalry, riflemen or infantry ... shall at no time exceed two hundred and fifty: that they may be attached at the discretion of the President ... as students at the military academy, and be subject to the established regulations thereof; that they shall be arranged into companies ... and the said corps shall be trained and taught all the duties of a private, non-commissioned officer, and officer: be encamped at least three months of each year, and taught all the duties incident to a regular camp: that the candidates for cadets be not under the age of fourteen, nor above the age of twenty-one years; that each cadet, previously to his appointment by the President ... shall be well versed in reading, writing and arithmetic.... .

> SEC. 4.... when any cadet shall receive a regular degree from the academical staff, after going through all the classes, he shall be considered as among the candidates for a commission in any corps ... and in case there shall not at the time be a vacancy in such corps, he may be attached to it by brevet of the lowest grade, as a supernumerary officer ... .

> SEC. 6.... so much of the [Act of 16 March 1802] as confines the selection of the commander of the corps of engineers to the said corps ... is hereby repealed.(51)

Colonel Williams must have been pleased by this legislation, which appeared at last to presage better days for both the Corps of Engineers and the Academy. His own fortunes, too, appeared brighter when he received a letter from the Secretary in early May regarding the defenses of New York City. "Within a short time (it is expected)," wrote Eustis, "a Commanding General will be charged with the defence of the City, to whom will necessarily be confided the general means of Defence."(52) Although Colonel Burbeck, then commanding the garrisons in the harbor, was considerably senior to

Williams, the Chief Engineer seems to have inferred that he would receive a promotion and the command of his favorite fortifications. In this expectation he was to be bitterly disappointed.

The nation was now sliding slowly but inexorably into war with the greatest naval power in the world. On 14 April Congress, at Madison's urging, passed another Embargo Act, this one to last until an American naval vessel brought definite word that Britain still refused to rescind the Orders in Council—at which time the President would ask Congress to declare war. Nothing, however, was being done to make specific plans for a war; there was simply an accepted idea that somehow the United States would invade and seize Canada as a hostage to force Britain to come to terms. The invasion would be carried out, in ways yet to be specified, by Major General Henry Dearborn's force, beginning to assemble around Albany, and a smaller collection of volunteers and militia under Brigadier General William Hull, gathering south of Detroit.

In the South, there were vague plans to seize the rest of Spanish Florida. Lieutenant Colonel Alexander Macomb, acting as Adjutant General, probably knew as much as anyone about the proposed invasion of Canada, and he decided to apply for a more active assignment. Seeing no chance for promotion in the Engineers, Macomb applied to Secretary Eustis for appointment to the unfilled colonelcy of the 3d Artillery. Eustis appreciated Macomb's desire for promotion and for a command in the line, and failed to assess the loss of a trained engineer to the Army. On the Secretary's recommendation the President made the nomination, and in May Alexander Macomb became colonel of the newest artillery regiment.(53) Although Macomb had no way of knowing it, had he waited a few months he would have become colonel and Chief Engineer.

With Colonel Macomb lost permanently to the Corps of Engineers, his vacant lieutenant colonelcy was at once filled by the promotion of Major Joseph G. Swift, who was commanding and supervising last-minute construction at Fort Johnston, North Carolina. Secretary Eustis continued to violate the prohibition against Engineer officers commanding line troops: on 8 May he notified Governor Tompkins of New York that Lieutenant Colonel Swift would supersede Captain Nathaniel Leonard of the Artillerists in command of Fort Niagara on the Canadian frontier.(54) Events, however, were to negate this assignment.

On 14 May Congress at last enacted legislation creating an Ordnance Department, to be headed by a colonel as commissary general, with a major as assistant, four captains as deputies, and assistant deputies as needed. The duties of the Commissary General of Ordnance were "to direct the inspection and proving of all pieces of ordnance, cannon balls, shells and shot, procured for the use of the army … ; and to direct the construction of all carriages … ammunition wagons, pontoons and travelling forges; also the direction of the laboratories, the inspection and proving the public powder, and preparing all kinds of ammunition for garrison and field service … ." Once the items were procured, it would be the function of the Commissary General of Ordnance to forward them to the appropriate "armies, garrisons, magazines and arsenals."(55)

Pending the organization of the Ordnance Department, Colonel Burbeck of the Artillerists continued to supervise ordnance functions in addition to his command of the troops in New York Harbor. Secretary Eustis had notified General Dearborn in Albany that he could look to Burbeck for ordnance supplies, and as late as 16 June the Secretary reminded Burbeck that he was still in charge of ordnance matters, asking him to assist in the organization of the new Ordnance Department.(56) The following week an officer was chosen to become the assistant commissary general: Captain George Bomford of the Engineers, at 30 considered too young for the top position, was a natural choice for the post of principal assistant. Bomford accepted with enthusiasm, but with the cautious proviso that he not vacate his permanent commission in the Corps of Engineers.(57) To be Bomford's chief, the commissary general, the Administration turned to a former officer who had twice resigned his commission—Decius Wadsworth of Connecticut. The irascible, occasionally devious, but undeniably talented Wadsworth, now 44 and in the fur trade in Canada, was probably as well qualified for the position as any officer or former officer of the Army. He had been a particular favorite of Secretary Dearborn from 1801-05, and it may have been General Dearborn who urged Wadsworth's appointment, as of 2 July, as Commissary General of Ordnance.

Last Preparations for Seacoast Defense

At the end of May the American naval vessel that was to report Britain's final position on the Orders in Council still had not arrived, and the United States remained officially at peace. Most of the nation was determined to resort to war, but few individuals, in official positions or otherwise, had given much thought to how such a war would be fought, beyond the vague but comforting idea that Canada would soon be American property. In the last weeks of May, however, thoughts began to turn to defensive measures against naval onslaught once war was declared. Suddenly the embryonic plans to invade Canada took second place, and all attention turned once again to the problems of defense of the maritime frontier. The result was that while it was too late to do much about seacoast defense, the outbreak of war on 18 June found no army properly organized and equipped to invade Canada. Three weeks before the declaration of war, Secretary Eustis wrote General Dearborn in Albany to advise him of the sudden change in priorities:

> ... the President has been pleased to direct that the fortifications on the Sea Board be immediately put in the best state of defence. Orders to this effect have been given to Genl Pinckney for the Southern Department - and General Bloomfield has been directed to take command in the City & Harbour of New York.... Under these arrangements you will perceive the necessity of ... the delay which will be occasioned in forming the Encampment at Albany, as your particular attention will be required to the maritime frontier of New England ....(58)

At the beginning of June the seacoast fortifications all had garrisons of one sort or another, ranging from well-established companies of artillerists to handfuls of recruits from various regiments of all arms. The command structure that should have coordinated the many defenses, however, was still far from adequate. The garrisons from Boston northward were again placed under Colonel John P. Boyd of the 4th Infantry, back on the seaboard after his services at Tippecanoe. The fortifications in southern Massachusetts, Rhode Island, and Connecticut were entrusted to Colonel Moses Porter of the Light Artillery. Colonel Burbeck, still occupied with ordnance duties, continued in New York, but the command of New York Harbor and the surrounding area was assigned to Brigadier General Joseph Bloomfield—to the great chagrin of Colonel Williams, who desired that post above all others. In General Pinckney's Southern Department Lieutenant Colonel Constant Freeman commanded the defenses of Norfolk, and newly-promoted Major James Read—filling Porter's old majority—was transferred from Fort Mifflin to the command of the fortifications in Charleston Harbor. Major William MacRea continued in command of the defenses of New Orleans and the mouth of the Mississippi. Two of the four majors of Artillerists were lost to the regiment: Abimael Y. Nicoll remained in Washington as principal assistant to the yet-unnamed Adjutant General, while Amos Stoddard, a member of a temporary board of officers in Washington, was soon to be pressed into service as a deputy quartermaster general. (59)

In a report to the Secretary of War on 6 June, Major Nicoll noted that 1,874 troops of "the Peace Establishment and Additional Military Force of 1808, including recruits," were manning the seacoast

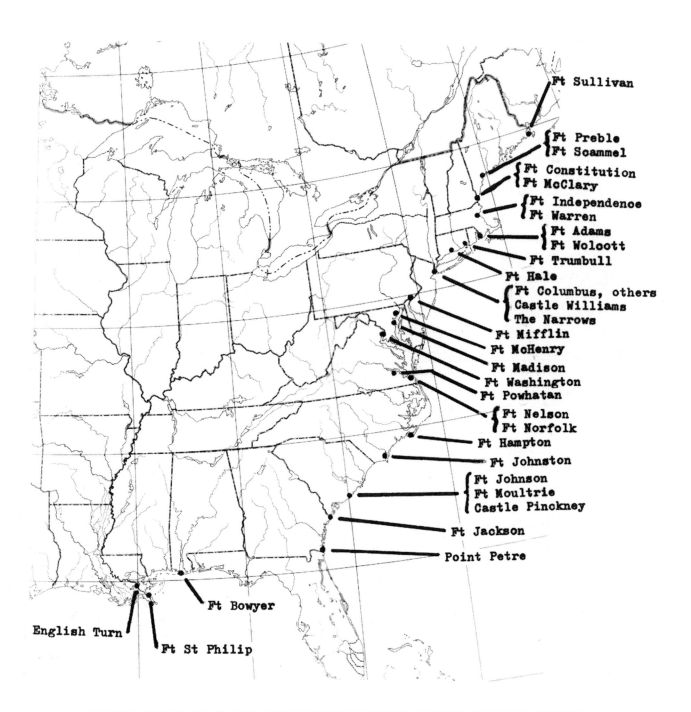

Ft Sullivan

Ft Preble
Ft Scammel

Ft Constitution
Ft McClary

Ft Independence
Ft Warren

Ft Adams
Ft Wolcott

Ft Trumbull

Ft Hale

Ft Columbus, others
Castle Williams
The Narrows

Ft Mifflin

Ft McHenry

Ft Madison

Ft Washington

Ft Powhatan

Ft Nelson
Ft Norfolk

Ft Hampton

Ft Johnston

Ft Johnson
Ft Moultrie
Castle Pinckney

Ft Jackson

Point Petre

Ft Bowyer

English Turn

Ft St Philip

MAJOR FEDERAL SEACOAST FORTIFICATIONS OF THE SECOND SYSTEM
1807-1813

defenses. He added, on what authority is not evident, that "it is computed that three thousand men are sufficient to man the works in the city and harbor of New York, exclusive of the works of the Narrows … and that seven hundred and fifty men are sufficient for the works in the harbor of Newport, Rhode Island."(60) Obviously, to provide garrisons for the entire seaboard on a scale of 3,000 men for New York and 750 for Newport would require extensive use of local militia.

Preliminary steps were taken before the declaration of war to provide for militia for some of the seacoast fortifications. As early as 20 April Secretary Eustis had written Governor Tompkins, requesting that "provision may be made for the immediate organization of six companies of Artillery with two majors, to man the works in the harbour of New York … ."(61) Down in Savannah Captain William McRee of the Engineers had almost completed the construction of Fort Jackson, and at General Pinckney's direction he made formal application to the governor of Georgia for four companies of militia. But while waiting for the administrative wheels to turn, McRee wrote on his own to the mayor of Savannah, advising that "Fort Jackson has eight guns mounted - but not one soldier for its defence, or to secure it from insult," and asked for the immediate assignment of a militia company, to include a detachment of artillerymen.(62) As it turned out, provision of militia would be no problem in New York and Georgia and in the region between, but the same would not be true in die-hard Federalist New England.

On 18 June Major Nicoll issued his last peacetime order, providing for the first time for an overall commander for the defenses of Maryland within Chesapeake Bay. Captain Lloyd Beall of the Artillerists, already commanding at Fort Washington, was appointed to command "the District comprehending Fort McHenry, Baltimore, Forts Madison and Severn, Annapolis, and Fort Washington on the Potomack."(63) Thus on the very eve of war all of the seacoast garrisons, with the single exception of Fort Mifflin at Philadelphia, were assigned to a supervisory district of some sort.

President Madison, convinced that Britain would make no concessions, asked Congress for a declaration of war on 1 June. The House passed a war bill on 4 June, but the Senate debated the matter in secret for two weeks, finally voting for war on 18 June; that afternoon the President signed a formal declaration of war against the Mistress of the Seas. Secretary Eustis at once sent off messages to the senior military commanders, by express to those within riding distance and by regular post to the others, advising them to "make such arrangements and adopt such measures as the occasion requires."(64) The following day Major Nicoll sent a circular to all post commanders, notifying them of the state of war and advising each to "make the best disposition of the means within your control to meet the event."(65) More general and less helpful directives could hardly have been devised; there was about them a certain air of *sauve gui peut*. While everyone was probably relieved that the long-expected war had finally come, those who knew the state of the military forces and particularly the manning of the seacoast defenses must have felt some trepidation at the thought of the British reaction that must surely come.

CHAPTER XII
THE CRUCIBLE OF COMBAT
1812-1815

The Second System of American seacoast fortifications construction, as a concerted program, was essentially completed prior to the declaration of war on 18 June 1812. A few additional defenses were erected during the war, in cooperation with local authorities, to strengthen the protection of such cities as Baltimore and Norfolk, and in a few instances, notably at the Narrows in New York Harbor, state-constructed works were ceded to the federal government. To these should be added those fortifications included in the acquisition of new territory, of which Fort Bowyer at the entrance to Mobile Bay is an example.

This history of the First and Second Systems of seacoast defense, and of the Artillerists and Engineers who contributed to the construction and manning of the fortifications, should properly terminate with the outbreak of War in 1812. For many reasons, however, it is impracticable to end the story abruptly on 18 June 1812. The seacoast fortifications erected between 1794 and 1812 were designed with the hope that they would deter enemy attack; if the enemy pressed an attack, the forts were to destroy his warships and turn him back. We know in retrospect that no enemy attack got beyond the planning stages in 1794 and in 1798; we know also that a very possible French attack on the mouth of the Mississippi in 1802 was diverted to another objective. The war of 1812-15, however, presented exactly the threat that the seacoast fortifications of the United States were designed to meet—defense against the greatest naval power in the world. The question, then, is whether or not these defenses were successful, whether or not they accomplished the purpose for which they were designed and on which comparatively large sums had been expended. This final chapter will undertake to examine this question and to assess the effectiveness of the American seacoast fortifications under wartime conditions.

It is also hoped that the reader who has followed the fortunes of the officers of the Artillerists and Engineers thus far will wish to know what happened during the war to Henry Burbeck and Jonathan Williams and the officers of their two corps. As might be expected, some succeeded brilliantly, a few failed, some dropped out of sight; most of them carried out their duties conscientiously and without fanfare. We begin this last chapter with a brief look at what happened to the leadership and structure of the Corps of Engineers.

The Corps of Engineers During the War

Less than a week after the declaration of war President Madison supported a decision which, while possibly necessary under urgent wartime needs, contradicted the basis on which the Corps of Engineers had been created ten years earlier. Writing to the department and district commanders, Secretary of War William Eustis advised them of the President's authorization that "whenever the Exigencies of the Service may require the talents & knowledge of the Officers of the Corps of Engineers beyond the line of their immediate profession, you may assign to those under your Command such duties in the Line of the Army, as may comport with their Rank."(1)

Colonel Jonathan Williams apparently learned in advance of this change of policy, and determined to be its first beneficiary. The Chief Engineer felt his position in New York anomalous; with General Bloomfield commanding the district and Colonel Burbeck the harbor fortifications, Williams remained only the supervising engineer of construction that was virtually completed. On 21 June he wrote directly to President Madison on the subject:

While the Peace establishment alone existed I had but 3 Superior Officers (Genl Wilkinson, Colonels Burbeck and Cushing), I have now 14 Superiors, and while I cannot assume the command of a Sub-altern, I am expected to perform professional duties where a Subaltern commands. War being now declared, my Situation in this Harbor becomes humiliating to the last degree. Works that have been constructed by me become inhabited and commanded by my inferiors, while I appear to be mainly a Spectator, for in military command I have not the authority of a Serjeant.

I pray you Sir to relieve me from this unpleasant Situation, and by a Special order, which you alone can give, to place me in that, which my nominal rank naturally points out, and which my honour requires. I indulge a hope that ... I shall be placed in a command consistent with my Character, and such as I hope, also, is not unmerited by the public Services I have performed.(2)

Before Williams received a reply from the President, General Bloomfield had read Secretary Eustis's letter on the new policy, and seemingly assured Williams that he would be appointed to the command of New York Harbor. With this assurance, the Chief Engineer departed for Philadelphia to inspect Fort Mifflin. But as soon as word of the impending appointment circulated to the officers in the harbor garrisons, they banded together to protest strongly the assignment of an Engineer officer to a command in the line. As Colonel Burbeck stood to be displaced by Williams's assignment, it is possible that he had a hand in instigating the protest; the record here is silent. It was to Colonel Burbeck, however, that 18 junior officers of artillery and infantry, headed by Captain George Armistead of the Artillerists, addressed their "remonstrance":

We the undersigned officers of the line of the army ... beg leave respectfully to state to you, the Commander of the United States troops in the harbour of New York, the opinion we have individually and collectively formed of the arrangement which it is now in contemplation to adopt, touching the command of troops by a Corps of Officers who are by Law, universal custom, and the importance of their professional duties separated from the line of the army.

While we entertain the highest regard for ... the Commandant of the Corps of Engineers ... and also the junior officers of the Corps ... we cannot, must not view in Silence any encroachment upon our military rights or suffer the command to which we are entitled to be unjustly taken from us... .

We therefore respectfully solicit your influence, Sir, in arresting the progress of this arrangement... .

Call to view for a moment the rapid promotion which it has been the fortune of the officers of that Corps to receive, View with what unparralled [sic] rapidity they have ascended ... over the heads of those of the line, and we flatter ourselves Sir that you will be sensible that the only consolation the latter have had, and the only reason they can have to render their Situation tolerable is the assurance that the former will be retained in the Line of their profession.

For the precedent once established of calling them to command on the first rumour of approaching hostilities will completely jeopardize the dearest of our military rights... .(3)

As Captain Armistead could have pointed out, he was still a captain after thirteen years' service, while Joseph G. Swift of the Engineers, as an example, was a lieutenant colonel after less than ten. The officers of the line could view such rapid promotion with detachment as long as Engineer officers remained technical specialists, but they objected strongly to young field officers of that Corps being placed in command positions over them. Colonel Williams, at 62, was not the real object of their protest, but the line officers knew that his appointment to command would set a most undesirable precedent.

Colonel Burbeck took the memorial to General Bloomfield, who seems to have been impressed by its argument; he suspended the orders assigning Colonel Williams to command. When Williams returned from Fort Mifflin and learned of the protest, he did not attempt to counter its legal aspect; rather, he seemed to consider himself as a special exception, and he wrote to President Madison again on 10 July to force the issue:

> Far be it from me, Sir, to create any diversion among men whose profession of all others should form a well connected & affectinate Brotherhood; but I must be permitted to judge for myself in what relates to me personally, therefore it only remains to do the last, and only, act that can be done consistently with my honor, and a desire to preserve harmony among the officers of the Army, and I hereby resign my Commission.

> ... after having resigned upon a former occasion, I was called again into Service upon an express Stipulation which was afterwards made law by the 63d Article of the Rules and Regulations for the Government of the Army.(4) This being the condition, *upon which alone* I accepted my commission. I hold myself absolved- from all obligation the moment it ceases to operate. The loss of an officer in his Sixty third year may not be considered of great importance when compared with that of eighteen officers in the vigor of youth ...(5)

There are good reasons to believe that Williams hoped, by this threat of resignation, to force the President to appoint him specifically to the command of New York Harbor. Secretary Eustis notified Williams a few days later that he was instructed by the President "to inform you that your letter of Resignation is under his consideration," and went on to ask Williams to prepare a specific report on the practicability of suspending a chain across the Narrows.(6) This seemed to indicate that the President was unwilling to accept Williams's resignation, but it was misleading, for Madison decided not to accede to the wishes of the elderly Chief Engineer. Taking Williams's resignation at face value, the President accepted it as of 31 July, and so for the second and last time Jonathan Williams left the United States Army.

Williams was not long unemployed, however, for Governor Tompkins almost immediately appointed him a supernumerary brigadier general of New York militias and he became a consulting engineer for the state fortifications under construction at the Narrows. After these forts were completed and turned over to the federal government the following year, Williams returned to his home in Philadelphia, lending his expertise to plans for defensive works on the Schuylkill River. He ran for Congress from Philadelphia in 1814 and was elected, but died in May 1815, just short of his 65th birthday, without taking his seat in the House.(7)

The resignation of Colonel Williams left the newly-promoted lieutenant Colonel Joseph G. Swift as the senior officer of the Corps of Engineers. Secretary Eustis was reluctant to appoint Swift, at the age of 28, to the post formerly held by the 62-year-old Williams; he could imagine the caustic comments of the officers who had signed the protest in New York Harbor. Swift was then in Charleston as chief engineer of the Southern Department; he received, as he put it, "letters from Washington, advising of the resignation of Colonel Williams, but no order signifying my consequent advancement."(8) There are indications that Eustis tried to find a prestigious civilian engineer to succeed Jonathan Williams, and Swift believed that Eustis recommended Robert Fulton to head the Corps of Engineers, but that the President would not agree.(9) Finally, on 30 November, the Secretary recommended Swift for promotion; with Madison's nomination and Senate approval, Joseph Gardner Swift became Chief Engineer with the rank of colonel, to date from Williams's resignation on 31 July. Promoted at the same time were Walker K. Armistead to lieutenant colonel, William McRee to major, and Joseph G. Totten and Samuel Babcock to captain. Excluding brevet honors, this was the last substantial promotion of Engineer officers for the duration of the war.(10)

During the late summer and fall of 1812 the Engineer officers were assigned to the armies in the field and to the two departments. In the latter case they were still concerned with seacoast fortifications, but with the shortage of Engineers more and more reliance was placed on local civilian engineers. Major McRee was initially assigned as chief engineer of the Southern Department, while Captain Charles Gratiot became the engineer for the new army in the northwest under General Harrison, formed to replace the force surrendered by Hull at Detroit; Gratiot thus succeeded Lieutenant William Partridge, Hull's engineer, who died a prisoner of war at Detroit on 20 September.(11)

On 19 March 1813 the Army was organized into nine military districts, and the officers of the Corps of Engineers were divided among most of them. Colonel Swift, instead of remaining in Washington, was assigned as chief engineer of the Ninth Military District in northern New York, which was actually a field army whose two wings were commanded by James Wilkinson and Wade Hampton, both now major generals; also assigned there were Major McRee, Captain Totten, and 1st Lieutenant Sylvanus Thayer. Lieutenant Colonel Armistead and Captain Babcock were assigned to the Fifth Military District in Maryland and Virginia. Captain Prentiss Willard became chief engineer for General Pinckney's Sixth Military District, the Carolinas and Georgia, but died at Beaufort, S.C., in October 1813. Captain Eleazer D. Wood joined Gratiot in General Harrison's army, then the Eighth Military District. Captain Alden Partridge remained in virtual charge of the Military Academy during the war, with a faculty of three professors and two teachers. At the end of 1813 there were 99 cadets on the rolls; only one was graduated in 1813, but in 1814 the number was 30, and in the first months of 1815 another 40 were commissioned, virtually exhausting the supply of cadets—there was no Class of 1816.(12) During the course of the war six 2d lieutenants of Engineers were appointed from civil life.

Several officers of Engineers were particularly distinguished during the war. Colonel Swift was brevetted brigadier general in early 1814 for generally meritorious service. Major Bomford, on Ordnance duty, was brevetted lieutenant colonel for meritorious service at the end of 1814, and promoted to lieutenant colonel of Ordnance at the end of the war. Major McRee was brevetted twice, to lieutenant colonel for gallant conduct at Niagara and to colonel for distinguished service in the defense of Fort Erie. Captain Wood was also brevetted twice, to major for distinguished service in the defense of Fort Meigs and to lieutenant colonel for gallant conduct at Niagara; Wood was killed leading a sortie from Fort Erie in September 1814—the work on Bedloe's Island in New York Harbor was named Fort Wood in his honor. Captain Totten was brevetted to major and lieutenant colonel for his services at Fort George in 1813 and at Plattsburg in 1814. And Captain Thayer, a future Superintendent of the Military Academy, was brevetted major for his services in the defense of the Norfolk region during 1814.(13)

It is interesting to note that after the rapid promotion of the period 1802-1812, about which the line officers were aggrieved, promotions in the Corps of Engineers ground almost to a halt during the war. The junior 2d lieutenant at the end of 1813 did not become a 1st lieutenant until the end of 1817; when he died in 1858, after 45 years' service, he was only a major.

It is illustrative of the longevity of some of the officers of the Corps that successive Chief Engineers until near the end of the Civil War—Swift, Armistead, Macomb, Gratiot, and Totten—all came from officers appointed prior to the War of 1812, veterans all of the Second System of seacoast fortification construction.

The Wartime Dispersal of the Artillerists

The simultaneous need to man the seacoast defenses and to organize field armies to invade Canada in 1812 had led to the decision to utilize local militia units as seacoast garrisons, but with at least one officer of regular Artillery to command each of the major defenses.(14) The calls for militia were answered promptly everywhere except in Massachusetts and Connecticut, which together had the bulk of the exposed New England coastline. The die-hard Federalist administrations of those states were determined not to support "Mr. Madison's War," and Connecticut replied to General Dearborn's call that "the Governor is not informed that the United States are in imminent danger of Invasion"; Massachusetts made substantially the same reply. Secretary Eustis wrote frantically to both states, assuring them that the President considered the "danger to be actual," but neither state cooperated.(15) Thus Dearborn's hope of pulling out all regular troops to augment his field army was frustrated, and to some extent the subsequent failure of that army had its basis here. The unwillingness of Massachusetts and Connecticut to organize strong militia garrisons along their coasts at the outset was to cause both states much grief when British raiding expeditions later took place.

The death of Brigadier General Peter Gansevoort in July and Congressional authorization for additional brigadier generals brought several appointments during the summer of 1812. Thomas Flournoy of Georgia and John Chandler of Maine, both active militia generals, and John Armstrong, Revolutionary War intriguer and recent minister to France, were appointed in July, and the following month Colonel John P. Boyd of Tippecanoe fame was promoted to brigadier general. It was decided also to utilize the authority for two brigadier generals of the staff: Colonel Thomas H. Cushing of the 2d Infantry and Colonel Alexander Smyth of the Regiment of Riflemen were promoted for the offices of Adjutant General and Inspector General respectively.(16)

Boyd, Cushing, and Smyth had all been junior to Henry Burbeck of the Artillerists, and it was obvious to Secretary Eustis that Burbeck, the senior colonel of the Army, certainly deserved promotion as much as Cushing or Smyth. But there was no other staff position authorized the higher grade, and Burbeck had insufficient political backing for a generalcy in the line. Eustis found the solution in the fourth section of the Act of 6 July 1812, which provided that the President was authorized to confer brevet rank on "such officers of the army as shall distinguish themselves by gallant actions or meritorious conduct, or shall have served ten years in anyone grade.,"(17) There were in the old Regiment of Artillerists—now officially the 1st Regiment of Artillery—five officers who had been serving in grade for over ten years, and during the summer of 1812 they were brevetted to the next higher grade: Henry Burbeck to brigadier general, Constant Freeman to colonel, William MacRea to Lieutenant colonel, and Nehemiah Freeman and Lloyd Beall—the two remaining captains dating from 1802—to major. To those who were to exercise district or seacoast command positions, the brevet promotions brought the full pay and emoluments of the higher grade.

By September the news of three catastrophes in the northwest had reached Washington: the surprise capture of Michilimackinac, whose commander had not even known war was declared; the surrender of Fort Dearborn at Chicago and the massacre of its garrison by British-allied Indians; and the disgraceful surrender of Detroit and most of his army by General Hull. It soon became apparent that the blame for these disasters was to be laid at the door of the Secretary of War. For some time William Eustis had lacked rapport with Congress, although most of the criticism came from Federalists and other factions trying to discredit the Madison administration. No one was more to blame for the deficiencies of the War Department and the Army than Congress itself; Eustis had recognized as soon as he took office in 1809 the deficient staff organization he had inherited, but his repeated pleas to Congress

Defenses of New York Harbor, Showing the Fortifications of the Inner Harbor and The Narrows, ca. 1811.

to revitalize the staff went unheeded until the very eve of war. The similar stubborn refusal by Congress to provide one or two assistant secretaries to share the administrative burden doomed Eustis to continual overwork, for the staff organization finally authorized was not organized and able to render any real assistance to the Secretary until 1813. The combination of overwork and the knowledge that he lacked the confidence of Congress—and some members of the Administration—made up Eustis's mind, and on 3 December he submitted his resignation to the President. Madison accepted it, praising his past services, and asked Eustis to stay on until a successor could be found. Secretary of State James Monroe took over the War Department duties in addition to his own about 24 December, but declined the position on a permanent basis. The President offered the secretaryship to former secretary Dearborn, General Harrison, Governor Tompkins, and several senators; all declining with thanks, Madison appointed General Armstrong, who accepted with alacrity and took office early in February.(18)

In the reorganization of the Army into military districts in March 1813, Brevet Brigadier General Burbeck was assigned command of the Second District, the states of Rhode Island and Connecticut, which gave him effective supervision of the seacoast defenses of Narragansett Bay and the Connecticut coast. Subsequently, however, he was reassigned to inland districts supporting the field armies in the north, and ceased to have any direct connection with the maritime frontier. But by mid-1813 few regular troops were assigned to seacoast duties; most of the companies of the three regiments of artillery and the light artillery were serving as field artillery or in the forts along the Canadian frontier. Many of the officers of the old Artillerists were assigned administrative positions. Major Nicoll was named an inspector general in March 1813, as a temporary colonel, and Captain John DeB. Walbach, long-time commander of Fort Constitution, also became a temporary colonel as adjutant general of Wilkinson's army in the summer of 1813. Major Stoddard rejoined the 1st Artillery on the northwest frontier, where he died of wounds received at Fort Meigs, Indiana, in May 1813. Major James Read died at Pittsburgh in October 1813. Two captains benefited by transfer: James House was appointed lieutenant colonel of the 3d Artillery, which had never been completely organized, in March 1813, and George Armistead became a major of that regiment at the same time.

By the spring of 1814 the three regiments of artillery were widely scattered and leaderless—Henry Burbeck was commanding a district, George Izard of the 2d had become a mediocre major general, and Alexander Macomb of the 3d was an eminently successful brigadier general. At this time the decision was taken to consolidate the many separate artillery companies so as to reduce the number from 60 to 48, at the same time abolishing the regimental organization. The Act of 30 March provided for a Corps of Artillery, with no commander, to be organized into 12 battalions; in order not to have to promote too many majors, the legislation directed that six battalions be commanded by lieutenant colonels and six by majors! Little was done to organize these battalions, however, until after the war.(19) One ironic result of this reorganization was that Henry Burbeck, while retaining his brevet of brigadier general, saw, his permanent colonelcy abolished; in the post-war reduction of 1815, as Congress still declined to authorize a colonel for the Corps of Artillery, Burbeck was discharged as supernumerary. He retired to Connecticut, where he lived until his death in 1848 at the advanced age of 94.

Wartime Operations Against Seacoast Fortifications

Despite American fears of a British invasion as early as the fall of 1812, both Britain's naval and land forces were too preoccupied with Napoleon to attempt a seaborne assault that year or the next. British and American vessels clashed at sea in 1812 and 1813, with American ships fully holding their own, but the only serious threat to the seacoast during 1813 was a British squadron that sailed the length of Chesapeake Bay with relative impunity, blockading Baltimore and making a desultory attempt to take Norfolk. Without an adequate landing force, however, the Royal Navy was not prepared to launch a full-scale amphibious assault in 1813.

In mid-1813 Congress asked Secretary of War John Armstrong for his views on the state of the seacoast defenses. Armstrong replied prudently that the maritime defenses were insufficient, but his specific proposals for strengthening them were quite modest; he proposed minor earthworks at the mouth of the Delaware River, on the Potomac below Fort Washington, and on Craney Island at the mouth of the Elizabeth River near Norfolk, together with a strengthening of the outworks of Fort Jackson at Savannah. In general, Armstrong was satisfied with the defenses of Charleston and concluded that no additional work was necessary in and around New Orleans.(20) A month later the Senate specifically asked about the defenses of Washington. In view of what was to come in 1814, Secretary Armstrong's confident reply is of interest:

> ... on the water line, the means of defence are of two kinds, naval and military; that there are of the former, one frigate; two schooners, and three gunboats, so stationed as to co-operate with Fort Washington; that this fort and its covering work have been recently put into a state of thorough repair, are well equipped with heavy cannon, furnaces, &c. &c., and are now occupied by a competent garrison of United States' artillerists; that, to any attempts on the land side, we can oppose [elements of four infantry regiments] and one battalion of militia; the whole amounting to 1,600 effectives ... .(21)

In the spring of 1814 came the first real tests of the American seacoast defenses. The defeat of Napoleon at Leipzig near the end of 1813 forecast his abdication the following spring and the apparent end of the Napoleonic Wars. Almost at once Britain made plans to send additional warships and veteran troops of Wellington's army across the Atlantic, to terminate decisively the war with American that had dragged on for nearly two years. Even before the arrival of these reinforcements, British ships and troops at Halifax signalled the arrival of spring by a descent on the coast of New England. For the next nine months the American seacoast defenses became, for the first time in the war, an important if not crucial factor. The effectiveness of the coastal fortifications and their garrisons, however, varied widely. Their story during 1814 and early 1815 can be told geographically with little loss of chronology, for the British attacks against the seacoast defenses moved generally from northeast to southwest during that period.

An object of British imperial policy since 1783 had been to control the land, now part of the Maine District, along the route that connected Halifax with Quebec in a straight line. On 5 July an expedition left Halifax for Passamaquoddy Bay, and five days later appeared off Eastport on Moose Island, the easternmost town in the United States. An officer was sent ashore on 11 July to demand the surrender of Fort Sullivan, a small stone battery now garrisoned by a detachment of the newly-raised 40th Infantry. The commander, Major Perley Putnam, reportedly wanted to resist, but was persuaded by the townspeople that the fleet offshore could destroy not only the fort but the town of Eastport as well. Fort Sullivan's surrender without firing a shot opened the entire region to British annexation; the local populace swore allegiance to George III, and the area was not returned to the United States until 1818.(22)

Britain had no strategic need for all of the Maine coast, but raided up the Penobscot River to control that region as the southwest anchor of the 100 miles of coastline that reverted temporarily to the British empire. Although both towns had frequent alarms, neither Portland, defended by over 30 heavy guns in Forts Preble and Scammel, nor Portsmouth, protected by some 50 heavy guns in Forts Constitution and McClary, were attacked.

Although the coast off Boston was blockaded, no attack was made against the city itself—possibly

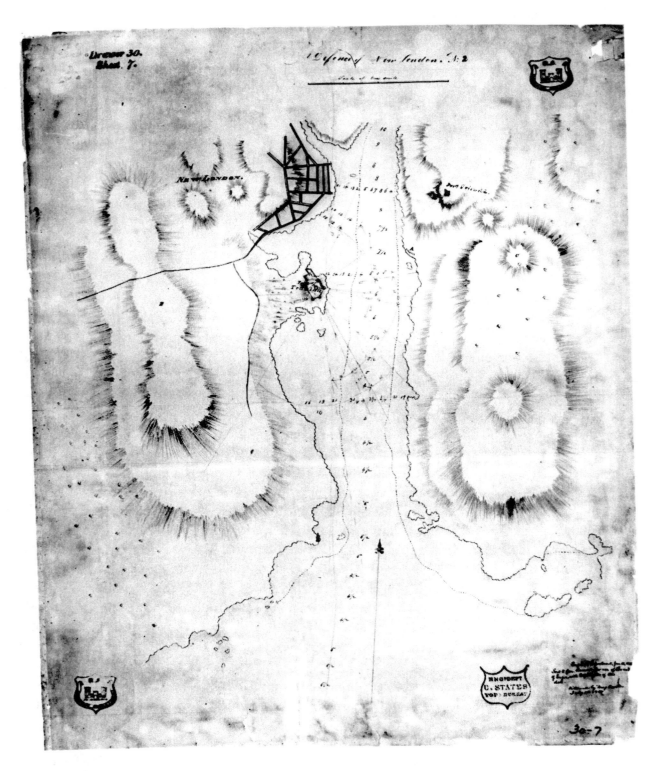

Defenses of New London, Connecticut, Showing Fort Trumbull on the West Bank of the Thames River and Fort Griswold, Completed during the Third System, across the River.

so as not to extinguish Massachusetts's strong antiwar sentiment. However, the main channel into the port was defended by Forts Independence and Warren, mounting a total of about 60 heavy guns; if the forts had been adequately manned by militia artillery, they would have been a strong deterrent to the passage of warships. In September, at the height of British activity to the south, citizens of Boston erected several additional defensive works, the most important of which was a battery on Noddle's Island named Fort Strong in honor of the governor.(23)

Surprisingly, British squadrons made no determined effort to penetrate Narragansett Bay and attack Newport, but the inadequate garrisons of Forts Wollcott and Adams were alerted several times, and called upon militia forces to be ready to reinforce their 55 heavy guns. The same general situation was true along the Connecticut coast: it was continually ravaged by British raiding parties, but never subjected to an amphibious assault. Fort Trumbull at New London, mounting about 20 guns, was never attacked; Fort Hale at New Haven reportedly drove off raiders with its six-gun battery, but was not subjected to naval bombardment.(24)

Almost to the regret of the historian, the defenses of New York Harbor were not tested during the war. Any British squadron attempting to enter the port would have encountered first the still incomplete defenses at the Narrows; on the Staten Island side were Fort Tompkins and Battery Morton on the heights, Fort Richmond at the water line, and Battery Hudson in between, but on the Brooklyn side was only a modest earthwork called Fort Lewis. The total number of guns mounted at the Narrows in 1814 was at least 60, for Fort Richmond alone was designed for 27. Had the enemy fleet penetrated the Narrows into the upper bay, it would have faced 60 heavy guns in Fort Columbus, about 100 guns in two tiers in Castle Williams, 28 in a single tier in the work now called Castle Clinton at the tip of Manhattan, and a total of some 40 guns and mortars in the works on Bedloe's and Ellis's Islands (subsequently Forts Wood and Gibson). An attempt to push up the Hudson would have been met by 16 guns in the work off Hubert Street, called the Red Fort from its sandstone walls, and 20 in a newer work named Fort Gansevoort, built in late 1812 at the site of George Bamford's old "laboratory." Discounting any guns on travelling carriages, the inner harbor thus held over 260 heavy guns and mortars; how well these weapons would have been manned in the event of sudden attack can only be conjectured. While an enemy fleet would unquestionably have suffered severe damage in a duel with the many forts, it must be conceded that the city itself would probably have been heavily bombarded at the same time.(25)

Had Philadelphia still been the national capital in 1814, it is probable that the British squadron standing off the entrance to Chesapeake Bay would have made an attack up the Delaware River, if only for morale and propaganda purposes. As it was, Philadelphia did not become an enemy target, and Fort Mifflin, which with its water battery mounted 37 heavy guns at the outbreak of war, remained undisturbed.

The Chesapeake Bay region was the scene of much enemy activity in the summer of 1814. British operations there a year earlier had been only tentative, but Baltimore and Washington were thought to be securely guarded on their water approaches, and it was felt that local militia could deal with any attacks by land. Norfolk was still vulnerable, but comfort was taken in the fact that a minor attack on the navy yard in 1813, by some 1,300 British sailors and marines, had been turned back by state forces and a seven-gun battery on Craney Island.(26) In 1814 there was no question of surprise, for the augmentation of British forces by warships and by Wellington's veterans was well known. By 1 July President Madison told his cabinet that he expected an attack on Washington, and directed the creation of the Tenth Military District, consisting of Maryland, the District of Columbia, and Virginia north of the Rappahannock.(27) Secretary Armstrong wanted to place the new command under the experienced

Moses Porter, now a brevet brigadier general, but the President preferred Brigadier General William H. Winder, a close relative of the governor of Maryland.

The British campaign against Baltimore and Washington, which resulted in the capture and burning of Washington and a complete repulse at Baltimore, concerns us here only as regards the defenses at Fort Washington, on the Potomac, and at Fort McHenry and its outworks guarding Baltimore.

Fort Washington had received some attention after the British activity on the lower Potomac in 1813, and Secretary Armstrong thought the fort was adequately armed and garrisoned. But in July of 1814 the temporary commander, Lieutenant James L. Edwards, 2d Artillery, reported that the post was in poor condition, noting particularly that the water battery had weak parapets, gun carriages and platforms were in disrepair, and the guns for the tower overlooking the fort had not been mounted. (28) When the permanent commander, Captain Samuel T. Dyson, resumed command, a few deficiencies were rectified, but no sense of urgency prevailed; Captain Dyson was a veteran of nearly 18 years' service, but his conduct showed a marked lack of energy, if not of courage. In August, on the eve of the British attack, the main battery of Fort Washington contained two 50-pounders, two 32-pounders, and nine 24-pounders, all barbette-mounted on three-wheeled carriages. Seven smaller guns on travelling carriages were in exposed positions outside the fort, while the water battery consisted of five 18-pounders on truck carriages, almost totally exposed to fire from the river. The fact that adequate earthen parapets had not been erected for all exterior guns was inexcusable.

The main British attack against Washington came not by way of the Potomac, but up the Patuxent River and then overland against Washington from the rear. General Winder made it clear to Captain Dyson that he could not reinforce the 50-man garrison of Fort Washington, and Dyson later claimed that Winder's aide-de-camp had instructed him that if his post were attacked by land from the rear, he was to blow up the fort and withdraw the garrison across the Potomac. On 27 August, just after the British main body had captured Washington, a small British squadron, which had laboriously worked its way past the shoals of the Potomac, appeared before Fort Washington. This force, consisting of two frigates, three bomb ketches, and four smaller vessels, mounted about 133 guns; given enough time and willingness to accept casualties, it probably could have reduced the fort. But what might have happened will never be known, for at the sight of the enemy flotilla in his front, Captain Dyson spiked his guns, blew up the fort, and withdrew his men to Macon's Island up the Potomac.(29)

Queried later, Dyson claimed that he had heard that enemy forces were also approaching the fort from the rear. This inadequate reply brought him a court-martial on 10 October, charged with misbehavior in the face of the enemy; one specification alleged that he was drunk at the time. Dyson was absolved of the charge of drunkenness, but was found guilty of the charges of abandoning his post without any attempt to defend it, and was dismissed the service. His defense, however, brought out clearly that many of his superiors had been aware of the poor condition of the fort, including Secretary Armstrong.(30)

Meanwhile the major element of the British fleet and its landing force, after the easy capture of Washington, turned toward the commercially more important port of Baltimore. The British plan was an overland attack, landing at the mouth of the Patapsco River to advance against Baltimore from the east, while the fleet would proceed up the Patapsco to reduce Fort McHenry on Whetstone Point. But much had been accomplished in the defenses of Baltimore since the 1813 threat, most of it due to the energy and leadership of the local major general of Maryland militia, U.S. Senator Samuel Smith. Fort McHenry itself had been strengthened, and ship hulks were sunk in the channel as obstacles. Captain Samuel Babcock of the Engineers had erected two works west of Fort McHenry, known as Forts Covington and Babcock, with a circular battery on the heights behind them. A long and effective water battery was thrown up in front of Fort McHenry, and among its armament were several 42-pounders borrowed from a French frigate in the harbor. Baltimore authorities prevailed upon Secretary Armstrong to replace the commander of Fort McHenry, Brevet Major Lloyd Beall of the Artillerists, in whom they had little confidence, by recalling Major George Armistead, now of the 3d Artillery, who had commanded Fort McHenry before the war.(31) .On the eve of the British attack on 13 September, Major Armistead's garrison at Fort McHenry consisted of one company of federal artillery, small detachments of four infantry regiments, three companies of militia artillery and two of "sea fencibles," and a detachment of sailors from the Navy. The armament of the fort was composed of 21 guns up to 24-pounders, but the adjacent water battery contained about 40 guns, ranging from 18-pounders to the borrowed French 42-pounders.

During the night of 12 September 16 British vessels moved up the Patapsco, and by daylight of the 13th were in position about two miles from Fort McHenry; shallow water prevented a closer approach, but at this position the heavier British bomb ketches and mortar vessels could reach the fort and yet remain outside the range of the American guns, with the possible exception of the 42-pounders. The British bombardment began just after the daylight, and lasted until about 0700 the following day. The operation could hardly be called an artillery duel, for while the British reported firing over 1,000 shells and "bombs, " the garrison of Fort McHenry could make only token reply. The heavier guns of the water battery contributed to keeping the fleet at a distance, but most of the fort's ordnance fired from time to time just to prove that the fort had not been destroyed. In fact, according to eyewitness reports, no more than half a dozen of the high-trajectory bombs or rockets burst within Fort McHenry, and only four of Armistead's men were killed and 24 wounded during the entire bombardment.(32) More importantly, the land attack against Baltimore collapsed after death of its commander, General Ross, and the fleet, unwilling to continue the apparently unproductive bombardment of Fort McHenry or to close to more effective but more dangerous range, broke off the engagement and withdrew. Thanks in part to Francis Scott Key's stirring poem, Fort McHenry gained a somewhat exaggerated reputation for invulnerability; nevertheless, particularly when contrasted to the fate of Fort Washington, the successful defense of Fort McHenry, led by a determined commander, justified to some extent the entire seacoast fortifications system.

There were no attacks of any significance along the south Atlantic coast during the entire war. Charleston, guarded by Forts Moultrie and Johnson and Castle Pinckney, mounting at least 80 heavy guns, would probably have given a good account of itself if needed. The mouth of the Savannah River, protected only by the recently-completed Fort Jackson, was far more vulnerable, but its defenses were not tested. In January of 1815 British forces, unaware of the signing of the Treaty of Ghent, invaded Cumberland Island off the south Georgia coast, attacked and overpowered the 90-man garrison of riflemen at Point Petre, and took the town of St. Mary's. Further British operations here ceased with the news of the end of the war.(33)

The new possessions of the United States along the Gulf of Mexico, however, were subjected to several large-scale attacks in 1814 and early 1815, and the new seacoast defenses there were thoroughly tried.

The region around Mobile on the Gulf was still claimed and controlled by Spain at the outbreak of war, but American claims on the area, based on the Louisiana Purchase, were sharpened when Spanish authorities allowed Britain to use Pensacola and Tampa as bases of operations against American commerce. In 1813, at President Madison's direction, General Wilkinson had organized an expedition against Mobile, under the immediate command of Lieutenant Colonel John Bowyer of the 2d Infantry, which captured and secured Mobile Bay on 13 April. In order to bar the bay to British vessels, Colonel Bowyer began construction of a fort on Mobile Point, at the eastern entrance to the bay, which was completed in May 1814 and named Fort Bowyer. Of Vauban design, it consisted of a semicircular battery with parapet walls 15 feet thick; the landward side was covered by a bastion connected to the battery by 180-foot curtains. Constructed of sand revetted with pine logs, the entire work was surrounded by a ditch 20 feet wide, with a glacis slope for concealment. The main battery consisted of three 32-pounders, eight 24-pounders, and 11 smaller field guns; the bastion mounted one 24-pounder and two field guns. The garrison posted there totaled 134 men of the 2d Infantry, commanded by Major William Lawrence.(34)

Attempting to regain control of Mobile Bay, the British launched a modest amphibious assault on Fort Bowyer on 12 September 1814. A force of 100-odd marines, with Indian allies, landed to attack Fort Bowyer from the landward side, while two days later a flotilla of four warships moved up to bombard the fort from the gulf side. Because of adverse winds and tide the flotilla was unable to support the land attack, and Major Lawrence's defenders easily beat off the attack against their rear by combined small-arms fire and the use of grapeshot from the bastion. On 15 September the British naval commander moved into the bay and attempted to reduce the fort by bombardment with his 78 guns, only about half of which could bear on the fort. Anchoring opposite Fort Bowyer's main battery, the fleet began a bombardment of several hours' duration. Here, however, the fire of the American guns was extremely effective; the anchor cable of the British flagship was cut, the vessel came under the full raking fire of the fort, and was driven onto the shoals in badly damaged condition. Unable to extricate his ship, the captain set it afire and it blew up with some loss of life. The British expedition, unable to pass Fort Bowyer or to reduce it, withdrew with relatively high casualties. Major Lawrence's loss was four men killed and five wounded.(35) The defense of Fort Bowyer was probably the most successful seacoast-defense action of the war, but there would be a less fortunate sequel some months later.

Another defensive fortification saw heavy action during the British campaign against New Orleans in December 1814 and January 1815. Fort St. Philip, at Placquemines, some 70 miles below New Orleans, was the principal defense against a British fleet seeking to ascend the Mississippi. Major General Andrew Jackson, who reached New Orleans on 1 December to conduct the defense of the city, visited Fort St. Philip with Lieutenant Colonel William MacRea; they found the ramparts, mounting 28 24-pounders, in generally good repair. Jackson ordered the inflammable wooden barracks destroyed, directed the augmentation of the garrison, and told Colonel MacRea to transfer additional guns there from defenses nearer New Orleans. Had the British fleet initially moved up the Mississippi, it might have reduced the undermanned fort; the ground behind the fort, however, was so marshy that a land attack against its rear was impossible, and for this and other reasons the British attack against New Orleans came by way of Lake Borgne. This led to the celebrated defense of New Orleans on 8 January 1815, which resulted in the complete repulse of the attackers.(36)

In early January the British fleet, lying off Cat Island at the entrance to Lake Borgne, belatedly attempted to facilitate British land operations by clearing the Mississippi. Fort St. Philip had now been substantially strengthened. Its garrison included two companies of the Corps of Artillery under Captains Charles Wollstonecraft and Thomas Murray, and a detachment of the 7th Infantry from New Orleans, the whole amounting to 366 men. The fort was commanded by Major Walter H. Overton of the 3d Regiment of Riflemen, who had been in New Orleans on leave when the British attack came; volunteering his services to General Jackson, he was given the important command of Fort St. Philip. On the morning of 9 January an advance British flotilla of five bomb vessels and supporting craft approached Fort St. Philip and anchored about two miles below the fort. The fort's armament had been augmented to two 32-pounders, 29 24-pounders, and several mortars and small howitzers, while a

Navy gunboat had been warped up the bayou to protect the rear of the fort. Two British barges sent upriver to take soundings near the fort were fired on by the American gunboat and driven back. In mid-afternoon two British bomb vessels opened fire with four heavy mortars from a range that was just beyond that of Wollstonecraft's and Murray's guns, and this bombardment continued for the next eight days, with over a thousand heavy shells being thrown into and around the fort. Major Overton kept his men under cover whenever possible, and most of the British shells buried themselves in the sand and mud before exploding, causing few American casualties. The American artillery kept up a steady fire whenever the British vessels tried to move forward; although several carriages were smashed and one 32-pounder was hit five times, Overton's men repaired them and kept the guns in action. The flotilla made one attempt, during a favorable wind, to run past the fort, but the American fire was too heavy and the attempt was not repeated. Just before dawn on 18 January the British ships ceased firing and began to drop down the river. Major Overton reported his casualties as only two killed and seven wounded.(37)

After the disastrous repulse at New Orleans the British commanders determined to salvage some strategic advantage by attempting once again to take Mobile. Still in ignorance of the treaty ending the war, a British fleet of 38 ships, carrying 7,500 troops, appeared off Fort Bowyer on 7 February. Major Lawrence, the hero of the successful defense the previous September, now had a garrison of some 370 men, but he was faced with an overwhelming enemy force. The British landing force of over 7,000 men, coming ashore at several points, combined on Mobile Point to attack Fort Bowyer from the rear. The entire fleet took up positions to bombard the fort, with 25 ships on the gulf side and 13 on the bay side. Under cover of heavy naval gunfire the land attack advanced to within 700 yards of Fort Bowyer's landward bastion before resorting to siege operations. It is noteworthy that the defense was considered too strong for the attackers to launch an all-out assault at the outset. By the fifth day the siege lines were 40 yards from the fort, which was completely cut off by land and sea from any hope of relief. After he had lost one killed and ten wounded—British losses were about 40—Major Lawrence felt compelled to surrender the fort. Shortly after the surrender the British commander finally learned of the signing of the Treaty of Ghent, and allowed Major Lawrence and the garrison to march to Mobile. On 1 April the British forces evacuated Fort Bowyer, boarded the fleet, and sailed out of Mobile Bay.(38)

Some Conclusions and Observations

The fact that only a very small number of American seacoast fortifications came under hostile fire during the War of 1812, with results ranging from brilliant defense to abject surrender, means that there is a rather thin basis for establishing by any scientific method the true value of the maritime defenses up to 1815. Even if it can be assumed that the comparatively strong defenses of Boston, New York, and Charleston were known to the enemy and were factors in his planning, it is impracticable from the existing records to quantify those factors so as to arrive at what would today be called a "cost-effectiveness" analysis of the worth of the seacoast defenses during the era of the First and Second Systems.

What *can* be assessed, however, is the feeling by the American public, after the War of 1812, that the seacoast fortifications had indeed been worthwhile; that despite their many deficiencies, they had made a significant contribution to the security of the nation. This is quite clear from the fact that, within months of the end of the war, Congress determined to begin construction of a better and more permanent system of coast defenses, and established in 1816 a Board of Engineers to study and make recommendations for what was to become the Third System of seacoast fortifications. So accepted, in fact, was the idea of the necessity for strong seacoast defenses, that the United States was to pursue the subject with increasing enthusiasm and increasing willingness to expend large sums on coastal fortifications, until by the end of the 19th century the country became, with Great Britain and Russia, one of the three leading exponents of the art of seacoast defense.(39) Indeed, by the middle of the 20th century, when rapid advances in long-range aircraft made all surface coastal defenses obsolete, the United States was the possessor of the finest seacoast fortifications in the world, stretching from Maine to Texas, along the Pacific coast, and including its possessions in the Panama Canal Zone, Hawaii, and the Philippines.

But the road to that state of preeminence was by no means as easy as it can be made to sound, and the student of the American seacoast defenses from the Third System forward will certainly recognize in his researches many of the same problems and difficulties that plagued the Army and the successive political administrations during the First and Second Systems. Even from the vantage point of 1815, it was possible to look back and, with the benefit of hindsight, see how the entire problem of seacoast defense might have been simplified and the defenses themselves improved.

In the most basic terms, seacoast defenses consist of forts, guns, and men. Let us now review the First and Second Systems of seacoast fortification from the point of view of each of those elements.

Fortifications design and construction during the First System was almost entirely in the hands of European-trained engineers. Within the limits of meager appropriations, and always in considerable haste both in 1794 and 1798, Rochefontaine and his countrymen produced very satisfactory results. Building on existing colonial works in most cases, and constrained often by the irregular traces of the earlier works, they carried out in the New World the time-tested principles of Vauban and the French school of the first half of the 18th century. Second System design and construction was in the hands of American engineers, almost all members of the newly-created Corps of Engineers and all but a few products of the infant Military Academy. Under the tutelage of Jonathan Williams, the new breed of engineers followed generally in the well-worn path of their foreign-born predecessors, but they were bound less by the Vauban tradition and were willing to experiment. The younger Engineer officers like Alexander Macomb and Joseph G. Swift grumbled about the outmoded designs forced upon them from Washington, but they arranged to produce works that were relatively effective blends of old and new theory. It was during the Second System that the modified Montalembert designs, the perpendicular casemated "castles," came into vogue.

Comparing the two design theories under wartime conditions, is apparent that the Vauban-type fortifications stood the test of battle well. Fort McHenry, Fort Bowyer, and Fort St. Philip, all of which resisted full-scale bombardment so well, were basically horizontal Vauban designs. The fortifications embodying the Montalembert principles never came under enemy fire, although Castle Williams in New York Harbor emerged relatively unscathed from the point-blank fire of two American warships just before the war. Nevertheless, proceeding from theory rather than experience, it was the casemated, multi-tiered castle that formed the basis for Third System design, beginning in 1816. The most advanced example of this design, Castle Williams, was the model for all major fortifications constructed over the next 50 years.(40) While the creation of the Corps of Engineers was a great step forward toward standardization of fortifications design, its influence was not fully felt until the Third System. In retrospect, the Corps was not entirely effective until after the War of 1812 because no one was really in charge; Jonathan Williams was designated Chief Engineer, but he was increasingly concerned only with the Military Academy and the defenses of New York Harbor. The best discussions of fortifications theory and its application to American needs took place not in an Engineer office in Washington, but in the meetings of the United States Military Philosophical Society at various locations. Not until the Chief Engineer established his office in Washington after the war would there be centralized direction of engineering effort and increasing standardization of design.

The guns provided for the fortifications of the First and Second Systems would have been quite recognizable to veterans of the Seven Years' War. Relatively few innovations appeared prior to the War of 1812, and most of the guns mounted in the coastal forts were either relics of the Revolution or almost direct copies. The lack of an Ordnance Department until 1812 inhibited design research, and threw almost all ordnance matters into the hands of the senior officer of Artillerists, who had little time to devote to ordnance research. The private cannon foundries, of which Henry Foxall's Columbia Foundry was the most effective, had little difficulty in producing such cannon as the limited appropriations permitted; they were perfectly willing to experiment occasionally with larger weapons, but there was no money for research and no officers available to sponsor it, even had the concept of "pure" research been understood at the time.

An analysis of the individual fortifications yields the conclusion that the forts of the First and Second Systems were generally under-gunned. There is no absolute standard for the number of guns needed by a seacoast fortress, although in broad terms a major fort should be able to match the firepower of at least the broadside of a first-class warship—at that period, 37 guns averaging 24-pounders of the line-of-battle 74. Few American forts were able to bring that many guns, 24-pounders or larger, to bear on a single target. Certainly the forts in New York Harbor had adequate numbers of guns, and this may have contributed to the fact that they were never attacked. But the forts that came under naval gunfire—or were threatened, in the case of Fort Washington—were not sufficiently armed to engage in protracted duels with enemy warships. Most of them relied on medium-weight guns, 24- and even 18-pounders, and the mounting of 32-pounder was a cause for celebration. Particularly lacking were long-range, high-trajectory mortars to counter the British bomb ketches and mortar vessels that stood out of range of the flat trajectory guns of the American forts; the few American mortars available were mounted primarily in New York Harbor.

It has been theorized that because the production of artillery weapons during the Second System included many heavier guns, the overall average of the armament was increased in terms of caliber. (41) This is true, but the average was distorted because the bulk of the heavier guns went to only a few selected forts; about two dozen of the experimental 50-pounders were mounted in Castle Williams alone. Yet the conclusion that heavier, longer-range guns were needed in the seacoast fortifications was not one of the accepted lessons of the war.

The fact is that the heaviest guns were not considered with favor, balancing their greater range and effectiveness against their cost and against the difficulty of transport and mounting. Two years after the war the Commissary General of Ordnance, Colonel Decius Wadsworth, submitted a recommendation for standardizing armament; he included nothing larger than 24-pounders, plus 8-inch howitzers and 8- and 10-inch mortars.(42) Wadsworth admittedly was trying to reduce the multiplicity of types and calibers, but the conclusion from the war seemed to be that the best guns for seacoast artillery were simply the largest sizes procured for field artillery. As late as 1822, when George Bomford headed the Ordnance service—by then abolished as a separate corps—he reported that the total weapons issued to fortifications, both seacoast and frontier, included 228 18-pounders, 413 24-pounders, 226 32-pounders, and only 28 42-pounders.(43) (Of the 42-pounders, 27 were mounted in New York Harbor; the other, curiously, was at Fort Sewall in Marblehead.)

The weakest aspect of the seacoast defenses of the First and Second Systems was the garrisons of the fortifications. From the beginning of the First System, few if any forts were adequately manned by trained federal troops. During the period 1796-98 the garrisons were purposely kept small in order to attempt some form of professional training at West Point, while during the era of the Provisional Army too many companies of Artillerists and Engineers were held out for potential use with the field army, which existed mostly on paper and in Hamilton's mind. It is no exaggeration to say that from 1802 to 1809, the seacoast garrisons were little more than caretakers; after the augmentation of 1808-09, such additional troops as the coast defenses received were usually recruits of infantry or riflemen, while many trained artillerists were assigned to the frontiers. Secretary Eustis's estimate of 13 men per gun for the seacoast defenses far exceeded the resources of the Regiment of Artillerists, even had that regiment been assigned exclusively to the coastal fortifications.

The promising geographical command structure finally achieved in 1811, with field officers of Artillerists commanding seacoast-defense districts, was swept away within the first few months of the war. The concentration on invading Canada in 1812 meant that almost all federal artillery companies were withdrawn from seacoast garrisons to support the field armies, to be replaced by militia units or volunteers. Many of the officers of the old Regiment of Artillerists, and of the two new regiments raised in 1812 by George Izard and Alexander Macomb, made fine records during the war, serving with the field armies or in the forts along the Canadian frontier. Few of them saw seacoast defense service after 1812. In the four principal confrontations analyzed earlier, artillery officers commanded at the defense of Fort McHenry and the surrender of Fort Washington, while infantry officers of high quality commanded the successful defenses of Fort Bowyer and Fort St. Philip—although the latter defense depended heavily upon two regular companies of artillery. The result of the lack of wartime seacoast-defense experience by regular officers was that no body of expertise and doctrine was accumulated. With no centralized direction of the defenses of the seacoast, no commander or staff officer was able to pass to other defenses the lessons learned at Fort Washington or Fort McHenry. The Army entered the Third System of fortification in 1816 with very definite theories on construction and an adequate approach to ordnance problems, but with almost no doctrine for the organization, training, and assignment of artillery companies to coastal fortifications. This latter deficiency was to last, to some extent, throughout the 19th century.

It has been said that in a democracy the people get the types of institutions they deserve. Certainly the voting public gets the type of army it deserves, and in the early years of the Republic the American people probably got the seacoast defenses they deserved. Yet they learned the basic lessons, and beginning with the Third System the American people began to demand, and pay for, and get an increasingly adequate degree of coastal protection. This process was not continuous; there were rich years and lean years throughout the 19th century, but at the end of that century, and indeed until the need was no longer realistic, the American system of seacoast defense was the best in the world.

This has been simply the story of how it began.

NOTES TO CHAPTER I

1. Act of 3 June 1784, in Worthington C. Ford (ed.), *Journals of the Continental Congress* (Washington, 1904-37), XXVII, 530-531.

2. *Ibid.*, XXXI, 891-893; XXXII, 153-154.

3. John Doughty had resigned in early 1791. Ebenezer Denny, *Military Journal of Major Ebenezer Denny* (Philadelphia, 1859), 172. Good general accounts of the Harmar and St. Clair campaigns are in James R. Jacobs, *The Beginning of the U.S. Army, 1783-1812* (Princeton, 1947), and William H. Guthman, *March to Massacre* (New York, 1975).

4. Burbeck had entered postwar service as captain of one of the Massachusetts artillery companies raised for Shays's Rebellion. Orders, 4 Sept 1792. Orderly Books of Major General Anthony Wayne, I; Francis B. Heitman, *Historical Register and Dictionary of the United States Army, 1789-1903* (Washington, 1903), I, 139-140.

5. Thomas A. Bailey, *A Diplomatic History of the American People* (New York, 1958), 72-73; John C. Miller, *The Federalist Era* (New York, 1960), 140-141.

6. Of the very few works on seacoast fortifications in colonial America, most center on Louisbourg in Nova Scotia. A few pages (14-17) of Emanuel Raymond Lewis, *Seacoast Fortifications of the United States: An Introductory History* (Washington, 1970), are devoted to the colonial period. For interesting details of fortifications of major ports prior to 1759, see Carl Bridenbaugh, *Cities in Revolt* (New York, 1955), 22-24. The best references for the colonial period are a series of articles by Major Robert Arthur in *The Coast Artillery Journal* (hereafter *CAJ*) between 1923-1929, referred to in specific notes below.

7. Duportail to Washington, 30 Sept 1783, quoted in William E. Birkhimer, *Historical Sketch of the ... Artillery, United States Army* (New York, 1884), 17-18. (Cited hereafter as Birkhimer, *Artillery*.)

8. Birkhimer, *Artillery*, 19.

9. *American State Papers, Military Affairs* (Washington, 1832-61), I, 61-62. (Cited hereafter as *ASP, MA.*)

10. [Robert Arthur], "Early Coast Fortifications." *CAJ* (Feb 1929), 134; United States Military Academy, *Notes on Permanent Land Fortifications* (West Point, N.Y., 1952), 4; Harold L. Peterson, *Forts in America* (New York, 1964), 24-25, 37.

11. Arthur, *loc. cit.*, 134-135; Harold I. Peterson, *Round Shot and Rammers* (New York, 1969), 72.

12. George W. Cullum, "History of the Sea-Coast Fortifications of the United States: Narragansett Bay," *Journal of the United States Artillery*, VIII (1897), 187; John B. MacMaster, *History of the People of the United States* (New York, 1885), II, 170-173.

13. *ASP, MA*, I, 62-63.

14. *Statutes at Large and Treaties of the United States of America, 1789-1873* (Boston, 1845-73), I, 345. (Cited hereafter as I *Stat.* 345.)

15. Edgar B. Wesley, "The Beginnings of Coast Fortifications," *CAJ* (Oct 1927), 282.

16. Knox to Rochefontaine, 29 Mar 1794, *ASP, MA*, I, 72-74.

17. Just who first used this terminology is not clear. It was employed officially by Joseph G. Totten, *Report of General J. G. Totten, Chief Engineer, on the Subject of National Defence* (Washington, 1851), 50-51.

18. Knox to House of Representatives, 19 Dec 1794, *ASP, MA*, I, 71-72; Knox to same, 28 Nov 1794, NA RG 107, Copies of War Department Correspondence and Reports, 1791-96 (microcopy T932, roll 1) (cited hereafter as Knox Report, 28 Nov 1794).

19. Knox Report, 28 Nov 1794; *ASP, MA,* I, 107, 116; Robert Arthur, "Coast Forts in Colonial Maine," *CAJ* (Apr 1923), 236; *Portland City Guide* (Portland, 1949), 284. Fort Sumner is thought to be the "Fort upon the hill" of Longfellow's poem, "My Lost Youth."

20. *ASP, MA,* I, 116, 158; Robert Arthur, "Coast Forts in Colonial New Hampshire," *CAJ* (June 1923), 549-552; George B. Griffith (ed.), *History of Fort Constitution and "Walbach Tower," Portsmouth Harbor, N.H.* (Portsmouth, 1865), 3; Harriet S. Lacy, "Fort William and Mary Becomes Fort Constitution," *Historical New Hampshire,* XXIX (Winter 1974), 281-293.

21. Knox Report, 28 Nov 1794; *ASP, MA,* I, 61-62; Arthur, "Early Coast Fortifications," 139.

22. Knox Report, 28 Nov 1794; *ASP, MA,* I, 141; Arthur, *ibid.*; *Essex Institute Historical Collections,* V, 258-260.

23. *ASP, MA,* I, 141; Arthur, *ibid.*; Wesley, *loc. cit.,* 284.

24. Knox Report, 28 Nov 1794; *ASP, MA,* I, 61-62; Lewis, *Seacoast Fortifications,* 15, 40; Robert Arthur, "Coast Forts of Colonial Massachusetts," *CAJ* (Feb 1923), 113-119.

25. Knox Report, 28 Nov 1794; *ASP, MA,* I, 71-72; Arthur, "Early Coast Fortifications," 139-140; Cullum, "Narragansett Bay," *loc. cit.,* 187-188.

26. Knox Report, 28 Nov 1794.

27. *ASP, MA,* I, 72, 116; Arthur, "Early Coast Fortifications," 140; McMaster, *History,* II, 173.

28. Knox Report, 28 Nov 1794.

29. *ASP, MA,* I, 61-62; Arthur, "Early Coast Fortifications," 140-141; McMaster, *History,* II, 173; Edmund Banks Smith, *Governors Island: Its Military History Under Three Flags, 1637-1913* (New York, 1913), 53-54; Ames W. Williams, "The Old Fortifications of New York Harbor," *Military Collector and Historian,* XXII, 2 (1970), 38-39.

30. *ASP, MA,* I, 61-62; Arthur, "Early Coast Fortifications," 141; Wesley, *loc. cit.,* 284; *Statutes at Large of Pennsylvania* (Harrisburg, 1911), XV, 293-294; *Dunlap and Claypool's American Daily Advertiser,* 2 Sept 1795.

31. Arthur, "Early Coast Fortifications," 141; Wesley, *loc. cit.,* 285; Knox Report, 28 Nov 1794.

32. Harold I. Lessen and George C. MacKenzie, *Fort McHenry* (Washington, 1954), 2; Arthur, *ibid.*; McMaster, *History,* II, 173.

33. *ASP, MA,* I, 61-62; Robert Arthur, "Tidewater Forts of Colonial Virginia," *CAJ* (Jan 1924), 18; Knox Report, 28 Nov 1794.

34. *ASP, MA,* 1, 71; Arthur, "Early Coast Fortifications," 142; Wesley, *loc. cit.,* 285-286; Blackwell P. Robinson (ed.), *The North Carolina Guide* (Chapel Hill, 1955), 269-270.

35. *ASP, MA,* I, 61-62; Arthur, "Early Coast Fortifications," 142.

36. Arthur, *ibid.,* 142-143; Ralston B. Lattimore, *Fort Pulaski National Monument* (Washington, 1954), 3; Richard K. Murdoch, *The Georgia-Florida Frontier, 1793-1796* (Berkeley, CA, 1951), 35ff.

37. Bailey, *Diplomatic History,* 74; I *Stat.* 352.

38. Knox to Wayne, 31 Mar 1794, Richard C. Knopf (ed.), *Anthony Wayne, A Name in Arms* (Pittsburgh, 1960), 318-319.

NOTES TO CHAPTER II

1.   Knox to Washington, 7 Apr 1894, and Washington to Knox, same date, John C. Fitzpatrick (ed.), *The Writings of George Washington* (Washington, 1941), XXXIII, 317.

2.   The company was commanded by Capt. Cornelius R. Sedam of the 1st Sublegion. Smith, *Governors Island*, 53.

3.   I *Stat.* 366.

4.   See, for example, references to Jacob Melcher of Pennsylvania and John Morgan of New Jersey as cadets, in Ebenezer Denny, *Journal of Major Ebenezer Denny* (Philadelphia, 1859), 111, 125.

5.   Knox to Wayne, 16 May 1794, Knopf (ed.), *Anthony Wayne*, 331.

6.   Orderly Book of the Corps of Artillerists and Engineers at West Point (cited hereafter as OB CA&E), I, various entries for 1794; Heitman, *Register*, I, passim; Charles K. Gardner, *Dictionary of All Officers in the Army of the United States* (New York, 1853), passim.

7.   John F. Ficken, *Michael Kalteisen, Captain of United States Artillery* (Charleston, 1910), 5, 11; Gabriel E. Manigault, "The Military Career of General George Izard," *Magazine of American History*, XIX (1886), 462-465.

8.   Knox to Speaker HR, 28 Nov 1794, NA RG 107, Copies of War Department Correspondence and Reports, 1791-96 (microcopy T982, roll 1).

9.   *ASP, MA*, I, 68.

10.   "Opinion of the General Officers," undated [c. Feb 1792], Fitzpatrick (ed.), *Writings of Washington*, XXXI, 509-515.

11.   James R. Jacobs, *The Beginning of the U.S. Army, 1783-1812* (Princeton, 1947), 157-158; Heitman, *Register*, I, 790.

12.   The voluminous Pickering Papers in the Massachusetts Historical Society contain much correspondence between Pickering and officers of the Army after early 1796, and are a prime source for the history of the Corps of Artillerists and Engineers.

13.   For Henry Burheck's antecedents and wartime career, see Asa Bird Gardner, "Henry Burbeck," *Magazine of American History*, IX, 4 (Apr 1883), 251-265; for his dealings with Governor Quesada in 1791-92, Richard K. Murdoch, "The Case of the Three Spanish Deserters, 1791-1793," *Georgia Historical Quarterly*, XLIV (Sept 1960), 278-305.

14.   Heitman, *Register*, I, 50.

15.   *Ibid.*; *ASP, Indian Affairs*, I, 390ff.

16.   The grade of lieutenant colonel commandant was adopted in 1779, primarily because there were no line colonels in the British Army in America with whom equivalent-rank prisoner exchange could be effected. Congress decided that no new colonels would be appointed to command regiments, and that lieutenant colonels commandant—who were senior to other lieutenant colonels—could be promoted directly to brigadier general. Josiah Harmar's grade in 1784 was lieutenant colonel commandant, although he was subsequently brevetted brigadier general, and no colonels were appointed in the United States Army until 1802. See John W. Wright, "Some Notes on the Continental Amy," *William and Mary College Quarterly Historical Magazine*, X (Apr. 1931), 96-97.

17.   Ford (ed.), *Journals of the Continental Congress*, XII, 926.

18.   Edward H. Hall, "Lieutenant Colonel Stephen Rochefontaine," *26th Annual Report of the American Scenic and Historical Preservation Society* (Albany, N.Y., 1922), Appendix B, 245-262; this is the only known biographical sketch of Rochefontaine in English.

19. Washington to James McHenry, 15 Oct 1798, Fitzpatrick (ed.), *Writings of Washington*, XXXVI, 438-489.

20. Rivardi to Pickering, 16 May 1798, Pickering Papers, XXII, 160; Rivardi to Hamilton, 21 May 1799, Harold C. Syrett (ed.), *The Papers of Alexander Hamilton*, XXII (New York, 1975), 572.

21. See the listing of French officers in Francis B. Heitman, *Historical Register of Officers of the Continental Army* (Washington, 1893; revised 1914), 644-668. Heitman's *Register of the U.S. Army*, I, 833, credits Rivardi with no military service prior to 26 Feb 1795. Rivardi himself later wrote that "I Served in the Most despotic of all Armies," presumably the Russian; Syrett (ed.), *Papers of Alexander Hamilton*, XXII, 571.

22. Rivardi referred to himself as "the only Officer in the army whose wife has no relations in America"; Rivardi to Hamilton, 21 Nov 1799, Syrett (ed.), *Papers of Alexander Hamilton*, XXII. 572.

23. Norman B. Wilkinson, "The Forgotten 'Founder' of West Point," *Military Affairs*, XXIV (Winter 1960-61), 177-178; Edward L. Tinker, "Anne Louis de Tousard," *Dictionary of American Biography* (New York, 1964), IX, Pt. 2, 605-606. It is curious that of the five field officers of the Corps of Artillerists and Engineers, including the American-born Henry Burbeck and Constant Freeman, only Tousard has a sketch in the *D.A.B.*

24. William Lee (ed.), "Record of the Services of Constant Freeman, Captain of Artillery in the Continental Army," *Magazine of American History*, II (1878), 349-359; Freeman's activities in Georgia are referred to in *ASP, Indian Affairs*, I, 390ff, 499-500.

25. Appendix A is based on OB CA&E, I-IV; Heitman, *Register*, I; Gardner, *Dictionary of the Army*; William H. Powell, *List of Officers of the Army of the United States from 1779 to 1900* (New York, 1900); and miscellaneous fragmentary sources. Most of the captains listed were present for duty, but the same was not true of the lieutenants; George Izard, for example, was still in France.

26. OB CA&E, I; Smith, *Governors Island*, 53-54.

27. Dunlap and Claypool's *American Daily Advertiser*, 2 Sept 1795, p. 3.

28. Bruff to Stone, 2 Feb 1795, Papers of James Bruff, Maryland Historical Society.

29. Bruff to Stone, 11 Apr 1795, *loc. cit.*

30. Entry for 5 Jan 1798, OB CA&E, IV.

31. Ficken, *Michael Kalteisen*, 5. Kalteisen was, however, offered promotion to major at the end of 1804, but declined in order to remain at Fort Johnson; SecWar to Kalteisen, 24 Jan 1805, NA RG 107, SecWar Military Book No. 2, letters Sent Relating to Military Affairs, 1803-1806 (microcopy M6, roll 2).

32. Octavius Pickering, *The Life of Timothy Pickering* (Boston, 1873), III, 158-159.

33. *ASP, MA*, I, 107.

34. Pickering to Hayne, 27 June 1795, Knopf (ed.), *Anthony Wayne*, 429.

35. Same, 29 June 1795, *ibid.*, 434.

36. Waste Book for the Quartermaster Stores, West Point, 1794-1806, USMA Archives. The issue was made to "Colonel" Tousard, the title by which he was sometimes referred because of the brevet of lieutenant colonel conferred by Congress in 1778; no other officer of artillerists and engineers held a wartime brevet higher than his lineal rank in 1795.

37. OB CA&E, I; West Point Clothing Account Book, 1795-1796, USMA Archives. Heitman, *Register*, I, lists Landais and Rodrigue as French-born, and Triplett as from Virginia; it is probable that the three cadets were former soldiers of the Legion.

38. Entries for 25 June and 9 July 1795, OB CA&E, I, and for 5 Jan 1798, *ibid.*, IV. The uniform regulations for the Battalion of Artillery are from the Order and Letter Book of Henry Burbeck, 1787-1800, USMA Archives.

39. Pickering to Wayne, 17 July 1795, Knopf (ed.), *Anthony Wayne*, 439.

40. Rivardi to Pickering, 3 Oct 1795, *Pickering Papers,* XX, 66.

41. OB CA&E, I; Fitzpatrick (ed.), *Writings of Washington,* XXXIV, 355.

42. OB CA&E, II; West Point Clothing Account Book, entry for 6 Jan 1796.

NOTES TO CHAPTER III

1. Forwarded to Congress 3 Feb 1796, *ASP, MA,* I, 113.

2. This was almost certainly *A Treatise Containing the Elements of Fortification* by John Muller, professor of fortifications and artillery at the Royal Military Academy, Woolwich. This work, originally published in London in 1746, was unquestionably the best available in English. Few copies would have been available at West Point, and presumably the officers were set to "copying the author" so as to have their own textbooks.

3. Orders, 10 Feb 1796, OB CA&E, II.

4. Rochefontaine to Pickering, 23 Feb 1796, Pickering Papers, XX, 131.

5. Same, 19 Feb 1796, *ibid.*, 129.

6. Same, 5 May 1796, *ibid.*, 134.

7. Warin to Pickering, 24 May 1796, *ibid.*, 142.

8. James McHenry to Anthony Wayne (private), 25 May 1796, Knopf (ed.), *Anthony Wayne,* 481-482.

9. For a summary of the Collot-Warin mission, see Dale Van Every, *Ark of Empire* (New York, 1963), 339-340. Much of the McHenry-Wayne correspondence in May and June 1796 concerns the possibility that Collot was engaged in a conspiracy with Brig Gen James Wilkinson, Wayne's second-in-command; see Knopf, *Anthony Wayne.* Some of the excellent maps produced by Joseph Warin are reproduced in David Lavender, *The American Heritage History of the Great West* (New York, 1965), 54-55.

10. Rochefontaine to Pickering, 12 Apr 1796, Pickering Papers, XX, 150.

11. Quoted by Edward S. Holden in "Origins of the United States Military Academy, 1777-1802," *Centennial of the United States Military Academy, 1802-1902* (Washington, 1904), I, 212-214.

12. Rochefontaine to Hamilton, 28 Apr 1796, ms. in USMA Archives; see also Rochefontaine to Pickering, 26 Apr 1796, Pickering Papers, XX, l56ff.

13. Holden, *loc. cit.,* 214.

14. James A. Huston, *The Sinews of War: Army Logistics, 1775-1953* (Washington, 1966), 95; Constance McL. Green, *Eli Whitney and the Birth of American Technology* (Boston, 1956), 116; Wadsworth to Sec-War Armstrong, 6 June 1814, *A Collection ... Relating to the Ordnance Department* (Washington,1878), I, 15-16. Decius Wadsworth would become an engineer officer in 1802, and would serve as head of the Ordnance Department from 1812-1821.

15. McHenry to Wayne, 12 May 1796, Knopf (ed.), *Anthony Wayne,* 481.

16. Rochefontaine to Pickering, 28 May 1796, Pickering Papers, LIII, 269. The other members of the court were Maj William Peters and Capt Daniel Britt; the judge advocate was Lieut William K. Blue, who had acted as judge advocate for the Legion.

17. Orders, 23 May 1796, OB CA&E, II.

18. The record of the court, "Proceedings of a Court of Inquiry held at West Point by order of Major Genl Wayne on the 23d of May 1796," was presumably destroyed in the War Dept fire of Nov 1800. The only known copy is the one authenticated by Rochefontaine and sent by him to Pickering, filed in the Pickering Papers, LIII, 269-303. As Pickering could have had access to the original record sent to SecWar McHenry, there is no reason to question the essential accuracy of Rochefontaine's "true copy."

19. Rochefontaine to Pickering, 28 May 1796, Pickering Papers, XX, 180.

20. Same, 5 June 1796, *ibid.*, 198-199, enclosing note Blue to Rochefontaine, 2 June 1796.

21. Same, 7 June 1796, *ibid.*, 203.

22. Same, 19 June 1796, *ibid.*, 220; McHenry to Rochefontaine, 18 June 1796, OB CA&E, III.

23. Orders, 6 June 1796, OB CA&E, III. It is not clear whether Wilson's transfer was directed by SecWar, or by Maj Tousard, who was in command of the garrison as well as of the CA&E on 6 June.

24. McHenry to Wadsworth, 1 July 1796, Bernard C. Steiner, *The Life and Correspondence of James McHenry* (Cleveland, 1907), 184.

25. Rochefontaine to Pickering, 1 July 1796, Pickering Papers, XX, 247.

26. McHenry to Wayne, 22 July 1796, Knopf (ed.), *Anthony Wayne*, 500.

27. The full text was reprinted in the *Columbian Centinel* of Boston on 17 Aug (copy in USMA Archives).

28. Rochefontaine to Pickering, 31 May 1796, Pickering Papers, XX, 181.

29. Rivard; to Pickering, 2 June 1796, *ibid.*, 190.

30. "Fort Ontario [originally Fort Oswego], New York," NA RG 98, Records of United States Army Commands (Army Posts) (microcopy T912, roll 1). Lieut Elmer's role is not mentioned in OB CA&E.

31. OB CA&E, III; Clarence E. Carter (ed.), *The Territorial Papers of the United States* (Washington, 1934), II, 561.

32. Rivardi's initial assignment to Michilimackinac does not appear in OB CA&E, but is mentioned in Rivardi to Hamilton, 21 Mar 1799, Syrett (ed.), *Papers of Alexander Hamilton*, XXII, 569.

33. Rivardi to Pickering, 6 Aug 1796, Pickering Papers, XX, 315.

34. Rochefontaine to Pickering, 2 Sept 1796, *ibid.*, 347.

35. Rivardi to Pickering, 23 Aug 1796, *ibid.*, 338; Rivardi to Hamilton, 21 Mar 1799, *Papers of Alexander Hamilton*, XXII, 569.

36. Pickering to Committee on the Military Establishment, HR, 3 Feb 1796, *ASP, MA,* I, 113.

37. Tabular summary of 29 Mar 1796, *ibid.*, 115.

38. For a summary of the debate, Edgar B. Wesley, "The Beginning of Coast Fortifications," *CAJ* (Oct 1927), 286-287.

39. I *Stat.* 483.

40. Heitman, *Register,* II, 562-563.

41. Washington to McHenry, 25 July 1796, Fitzpatrick (ed.), *Writings of Washington*, XXXV, 151-152.

42. Same, 3 Aug 1796, *ibid.*, 164.

43. OB CA&E, III; McHenry to Wayne, 22 July and 27 Aug 1796, Knopf (ed.), *Anthony Wayne*, 500, 501.

44. Wayne to McHenry, 8 Oct 1796, *ibid.*, 534-535.

45.   Richard Whiley served as an officer for almost 15 years. As a captain of artillerists in Jan 1808, he presented to the United States Military Philosophical Society at West Point four volumes of the orderly books of Gen Wayne during his command of the Legion; how these important records came into Whiley's possession is unknown.

46.   Five other lieutenants were appointed with rank from 19 Dec 1796, but they did not report to West Point until mid-1797.

47.   Order and Letter Book of Henry Burbeck, 1787-1800, USMA Archives.

48.   *ASP, MA*, I, 117; OB CA&E.

49.   OB CA&E, III.

50.   For the political and diplomatic background of the breach with France, Alexander DeConde, *The Quasi War: The Politics and Diplomacy of the Undeclared with War with France, 1797-1801* (New York, 1966), 3-17.

51.   McHenry to Richard Stockton, 3 June 1797, *ASP, MA*, I, 118.

52.   Act of 3 Mar 1797, I *Stat.* 508.

53.   Debate of 16 June 1797, *Annals of Congress*, 5th Cong., 1st Sess., HR, 325-331.

54.   Holden in *Centennial of the USMA*, I, 214.

55.   Waste Book for the Quartermaster Stores, West Point, 16 Dee 1797.

56.   OB CA&E, III; Wilkinson to Burbeck, 19 Aug 1797, Burbeck O&L Book; Rivardi to Hamilton, 21 Mar 1799, *Papers of Alexander Hamilton*, XXII, 569.

57.   Thomas R. Hay and M.R. Werner, *The Admirable Trumpeter: A Biography of General James Wilkinson* (Garden City, N.Y., 1941), 166. For Freeman's activities in early 1798, see Isaac Guion to William Kersey, 12 May 1798, in *Seventh Annual Report of the Director at the Department of Archives and History of the State of Mississippi* (Nashville, Tenn., 1909), 71-72.

58.   OB CA&E, III.

NOTES TO CHAPTER IV

1.   See Alexander DeConde, *The Quasi-War* (New York, 1966), 36-73, and Ralph Adams Brown, *The Presidency of John Adams* (Lawrence, Kans., 1975), *passim*.

2.   Hamilton to Pickering, 17 Mar 1798, Harold C. Syrett (ed.), *The Papers of Alexander Hamilton*, XXI (New York, 1974), 364-366.

3.   McHenry to Samuel Sewall, 27 Feb 1798, *ASP, MA*, I, 119-120.

4.   Orderly Books, Corps of Artillerists and Engineers, III and IV; Order and letter Book of Henry Burbeck; letters of Capt Isaac Guion from Natchez, Jan-Mar 1798, *Seventh Annual Report of the Director of the Department of Archives and History of the State of Mississippi*; various miscellaneous correspondence in the Pickering Papers.

5.   F. B., Heitman, *Register*, I, 840.

6.   The charges were later summarized by SecState Pickering to Pres Adams, 28 Apr 1798, Pickering Papers, VIII, 371.

7.   McHenry to Adams, 6 Apr 1798, copy in Pickering Papers, VIII, 373.

8.   Wolcott to Adams, 23 Apr 1798, copy *ibid.*, 375.

9.   Pickering to Adams, 28 Apr 1798, *ibid.*, 371.

10. Rochefontaine to Pickering, 27 Apr 1798, *ibid.*, XXII, 143.

11. Same, 30 Apr 1798, *ibid.*, 146.

12. Orders, 10 May 1798, 08 CA&E, IV; this is the only reference in the Orderly Books to Rochefontaine's departure.

13. Edward M. Hall, "Lieutenant Colonel Stephen Rochefontaine," *Twenty-Sixth Annual Report of the American Scenic and Historic Preservation Society*, 1921 (Albany, N.Y., 1922), 264-266.

14. McHenry to Sewall, 9 Apr 1798, *ASP, MA*, 1,120-121.

15. Act of 27 Apr 1798, 1 *Stat.* 552.

16. McHenry to Sewall, 28 Jun 1798, *ASP, MA*, I, 128-129.

17. The organization of the Provisional Army is given in detail in Carlos E. Godfrey, "Organization of the Provisional Army of the United States in the Anticipated War with France, 1798-1800," *Pennsylvania Magazine of History and Biography*, XXXVII (1914), 129-182. Good general coverage is in John C. Miller, *Alexander Hamilton and the Growth of the New Nation* (New York) 1959), Part IV; see also Miller's *The Federalist Era, 1799-1801* (New York, 1960), Chap. XII, and DeConde, *The Quasi-War*, 89-123 and passim. On whether the Provisional Army should properly be called the "Eventual Army," see Richard H. Kahn, *Eagle and Sword: The Federalists and the Creation of the Military Establishment in America, 1783-1802* (York, 1975), 229, but this argument does not affect the artillerists and engineers. For the Act of 28 May 1798, 1 *Stat.* 558.

18. Washington continued to use the term Commander-in-Chief in its traditional military sense, rather than as referring to the President, who was Commander-in-Chief of the Army and Navy under the Constitution. The use of the term "General Staff" at this period referred only to the heads of staff departments such as the Adjutant General and the Quartermaster General; the United States would not have a true General Staff for over a century.

19. Washington to McHenry, 4 July 1798, Fitzpatrick (ed.), *Writings of Washington*, XXXVI, 308-310.

20. Washington to Adams, 4 July 1798, *ibid.*, 315.

21. DeConde, *The Quasi-War*, 102.

22. 1 *Stat.* 604; Orders, 2 Aug 1798, OB CA&E, IV. Young Cross would not be commissioned until Feb 1801.

23. Washington to McHenry, 22 July 1798, Fitzpatrick (ed.), *Writings of Washington*, XXXVI, 360.

24. For a good discussion of the political attributes of the Provisional/Eventual Army, see Kahn, *Eagle and Sword*, Chaps. 11-12.

25. Washington to Hamilton, 9 Aug 1798, Fitzpatrick (ed.), *Writings of Washington*, XXXVI, 395.

26. Washington to McHenry, 15 Oct 1798, *ibid.*, 488-489.

27. Heitman, *Continental Register*, 122, 300, 315; Hamilton to McHenry, 19 Oct 1798, Syrett (ed.), *Papers of Alexander Hamilton*, XXII, 202-203.

28. Hamilton to McHenry, 20 Dec 1798; McHenry to Hamilton, 28 Dec 1798, *ibid.*, 378-379, 397.

29. Order and Letter Book of Henry Burbeck; the Dayton nomination is discussed in William E. Birkhimer, *Historical Sketch of the ... Artillery: United States Army* (New York, 1884), 32.

30. Washington to McHenry, 13 Dec 1798, Henry Cabot Lodge, *Works of Alexander Hamilton* (New York, 1904), VII, 14-15. This letter, drafted by Hamilton, is the first of two Washington-to-McHenry letters of that date.

31. Hamilton's original ideas were incorporated in Washington to McHenry, 13 Dec 1798, Lodge, *Works of Hamilton*, VII, 22-37; McHenry's final version, as forwarded by the President to Congress, as in *ASP, MA.* I, 124-126.

32. Isaac Guion to James Wilkinson, 30 July 1798, Guion Letters, *loc. cit.*; OB CA&E, IV; Heitman, *Register*, I, *passim.*

33. OB CA&E, IV; Heitman, *Register*, I, 682.

34. William W.H. Davis, *The Fries Rebellion, 1798-99* (Doylestown, Pa., 1899), is the best published source; the calling-out of troops is covered in Chap. VIII.

35. Hamilton queries Jonathan Dayton of New Jersey as to Major Ford's political ideology: Hamilton to Dayton, 18 May, and Dayton to Hamilton, 20 Mar 1799, quoted in Broadus Mitchell, *Alexander Hamilton: The National Adventure, 1788-1804* (New York, 1962), 435.

36. Davis, *The Fries Rebellion*, 79-81. Elliott's and Henry's companies apparently came from Rhode Island, and Irvine's from around Fort Mifflin. In May the OB CA&E, IV, listed the three companies as detached at Reading.

37. For a recent evaluation of the role of federal troops in the Fries Rebellion, see DeConde, *The Quasi-War*, 196-198.

38. McHenry to Hamilton, 4 Feb 1799, John C. Hamilton (ed.), *The Works of Alexander Hamilton* (New York, 1851), 199-207.

39. Act of 2 Mar 1799, 1 *Stat.* 725.

40. Act of 3 Mar 1799, 1 *Stat.* 749.

41. This was the title conferred upon Gen John J. Pershing after World War I, and is usually considered as unique and without precedent. Although Congress unquestionably authorized the grade in 1799, there is no record that it was actually conferred upon Washington before his death in December.

42. 1 *Stat.* 521; *ASP, MA*, I, 141; Edgar B. Hesley, "The Beginning of Coast Fortifications," *Coast Artillery Journal* (Oct 1927), 288-89; *Annals of Congress*, 5th Cong., 2d Sess., 1394-1402.

43. Report of SecWar, *ASP, MA*, 1, 141; expenditures, shown to the nearest dollar, were through 1 Oct 1799. This table is presented only as a rough guide to priorities, for other sources give somewhat different amounts expended, particularly at Norfolk.

44. Hamilton to Gates, 5 Jun 1799, Order Book of Capt Lemuel Gates's Company[2d A&E], USMA Archives.

45. "Battalion Orders, Castle William," 4 Jun 1799, *ibid.*

46. *Eastern Herald and Gazette of Maine*, 18 Jun 1793, and *Portland Gazette*, 1 and 23 Oct 1798, quoted in Frank E. Southard, "The Portland Federal Volunteers, 1793-1803," *Military Collector and Historian*, XII (1959), 44-46; Gates's Order Book; Joseph G. Swift, *The Memoirs of Gen. Joseph Gardner Swift, U.S.A.* (Worcester, Mass., 1890), 19-20.

47. *Essex Institute Historical Collections* (Salem, Mass.), V, 260.

48. George W. Cullum, *Historical Sketch of the Fortification Defenses of Narragansett Bay* (Washington, 1884), 21-22.

49. *Connecticut Gazette* of New London, 4 July 1798 and 10 July 1799.

50. Gates's Order Book, 1 Nov 1799.

51. Edmund Banks Smith, *Governors Island* (New York, 1913), 54; Syrett (ed.), *Papers of Alexander Hamilton*, XXII, 59-60n; Talbot Faulkner Hamlin, "Joseph Francois Mangin," *D.A.B.*, V, Pt. 2, 231-232.

52. OB CA&E, IV; Gates's Order Book, 26 Aug 1799; Stevens to Hamilton, 15 and 23 Nov 1798, Syrett (ed)., *Papers of Alexander Hamilton*, XXII, 249, 263-264; Thomas F. Pitkin, *Keepers of the Gate* (New York, 1975), 4.

53. Stevens to Hamilton, 23 Feb 1799, *ibid.*, 298-299; OB CA&E. IV.

54. Order and Letter Book of Henry Burbeck; Heitman, *Register*, I, 595.

55. Lessen and MacKenzei, *Fort McHenry National Monument*, 2.

56. Order and letter Book of Henry Burbeck.

57. *Ibid.; ASP, MA*. I, 141.

58. OB CA&E, IV; *Hall's Wilmington Gazette*, I, 37 (14 Sept l797).

59. *Hall's Wilmington Gazette*, 8 Aug and 26 Sept 1799, 9 Jan 1800.

60. Huger was one of the instigators of Lafayette's brief escape from Olmutz prison in 1794; see John G. Van Deusen, "Francis Kinloch Huger," *D.A.B.*, V, Pt. 1, 344.

61. Gabriel E. Manigault,"The Military Career of General George Izard," *The Magazine of American History*, XIX (1886), 465; Gardner, *Dictionary of the Army*, 239, 247.

62. *ASP, MA*, I, 117; OT'der and Letter Book of Henry Burbeck.

63. Asa Bird Gardner,"Henry Burbeck," *Magazine of American History*, IX (1883), 258.

64. Appendix C has been constructed primarily from OB CA&E, IV; Order and letter Book of Henry Burbeck; and orders from Maj Gen Hamilton copied into Gate's Order Book during 1799.

NOTES TO CHAPTER V

1. Hamilton to Pinckney, Dec 1799, Henry Cabot Lodge, *Works of Alexander Hamilton* (New York, 1904), VII, 190.

2. See the aptly-titled Chap 32, "The Effort to Avert Peace," in John C. Miller, *Alexander Hamilton and the Growth of the New Nation* (New York, 1959).

3. Hamilton to McHenry, 23 Nov 1799, Lodge, *Hamilton,* VII, 179-180.

4. *Ibid.*, 183-184.

5. Washington to Hamilton, 12 Dec 1799, original in USMA Archives.

6. Incorporated in Report of SecWar, 5 Jan 1800, *ASP, MA*, I, 135-138.

7. Order Book of Capt Lemuel Gates's Company [2d A&E], USMA Archives.

8. 2 *Stat*. 85.

9. Hamilton to Izard, 27 Feb 1800, quoted in Broadus Mitchell, *Alexander Hamilton: The National Adventure, 1788-1804* (New York, 1962). 465.

10. General order dated July 1800, Lodge, *Hamilton*, VII, 224; Hamilton to McHenry, 2 July 1800, *ibid.*

11. For correspondence on Smith's pretensions and Tousard's appointment, Charles Francis Adams, *The Works of John Adams* (Boston, MA), IX, 61-63; see also Mitchell, *Hamilton*, 452.

12. Heitman, *Register*, I, 50-51.

13. Cushing's correspondence is in NA RG 94 and 107 (combined in microcopy M565, roll 1), under the inexact title of letters Sent by the Office of the Adjutant General, 1800-1803. (Cited hereafter as Letters Sent, AGO.)

14. Cushing to SecWar, 10 Jan 1801, Letters Sent, AGO.

15. General Orders, 1 Dec 1800, quoted in Asa Bird Gardner,"Henry Burbeck," *Magazine of American History*, IX (1883), 259.

16. Cushing to Tousard, Sept 1800, letters Sent, ASJ; General Orders. 30 Nov and 1 Dec 1800, General James Wilkinson's Order Book,1795-1808, in NA RG 94 (microcopy M654, roll 3) (cited hereafter as Wilkinson Order Book).

17. Dexter to James Taylor, 19 Nov 1800, Military Book No. 1, 1800-1802, War Office, in NA RG 107, Letters Sent by the SecWar Relating to Military Affairs (microcopy M6, roll 1). (Cited hereafter as Military Book No. 1.)

18. Maj Cushing's letters-sent book, 1800-1803, was not destroyed in the fire, but was later misplaced and not discovered until 1902; it was therefore not available for use in compiling the *American State Papers*.

19. *Annals of Congress*, Ser. I, Vol. X, 825-836 (17 Dec 1800); the quotation is from Joseph Varnum of Massachusetts.

20. Cushing to Dexter, 10 Feb 1801, Letters Sent, AGO; on Griswold, see Gardner, "Henry Burbeck," *loc. cit.*, 259.

21. Adams to McHenry, 16 Apr 1799, C.F. Adams, *John Adams*, VIII, 632-633.

22. Arthur P. Wade, "A Military Offspring of the American Philosophical Society," *Military Affairs*, XXX-VIII (1974), 103-104.

23. See, for example, Maj Cushing's letter of welcome to Maj Williams, 2 Mar 1801, Letters Sent, AGO, which Cushing signs "with sincere regard, yr friend & brother soldier."

24. Cushing to Freeman, 6 Feb 1801, and Cushing to Wilkinson, 26 Feb 1801, letters Sent, AGO.

25. The Senate by 18-14, the House by 69-36.

26. Heitman, *Continental Register*, 190; Julius W. Pratt, "Henry Dearborn," *D.A.B.*, III, Pt. I, 174-176. There is no published biography of Dearborn, and his generally valuable services as Secretary of War have been overshadowed by his mediocre performance as a major general in the War of 1812.

27. Dearborn to Tousard, 18 Mar 1801, Military Book No. l.

28. Dearborn to Morris, 10 Apr; Dearborn to Rivardi, 21 Apr and 1 May 1801, *ibid.*

29. Dearborn to Burbeck, 1 Apr 1801, *ibid.*

30. Dearborn to Cushing, 6 July 1801, *ibid.*; Wadsworth, after a period out of service, would become Commissary General of Ordnance in 1812.

31. Dearborn to Tousard, 4 Apr 1801, *ibid.*

32. Enclosure to Dearborn to Tousard, 14 Apr 1801, *ibid.*

33. *Journals of the Continental Congress* (20 June 1777), VIII, 485, quoted in Sidney Forman, "Why the United States MilitaryAcademy was Established in 1802," *Military Affairs*, XXIX (1965), 19. Forman's article gives a good synopsis of some of the wartime attempts at military education.

34. *ASP, MA*, I, 133-144; Forman, *loc. cit.*, 24-25.

35. Tenney L. Davis, "Benjamin Thompson," *D.A.B.*, IX, Pt. II, 451; C.F. Adams, *Works of John Adams*, VIII, 660.

36. Norman B. Wilkinson, "The Forgotten 'Founder' of West Point," *Military Affairs*, XXIV (1960-61), 178-182; Wilkinson quotes at some length from Tousard's memoir to McHenry, but does not make clear what happened to it.

37. Gardner, "Henry Burbeck," *loc. cit.*, 258-259. Gardner does not so state, but presumably the original of Burbeck's proposal was destroyed in the War Depariment fire of 8 November 1800.

38. Several biographers claim on behalf of their subjects the title of "Founder" of the United States Military Academy, among them Wilkinson for Tousard and Gardner on behalf of Burbeck. Similar claims could perhaps be made for Hamilton or even Rochefontaine. In fact there is no single accepted "Founder" of the Military Academy; the so-called "Father of the Military Academy, Sylvanus Thayer, who was superintendent from 1817-1833, might be considered the "Re-Founder" of the Academy, which by 1817 had fallen on hard times.

39. Adams to Dexter, 25 July 1800, C.F. Adams, *Works of John Adams*, IX, 65-66.

40. Same, 13 Aug 1800, *ibid.*, 76.

41. Joseph G. Swift, *The Memoirs of Gen. Joseph Gardner Swift, U.S.A.* (Worcester, Mass., 1890), 19-24.

42. SecWar to Burbeck, 27 May 1801, Military Book No.1.

43. According to the semi-official *Centennial of the United States Military Academy* (Washington, 1904), I, 52, Baron's appointment was dated 6 Jan 1801, although no source is given. Most of the information on Baron comes from Swift's *Memoirs*.

44. Swift, *Memoirs*, 25; John Nehman, Chief Clerk War Dept, to Cushing, 3 Mar 1801, Military Book No.1.

45. SecWar to Tousard, 14 Apr 1801, *ibid.*

46. Sedlar to CO, West Point, 15 Apr 1801, *ibid.*

47. Cushing to Wilkinson, 1 May 1801, Letters Sent, AGO.

48. Dearborn to Wilkinson, 12 May 1801, Military Book No.1.

49. SecWar to G. Fleming, 26 May 1801, *ibid.*

50. Cushing to Burbeck, 20 July 1801, Letters Sent, AGO. Joseph B. Wilkinson, the General's younger son, was deferred because he had already enrolled in the College of New Jersey at Princeton; he remained at that school and allowed his cadet warrant to lapse; see James R. Jacobs, *Tarnished Warrior* (New York, 1938), 198.

51. Swift, *Memoirs,* 26.

52. N.B. Wilkinson, "Forgotten 'Founder'," *loc. cit.,* 186; Gardner, *Dictionary of the Army*, 280.

53. SecWar to Williams, 24 Dec 1801, Military Book No. 1.

54. *Centennial of the United States Military Academy*, I, 221-222; *Register of Graduates and Former Cadets of the United States Military Academy, 1802-1970* (Chicago, 1970), 205. Young Lillie finally surrendered his sinecure in December 1805; he is listed, together with Ambrose Porter, as a non-graduate of the Class of 1805.

55. SecWar to Cushing, 19 Oct 1801, Military Book No.1.

56. Cushing to Burbeck, 19 Oct 1801, Letters Sent, AGO.

57. SecWar to Cushing, 12 Nov and 2 Dee 1801; SecWar to Worrell, 19 Nov 1801, Military Book No.1.

58. N.B. Wilkinson, "Forgotten 'Founder'," *loc. cit.*, 186.

59. SecWar to Williams, 14 Dec 1801, Military Book No.1.

60. SecWar to Swift, 30 Oct and 18 Nov 1801, *ibid.*; Swift, *Memoirs,* 27-28.

61. SecWar to Swift, 5 Dee 1801, *ibid.*

62. Several secondary works refer to 12 cadets at West Point in Dec1801. Based on a study of the official correspondence of the Inspector of the Army, I am able to identify only 11 by name: J.G. Swift, S.M. Levy, H.B. Jackson, S. Gates, W. Gates, J.P. Proveaux, J. Taylor, A. Porter, S. Clark, W.K. Armistead,

and J. Lillie. The possible 12th, J.E. Morrison, had resigned in May 1801; see John Nevman, Ch Clk War Dept, to Cushing, 5 May 1801, Military Book No.1. Of the 11 listed above, only Swift, Levy, Armistead, Jackson, and the Gates brothers were to "graduate." Simon Levy was the only one of the former NCOs to complete the course successfully.

63. SecWar to Williams, 18 Dec 1801, Military Book No.1.

64. Same, 11 Feb 1802, *ibid.*

NOTES TO CHAPTER VI

1. James D. Richardson, *A Compilation of the Messages and Papers of the Presidents, 1789-1902* (Washington, 1905), I, 329-330.

2. SecWar Dearborn to Williams, 19 Dec 1801, Military Book No. 1.

3. Dumas Malone, *Jefferson the President: First Term, 1801-1805* (Boston, 1970), 240-248.

4. War Dept, 23 Dec 1801, *ASP, MA,* I, 156; the format of the original listing has been slightly modified for clarity.

5. *Annals of Congress,* XI (7th Congr., HR), 427-431.

6. Cushing to Morris, 25 Jan 1802, Letters Sent, AGO.

7. Cushing to Wilkinson, 28 Jan 1802, *ibid.*; the 1st Inf was stationed mainly at posts on the Great Lakes.

8. Act of 16 Mar 1802, 2 *Stat.* 132.

9. SecWar to Tousard, 18 Mar 1802, Military Book No.1.

10. See, for example, Cushing to Ford, 19 June 1801, Letters Sent, AGO, on the subject of Ford's repeated failure to submit returns for the troops under his command. In 1799, during the Fries Rebellion, Ford had been regarded as an Ultrafederalist; see Broadus Mitchell, *Alexander Hamilton: The National Adventure, 1788-1804* (New York, 1962), 435.

11. See SecWar to Ford, Rivardi, and others, 1 Apr 1802, Military Book No.1; on severance pay, 2 *Stat.* 137 and Sedlar to Paymaster of the Army, 29 Mar 1802, Military Book No.1.

12. Gardner, *Dictionary of the Army*, 382; N.B. Wilkinson, "The Forgotten 'Founder' of West Point," *Military Affairs*, XXIV (1960-6l), 187-188; Edward L. Tinker, "Anne Louis de Tousard," *D.A.B.*, IX, Pt. 2, 606. Tousard's work has retained historical interest, and was recently reprinted as *American Artillerist's Companion, or Elements of Artillery* (New York: Greenwood Press, 1968), in three volumes.

13. SecWar to Williams, 9 Mar; to Mansfield, 4 May; to Cushing, 21 Apr 1802, Military Book No.1.

14. The *Register of Graduates of the USMA* carries Ambrose Porter, together with John Lillie, Jr., as nongraduates admitted in 1801, but makes no mention of Taylor or Clark. However, while the *Register* is the definitive work for graduates of the Military Academy, it makes no such claim for the many nongraduates, particularly prior to 1821.

15. SecWar to Adjutant and Inspector (hereafter A&I), 27 Apr 1802, Military Book No.1.

16. SecWar to Williams, 26 May and 28 July 1802, *ibid.*

17. SecWar to Williams, 8 July 1802; SecWar to Wadsworth, same date, *ibid.*

18. SecWar to Williams, 9 July 1802, *ibid.* The books that Williams turned over to the Military Academy, and for which he was apparently reimbursed, included many volumes he had inherited from the library of his great-uncle, Benjamin Franklin; several of these, with Franklin's bookplate, survive in the Special Collections of the USMA Library.

19. SecWar to Lt J. Saunders, Ft Nelson, 7 Aug 1802, Military Book No.1.

20. SecWar to Cushing, 12 Oct 1802, *ibid.*; Julius W. Pratt, "Alexander Macomb," *D.A.B.*, VI, Pt. 2., 155-157.

21. SecWar to Swift and Levy, 12 Oct 1802, Military Book No.1; *Register of Graduates of the USMA*, Class of 1802.

22. Gardner, *Dictionary of the Army*, 451; William A. Ganoe, Joseph Gilbert Totten," *D.A.B.*, IX, Pt. 2, 598-599.

23. Something of this feeling of separation from the Army proper exists today, particularly in that part of the Corps of Engineers charged with supervision of Civil Works.

24. The attempt to have a distinctive uniform survives today in the fact that officers of the Corps of Engineers wear brass buttons stamped with the seal of the Corps and the motto *Essayons*, while the rest of the Army's buttons bear the spread eagle.

25. Slightly paraphrased from the listing in SecWar to Cushing, 18 Mar 1802, Military Book No.1.

26. Cushing to Stoddard, 19 May 1802, Letters Sent, AGO.

27. SecWar to Barron, 19 June 1801, Military Book No. 1.

28. SecWar to Jackson, 1 Mar 1802, *ibid.*

29. SecWar to Lt J. Saunders, 21 May 1802, *ibid.*

30. SecWar to C. Freeman, 6 Aug 1802, *ibid.* 153

31. SecWar to Freeman, 14 Aug 1802, *ibid.* Nicoll had received the same authority while commanding at Ft St Tammany and Point Petre in 1800; SecWar Dexter to Capt H. McCall, 31 Dec 1800, *ibid.*

32. GO Hq Washington City, 9 Sept 1800, Wilkinson Order Book.

33. SecWar to Cushing (hereafter designated A&I), 29 Sept 1802, Military Book No. 1.

34. SecWar to Abrahams, 11 Nov 1802, Military Book No.1.

35. SecWar to Wilkins, 18 Mar 1802, *ibid.*

36. A&I to Wilkinson, 17 Aug 1802, Letters Sent, AGO.

NOTES TO CHAPTER VII

1. Richardson (comp.), *Messages and Papers of the Presidents*, I, 343-345.

2. SecWar to Stoddard, 19 Feb 1803, Military Book No. 1 (NA RG 94, microcopy M6, roll 1).

3. A&I [Adjutant and Inspector] to Cooper, 14 Mar 1803, Letters Sent, AGO.

4. A&I To MacRea, 14 Mar 1803, *ibid.*

5. A&I To Muhienberg, 14 Mar 1803, *ibid.*

6. SecWar to Wilkinson, 7 Mar 1803, Military Book No. 1.

7. *Ibid.*

8. SecWar to A&I, 24 Mar 1803, *ibid.;* A&I to Jackson and Freeman, 28 Mar 1803, Letters Sent, AGO. On 25 May the SecWar authorized Salem and Marblehead to be manned by "one sober man for each Post."

9. A&I to Blackburn, 14 Apr 1803, Letters Sent, AGO.

10. SecWar to Jackson, 19 Apr 1803, Military Book No. 1.

11. A&I To Blackburn, 22 Apr 1803, Letters Sent, AGO.

12. Gardner, *Dictionary of the Army*, 70, indicates Blackburn's death as at Fort Adams; correspondence in connection with the Butler court-martial, however, appears to show that Blackburn had not sailed for Mississippi Terr.

13. SecWar to Burbeck, 23 May 1803, Military Book No. 1. One reason for Burbeck's selection may have been that Dearborn wanted to entrust him with a favorite project, the establishment of what became Fort Dearborn at Chicago, which Hamtramck had begun before his death.

14. Cushing to Burbeck (unofficial), 22 May 1803, Letters Sent, AGO.

15. A&I to Hunt, 28 May 1803, Letters Sent, AGO; on Burbeck's route, A.B. Gardner, "Henry Burbeck," *Magazine of American History*, IX (1883), 263.

16. See Chap.V.

17. Gabriel E. Manigault, "The Military Career of General George Izard," *Magazine of American History*, XIX (1888), 467.

18. A&I to SecWar, 25 Sept 1802, Letters Sent, AGO.

19. A&I to Williams and Izard, 27 Sept 1802, *ibid.*; the text of the SecWar letter was not copied into the A&I letter book, nor does it appear in Military Book No.1, but see note following.

20. Henry L. Abbott, "The Corps of Engineers," *Journal of the Military Service Institution of the United States*, XV (1894), 424-425. General Abbott does not document his source exactly, and his quotation sounds paraphrased, but there is no reason to doubt its basic authenticity.

21. *Ibid.*; Sidney Forman, "The United States Military Philosophical Society, 1802-1813," *William and Mary Quarterly*, 3d Ser., II (1945), 276-277.

22. SecWar to Williams, 26 Feb 1803, Military Book No.1.

23. Jonathan Williams, "Report of the Superintendent of the U.S. Military Academy, 1810," in George W. Cullum, *Biographical Register of the Officers and Graduates of the United States Military Academy* (Boston, 1891), III, 549-550.

24. For details of the early years of the Society, see Forman, *loc. cit.*, and Arthur P. Wade, "A Military Off-spring of the American Philosophical Society," *Military Affairs*, XXXVIII (1974),103-107.

25. SecWar to A&I, 20 Apr 1803, Military Book No. 1; Heitman, *Register*, I, 556. George Izard remained in civil life until 1812, when he was offered the colonelcy of a newly-authorized regiment of artillery.

26. By Abbott in "The Corps of Engineers," *loc. cit.*, among others.

27. SecWar to Barron, 26 May 1803, Military Book No. 1.

28. SecWar to Williams, 15 March and 20 Apr 1803, *ibid.*

29. SecWar to Wadsworth, 21 June 1803, *ibid.*

30. SecWar to Barron, 21 June 1803, *ibid.*

31. Act of 28 Feb 1803, 2 *Stat.* 206.

32. Dumas Malone, *Jefferson the President: First Term, 1801-1805* (Boston, 1970), xxviii.

33. SecWar to Wadsworth, 10 July 1803, Military Book No. 2 (Office of the SecWar, Letters Sent Relating to Military Affairs, 1803-1806), NA RG 107 (microcopy M6, roll 2).

34. SecWar to Stoddard, 19 July 1803, Military Book No.2.

35. Amos Stoddard, *Sketches, Historical and Descriptive, of Louisiana* (Philadelphia, 1812).

36.   Richardson, *Messages and Papers of the Presidents*, I, 360.

37.   SecWar to Wilkinson, 31 Oct 1803, Military Book No. 2.

38.   A&I to Pasteur *et al.*, 8 July 1803, Letters Sent, AGO. For details of the charges, T.R. Hay and M.R. Werner, *The Admirable Trumpeter: A Biography of General James Wilkinson* (Garden City, N.Y., 1941), 228-230.

39.   A&I to Burbeck, 12 July 1803, Letters Sent, AGO.

40.   A&I to Ingersoll and Wollstonecraft, 19 Sept 1803, *ibid.* Joseph G. Swift, *Memoirs*, 41-42, says that Ingersoll retaliated by charging Wollstonecraft with shooting his ducks; Swift also claims that Lt Wollstonecraft, a native of England, was a brother of Mary Wollstonecraft Godwin.

41.   A&I to SecWar, 5 Nov 1803, Letters Sent, AGO. Sec. I of the Articles of War approved by Congress on 31 May 1786 provided that "General Courts-Martial may consist of any number of Commissioned Officers from five to thirteen inclusively; but they shall not consist of less than thirteen where that number can be convened without manifest injury to the service." (*Journals of the Continental Congress*, XXX, 316-317.)

42.   Swift, *Memoirs*, 42.

43.   A&I to SecWar, 27 Nov 1803; A&I to Post Comdrs, 2 Dec 1803, Letters Sent, AGO.

44.   SecWar to A&I, 31 Jan 1804, Military Book No.2.

45.   SecWar to Wilkinson, 2 Feb 1804, *ibib.*

46.   A&I Circular, 19 Jan 1804; A&I to Burbeck, 10 Jan 1804, Letters Sent, AGO.

47.   SecWar to Freeman, 31 Jan 1804, Military Book No.2.

48.   SecWar to Wadsworth, 13 Feb 1804, *ibid.*; Wadsworth to SecWar, 25 May 1804, The Buell Collection of Historical Documents Relating to the Corps of Engineers, 1801-1819, UA RG 77 (microcopy M417, roll 1), cited hereafter as Buell Collection.

49.   A&I to Wilkinson, 12 Aug and 15 Sept 1804; to Read, 2 Oct 1804; to P. Muhlenberg, 26 Oct 1804, Letters Sent, AGO. Capt Muhlenberg had been tried and convicted of neglect of duty at New Orleans in Jan 1804, but the President disapproved the sentence of dismissal and Muhlenberg was transferred to Ft. McHenry (GO Hq Washington, 20 June 1804, Wilkinson Order Book).

50.   A&I to Wilkinson, 2 Oct 1804, and to Luckett, 11 Oct 1804, Letters Sent, AGO. 178

51.   SecWar to Pres. Jefferson, 24 Oct 1804, Letters Sent to the President by the SecWar, Vol 1. (1800-1820), NA RG 107 (microcopy M127, roll 1), cited hereafter as letters to President by SecWar, Vol. 1.

52.   A&I to Ingersoll, 21 Oct 1804, Letters Sent, AGO.

53.   A&I to Wilkinson, 18 Dec 1804, *ibid.*

54.   SecWar to Mansfield, 13 Jan 1804, Military Book No. 2.

55.   SecWar to Levy, 12 Mar 1804, *ibid.*

56.   SecWar to Barron, 20 Apr 1804, *ibid.*

57.   SecWar to Hook, 3 Aug 1803; SecWar to Lewis, 26 Mar 1804, *ibid.* For a slightly distorted view of Clark's captaincy, see Richard Dillon, *Meriwether Lewis: A Biography* (New York, 1965), 48.

58.   SecWar to Wadsworth,17 July 1804, Military Book No. 2.

59.   Same, 8 Jan 1805, *ibid.*; see also Stephen E. Ambrose, *Duty, Honor, Country: A History of West Point* (Baltimore, 1966), 28-29.

60. Wadsworth to SecWar, 31 Jan 1805, Buell Collection; SecWar to Wadsworth, 8 Feb 1805, Military Book No. 2.

61. SecWar to Williams, 22 Apr 1805, *ibid.*

62. SecWar to Levy, 5 Mar and 15 May 1805; SecWar to Williams, 12 June and 12 Aug 1805, *ibid.*

63. Gardner, *Dictionary of the Army*, 278.

64. SecWar to Pres. Jefferson, 14 May 1805, letters to President by SecWar, Vol. 1; SecWar to Williams, 17 May1805, Military Book No. 2.

65. SecWar to Williams, 19 June 1805, *ibid.*

66. Williams to SecWar, 29 June 1805 (certificate enclosed), Letters Received by the Secretary of War, NA RG 107 (microcopy M221, roll 2).

67. SecWar to Williams, 19 Aug, 26 Sept, and 3 Oct 1805, Military Book No. 2.

68. SecWar to Wilson, 21 Nov 1805 and 22 Feb 1806, *ibid.*

NOTES TO CHAPTER VIII

1. By Mar 1806 there had been 13 graduates, of whom six—Joseph G. Swift, Simon M. Levy, Walker K. Armistead, George Bomford, William McRee, and Joseph G. Totten—were appointed to the Corps of Engineers. Levy resigned in 1805, Totten in 1806.

2. Richardson, *Messages and Papers of the Presidents*, I, 383-384 .

3. Dumas Malone, *Jefferson the President: Second Term, 1805-1809* (Boston, 1974), 69-70.

4. Richardson, *Messages*, I, 385.

5. SecWar to Speaker HR, 13 Feb 1806, *ASP, MA*, I, 192-196.

6. Sandy Hook is on the New Jersey coast, outside the lower bay; it eventually became a prime gun site for the defense of New York Harbor, but at this period it would seem to have been impractical because of the limited range of the guns available.

7. SecWar to Williams, 22 May 1806, Military Book No. 3, Letters Sent by SecWar Relating to Military Affairs, 1806-1808, NA RG 107 (microcopy M6, roll 3).

8. SecWar to Clinton, 10 June 1806, Buell Collection; SecWar to Whiley , 10 June 1806. Military Book No. 3.

9. Sedlar to Kalteisen, 24 Jan 1805, Military Book No. 2.

10. SecWar to Macomb, 18 Apr 1806, *ibid.,* and 1 Sept 1806, Military Book No. 3; SecWar to Roger Nelson, 9 Dec 1806, *ASP, MA*, I, 206.

11. SecWar to Abrahams, 15 July 1806, Military Book No. 3.

12. SecWar to John Randolph, 9 Jan 1807, *ASP, MA*, I, 207.

13. Richardson, *Messages*, I, 405-507.

14. Howard I. Chapelle, *The History of the American Sailing Navy* (New York, 1949), 190.

15. Williams to Jefferson, 18 June 1805, quoted in Sidney Forman, "The United States Military Philosophical Society, 1803-1813," *William and Mary Quarterly*, 3d Ser., II (July 1945), 277.

16. See note 6.

17. The subjects discussed are summarized from the Society's printed record, known as *Extracts from the Minutes of Stated and Occasional Meetings*, now in the USMA Library. The three major meetings reported in some detail were on 6 October 1806 at West Point, 30 January 1808 in Washington, and 28 December 1809 in New York City.

18. See Chapter I.

19. Quentin Hughes, *Military Architecture* (New York, 1974). 133-139.

20. *Ibid.*, 140-141; U.S. Military Academy, *Notes on Permanent Land Fortifications* (West Point, N.Y.,1958), 3-6.

21. This fact is not recognized by the authors of the standard works on military architecture cited in this and earlier chapters.

22. Forman, "Military Philosophical Society," *loc. cit.*, 282.

23. Swift, *Memoirs*, 67.

24. Joseph G. Totten, *Report of General J.G. Totten, Chief Engineer, on the Subject of National Defences* (Washington, 1851), 33.

25. This was the second phase of the tragi-comic episode involving, among other things, Butler's refusal to cut off his Federal-style queue and to crop his hair in the approved Republican manner. There was, of course, much more to the story than the style of Butler's hair; for reasorably objective versions of the Butler case, see James R. Jacobs, *Tarnished Warrior: General James Wilkinson* (New York. 1938), 200-201, and Thomas R. Way and M.R. Werner, *The Admirable Trumpeter* [Garden City, N.Y., 1941), 229-232.

26. A&I to Murray, 9 Mar 1805, A&I circular to post commanders, 29 Apr 1805, A&I to Porter, 8 Nov 1805, Letters Sent, AGO.

27. GO Hq Camp Belle Fontaine, 30 Aug 1805, Wilkinson Order Book.

28. Swift, *Memoirs*, 42, 63.

29. GO Hq St. Louis, 8 Nov 1205, Wilkinson Order Book; A&I to Bruff, 27 Jan 1806, Letters Sent, AGO.

30. GO Hq St. Louis, 12 Mar 1806, Wilkinson Order Book.

31. GO Hq St. Louis, 7 May 1806, *ibid.*

32. GO Hq Natchitoches, 25, 27, and 29 Sept 1806, *ibid.*

33. SecWar to Wilkinson. 27 Nov 1806, Military Book No. 3.

34. GO Hq New Orleans, 4 and 6 Dec 1806, Wilkinson Order Book.

35. *ASP, MA*, I, 204-205.

NOTES TO CHAPTER IX

1. Norma Lois Peterson (ed.), *The Defence of Norfolk in 1807* (Chesapeake, Va., 1970), 15; L.B. Potter (ed.), *The United States and World Sea Power* (Englewood Cliffs, N.J., 1955), 222.

2. A description of the several types of gunboats, with detailed drawings, is in Chap. IV, "The Gunboat Navy, 1801-1812," of Howard I. Chapelle, *The History of the American Sailing Navy* (New York, 1949).

3. Richardson, *Messages and Papers of the Presidents*, I, 419-421.

4. Presidential message of 19 Feb 1807, *ibid.*, 421.

5. *ASP, MA*, I, 215.

6. Joseph G. Totten, *Report of General J.G. Totten, Chief Examiner on the Subject of National Defences* (Washington, 1851), 62.

7. Quoted without attribution in Ambrose, *Duty, Honor, Country*, 32. See also George W. Cullum, *Biographical Sketch of … Joseph G. Swift* (New York, 1877), 7. Swift himself (*Memoirs*, 66-67) says the arrest order originated in a letter from Colonel Williams.

8. Williams to SecWar, 2 May 1807, Buell Collection.

9. Same, 2 Jun 1807, *ibid.*; Chief Clerk WD to Williams, 15 June 1807, Military Book No. 3.

10. SecWar to Wilkinson, 4 Apr 1807; SecWar to Nicoll, 6 Apr 1807, Military Book No. 3; Cushing to Jacob Kingsbury, 8 May 1807, Letters Sent, AGO.

11. Peterson, *Defence of Norfolk*, 16-17, 31n.

12. SecWar to Burbeck, 3 July 1807 (two letters); SecWar circular to governors, 6 July 1807, Military Book No. 3.

13. Gallatin to Jefferson, 25 July 1807, Henry Adams (ed.), *The Writings of Albert Gallatin* (New York, 1879), I, 340-345.

14. SecWar to Irvine, 6 and 15 Aug 1807, Military Book No. 3.

15. Henry L. Abbott, *Course of Lectures Upon the Defence of the Sea-Coast of the United States* (New York, 1888), 136-139.

16. Ames W. Williams, "The Old Fortifications of New York Harbor," *Military Collector & Historian*, XXII, 2 (Summer 1970), 37.

17. Memorandum signed by SecWar, 21 July 1807, Buell Collection.

18. Williams to Selah Strong, 28 July 1807, *ibid.*

19. Tatham to Jefferson, 7 and 10 July 1807, Peterson, *Defence of Norfolk*, 25-26; for Tatham's views on Lynnhaven and Craney Island, *ibid.*, 102.

20. SecWar to Nacomb, 3 Aug 1807, Military Book No. 3.

21. Macomb to SecWar, 18 Aug 1807, Buell Collection.

22. Charleston *City Gazette*, 4 Nov 1807, as quoted in *South Carolina Historical Magazine*, XXXI (1930), 266.

23. Armistead to Williams, 25 Dec 1807, Buell Collection.

24. Richardson, *Messages and Papers of the Presidents*, I, 425-429.

25. SecWar to Williams, 31 Oct 1807, Military Book No. 3.

26. *ASP, MA*, I, 217-218; the SecWar report is *ibid.*, 219-222.

27. *Annals of Congress*, XV (10th Cong., 1st Sess.), 994.

28. *Ibid.*, 1227ff.

29. SecWar to Burbeck, 2 Jan 1808, Military Book No. 3.

30. SecWar to Jefferson, 26 Jan 1808, Letters to President from SecWar, Vol. 1. On graduation on 30 Oct 1806, Partridge had been appointed to a vacant 1st lieutenancy and Gratiot to a 2d lieutenancy. Jumping Gratiot over Partridge to captain in 1808 may have been in recompense; however, because of lack of further vacancies, it would be over two years before Partridge, who was on the Academy faculty, was promoted to captain.

31. All references are from *Extracts from the Minutes of the United States Military Philosophical Society, at an occasional meeting, held at Washington, January 30., 1803* (n.p., n.d.), USMA Library.

32.   SecWar to Foncin, 25 Jan and 16 Feb 1803, Military Book No. 3.

33.   Williams to SecWar, 29 Feb 1808, Buell Collection. On 14 March, however, the newly-reappointed Lt Totten was assigned to the "Eastern Department" under Major Swift; see Cullum, *Life of Genl Joseph G. Swift*, 8.

34.   *ASP, MA*, I, 228-230.

35.   So stated a committee of the House in 1834, *ASP, MA*, V, 349.

36.   Mildred E. Lombard, "Jonathan Williams," *D.A.B.*, X. Pt. 2, 220-282, believes that Williams was distrusted by the Administration because he was at heart a Federalist, an argument adopted by Ambrose in *Duty, Honor, Country*, 34. Considering Williams's membership on the committee of the American Philosophical Society that included both Jefferson and Wilkinson, and in view of the scientific detachment he affected, it is hard to think of Williams as a die-hard Federalist.

37.   *ASP, MA*, I, 227-228.

38.   2 *Stat.* 481.

39.   But see Chap. VIII on Wilkinson's organization in 1806 of two horse/mule-drawn companies of artillerists in Louisiana.

40.   Committee report, 19 Nov 1807, *ASP, MA*, I, 215.

41.   Frank Monaghan, "Henry Foxall," *D.A.B.*, III, Pt. 2, 573; SecState to SecWar, 11 Dec 1804, Letters Received by SecWar, 1803-1805 (J-W), NA RG 107 (microcopy M221, roll 2).

42.   Foxall, "Columbia Foundry," to Sedlar, Aug 1807, *ASP, MA*, I, 216.

43.   James A. Huston, *The Sinews of War* (Washington, 1966), 98.

44.   SecWar to Committee of HR, Aug 1807, *ASP, MA*, I, 217.

45.   SecWar to Burbeck, 2 June 1808, Military Book No. .3. The unsolved question of the origin of the columbiads is discussed in Harold L. Peterson, *Round Shot and Rammers* (New York, 1969), 76; see also Cary L. Tucker, "The Early Columbiads," *Military Collector & Historian*, X (1958), 40-42, and Emanuel Raymond Lewis, "The Ambiguous Columbiads," *Military Affairs*, XXVIII (Winter 1964), 111-112. See also Chap. X below.

46.   SecWar to Wilkinson, 5 July 1808, Military Book No. 3; A&I (Nicoll) to Wilkinson, 25 Aug 1808, Letters Sent, AGO.

47.   SecWar to MacRea. 6 June 1808, Military Book No. 3.

48.   Swift, *Memoirs,* 75-76; SecWar to Porter, 15 Apr 1808, Military Book No. 3.

49.   Swift, *Memoirs.* 76.

50.   SecWar to Jefferson, 14 May 1808, Letters to President from SecWar, 1

51.   Swift, *Memoirs,* 77.

52.   *Ibid.*, 78; Gardner, *Dictionary of the Army*, 581-582.

53.   Swift, *Memoirs,* 67.

54.   Armistead and Bomford to SecWar, June-Sept 1808, Buell Collection.

55.   Williams to Dearborn, 6 Feb 1808, *ibid.*

56.   Macomb to Sedlar, 1 Nov 1808, *ibid.*

57.   SecWar to Supt of Mil Stores, 24 Dec 1808, Military Book No. 4 (1808-1810), NA RG 107 (microcopy M6, roll 4).

58. SecWar to Jefferson, Oct 1808, Letters to President from SecWar, Vol. 1.

59. Dearborn's report is in *ASP, MA*, I, 236-239.

NOTES TO CHAPTER X

1. Dumas Malone, *Jefferson the President: Second Term, 1805-1809* (Boston,1974), 520.

2. SecWar to Wilkinson, 2 Dec 1808, Military Book No. 3.

3. Same, 30 Nov 1808, *ibid.*

4. A&I to Kingsbury, 15 Feb 1809, and to Burbeck, same date, Letters Sent, AGO.

5. Edmund Kimball Alden, "John Parker Boyd," *D.A.B.*, I, Pt. 2, 526-527.

6. Totten to Williams, 1 Dee 1803, Buell Collection.

7. Actg SecWar Smith to Humphreys, 1 Mar 1809, Military Book No. 4.

8. SecWar to Macomb, 11 Jan 1809, *ibid.*

9. A&I to Wilkinson, 13 Feb 1809, Letters Sent, AGO.

10. A&I to "John Smith Esqr, Acting Secretary of War," 24 Feb 1809, *ibid.*

11. Actg SecWar to Kingsbury, 2 Mar 1809, Military Book No. 4.

12. A&I to Wilkinson, 10 Mar 1309, Letters Sent, AGO.

13. These were Knox, Pickering, Dexter, Dearborn, and Eustis; only McHenry, from Maryland, broke the pattern. On Eustis, see Claude M. Fuess in *D.A.B.*, III, Pt. 2, 193-194.

14. SecWar to Wilkinson, 27 Apr 1809, Military Book No. 4.

15. SecWar to Kingsbury, 10 Hay 1809, ibid.; *Kingsbury* had asked for another extension of his furlough.

16. SecWar to Williams, 26 Apr and 6 May 1809, *ibid.*

17. SecWar to Wilkinson, 30 Apr 1809, *ibid.* Many historians partly blame Eustis for the mortality rate of the troops in 1809-10, but it is hard to justify such blame in light of the existing situation when Eustis took office, and in view of the many actions taken by Eustis to revitalize the medical service and improve sanitary conditions for the troops under Wilkinson's command.

18. Richardson, *Messages of the Presidents*, I, 470.

19. SecWar to Rep. Gorman, HR, 30 May 1809, Military Book No. 4; see also *ASP, MA*, I, 244.

20. SecWar to Hampton, 8 June; to Simonds, 7 June; to Williams, 10 June; and to Gansevoort, 11 June 1809, Military Book No. 4; A&I to Lt Col R. Purdy, 17 June 1809, Letters Sent, AGO.

21. See Chapter IX above.

22. Actg SecWar to Villard, 19 July 1809, Military Book No. 4.

23. Many 19th century writers claim that the Columbiad was a hell gun invented by George Bamford; it is clear, however, that the term "Columbiad" was applied in 1803-09 to a gun firing solid shot, while the use of term in 1808 antedates Captain Bomford's connection with the testing of the new cannon. For claims that Bamford invented the Colurmbiad, see Thomas M. Spaulding's sketch of Bomford in *D.A.B.*, I, Pt. 2,427, and Charles K. Gardner's brief entry on Bomford in *Dictionary of the Army*, 74. Another story is that the name derived from Joel Barlow's epic poem, *The Vision of Columbus*, first published in 1787 and revised and expanded in 1807 as *The Columbiad*. While this legend is impossible to disprove, it is highly unlikely that the name derived from Barlow's turgid poem rather than from the Columbia Foundry. Recent discussions of the characteristics and paternity of the Columbiad

are in Harold L. Peterson, *Round Shot and Rammers* (New York, 1969), 76; Cary S. Tucker, "The Early Columbiads," *Military Collector and Historian*, X (1958), 40-42; and Emanuel Raymond Lewis, "The Ambiguous Columbiads," *Military Affairs*, XXVIII (Winter 1964), 111-122.

24. Actg A&I to SecWar, 22 Sept 1809, Letters Sent, AGO.

25. SecWar to C. Irvine, 10 Nov 1809, Military Book No. 4.

26. Swift, *Memoirs*, 85. Despite frequent references in 1809-10 to the "Burbeck carriage," Swift's reference to three wheels is the only description I have found. The carriage was probably at least similar to those shown in Peterson, *Round Shot and Rammers*, 73, which are based on descriptions by De Scheel and Tousard. The replacement of the four naval-type truck wheels by two large spoked wheels and a smaller rear wheel would seem to have made possible the use of this carriage as a barbette as well as a casemate mount.

27. Swift to SecWar, 13 Nov 1809, Buell Collection.

28. Swift, *Memoirs*, 84.

29. Totten to Williams, 30 Nov 1809, Buell Collection; on naming Fort Wooster, Totten to SecWar, 19 July 1809, *ibid.*

30. Williams to Capt R. Whiley, 7 Dec 1809, *ibid.*

31. *Ibid.*; Report of SecWar, 19 Dec 1809, *ASP, MA*, I, 245-246.

32. Williams to Col J. Simonds, 8 Aug 1809, Buell Collection.

33. Bomford to SecWar, 1 Dec 1809, *ibid.*

34. Report of SecWar, 19 Dec 1809, *ASP, MA*, I, 245-246.

35. *Ibid.*

36. This is Beaufort (bofort), N.C., not to be confused with Beaufort (bewfort), S.C.

37. Swift, *Memoirs*, 87-89; Report of SecWar, 19 Dec 1809, *ASP, MA*, I, 246.

38. Actg SecWar to Hampton, 10 Sept 1809, Military Book No. 4.

39. SecWar to Macomb, 1 Nov 1809, *ibid.*

40. Report of SecWar, 19 Dec 1809, *ASP, MA*, I, 246.

41. *Ibid.*; Gardner, *Dictionary of the Army*, 581.

42. Macomb to SecWar, 30 Oct 1809, Buell Collection; SecWar to MacRea, 13 and 22 Nov 1809, Military Book No. 4.

43. SecWar to MacRea, 22 Nov 1809, *ibid.*; Report of SecWar, 19 Dec 1809, *ASP, MA*, I, 246.

44. Richardson, *Messages* of the Presidents, I, 473,476.

45. Printed in *ASP, MA*, I, 245-246.

46. United States Military Philosophical Society, *Extracts from the Minutes of Stated and Occasional Meetings* …. (n.p., n.d.), USMA Library.

47. *Ibid.*; *Transactions of the American Philosophical Society*, VI, Pt. II (Philadelphia, l809), xxii-xxiii, xxxviii, xliii-xliv.

48. On the fate of the Society and the eventual disposition of its treasury, Arthur P. Wade, "A Military Offspring of the American Philosophical Society," *Military Affairs*, XXXVIII, 3 (Oct 1974), 105-106.

49. SecWar to Williams, 27 Dec 1809, Military Book No. 4.

50. SecWar to Hon. W.B. Giles, 1 Jan 1810, *ASP, MA*, I. 256-257.

51. This and similar correspondence seems to refute the accusation by several historians that Eustis was indifferent to the fate of the Academy.

52. SecWar to Mansfield, 4 Jan 1810, Military Book No. 4.

53. Actg SecWar to Mansfield. 25 Aug 1810, *ibid.*

54. SecWar to Stoddert [sic], 24 Nov 1809, *ibid.*

55. SecWar to Boyd, 6 Feb 1810, *ibid.*

56. A&I to Armistead, 11 Jan 1810, Letters Sent, AGO.

57. Report of SecWar, 5 Jan 1810, *ASP, MA*, I, 248.

58. Details of the proposed legislation, including a printed draft, are in the April 1810 section of the Buell Collection; as the bill failed, it has not been thought necessary to reproduce it in any detail here.

59. SecWar to Williams, 14 Mar 1810, Military Book No. 4; Stephen E. Ambrose, in *Duty, Honor, Country*, 34-35, feels that one reason for Republican opposition to the Military Academy in general was that "Williams was a Federalist." But Williams's appointment by John Adams in early 1801, after Adams's break with the High Federalists, and Williams's friendship with Jefferson, argue against Williams's being a very strong Federalist by 1810.

60. SecWar to Williams, 18 May 1810, enclosing Regulations dated 30 Apr 1810, Military Book No. 4.

61. They were Asa Payne, Joel Johnson, J.A. Lillington, and Joel Strong, indicated by acceptance of their resignations, May 1810, *ibid.*

62. SecWar to Williams, 4 June 1810, *ibid.*

63. Sedlar to Williams, 30 Nov 1810, Military Book No. 5 (Nov 1810-June1812), NA RG 107 (microcopy M6, roll 5).

64. All to Freeman, 29 Oct 1810, Letters Sent, AGO. Col. Pasteur resigned as of 30 May; Fort Johnston was added to Freeman's district on 18 Dec.

65. SecWar to Burbeck, 12 June 1810, Military Book No. 4.

66. SecWar to Williams, 13 June 1810, *ibid.*

67. Same, 19 June 1810, *ibid.*

68. Williams to SecWar, 27 June 1810, Buell Collection.

69. SecWar to Williams, 9 July 1810, Military Book No. 4.

70. Same, 23 Nov 1810, Military Book No. 5.

71. Buell Collection; see also Edmund Banks Smith, *Governors Island* (New York, 1913), 65.

72. Williams to SecWar, 27 Nov 1810, Buell Collection.

NOTES TO CHAPTER XI

1. Gaillard Hunt (ed.), *The Writings of James Madison* (New York, 1908), VIII, 128-129.

2. *ASP, MA*, I, 296-297.

3. Sec War to Madison, 25 Feb 1811, Letters Sent to President by SecWar, Vol. 1; SecWar to Macomb,6 Mar 1811, Military Book No. 5.

4. Macomb to SecWar, 3 Jan 1811; Macomb to Williams, 20 July 1811, Buell Collection; SecWar to C. Irvine, 5 Jan 1811, Military Book No. 5.

5. SecWar to Macomb, 26 Apr 1811, *ibid.*

6.	Macomb to SecWar, 20 July 1811, Buell Collection.

7.	A&I to Williams, 21 Jan 1811, Letters Sent, AGO.

8.	SecWar to Bomford, 26 Mar 1811, Military Book No. 5.

9.	Same, 17 May 1811, *ibid.*

10.	SecWar to Porter, 27 Mar 1811; SecWar to House, 14 Feb 1811, Military Book No. 5. On Maj. Porter's activities in Newport in 1810, SecWar to Porter, 7 Mar 1810, Military Book No. 4.

11.	SecWar to Porter, 17 May 1811, Military Book No. 5.

12.	SecWar to Williams, 15 Mar 1811, *ibid.*

13.	Williams to SecWar, 27 May 1811, Letters Received by the SecWar, 1810-1811 (U-Y), NA RG 107 (microcopy M221, roll 41).

14.	SecWar to Williams, 5 June 1811, Military Book No. 5.

15.	SecWar to (name illegible), 20 June 1811, *ibid.*

16.	SecWar to Hon. S. Smith, 9 Sept 1811, *ibid.*

17.	SecWar to Wood, 5 June 1811, *ibid.* On Thayer, see R. Ernest Dupuy, *Where They Have Trod* (New York, 1940), 46. Statistics on the Classes of 1810-1812 from *Register of Graduates and Former Cadets, USMA, 1802-1970* (Chicago, 1970), 207.

18.	A good account of the East Florida adventure is Rembert W. Patrick, *Florida Fiasco* (Athens, Ga., 1954).

19.	The extent of Army involvement in East Florida is indicated by correspondence from A&I to Lt Col John Smith in Charleston and to Capt (later Lt Col) Thomas A. Smith at Fort Hawkins, Coleraine, Ga., during Jan-Feb 1811, Letters Sent, AGO.

20.	Hunt (ed.), *Writings of James Madison*, VIII, 177n.

21.	A&I to Kingsbury *et al.*, 10 June 1811; to Gansevoort et al., 22 June and 12 July 1811, Letters Sent, AGO.

22.	SecWar to Supt of Mil Stores, 23 Apr; to Capt J. House, 19 Apr; to Boyd, 17 July 1811, Military Book No.5; A&I to Boyd, 19 Apr 1811, Letters Sent, AGO.

23.	SecWar to Boyd, 12 Dec 1811, Military Book No. 5.

24.	SecWar to Swett, 5 Sept 1811, *ibid.*; A&I to A. Eustis, 7 Sept. and to Laval, 1 Oct 1811, Letters Sent, AGO.

25.	SecWar to T. Coxe, 10 Aug; to Lt. H.A. Fay, 5 Sept; to MacRea, 7 Sept; and to C. Irvine, 10 Sept 1811, Military Book No. 5.

26.	SecWar to Madison, 13 Nov 1811, Letters sent to President by SecWar, Vol. 1; A&I to Fenwick, 7 Dec 1811, Letters Sent, AGO.

27.	SecWar to Gansevoort, 16 Dec 1811, Military Book No.5.

28.	Richardson, *Messages and Papers of the Presidents*, I, 493-494.

29.	*ASP, MA*, I, 303-305.

30.	SecWar to L. Cheves, HR, 3 Dec 1811, *ibid.*, 307.

31.	Same, 10 Dec 1811, *ibid.*, 307-311.

32.	A&I memorandum, 31 Dec 1811, Letters Sent, AGO.

33.	Madison to Jefferson, 7 Feb 1812, Hunt (ed.), *Writings of James Madison*, VIII, 176-177.

34. *Ibid.*, 177.

35. 2 *Stat.* 671.

36. Heitman, *Register,* I, 51.

37. SecWar to Dearborn, 9 Apr 1812, Military Book No .5.

38. SecWar to Pinckney, 30 Apr 1812, *ibid.*

39. SeeWar to Porter, 15 and 19 Mar 1812, *ibid.*

40. Heitman, *Register,* I, 52, 566.

41. Act of 28 Mar 1812, 2 *Stat.* 696.

42. SecWar to North, 28 Mar, and to Coxe, 26 May 1812, Military Book No. 5; SecWar to Madison, 1 Apr 1812, Letters sent to President by SecWar, Vol. l.

43. Williams to SecWar, 4 Apr 1812, Buell Collection.

44. George H. Richards, *Memoir of Alexander Macomb* (New York. 1833), 50, thinks Williams was offering to resign in favor of Macomb; subsequent Williams-SecWar correspondence indicates otherwise.

45. SecWar to Williams 6 Apr 1812, Military Book No .5.

46. SecWar to Williams, 10 Apr 1812, *ibid.*; Williams to SecWar, 13 and 15 Apr 1812, Bell Collection.

47. Lt. Partridge reached his new assignment just in time to be swept up in the catastrophe of Hull's surrender of Detroit; he died in Detroit the following month as a prisoner of war; Gardner, *Dictionary of the Army*, 350.

48. Williams to SecWar, 15 Apr 1812, Buell Collection; the newspaper article was copied in Williams's hand.

49. A&I to Capt. J. Gibson, 16 Apr 1812, letters Sent, AGO.

50. War Dept orders, 28 Apr 1812, Military Book No. 5.

51. Act of 29 Apr 1812, 2 *Stat.* 720.

52. SecWar to Williams, 1 May 1812, Military Book No. 5.

53. The date of Macomb's appointment is given as 6 July, but it is clear from contemporary correspondence that he assumed command of the 3d Artillery in early May, before his confirmation by the Senate.

54. SecWar to Tompkins, 8 May 1812, Military Book No. 5.

55. Act of 14 May 1812, 2 *Stat.* 732.

56. SecWar to Dearborn, 16 May; to Burbeck, 16 June 1812, Military Book No. 5.

57. Bomford to SecWar, 23 June 1812, Buell Collection.

58. SecWar to Dearborn, 28 May 1812, Military Book No. 5.

59. *Ibid.*; A&I to Read, 3 June 1812, Letters Sent, AGO; Gardner, *Dictionary of the Army*, 430.

60. *ASP, MA,* I, 320.

61. SecWar to Tompkins, 20 Apr 1812, Military Book No. 5.

62. McRee to Mayor of Savannah, n.d. (probably June 1812), Buell Collection .

63. A&I to Beall, 18 June 1812, Letters Sent, AGO.

64. SecWar to Dearborn, *et al.*, 18 June 1812, Military Book No. 5.

65. A&I circular, 19 June 1812, Letters Sent, AGO.

NOTES TO CHAPTER XII

1. SecWar to Bloomfield, 23 June 1812, Military Book No. 5.

2. Williams to Pres. Madison, 21 June 1812, filed with Letters Received by SecWar, Aug 1811-Dec 1812 (T-Z), NA RG 107 (microcopy M221, roll 49).

3. Memorial to Col. Henry Burbeck, 8 July 1812, copy enclosed, *ibid.*

4. The 63d Article of War, approved by Congress 10 Apr 1806: "The functions of the engineers being generally confined to the most elevated branch of military science, they are not to assume, nor are they subject to be ordered on any duty beyond the line of their immediate profession, except by special order of the President … ; but they are to receive every mark of respect, to which their rank in the army may entitle them, and are liable to be transferred, at the discretion of the President, from one corps to another, regard being paid to rank." *Annals of Congress*, XV (9th Cong.), 1246-1247.

5. Williams to Pres. Madison, 10 July 1812, filed with Letters Received by SecWar, Aug 1811-Dec 1812 (T-Z), *loc. cit.*

6. SecWar to Williams, 27 July 1812, Military Book No. 6, Letters Sent by SecWar Relating to Military Affairs, July 1812-June 1813, NA RG 107 (microcopy M6, roll 6).

7. Mildred E. Lombard, "Jonathan Williams," *D.A.B.*, X, Pt. 2, 280-282; see also the sketch in James B. Longacre and James Herring, *The National Portrait Gallery of Distinguished Americans* (Philadelphia, 1834), I, 151-158.

8. Swift, *Memoirs*, 104.

9. *Ibid.*, 106. No other reference to Fulton's candidacy has been found.

10. SecWar to Pres. Madison, 30 Nov 1812, Buell Collection; Heitman, *Register*, 1, *passim.*

11. SecWar to Gratiot, 16 Sept 1812, Military Book No. 6; Swift to McRee, 19 Sept 1812, Buell Collection.

12. *ASP, MA,* I, 424; *Register of Graduates, USMA,* 207-209.

13. Gardner, *Dictionary of the Army, passim.*

14. SecWar to Dearborn, 9 July 1812, Military Book No. 6.

15. SecWar to J.C. Smith, 14 July 1812, and Caleb Strong, 21 July 1812, *ibid.*

16. Act of 6 July 1812, 2 *Stat.* 784; Heitman, *Register*, I, 21; SecWar to Boyd, 26 Aug 1812, Military Book No. 6.

17. 2 *Stat.* 785. This act was the basis for the brevet system which was to be the curse of the officer corps for the next 50 years and more.

18. Irving Brant, *James Madison: Commander in Chief, 1812-1836* (Indianapolis, 1961), 120, 126-129; Madison to Eustis, 4 Dec 1812, Hunt, *Writings of Madison*, VIII, 232-233.

19. Act of 30 Mar 1814, 3 *Stat.* 113.

20. SecWar to Jos. Anderson, HR, 10 June 1813, *ASP, MA,* I, 383.

21. SecWar to Chairman Senate Military Comm., 12 July 1813, *ibid.*, 384.

22. John K. Mahon, *The War of 1812* (Gainesville, Fla., 1972), 265; Ames W. Williams, "Fort at Moose Island," *CAMP Periodical,* VII (1975), 9.

23. George W. Cullum, "History of the Sea-Coast Fortifications of the United States: Boston Harbor," *Journal of the United States Artillery*, VII, 3 (1896), 369.

24. George W. Cullum, *Historical Sketch of the Fortification Defenses of Narragansett Bay* (Washington, 1884), 24; John M. Hammond, *Quaint and Historic Forts of North America* (Philadelphia, 1915), 171-172.

25. Hugh Hastings (ed.), "Early Fortifications Around New York City," *Journal of the United States Artillery*, IX, 2 (1898), 206-208; Report of SecWar, Dec 1811, *ASP, MA,* I, 308-309; Ames W. Williams, "The Old Fortifications of New York Harbor," *Military Collector & Historian*, XXII, 2 (1970), 38-40.

26. Maurice Matlof (ed.), *American Military History* (Washington, 1969), 138-139; Mahon, *War of 1812,* 119.

27. Raphael P. Thian, *Notes Illustrating the Military Geography of the United States* (Washington, 1881), 34.

28. *ASP, MA,* I, 545.

29. James R. Hinds, "Potomac River Defenses: The First Twenty Years," *CAMP Periodical,* V, 3 (Fall 1973), 7-15.

30. *Ibid.*

31. Harold I. Lessen and George C. MacKenzie, *Fort McHenry National Monument* (Washington, 1954), 5-6; Frank A. Cassell, "Baltimore in 1813: A Study of Urban Defense in the War of 1812," *Military Affairs.* XXXIII, 3 (Dec 1969), 358-359.

32. Lessen and MacKenzie, *Fort McHenry,* 6-8.

33. Mahon, *War of 1812,* 371, 383.

34. E.J. Cullen, "Under Five Flags: The History of the Fortification at Mobile Bay," *The Coast Artillery Journal,* LIX, 3 (Sept 1923), 225-226.

35. Accounts of British casualties vary. Cullen, *ibid.*, adopts the figure of 162 killed and 70 wounded carried in Gardner, *Dictionary of the Army,* 571. The official British report listed 27 killed and 45 wounded, accepted by Wilburt S. Brown, *The Amphibious Campaign for West Florida and Louisiana, 1814-1815* (University, Ala., 1969), 45.

36. Two recent and authoritative accounts of the New Orleans campaign, both based on official British sources, are Brown, *ibid.*, and Robin Reilly, *The British at the Gates* (New York, 1974). Brown, a retired major general of the Marine Corps, is particularly sound in his analysis of British operations in the light of modern amphibious doctrine.

37. The best account is Reilly, *The British at the Gates,* 303-304; losses are from Gardner, *Dictionary of the Army,* 572.

38. Cullen, "Under Five Flags," *loc. cit.,* 226-227.

39. This view is held by, among others, the British writer Quentin Hughes, in *Military Architecture* (New York, 1974), 178.

40. Lewis, *Seacoast Fortifications,* 31-32.

41. *Ibid.,* 32-33.

42. Wadsworth to SecWar, 23 Jan 1817, *A Collection of Annual Reports and Other Important Papers, Relating to the Ordnance Department* (Washington, 1878), I, 26-30.

43. Enclosure A to Bomford to SecWar, 29 Jan 1822, *ibid.,* 67.

SELECTED BIBLIOGRAPHY

I - Manuscript Sources
A - National Archives and Records Service

Records of the Office of the Secretary of War (RG 107):

> Letters Sent by the Secretary of War Relating to Military Affairs, 1800-1889 (microfilm publication M6).

> Letters Received by the Secretary of War, Main Series, 1801-1870 (microfilm publication M221).

> Copies of War Department Correspondence and Reports, 1791-1796 (microfilm publication T982).

> Letters Sent to the President by the Secretary of War, 1800-1863 (microfilm publication M127).

> Reports to Congress from the Secretary of War, 1803-1870 (microfilm publication M220).

Records of the Adjutant General's Office (RG 94 and RG 407):

> Letters Sent by the Office of the Adjutant General, Main Series, 1800-1890 (microfilm publication M565).

> General James Wilkinson's Order Book, December 31, 1796-March 8, 1808 (microfilm publication M654).

Records of the Office of the Chief of Engineers (RG 77):

> Buell Collection of Historical Documents Relating to the Corps of Engineers, 1801-1819 (microfilm publication M417).

> Headquarters Map File

> Fortifications Map File

Records of United States Army Commands (RG 393):

Historical Information Relating to Military Posts and Other Installations, ca. 1700-1900 (microfilm publication M661).

Brief Histories of United States Army Commands (Army Posts) and Descriptions of Their Records (microfilm publication T912).

B - Other Archival Sources

Order and Letter Book of Henry Burbeck, 1787-1800. United States Military Academy Library.

Timothy Pickering Papers. Massachusetts Historical Society.

Orderly Book of Major General Anthony Wayne. United States Military Academy Library (microfilm)

Waste Book for the Quartermaster Stores. West Point, 1794-1806. United States Military Academy Library.

West Point Clothing Account Book, 1793 [1795-1796]. United States Military Academy Library.

Orderly Book of the Corps of Artillerists and Engineers, West Point, N.Y., 4 volumes, 1795-1799. United States Military Academy Library.

Orders-Received Book of the Company of Captain Lemuel Gates [2d Regiment of Artillerists and Engineers], 1799-1806. United States Military Academy Library.

II - Primary Sources
A - Books and Pamphlets.

Adams, Charles Francis. *The Works of John Adams, Second President of the United States.* 10 vols. Boston: Little, Brown and Company, 1853.

Adams. Henry (ed.). *The Writings of Albert Gallatin.* 4 vols. Original publication 1879. New York: Antiquarian Press Ltd., 1960.

American Philosophical Society. *Transactions of the American Philosophical Society, Held at Philadelphia, for Promoting Useful Knowledge.* Vol. VI. Part II. Philadelphia: Jane Aitken, 1809.

Carter. Clarence E. (ed.). *The Territorial Papers of the United States,* Vol. II. *The Territory Northwest of the River Ohio, 1787-1803.* Washington: Government Printing Office,1934.

Cullum, George W. (Comp.). *Biographical Register of the Officers and Graduates of the United States Military Academy.* 9 vols. and supplements. Various places and dates of publication.

Denny, Ebenezer. *Military Journal of Major Ebenezer Denny. An Officer in the Revolutionary and Indian Wars, with an Introductory Memoir.* Philadelphia: J.B. Lippincott & Co., for the Historical Society of Pennsylvania,1859.

Fitzpatrick, John C. (ed.). *The Writings of George Washington from the Original Manuscript Sources, 1745-1799.* 37 vols. Washington: Government Printing Office, 1941.

Fort, Worthington C., et al. (comps.). *Journals of the Continental Congress, 1774-1789.* 34 vols. Washington: Government Printing Office, 1904-1937.

Gardner, Charles K. (comp.). *Dictionary of All Officers, Who have been Commissioned, or Have Been Appointed and Served, in the Army of the United States, Since . . . 1789, to the First January l853 . . . .* New York: G.P. Putnam and Company, l853.

Guion, Isaac. Letters of Captain Isaac Guion, 3d U.S. Infantry, 1797-1799, printed and bound with *Seventh Annual Report of the Director of the Department of Archives of the State of Mississippi.* Nashville, Tenn.: Brandon Printing Company, 1909.

Hamilton, John C. *The Works of Alexander Hamilton: Comprising His Correspondence and His Political and Official Writings, exclusive of The Federalist, Civil and Military.* 7 vols. Published from the original manuscripts deposited in the Department of State, by order of the Joint Library Committee of Congress. New York: John F. Trow, Printer, 1851.

Heitman, Francis B. (comp.). *Historical Register and Dictionary of the United States Army . . . 1789-1903.* 2 vols. Washington: Government Printing Office, 1903.

_____ . *Historical Register of the Officers of the Continental Army during War of the Revolution, April 1775 to December 1783.* Washington: Government Printing Office, 1833, 1914.

Hunt, Gaillard (ed.). *The Writings of James Madison, Comprising His Public Papers and His Private Correspondence . . . .* 9 vols. New York: G.P. Putnam's Sons, 1908.

Knopf, Richard C. (ed.). *Anthony Wayne, A Name in Arms: Soldier, Diplomat, Defender of Expansion Westward of a Nation.* The Wayne-Knox-Pickering-McHenry Correspondence. Pittsburgh: University of Pittsburgh Press,1960.

Lodge, Henry Cabot (comp.). *The Works of Alexander Hamilton.* 12 vols. New York: G.P. Putnam's Sons, 1904.

Mordecai, Alfred. *Artillery for the United States Land Service, as Devised and Arranged by the Ordnance Board, with Plates.* Prepared under the instructions of the Colonel of Ordnance. Washington: J. and G.S. Gideon, Printers, 1849.

Peterson, Norma Lois (ed.). *The Defence of Norfolk in 1807, as Told by William Tatham to Thomas Jefferson.* Chesapeake, Va.: Norfolk County Historical Society, 1970.

Powell, William H. *List of Officers of the Army of the United States from 1779 to 1900.* New York: L.R. Hamersly and Co., 1900.

Richardson, James D. (comp.). *A Compilation of the Messages and Papers of the Presidents, 1739-1902.* Washington: Bureau of National Literature and Art, 1905.

Scheel, M. de. *Memoires d'artillerie contenant l'artillerie nouvelle ou les changements fait dand l'artllerie francaise en 1765 (Copenhage, 1777),* translated by Jonathan Williams as *A Treatise of Artillery Conaining a New System, or the Alterations made in the French Artillery Since 1765.* Philaephlia: Aitken [?], 1800.

Steiner, Bernard C. *The Life and Correspondence of James McHenry.* Cleveland: The Burrows Brothers Company, 1907.

Steuben, Frederick W. von. *Regulations for the Order and Discipline of the Troops of the United States.* Originally published 1779. Philadelphia: Ray Riling Arms Books Co., 1966.

Swift, Joseph G. *The Memoirs of Gen. Joseph Gardiner Swift, LL.D., U.S.A., First Graduate of the United States Military Academy, West Point, Chief Engineer U.S.A. from 1812 to 1818* [1800-1855] Worcester, Mass.: F.S. Blanchard & Co., Printer, 1890.

Syrett, Harold C. (ed.). *The Papers of Alexander Hamilton.* 22 vols to date. New York: Columbia University Press, 1961-1975.

Totten, Joseph G. *Report of General J.G. Totten, Chief Engineer, on the Subject of National Defences.* Washington: A. Boyd Hamilton, 1851.

United States Congress. *American State Papers: Documents, Legislative and Executive . . . .* 38 vols. Washington: Gales and Seaton, 1832-1861.

_____. *The Debates and Proceedings in the Congress of the United States . . . .* (3 March1789-27 May 1824) 42 vols. (Short title: *Annals of Congress*) Washington: Gales and Seaton, 1834-1856.

United States Government. *Statutes at Large and Treaties of the United States of America, 1789-1873.* 17 vols. Boston: Little, Brown and Co., 1845-1873.

United States Military Philosophical Society. *Extracts from the Minutes of Stated and Occasional Meetings,* including West Point, 6 October 1806; Washington, 30 January 1803; and 30 January 1808; and New York, 28 December 1809. No publisher's imprint. United States Military Academy Library.

United States [Army] Ordnance Department. *A Collection of Annual Reports and Other Important Papers Relating to the Ordnance Department, taken from the Records of the Office of the Chief of Ordinance, from Public Documents, and from Other Sources.* 4 vols. Washington: Government Printing Office, 1878.

West Point Alumni Foundation. *Register of Graduates and Former Cadets of the United States Military Academy, 1802-1970.* Chicago: R.H. Donnelly and Sons Co., 1970.

Wilkinson, James. *Memoirs of My Own Times.* 3 vols. Philadelphia: Abraham Small, 1816.

Williams, Jonathan. Report of the Superintendent of the U.S. Military Academy, 1810. Reprinted in Cullum, *Biographical Register* (cited above), III (Boston, 1891), 549-550.

B - *Newspapers*

City Gazette, Charleston, South Carolina (1807)

Columbian Centinel, Boston, Massachusetts (1796)

Connecticut Gazette, New London (1798-1799)

Dunlap and Claypool's American Daily Advertiser, Philadelphia (1795)

Easton Herald and Gazette of Maine, Easton, Maine (1798)

Hall's Wilmington Gazette, Wilmington, North Carolina (1797-1800)

National Intelligencer, Washington, D.C. (1812)

Portland Gazette, Portland, Maine (1798)

III - *Secondary Works*

A - *Books and Pamphlets*

Abbott, Henry L. *Course of Lectures Upon the Defense of the Sea-Coast of the United States, Delivered Before the Naval War College: November 1887.* New York: D. Van Nostrand, 1888.

Abernethy, Thomas Perkins. *The Burr Conspiracy.* New York: Oxford University Press, 1954.

Ambrose, Stephen E. *Duty, Honor, Country: A History of West Point.* Baltimore: The Johns Hopkins Press, 1966.

Arthur, Robert. *The Coast Artillery School, 1824-1927.* Fort Monroe, Va.: Coast Artillery School Press, 1928.

Bailey, Thomas A. *A Diplomatic History of the American People.* New York: Appleton-Century-Crofts Inc., 1958.

Beirne. Francis. F. *Shout Treason: The Trial of Aaron Burr.* New York: Hastings House, Publishers, Inc., 1959.

Birkhimer, William E. *Historical Sketch of the Organization, Administration, Material and Tactics of the Artillery, United States Army.* New York: James J. Chapman, 1884.

Brant, Irving. *James Madison: The President, 1809-1812.* Indianapolis: The Bobbs-Merrill Company, Inc., 1956.

_____. *James Madison: Commander in Chief, 1812-1836.* Indianapolis: The Bobbs-Merrill Company, Inc., 1961.

Bridenbaugh, Carl. *Cities in Revolt: Urban life in America, 1743-1776.* Originally published 1955. New York: Capricorn Books, 1964.

Brown, Ralph Adams. *The Presidency of John Adams.* Lawrence: The University Press of Kansas, 1975.

Brown, Wilburt S. *The Amphibious Campaign for West Florida and Louisiana, 1814-1815: A Critical Review of Strategy and Tactics at New Orleans.* University, Ala.: University of Alabama Press, 1969.

Chapelle, Howard I. *A History of the American Sailing Navy: The Ships and Their Development.* New York: Bonanza Books, 1949.

Clarke, Sir George Sydenham. *Fortification: Its Past Achievements, Recent Development, and Future Progress.* 2d ed. London: John Murray, 1907.

Cullum, George W. *Biographical Sketch of Brigadier General Joseph G. Swift, Chief Engineer of the United States Army, July 31, 1812, to Nov. 12, 1818.* New York: Charles A. Coffin, Printer, 1877.

_____. *Historical Sketch of the Fortification Defenses of Narraganset Bay, Since the Founding, in 1633, of the Colony of Rhode Island.* Washington: n.p., 1834.

Davis, William, W.H. *The Fries Rebellion, 1798-99: An Armed Resistance to the House Tax Law, Passed by Congress, July 9, 1793, in Bucks and Northampton Counties, Pennsylvania.* Doylestown, Pa.: Doylestown Publishing Co., 1899.

De Conde, Alexander. *The Quasi-War: The Politics and Diplomacy of the Undeclared War with-France, 1797-1801.* New York: Charles Scribners Sons, 1966.

Dillon, Richard. *Meriwether Lewis: A Biography.* New York: Coward-McCann, Inc., 1965.

Downey, Fairfax. *The Sound of the Guns: The Story of American Artillery. . . .* New York: David McKay Company, Inc., 1955.

Duffy, Christopher. *Fire & Stone: The Science of Fortress Warfare, 1660-1860.* New York: Hippocrene Books, 1975.

Dupuy, R. Ernest. *Where They Have Trod: The West Point Tradition in American Life.* New York: Frederick A. Stokes Company, 1940.

Essex Institute. Historical Collections. Salem, Mass.: Essex Institute, various dates.

Ficken, John F. *Michael Kalteisen, Captain of United States Artillery: An Historical Address Delivered . . . January 17, 1909.* Charleston, S.C.: Walker, Evans & Cogswell Co., 1910.

Gardner, Asa Bird. *Memoir of Brevet Brig-Genl Henry Burbeck.* New York: A.S. Barnes & Co., 1883.

Green, Constance McL. *Eli Whitney and the Birth of American Technology.* Boston: Little. Brown and Company, 1956.

Griffith, George B. (ed*.*). *History of Fort Constitution and "Walbach Tower," Portsmouth Harbor. N.H.* By a student of Dartmouth College. Portsmouth, N.H.: C.W. Brewster & Son, Printers, 1865.

Guthman, Willian H. *March to Massacre: A History of the First Seven Years of the United States Army, 1784-1791.* New York: McGraw-Hill Company, 1975.

Hammond, John Martin. *Quaint and Historic Forts of North America.* Philadelphia: J.B. Lippincott Company, 1915.

Hay, Thomas Robson, and M.R. Werner. *The.Admirable Trumpeter: A Biography of General James Wilkinson.* Garden City, N.Y.: Doubleday, Doran & Company, 1941.

Hogg, Ian V. *A History of Artillery.* London: Hamlyn Publishing Group, Ltd., 1974.

_____, and John H. Batchelor. *Artillery.* New York: Charles Scribner's Sons, 1972.

Hughes, Quentin. *Military Architecture.* New York: St. Martin's Press, 1974.

Huston, James A. *The Sinews of War: Army Logistics, 1775-1953.* Army Historical Series. Washington: Office of the Chief of Military History, United States Army, 1966.

Jacobs, James Ripley. *The Beginning of the U.S. Army, 1783-1812.* Princeton: Princeton University Press, 1947.

_____. *Tarnished Warrior: Major-General James Wilkinson.* New York: The Macmillan Company, 1938.

Jobe, Joseph (ed.). *Guns: An Illustrated History of Artillery.* New York: Crescent Books, 1971.

Kahn, Richard H. *Eagle and Sword: The Federalists and the Creation of the Military Establishment in America, 1783-1802.* New York: The Free Press, 1975.

Lattimore, Ralston B. *Fort Pulaski National Monument, Georgia.* National Park Service Historical Handbook Series No. 18. Washington: Government Printing Office, 1954.

Lavender, David. *The American Heritage History of the Great West.* Alvin M. Josephy. Jr ., Editor in Charge. New York: American Heritage Publishing Co., 1965.

Lessen, Harold I., and George C. MacKenzie. *Fort McHenry National Monument and Historic Shrine, Maryland.* National Park Service Historical Handbook Series No.5. Washington: Government Printing Office, 1954.

Lewis, Emanuel Raymond. *Seacoast Fortifications of the United States: An Introductory History.* Washington: Smithsonian Institution Press, 1970.

Lloyd, Alan. *The Scorching of Washington: The War of 1812.* London: David & Charles, n.d. [ca. 1975].

Longacre, James B., and James Herring. *The National Portrait Gallery of Distinguished Americans.* 4 vols. Philadelphia: Henry Perkins, 1834.

Mahon, John K. *The War of 1812.* Gainesville: University of Florida Press, 1972.

Malone, Dumas. *Jefferson the President: First Term, 1801-1805.* Boston: Little, Brown &-Company, 1970.

_____. *Jefferson the President: Second Term, 1805-1809.* Boston: Little, Brown & Co., 1974.

Manucy, Albert. *Artillery Through the Ages.* National Park Service Interpretive Series: History No. 3. Washington: Government Printing Office, 1949.

McDonald Forrest. *The Presidency of George Washington.* Lawrence: The University Press of Kansas, 1974.

McMaster, John B. *A History of the People of the United States from the Revolution to the Civil War.* 6 vols. New York: D. Appleton and Company, 1885.

Miller, John C. *Alexander Hamilton and the Growth of the New Nation.* Originally published as *Alexander Hamilton: Portrait in Paradox.* New York: Harper and Row, 1959.

_____. *The Federalist Era, 1789-1801.* New York: Harper & Row, 1960.

Mitchell, Broadus. *Alexander Hamilton: The National Adventure, 1788-1804.* New York: The Macmillan Company, 1962.

Murdoch, Richard K. *The Georgia-Florida Frontier, 1793-1796.* Berkeley: University of California Press, 1951.

Patrick, Robert W. *Florida Fiasco: Rampant Rebels on the Georgia-Florida Border, 1810-1815.* Athens: University of Georgia Press, 1954.

Peterson. Harold I. *Forts in America.* New York: Charles Scribner's Sons, 1964.

_____. *Round Shot and Rammers.* New York: Bonanza Books, 1969.

Pickering, Octavius, and Charles W. Upham. *The Life of Timothy Pickering.* 4 vols. Boston: Little, Brown & Co., 1867-1871.

Pitkin, Thomas M. *Keepers of the Gate: A History of Ellis Island.* New York: New York University Press, 1975.

Potter, E.B. (ed.). *The United States and World Sea Power.* Englewood Cliffs, N.J.: Prentice-Hall, Inc., 1955.

Quick, John. *Dictionary of Weapons and Military Terms.* New York: McGraw- Hill Book, 1973.

Reilly, Robin. *The British at the Gates: The New Orleans Campaign in the War of 1812.* New York: G.P. Putnam's Sons, 1974.

Richards, George H. *Memoir of Alexander Macomb, the Major General Commanding the Army of the United States.* NewYork: M'Elrath, Bangs & Co., 1833.

Ripley, Warren. *Artillery and Ammunition of the Civil War.* New York: Promontory Press, 1970.

Robinson, Blackwell P. (ed.). *The North Carolina Guide.* Chapel Hill: University of North Carolina Press, 1955.

Smith, Edmund Banks. *Governors Island: Its Military History Under Three Flags, 1637-1913.* New York: Published by the Author, 1913.

Thian, Raphael P. *Notes Illustrating the Military Geography of the United States*. Washington: Government Printing Office, 1881.

Tousard, Louis de. *American Artilleristt's Companion, or Elements of Artillery . . . .* 3 vols. Philadelphia: C. and A. Conrad and Co., 1809-1913. Reprinted New York: Greenwood Press, 1969.

United States Military Academy. *The Centennial of the United States Military Academy at West Point, New York, 1802-1902*. 2 vols. Washington: Government Printing Office, 1904.

_____ . *Notes on Permanent Land Fortifications*. West Point, N.Y.: Department of Military Art and Engineering, 1952.

Van Every, Dale. *Ark of Empire: The American Frontier, 1784-1802*. New York: William Morrow and Company, 1963.

Weinert, Richard P., Jr. *The Guns of Fort Monroe*. Fort Monroe, Va.: The Casemate Museum, 1974.

B - *Articles*

Abbott, Henry L. "The Corps of Engineers." *Journal of the Military Service Institution of the United States*, XV (1894), 415-427.

Allen, Richard S. "American Coastal Forts: The Golden Years. "*Periodical* of the Council on Abandoned Military Posts, V, 2 (Summer 1973), 2-6.

Arthur, Robert. "Coast Forts of Colonial Massachusetts." *The Coast Artillery Journal*, LVIII, 2 (Feb 1923), 101-121.

_____ . "Coast Forts in Colonial Maine." *The Coast Artillery Journal*, LVIII, 4 (Apr 1923), 217-237.

_____ ."Coast Forts in Colonial New Hampshire." *The Coast Artillery Journal*, LVIII, 6 (June 1923), 547-553.

_____ ." Tidewater Forts of Colonial Virginia." *The Coast Artillery Journal*, LIX, 1 (Jan 1924), 3-20.

_____ ."Colonial Coast Forts on the South Atlantic." *The Coast Artillery Journal*, LXX, 1 (Jan 1929), 3-17.

_____ ."Early Coast Fortifications." *The Coast Artillery Journal*, LXX, 2 (Feb 1929), 134-144.

Cassell, Frank A. "Baltimore in 1813: A Study of Urban Defense in the War of 1812." *Military Affairs*, XXXIII, 3 (Dec 1969), 349-36l.

Cullen, E[dward] J. "Under Five Flags: The History of the Fortification of Mobile Bay." *The Coast Artillery Journal*, LIX, 3 (Sept 1924), 223-234.

Cullum, George W. "History of the Sea-Coast Fortifications of the United States: Boston Harbor." *Journal of the United States Artillery*, VII, 3 (1896), 359-378.

_____ ."History of the Sea-Coast Fortifications of the United States: Narragansett Bay." *Journal of the United States Artillery*, VIII, 1-2 (1897), 186-204.

Finke, Detmar H. "Notes on Artillery Uniforms, 1801." *Military Collector & Historian* , IV, 1 (Mar 1952), 15 .

Forman, Sidney. "The United States Military Philosophical Society, 1802-1813." *William and Mary Quarterly*, 3d Ser., II, 3 (July 1945), 273-285.

_____ . "Why the United States Military Academy was Established in 1802. "*Military Affairs*, XXIX, 1 (Spring 1965), 16-28,

Freeman, James. "Record of the Services of Constant Freeman, Captain of Artillery in the Continental Army,"

William Lee, ed. *Magazine of American History*, II, 6 (June 1878), 349-360.

Gardner, Asa Bird. "Henry Burbeck: Brevet Brigadier-General United States Army—Founder of the United States Military Academy." *Magazine of American History*, IX, 4 (Apr 1883), 251-265.

Godfrey, Carlos E. "Organization of the Provisional Amy of the United States in the Anticipated War with France, 1798-1800." *Pennsylvania Magazine of History and Biography*, XXXVIII, 2 (1914), 129-182.

Hall, Edward H. "Lieutenant Colonel Stephen Rochefontaine." *26th Annual Report of the American Scenic and Historic Preservation Society* (Albany, N.Y.: J.B. Lyon Company Printers, 1922), 245-269.

Hastings, Hugh (ed.). "Early Fortifications Around New York City." Reprinted from *The Military Papers of Daniel D. Tompkins, Governor of New York, Written During the Second War with Great Britain. Journal of the of the United States Artillery*, IX, 2 (1898), 194-210.

Holden, Edward S. "Origins of the United States Military Academy, 1777-1802." *The Centennial of the United States Military Academy at West Point, New York, 1802-1902* (Washington, 1904), I.

Kirchner, D. P. "American Harbor Defense Forts." *United States Naval Institute Proceedings*, LXXXIV, 8 (Aug 1958), 93-101.

Lacy, Harriet S. "Fort William and Mary Becomes Fort Constitution." *Historical New Hampshire*, XXIX, 4 (Winter 1974), 281-293.

Lewis, Emanuel Raymond. "The Ambiguous Columbiads." *Military Affairs*, XXVIII, 2 (Winter 1964), 111-122.

Maine Historical Society. "The Ancient Defenses of Portland." Unsigned article in *Maine Historical Society Quarterly* (Jan 1896), reprinted in *Journal of the United States Artillery*, VII, 2 (1896), 193-206.

Manigault, Gabriel E. "The Military Career of General George Izard." *Magazine of American History*, XIX, 6 (1886), 462-478.

Mullin, John R. "Fortifications in America." *Periodical* of the Council on Abandoned Military Posts, Nos. 29, 30, and 31 (1973-1974).

Murdoch, Richard K. "The Case of the Three Spanish Deserters, 1791-1793." *Georgia Historical Quarterly*, XLIV, 3 (Sept 1960), 278-305.

Robinson, Willard B. "Fort Adams—American Example of French Military Architecture." *Rhode Island History*, XXXIV, 3 (Aug 1975), 77-96.

———————. "Military Architecture at Mobile Bay." *Journal of the Society of Architectural Historians*, XXX, 2 (May 1971), 119-139.

Schroeder. Alfred K. "Life and Times of a Harbor Fort." (Fort Warren, Massachusetts) *Periodical* of the Council on Abandoned Military Posts, VII, 3 (Fall 1975), 27-32.

Southard, Frank E. "The Portland Federal Volunteers, 1798-1803." *Military Collector & Historian*, XII (1959), 44-56.

Thibault, Jacqueline. "Deciphering Fort Mifflin." *Military Collector & Historian*, XXVII, 3 (Fall 1975), 101-112.

Tucker, Cary S. "The Early Columbiads." *Military Collector & Historian*, X (1958), 40-42.

Wade, Arthur P. "A Military Offspring of the American Philosophical Society." *Military Affairs*, XXXVIII, 3 (Oct 1974), 103-107.

Weller, Jack "The Artillery of the American Revolution." *Military Collector & Historian*, VIII, 3 (Fall 1956), 61-65, and VIII, (Winter 1956), 97-101.

Wesley, Edgar B. "The Beginnings of Coast Fortifications." *The Coast Artillery Journal,* LXVII, 4 (Oct 1927), 281-290.

Wilkinson, Norman B. "The Forgotten 'Founder' of West Point." (Louis Tousard) *Military Affairs,* XXIV (Winter 1960-61), 177-188.

Williams, Ames. H. "The Old Fortifications of New York Harbor." *Military Collector & Historian,* XXII, 2 (Summer 1970), 37-44.

Wright, John Womack. "Some Notes on the Continental Army." *William and Mary College Quarterly Historical Magazine,* 2d Ser., (five consecutive issues), 1931-32.

APPENDIX A

ORGANIZATION OF THE CORPS OF ARTILLERISTS AND ENGINEERS
July 1795

Commanding - Lieutenant Colonel Commandant STEPHEN ROCHEFONTAINE

1st Battalion - Major HENRY BURBECK

1st Co.: Capt Mahlon Ford	Lt Joseph Elliott	Lt Thomas Underwood
2d Co.: Capt John Peirce	Lt Piercy S. Pope	Lt Ebenezer Massey
3d Co.: Capt Moses Porter	Lt George Demlar	Lt James Sterrett
4th Co.: Capt George Ingersoll	Lt Peter Van Alen	Lt Frederick Dalcho

2d Battalion - Major LOUIS TOUSARD

1st Co.: Capt Griffith J. McRee	Lt John McClallen	Lt Joseph Guimpé
2d Co.: Capt Alexander Thompson	Lt Nehemiah Freeman	(vacant)
3d Co. : Capt Wm. Littlefield	Lt Theophilus Elmer	Lt John Saunders
4th Co.: Capt Donald G. Mitchell	Lt Robert Rowan	Lt George Hardy

3d Battalion - Major J.J. ULRICH RIVARDI

1st Co.: Capt Rich. S. Blackburn	Lt John P. Hale	Lt John M. Lovell
2d Co.: Capt Decius Wadsworth	Lt William Cox	Lt William Wilson
3d Co.: Capt Frederick Frye	Lt Horatio Dayton	Lt Peter Tallman
4th Co.: Capt Abimael Y. Nicoll	Lt Jonathan Robeson	(vacant)

4th Battalion - Major CONSTANT FREEMAN

1st Co.: Capt James Bruff	Lt Simon Geddes	Lt Nath'l Cudworth
2d Co.: Capt James Gamble	Lt David Hale	Lt Peter Dransy
3d Co.: Capt Michael Kalteisen	Lt George Izard	Lt William Morris
4th Co.: Capt Staats Norris	Lt Henry Muhlenberg	(vacant)

Medical Staff - Surgeon Charles Brown

Surgeon's Mates	Nathan Hayward	Francis G. Brewster
	John G. Coffin	Richard Griffith
	John R. Lynch	William Lawton

APPENDIX B

THE HAMILTON-HcHENRY PROPOSALS
FOR THE REORGANIZATION OF THE ARMY
December 1798

(Extracts Concerning the Artillery)

. . . [I]t is conceived that the organization of our military force would be much improved by modeling it according to the following plan . . . .

That a regiment of artillery consist of four battalions, each of four companies, and of the following officers and men, viz: one colonel; four majors; one adjutant; one quartermaster, and one paymaster, each of whom shall be a lieutenant. One surgeon, and two surgeon's mates; sixteen captains; sixteen first and sixteen second lieutenants, besides the three lieutenants abovementioned; thirty-two cadets, with the pay and emoluments as at present established; four sergeant majors; four quartermaster sergeants; sixty-four sergeants; sixty four corporals; one chief musician, and ten other musicians; and eight hundred and ninety-six privates, including to each company, eight artificers.

. . . .

The term lieutenant-colonel, in our present establishment, has a relative signification, without any thing, in fact, to which it relates: it was introduced during our revolutionary war to facilitate exchanges of prisoners, as our then enemy united the grade of colonel with that of general.

. . . .

The title of colonel, which has greater respectability, is more proper for the commander of a regiment . . . .

. . . .

The nature of the artillery service, being constantly in detachment, renders it proper to compose a regiment of a greater number of battalions than the other corps. This our present establishment has recognized . . . . The diminution of the number of musicians, while it will save expense, is also warranted by the peculiar nature of the artillery service. They answer in this corps few of the purposes they are applied to in the infantry.

. . . .

It is deeply to be lamented, that a very precious period of leisure was not improved, towards forming among ourselves engineers and artillerists; and that, owing to this neglect, we are in danger of being overtaken by war, without a competent number of characters of these descriptions. To form them suddenly is impracticable; much previous study and experiment are essential. . . . In the mean while, is conceived to be advisable to endeavor to introduce, from abroad, at least one distinguished engineer, and one distinguished officer of artillery. They may be sought for preferably in the Austrian, and next in the Prussian armies. The grade of colonels, with adequate pecuniary compensations, may attract officers of a rank inferior to that grade in those armies, who will be of distinguished abilities and merit . . . .

It is also suggested, than an inspector of fortifications is much wanted. In case of a legislative provision on this subject, the officer may be either drawn from the corps of artillerists and engineers, or it may be left discretionary with the President to choose him where he pleases. If, however, the choice is to be restricted to that corps, it will be proper, that withdrawing him from it shall not prevent his rise in it, and that his place in the corps should be filled by an officer of the same grade.

It will be easily imagined, that without such an officer the service may essentially suffer. To obviate this, the Department of War has always found it necessary to employ a person who has been paid out of the contingencies for performing that and some other duties of a military nature.

The importance of a faithful representation of the real state of the fortifications, public buildings, and barracks, the qualifications of the commandants of forts, the police they observe, and degree of attention they bestow on the works, magazines, and the like, can stand in need of no comment.

It is further submitted, whether it will not be proper, and conduce to the improvement of our artillery, to enlarge the field from which to select a fit character for inspector of artillery. As the law [Act of 16 July 1798] now is, the inspector must be chosen from the corps of artillerists and engineers, and would require one of its most experienced officers, all whose services are indispensable to the corps itself.

APPENDIX C

STATIONS AND NOMINAL ORGANIZATION
THE REGIMENTS OF ARTILLERISTS AND ENGINEERS
June 1799

1st Regiment - Lieutenant Colonel Commandant HENRY BURBECK (Michilimackinac)
  1st Battalion - Major J. J. Ulrich Rivardi (Fort Niagara)
    Porter's Company - Captain Moses Porter (Michilimackinac)
      Lieut Richard Whiley

    Thompson's Company - Captain Alexander Thompson (Fort Niagara)
      Lieut Theophilus Elmer
      Lieut Peter Tallman

  Western Army:
    Demlar's Old Company - Capt James Sterrett (enroute from Michilimackinac)
      Lieut Joseph Campbell (Natchez)
      Lieut Robert Parkinson

    Pope's Company - Captain Piercy S. Pope (Natchez)
      Lieut Andrew Marschalk
      Lieut Thomas T. Underwood

  2d Battalion - Major Louis Tousard (Newport)
    Ingersoll's Company - Capt George Ingersoll (West Point)
      Lieut Peter A. Dransy

    Elliott's Company - Captain Joseph Elliott (Fries Rebellion)
      Lieut James House
      Lieut William Yates

    Littlefield's Company - Captain William Littlefield (Newport)
      Lieut George T. Ross

    Freeman's Company - Captain Nehemiah Freeman (West Point)
      Lieut Philip Rodrigue
      Lieut Warham Shepard

  3d Battalion - Major Constant Freeman (Charleston)
    Frye's Company - Captain Frederick Frye (Fort Jay, N.Y.)
      Lieut Samuel Fowle

McClallen's Company - Captain John McClallen (Fort Mifflin, Pa.)
    Lieut Robert Rowan
    Lieut Staats Rutledge

Kalteisen's Company - Captain Michael Kalteisen (Charleston)
    Lieut George Izard
    Lieut Jonathan Robeson

Nicoll's Company - Captain Abimael Y. Nicoll (St. Mary's, Ga.)
    Lieut Howell Cobb

4th Battalion - Major Mahlon Ford (Fries Rebellion)
    Massey's Company - Captain Ebenezer Massey (Fort Mifflin, Pa.)
        Lieut Ebenezer Beebe

    Bruff's Company - Capt James Bruff (Fort McHenry, Md.)
        Lieut Henry M. Muhlenberg
        Lieut James P. Heath

    Morris's Company - Captain Staats Morris (Fort McHenry, Md.)
        Lieut Philip Landais
        Lieut Samuel T. Dyson

    Blackburn's Company - Captain Richard S. Blackburn (Norfolk)
        Lieut John Saunders
        Lieut James Triplett

2d Regiment - Lieutenant Colonel Commandant JOHN DOUGHTY (New York City)
    1st Battalion - Major Benjamin Brooks (New York City)
        Read's Company - Captain James Read (West Point)
            Lieut Theodore Meninger
            Lieut Robert W. Osborn

        Stillé's Company - Captain James Stillé
            Lieut Philip Stewart
            Lieut Patrick C. Harris (Fort Johnston, N.C.)

        Irvine's Company - Captain Callender Irvine (Fries Rebellion)
            Lieut Charles Wollstonecraft
            Lieut George W. Carmichael

        Cochrane's Company - Captain Walter L. Cochrane (Fort Jay, N.Y.)
            Lieut William L. Cooper
            Lieut Robert Heaton, Jr.

2d Battalion - Major Daniel Jackson (Boston)
     Wadsworth's Company - Captain Decius Wadsworth (New London)
          Lieut Francis Gibson
          Lieut Nathaniel Leonard

     Henry's Company - Capt John Henry (enroute Newport from Fries Rebellion)
          Lieut John W. Livingston
          Lieut John Knight

     Gates's Company - Captain Lemuel Gates (Boston)
          Lieut George W. Duncan
          Lieut George Waterhouse

     Stoddard's Company - Captain Amos Stoddard (Portland)
          Lieut William Steel
          Lieut Leonard Williams

3d Battalion - Major Adam Hoops (New York City)
     MacRea's Company - Captain William MacRea (Unknown)
          Lieut James White
          Lieut John Fergus. Jr. (Fort Johnston, N.C.)

     Huger's Company - Captain Francis K. Huger (Charleston)
          Lieut William F. DeVaux
          Lieut James B. Many

     Eddins's Company - Captain Samuel Eddins (Unknown)
          Lieut Alexander O. Pope
          Lieut John Leybourne

     Bishop's Company - Captain John Bishop (Unknown)
          Lieut John Hancock
          Lieut David Evans, Jr.

(4th Battalion authorized but not raised; no commander appointed)

APPENDIX D

STATIONS OF THE REGIMENT OF ARTILLERISTS
Summer-Fall 1802

Washington City
    Chief of Artillerists - Colonel HENRY BURRECK
        Paymaster - Lieut James House (Fort McHenry)
        ADC to Gen Wilkinson - Lieut John DeB. Walbach

Fort Sumner, Portland, Maine District
    Det., Stoddard's Co. - Lieut John Fergus, Jr.

Fort Constitution, Portsmouth, New Hampshire
    Stoddard's Co. (-) - Captain Amos Stoddard
        Lieut Pierson Titcomb

Fort Independence, Boston, Massachusetts
    Comdg Battalion and Post - Major Daniel Jackson
    Gates's Co. - Captain Lemuel Gates
        Lieut Leonard Williams
        Lieut William Wilson

    Freeman's Co. - Captain Nehemiah Freeman
        Lieut Joseph Cross
        Lieut Stephen Worrell

Fort Wolcott, Newport, Rhode Island
    Beall's Co. - Captain Lloyd Beall
        Lieut Nathaniel Leonard
        Lieut Lewis Howard

Fort Trumbull, New London, Connecticut
    Stille's Co. - Captain James Stille
        Lieut Charles Wollstonecraft
        Lieut Moses Swett

Fort Jay, New York Harbor
    Comdg Battalion and Post - Major George Ingersoll
    Livingston's Co. - Captain John W. Livingston
        Lieut Ebenezer Beebe
        Lieut William Yates

West Point, New York
    Izard's Co. - Captain George Izard
                Lieut Robert W. Osborn
                Lieut Kilian P. Van Rensselaer

Fort Mifflin, Philadelphia, Pennsylvania
    Bruff's Co. - Captain James Bruff (Comdg Post)
                Lieut George Waterhouse

    Muhlenberg's Co. - Captain Henry M. Muhlenberg
                Lieut Samuel Fowle (resd 27 Nov)
                Lieut William A. Murray

Fort McHenry, Baltimore, Maryland
    McClallen's Co. - Captain John McClallen
                Lieut Samuel T. Dyson
                Lieut Clarence Mulford

Fort Nelson, Norfolk, Virginia
    Blackburn's Co. - Captain Richard S. Blackburn
                Lieut John Saunders
                Lieut Addison B. Armistead

Fort Johnston, Cape Fear River, North Carolina
    Det., Kalteisen's Co. - Lieut John F. Powell

Charleston Harbor, South Carolina
    Comdg Battalion and Harbor - Lieut Colonel Constant Freeman
    Kalteisen's Co. - Captain Michael Kalteisen (Fort Johnson)
                Lieut John B. Barnes

    Robeson's Co. - Captain Jonathan Robeson (Fort Moultrie)
                Lieut Hezekiah W. Bissell (died 10 Nov)
                Lieut Louis Landais

Fort Greene, Savannah, Georgia
    Nicoll's Co. -   Captain Abimael Y. Nicoll
                Lieut Howell Cobb
                Lieut Peter Lamkin

Fort Niagara, New York
    Comdg Battalion and Post - Major Moses Porter
    Read's Co. - Captain James Read
                Lieut George Armistead
                Lieut George Peter

Detroit, Northwest Territory
    Tallman's Co. - Captain Peter Tallman
        Lieut William Cocks

Michilimackinac, Northwest Territory
    Dunham's Co. - Captain Josiah Dunham
        Lieut Richard Whiley

South West Point, Tennessee
    Comdg Battalion and Post - Major William MacRea
    Carmichael's Co. - Captain George W. Carmichael
        Lieut James B. Many

Fort Pickering, Chickasaw Bluffs, Tennessee
    Cooper's Co. - Captain William L. Cooper
        Lieut Samuel Welsh

Fort Adams, Mississippi Territory
    Sterrett's Co. - Captain James Sterrett
           Lieut Enoch Humphreys
           Lieut Augustus Strong

APPENDIX E

MEMBERSHIP OF
THE UNITED STATES MILITARY PHILOSOPHICAL SOCIETY
1807-1809

President - Jonathan Williams, Colonel of Engineers
Vice President - Charles Cotesworth Pinckney, Charleston, S.C.
Recording Secretary - Francis De Masson, Professor USMA
Corresponding Secretary - Joseph G. Swift, Major of Engineers
Treasurer - William Popham, New York City
Keeper of the Cabinet - George Bomford, Captain of Engineers

John Allen, Counselor at Law, Litchfield, Connecticut
John Quincy Adams, Senator U.S.
John Adams, Quincy, Massachusetts, late President U.S.
Walker K. Armistead, Captain of Engineers
John Armstrong, Minister of the U.S. in Paris

Samuel Babcock, Lieutenant of Engineers
William Bainbridge, Captain Navy U.S.
Joel Barlow, Washington
James A. Bayard, Senator U.S.
Lloyd Beall, Captain [of Artillerists] commanding at Rhode Island
Charles Biddle, late Vice President of Pennsylvania
Clement Biddle, formerly Quarter Master General
Russell Bissell, Major of Infantry [died Dec 1807]
Joseph Bloomfield, Governor of New Jersey
Joseph Blyth, George Town, S. Carolina
William R. Boote, Captain of Infantry (Okmulgee Old Fields, Georgia)
Stephen R. Bradley, Senator U.S.
John Brooks, Boston
James M. Brown
Daniel A.A. Buck, Lieutenant of Engineers
John Bullus, Navy Agent at New York
Henry Burbeck, Colonel Commandant of Eastern Division of Army U.S.

Thomas Cadwallader, Philadelphia
John Cassin, Captain Commanding Navy Yard
Samuel Champlain, Charleston
Isaac Chauncey, New York
William C.C. Claiborne, Governor of Territory New Orleans
Daniel Clark, Delegate in Congress from New Orleans
William Clarke [Clark?]
Eli B. Clemson, Captain Infantry U.S. (St. Louis, Louisiana)

Joseph Clay, of Philadelphia
DeWitt Clinton, Mayor of New York
George Clinton, Vice President of the United States
George Clinton, Jr., of New York
David Cobb, Taunton, Massachusetts
William Crane, of New Jersey
Thomas H. Cushing, Colonel of 2d Regiment of Infantry U.S.
William Cutbush, New-York
William Cutting, New-York

Samuel W. Dana
William R. Davie, late Governor N. Carolina and Minister to France
Jonathan Dayton, late Senator U.S.
Benjamin Dearborn, of Boston
Henry Dearborn, Secretary of War [to Feb 1809]
Stephen Decatur, Captain of the Navy U.S.
John H. Dent, Captain Navy U.S.
Rene Edward De Russy, Cadet of Engineers, USA
William DeSaussure, of Charleston

Thomas B. Earle, Adjutant Gen. State of N. Carolina
William Eaton, late General at Derne (Brimfield, Massachusetts)
William Eustis, Secretary of War [from Mar 1809]

James Fairley, New-York
John R. Fenwick, Lieutenant Marine Corps
Joachim Ferrere, New-York
Dr. Findlay, Beaufort, S.C.
George Fleming, late [military storekeeper], West Point
Constant Freeman, Lieut. Col. U.S. Artillery Natchitoches, Terr. Orleans
Nehemiah Freeman, Captain [of Artillerists], Commanding at Boston
Robert Fulton, New York

Peter Gansevoort, Military Agent at Albany
John Garnet, Brunswick, New Jersey
George Gibbs, Newport, Rhode-Island
Nicholas Gilman, Senator U.S.
Charles Gratiot, Captain of Engineers
John F. Grimke, Judge of Superior Court, S. Carolina

John Hall, Captain Marines
Paul Hamilton, Secretary of the Navy [from 1809]
Abijah Hammond, of New York
Wade Hampton, Brigadier General U.S. Army [1809]
Robert Goodloe Harper, Counselor at Law, Baltimore

William H. Harrison, Governor of Indiana Territory (Vincennes)
Ferdinand R. Hassler, Professor of Mathematics, West Point
Archibald Henderson, Marine Corps, Washington
John Hubbard, of Dartmouth College
Benjamin Huger, Georgetown, S.C.
Francis Huger, Georgetown, S.C.
Isaac Hull, Post-Captain U.S. Navy
William Hull, Governor at Detroit
David Humphreys, late envoy to Spain
Thomas Hunt, Colonel of 1st Infantry (St. Louis, Louisiana) [died Aug 1808]

George Izard, late Captain of Artillery

Thomas Jefferson, President of the United States
John Johnson, Lieutenant of Marines

Rufus King, late Minister of U.S. to Britain
Jacob Kingsbury, Lieut. Col. of 1st Infantry (Fort Adams, Miss. Terr.)
Francis Kinloch, Georgetown, S.C.

John Langdon, Governor of New Hampshire
Benjamin Latrobe, Director of Public Buildings U.S.
Tobias Lear, Consul of U.S. at Algiers
Louis LeCesne, Belleville, New Jersey
David Lenox, late Major, now President of Bank U.S.
Lawrence Lewis, New Haven
Meriwether Lewis, Governor of Louisiana (St. Louis)
Benjamin Lincoln, now Collector at Boston
Robert R. Livingston, late Minister U.S. to France

Alexander Macomb, Major of Engineers
Robert Macomb, Col. and Aid-de-camp to Governor of New-York
William MacPherson, now Naval Officer U.S. at Philadelphia
William MacRee, Captain of Engineers
James Madison, Secretary of State of U.S. [President 1809]
John Marshall, now Chief Justice U.S.
Jonathan Mason, of Boston, Massachusetts
Jared Mansfield, Lieut. Col. of Engineers, acting Surveyor General U.S.
William M'Creery, Member of Congress
Thomas M'Kean, Governor of Pennsylvania
John Milledge, Senator U.S.
Samuel L. Mitchill, M.D., Professor Natural History, N.Y.
James Monroe, late Minister U.S. to Britain
Jacob Morton, Brigadier Gen. of New York Artillery

Clarence Mulford, Charleston [Captain of Artillerists?]
John W. Mulligan, New-York
Alexander Murray, Captain U.S. Navy
John R. Murray, New York

Julian U. Niemcewicz, formerly of Poland, Citizen U.S.
William North, Late Adjutant Gen. U.S.

Presley N. O'Bannon, [late USMC], Artillery U.S. (Michilimackinac)
Aaron Ogden, late Colonel U.S.

William Paterson, late Judge of Supreme Court [died Sept 1806]
Alden Partridge, Lieut. of Engineers
William Partridge, Lieut. of Engineers
Robert Patton, late Capt. U.S. Army, Post Master, Philadelphia
Zebulon M. Pike, Major 6th Regiment of Infantry
Thomas Pinckney, late Major of U.S. Army
William Pinkney, Minister Plenipotentiary U.S. London
Ninian Pinkney, Captain of Infantry (Fort McHenry)
William Popham, late aid to Baron Steuben, Treasurer of USMPS, New, York
Moses Porter, Major of Artillery U.S.
Edward Preble, late Commodore U.S. [died Aug 1807]

Josiah Quincy, Member of Congress U.S.

David Ramsay, Charleston, S.C.
Thomas M. Randolph, of Virginia
Jacob Read, Charleston, S.C.
James Ricketts, of Elizabeth Town, N. Jersey
John H. Robinson, St. Louis, Louisiana
Hezekiah Rogers, of War Department, Secretary pro term USMPS
Jonathan Rogers, Commodore U.S. Navy
John Rutledge, Charleston, S.C.

John Saunders, Captain of Artillery U.S. (Norfolk, Va.)
Louis Simond, of New-York
James Simons, Charleston
Benjamin Smith, of Wilmington, N. Carolina
John Smith, Captain Navy U.S.
Robert Smith, Secretary of Navy [to 1809]
Samuel Smith, Senator U.S.
Nathaniel Smith, Dartmouth College
William Short, late Charge des Affairs at Madrid
William L. Smith, of Charleston, late Minister U.S. at Lisbon
Arthur St. Clair, of Pennsylvania

Daniel Stevens, of S. Carolina
Caleb Strong, late Governor of Massachusetts
Amos Stoddard, Major of Artillerists, Fort Adams [M.T.]
James Sullivan, Governor of Massachusetts
Thomas Sumter, Senator U.S.
Caleb Swan, Pay Master to the Army
Foster Swift, of Taunton, Massachusetts

Sylvanus Thayer, Lieut. of Engineers
Thomas Tillotson, of New-York
Thomas Tingey, Port Commodore, Washington
Daniel D. Tompkins, Governor State of New-York
Louis de Tousard, Lieut. Col. in the French Army [late 2d A&E]
John Trumbull, of New-York
Thomas Truxton, Commodore of the Navy U.S.
Thomas T. Tucker, Treasurer U.S.

Philip Van Courtland, of New York
K. Van Rensselaer, Member of Congress
Solomon Van Rensselaer, Adjutant Gen. Albany, N.Y.

John De B. Walbach, Capt. of Artillery, Commanding Fort Constitution
Bushrod Washington, Judge of Superior Court U.S.
William Washington, Charleston, S. Carolina
Samuel Webber, of Vermont
Samuel White, Senator U.S.
Eli Whitney, New Haven
Franklin Wharton, Lieut. Col. Commandant Marine Corps
Richard Whiley, Capt. of Artillery, Commanding Fort Columbus
Charles Wilkinson, Brigadier General Commandant of Army U.S.
Prentiss Willard, Lieut. of Engineers
Marinus Willett, New York
Alexander J. Williams, Cadet of Engineers, USMA
Henry J. Williams, Cadet of Engineers, USMA
John Williams, Professor, Cambridge
Samuel Williams, L.L.D., Rutland, Vermont
Eleazer D. Wood, Lieut. of Engineers

Christian E. Zoeller, Professor in the Military Academy

APPENDIX F

STATUS OF SEACOAST FORTIFICATIONS
December 1808

Extracts from Report of Secretary of War Henry Dearborn (*ASP, MA*, I, 236-239)

DISTRICT OF MAINE

PORTLAND HARBOR.—*Fort Preble*, a new enclosed work of stone and brick masonry . . . is completed. This work is erected on Spring point, and commands the entrance of this harbor, through the main channel.

Fort Scammel, also a new work of similar materials, is erected on House island, opposite fort Preble, and commands the main and other channels. It is now, completed . . . .

Fort Sumner battery, to the north of the town, has been repaired.

[Mention of minor batteries, generally for guns on traveling carriages, at Kennebeck, Sheepscutt, Damariscotta, St. George's River, Penobscot and Baggaduce River, and Machias.]

PASSAMAQUODDY.—A battery and block house have been erected, and a garrison placed in the works. Cannon have generally been mounted

[This became Fort Sullivan, at Eastport in Passamaquoddy Bay.]

NEW HAMPSHIRE

PORTSMOUTH HARBOR.—*Fort Constitution*, on New Castle point, at the entrance of this harbor, is an enclosed work, built principally of stone masonry. It is now complete . . . .

Fort McClary, a new strong work of masonry, has been erected on Kittery point, opposite fort Constitution. It is now finished . . . .

MASSACHUSETTS

NEWBURYPORT. — On the point of Plum Island, at the mouth of Merrimack River, a battery of wood, filled in with sand and surmounted with sod, has been erected. It . . . was constructed of wood on account or the shifting sands.

GLOUCESTER, CAPE ANN—The old fort of stone, in front of this place . . . has been repaired.

MARBLEHEAD.—The fort at this place [Fort Sewall] . . . has been repaired.

SALEM.—The fort [Fort Pickering] and block house . . . on a point at the entrance of this harbor, have been repaired. . . .

BOSTON HARBOR.—In addition to Fort Independence, the following works have been erected for the defense of this harbor.

Fort Warren.—On the summit of Governor's Island an enclosed star fort, of mason work . . . has been completed. Fort Warren battery, on the south point of the same island, is completed of stone, sod . . . .

Westhead battery is staked out and materials collected. On a point formed by Charles and Mystic rivers, a battery has been built of sod, on a stone foundation.

The old work on Gurnet head, near Plymouth, has been repaired, and platforms in front.

At the entrance of the inner harbor of New Bedford, two miles below the town, a small enclosed work has been erected of stone, brick, and sod. It commands the entrance into the harbor for a mile and a half in a direct line . . . .

RHODE ISLAND

NEWPORT HARBOR.—At fort Wolcott and fort Adams some repairs have been made, and the works extended so as to admit some additional guns.

. . .

On the main island, to the south of the town of Newport, a small battery has been erected, which commands the inner harbor between fort Wolcott and the town . . . .

CONNECTICUT

In this State directions were given . . . for the erection of a battery . . . for the defence of the harbor of New Haven; for the repair, improvement, and completion of Fort Trumbull, near New London; and for the erection of a small battery for the defence of Stonington. But the same want of engineers . . . has also prevented any more being done in this State than merely to select the proper sites for the defence of New Haven and Stonington, and the examination of the state of the works at Fort Trumbull . . . .

NEW YORK

Fort Jay . . . was demolished in 1806, except the walled counterscarp, the gate, sallyport, magazine, and two barracks; all the rest was removed as rubbish, to give place for a work composed of durable materials. On the site of the old fort, a new one (fort Columbus) has been erected, of the same shape, on three of its sides, as the former, with the addition of fourteen feet on each side. On the north side a ravelin has been added, with two retired casemated flanks. The new fort . . . is now nearly completed, and has fifty cannon mounted.

On a point of rocks, at the western extremity of Governor's Island, a circular castle, of durable mason work, to be connected with Fort Columbus by a zig-zag covered defile, has been commenced, and completed to the second floor, and is now ready to receive its first tier of guns . . . . The exterior diameter of this castle is two hundred and ten feet, and, when finished, will mount one hundred pieces of heavy ordnance.

On Bedloe's Island, a mortar battery commanding all the anchoring ground between Red Hook and the quarantine, and affording a protection to Ellis's island, has been commenced. Part of the redoubt in the rear has been excavated . . . .

On Ellis, or Oyster Island, advantageously situated for defending the entrance of North River, an open barbette battery for heavy ordnance on one platform . . . is now nearly completed. The platform is ready for the guns . . . .

. . . a battery in North river . . . off Hubert Street, has been commenced. The foundation is of stone, and has been carried up to high water mark . . . . This battery is connected with Hubert Street by a bridge 200 feet long and 30 wide.

Preparations have also been made for erecting a heavy battery on a stone foundation with a superstructure of solid mason work at the southwest point of the city. The point selected has a complete command from the whole range of North river on one side to the complete width of East river on the other . . . .

[Description also of a small arsenal behind the Custom House, and a larger arsenal and laboratory to be located about two miles from the city.]

PENNSYLVANIA

The works at Fort Mifflin have received considerable repair and the cannon mounted. Some further repairs of carriages . . . have been directed.

MARYLAND

Fort Washington, on the Potomac, between Alexandria and Mount Vernon, is a new enclosed work, of stone and brick masonry, to which is attached a strong battery of like materials. The whole is . . . ready for the reception of the cannon and garrison, which have been ordered, and have arrived at the fort. A stone tower has also been commenced on an eminence that overlooks the fort . . . .

A circular battery of mason work on Windmill point, for the protection and defence of Annapolis, is nearly completed—the cannon are mounted. Another battery on the bank of the Severn, below the town, is also nearly finished.

Fort McHenry, near Baltimore, is in a good state of defence.

VIRGINIA

Fort Nelson has been strengthened, and a large strong battery of mason work erected on the site of old Fort Norfolk . . . .

A site and materials for a strong battery at Hospital point, near Norfolk, have been procured . . . .

At Hoods [Bluff], on James River, a strong battery of mason work has been erected, and a regular enclosed work [Fort Powhatan], on an eminence commanding the battery, is in considerable forwardness . . . .

NORTH CAROLINA

A battery of mason work and barracks were ordered to be erected at Old Topsail Inlet, near Beaufort, N.C. [Fort Hampton]. . . . it is believed that the works are nearly completed.

The works at Fort Johnston, on Cape Fear river . . . are finished.

SOUTH CAROLINA

The works in the harbor of Charleston are progressing . . . .

A new fort on the site of old Fort Mechanic . . . was directed to be built of mason work. It is now completed and ready for the reception of a garrison; its situation is a commanding one.

The battery of Fort Johnston [i.e., Johnson] has been some time since finished, and is now completely mounted with heavy artillery.

Fort Moultrie, which is a little inferior in magnitude and importance to any work in the United States, is now enclosed, and ready to receive a garrison.

A new fort of mason work on the site of old Fort Pinckney is commenced, and in a rapid state of progress. . . .

A small battery for the immediate defence of Beaufort, S.C. . . . has been ordered to be erected on the site of old Fort Lyttleton. But the land being the property of the State and no cession having been made by her to the United States, nothing as yet has been done at this place.

A small battery . . . was directed to be built at Georgetown, S.C. The works are progressing and will soon be completed.

GEORGIA

Unavoidable delays in procuring the necessary sites have very much impeded the progress of the fortifications in this State.

As soon as a site could be obtained, a strong battery of mason work was commenced a few miles below the town of Savannah, at Five Fathom Hole, where large vessels generally take in their cargoes. This work will probably be completed in the course of a few weeks.

A regular enclosed fort of mason work was directed to be built on the site of old Fort Wayne, near the town of Savannah, with a battery in front; a battery and redoubt or strong block house on Point Petre, at the mouth of the St. Mary's river; and a small battery near Sunbury. The site for the fort near the town has been obtained [but] no sites have yet been obtained for the proposed works at Point Petre and Sunbury.

TERRITORY OF ORLEANS

Fort St. Charles, at the lower end of the city of New Orleans, and immediately on the bank of the river, is now in a good state of repair, with all its cannon mounted . . . .

At the mouth of Bayou St. John, a strong new battery has been erected, which commands the passage from lake Ponchartrain to the city of New Orleans. The battery of mason work . . . at English Turn [will] require but a few weeks for its completion.

A new fort of substantial mason work, has been commenced on the site of fort St. Philip at Placquemines; the two main bastions are completed and the cannon mounted [and] the fort will be completed in two or three months.

When the above works shall have been finished, it is believed that, with suitable garrisons and the number of gun boats destined for that quarter, they would afford such protection as has been contemplated.

*   *   *   *

The following sums have been advanced for the erection and repair of fortifications, and the construction of gun carriages, during the year 1808, viz:

For New Orleans:	$80,373
Georgia, North and South Carolina:	$204,289
Virginia and Maryland:	$111,432
Delaware, Pennsylvania, and New Jersey:	$5,000
New York:	$379,133
Connecticut and Rhode Island:	$11,000
Massachusetts and New Hampshire:	<u>$223,475</u>
	$1,014,702

For completing the works already commenced, and for erecting such others as have been contemplated, or may be deemed expedient, it is believed that an additional appropriation [of] four hundred and fifty thousand dollars, will be necessary, exclusive of the expense of a line of block chains &c., across the harbor of New York. The chain and timber for these blocks have already been procured, at an expense of upwards of 40,000 dollars; but . . . to complete this plan, as heretofore proposed, would require an expenditure of one million of dollars.

APPENDIX G

REPORT OF THE SECRETARY OF WAR
ON SEACOAST FORTIFICATIONS AND BATTERIES

December 1811 (*ASP, MA*, I, 307-311)

DISTRICT OF MAINE

Passamaquoddy - A circular battery of stone; with four guns mounted; covered by a blockhouse; with wooden barracks for 50 men . . . [Fort Sullivan].

Machias - The same, with wooden barracks for 40 men . . . .

Penobscot - A small enclosed battery; with four heavy guns mounted.

Georges, on Georges River - Same, with three heavy guns mounted.

On Damariscotta River - A small enclosed battery; with three heavy guns mounted, covered by a block house . . . .

Edgecomb, on Sheepscot river - The same, with six heavy guns mounted.

Georgetown, Kennebec river - An enclosed work; with a battery of six heavy guns mounted, a small magazine, and wooden barracks for 40 . . . .

Portland Harbor:

Fort Preble, situated on Spring Point, at the entrance of the harbor; an enclosed star fort of masonry, with a circular battery with flanks; mounting 14 heavy guns . . . barracks for one company.

Fort Scammel; (opposite) a circular battery of masonry with circular flanks, mounting fifteen heavy guns, is covered in the rear with a wooden block house, mounting six guns . . . .

At the north end of the town is a battery of five guns mounted [and] four eighteen pounders mounted on travelling carriages.

NEW HAMPSHIRE

Portsmouth Harbor:

Fort Constitution, situated on the eastern point of New Castle Island at the entrance of Piscataqua river, three miles below Portsmouth; an enclosed irregular work of masonry, mounting thirty-six heavy guns . . . and brick barracks for two companies . . . .

Fort McClary, (opposite) on the Kittery side; a circular battery of masonry, enclosed by earth and palisades, mounting ten heavy guns [with] barracks of brick and wood for one company . . . . In the town of Portsmouth; a brick arsenal with three 24 and three 18 pounders, mounted on field carriages . . . .

MASSACHUSETTS

Newburyport - On the east point of Plum Island, at the entrance of the harbor; an enclosed battery, built of earth and timber, mounting five heavy guns . . . .

Cape Ann, Gloucester - At the head of the harbor; an enclosed battery, mounting seven guns, covered by a block house . . . .

Salem - Fort Pickering, situated on the west side of the entrance into the harbor; an enclosed work of masonry and sods, mounting six heavy guns, covered by a block house . . . .

Marblehead - Fort Sewell [Sewall]; situated on the west point of the entrance into the harbor; an enclosed work of masonry and sods, mounting eight heavy cannon, covered by a block house . . . .

Boston Harbor:

Fort Independence, situated on Castle Island, on the South side of the inner harbor; a regular pentagon, with bastions of masonry, mounting forty-two heavy cannon, with two batteries for six guns [and] brick barracks for two companies . . . also an old wooden barrack, which has quartered six companies . . . .

Fort Warren, opposite, on Governor's Island; a star fort of masonry, mounting twelve guns . . . and brick barracks for 40 men . . . . On the West head, a circular battery of ten guns mounted [and] on the South point, a circular battery, calculated for ten guns . . . .

Also at Charlestown, near the navy yard; a circular battery of earth for eight heavy guns . . . .

Plymouth harbor - At the Gurnet Point, the entrance of the harbor; the old enclosed fort has been repaired with stone and sods, mounting five heavy guns . . . .

New Bedford - At Eldridge Point, which commands the entrance of the harbor; an enclosed work of masonry, mounting six heavy guns . . . .

RHODE ISLAND

Harbor of Newport:

Fort Adams, situated on Briton [Brenton's] Point, east side of the entrance of the harbor; an irregular star fort of masonry, with an irregular indented work of masonry adjoining it, mounting seventeen heavy guns. . . . The barracks are of wood and bricks, for one company . . . .

Fort Wolcott, situated on Goat Island, in the centre of the harbor; a small enclosed work, with open batteries, extending from two opposite flanks, of stone, earth sods, &c. mounting thirty-eight heavy guns . . . . The barracks are of bricks and wood, for one company . . . .

Rose Island, situated to defend the north and south passages of the harbor; a regular unfinished work of masonry of four bastions, two of which are circular. Within the works are a range of stone barracks, or arched rooms, sufficient for 300 men . . . . The works were commenced in 1798—unfinished.

At the north point of the town, on a piece of ground rented by the United States, called Easton's Point, an elliptical stone battery has been erected, but now in a state of ruin . . . .

On a bluff of rocks, called the Dumplins, on Conanicut Island, nearly opposite to Fort Adams; a circular tower of stone, with casemates . . . with a small expense, there can be mounted six or eight heavy guns; and now in an unfinished state.

CONNECTICUT

New London Harbor - Fort Trumbull, situated on the west side of the harbor; an irregular enclosed work of masonry and sod, mounting eighteen heavy guns; . . . a brick barracks for one company . . . .

New Haven - Fort Hale, situated on the eastern side of the harbor of New Haven; an elliptical enclosed battery of masonry; mounting six heavy guns; . . . brick barracks for fifty men . . .

At Stonington; a brick arsenal, with four eighteen pounders mounted on travelling carriages.

STATE OF NEW YORK

New York Harbor:

Fort Columbus, situated on Governor's Island, within half a mile of the city; a regular enclosed work of masonry, comprehending four bastions and a ravelin, with sixty heavy guns mounted, a brick magazine that will contain 500 barrels of powder, and brick barracks for two companies . . . .

On a projecting point of the island stands a stone tower, called Castle Williams, with fifty-two [42- and 32-] pounders, mounted on two tiers, under a bomb [proof] roof, and on the terrace above is intended to mount twenty-six fifty pound Columbiads. Two stone magazines, which will contain 250 barrels of powder, and the arches of the second tier will answer for barracks for 300 men; also on the island . . . a wooden barrack for 300 men and officers.

Bedloe's Island, nearly opposite; a star fort of masonry, mounting twenty-four heavy guns; . . . a brick barrack for one company . . . .

Ellis's Island, opposite Fort Columbus; an enclosed circular battery of masonry, mounting fourteen heavy guns, with a barracks of stone and wood for one company . . . .

About one hundred yards in front of the west head of the grand battery, in the city of New York, an enclosed circular battery of stone, with twenty-eight heavy guns mounted . . . .

North battery, one mile up North river; an enclosed circular stone battery, with sixteen heavy guns mounted . . . .

Three miles out of the city; a brick arsenal . . . and a brick laboratory for making and repairing of ammunition, &c.

At Sagg Harbor, on Long Island, a brick arsenal, with four 18 pounders mounted on field carriages, with implements.

PENNSYLVANIA

Fort Mifflin, situated on the west side of the Delaware river, seven miles below Philadelphia; an irregular enclosed work of masonry, defended by bastions, demi-bastions, &c. mounting 29 heavy guns, with a water battery without the works, mounting eight heavy guns . . . with brick barracks for 100; within 3/4 of a mile are public buildings, called the Lazaretto, which are good barracks for 400 men.

DELAWARE

Wilmington - An arsenal of brick . . . with four 12 pounders mounted on field carriages . . . .

Newcastle - An arsenal of brick . . . with four heavy cannon mounted on field carriages . . . .

MARYLAND

Harbor of Baltimore - Fort McHenry, situated at the entrance of the harbor; a regular pentagon of masonry, calculated for 30 guns, a water battery with ten heavy guns mounted . . . with brick barracks for two companies; without the fort, a wooden barrack for one company . . . .

Annapolis - Fort Madison, situated at the eastern entrance into the harbor; an enclosed work of masonry, comprehending a semi-elliptical face, with circular flanks, calculated for 13 guns, with . . . brick barracks for one company. At the Windmill point, a circular battery of masonry, for 8 heavy guns; in the rear are quarters for two companies.

On Potomac - Fort Washington, situated at Warburton, on the east side of the river; an enclosed work of masonry, comprehending a semi-elliptical face, with circular flanks, mounting 13 heavy guns; it is defended in the rear by an octagon tower of masonry, mounting six cannon; . . . brick barracks for one company . . . .

VIRGINIA

Norfolk Harbor:

Fort Nelson, situated on the western side of Elizabeth river, and opposite that part of Norfolk called the Point; an irregular work, defended by whole and half bastions, &c., built of bricks and sod, and enclosed in the rear by a brick parapet, mounting 37 guns . . . brick barracks for one company . . . .

Fort Norfolk, situated on the northeastern side of Elizabeth river, one thousand yards distant from Fort Nelson; an irregular enclosed work of masonry, comprehending a semi-elliptical battery, defended on the flanks and rear by irregular bastions, mounting 30 heavy guns; . . . brick barracks for two companies.

On James River - Hood's Bluff; an unfinished work of masonry [Fort Powhatan], intended for 13 cannon, &c.; there are now barracks for one company.

NORTH CAROLINA

Wilmington - Fort Johnston, situated on the right bank of Cape Fear river, 28 miles from Wilmington; a flank battery of tapier [tapia], mounting eight heavy guns . . . a brick barrack for one company . . . .

Beaufort - Fort Hampton, of a circular form in front, and enclosed with a straight line in the rear, mounting five guns . . . and brick barracks for one company.

SOUTH CAROLINA

Harbor of Charleston - Fort Johnston [Johnson], situated in the harbor . . . a marine battery of irregular form, built of brick and wood, mounting 16 guns . . . . The barracks are built of wood and tapier . . . for 200 men and officers.

Fort Moultrie, situated at the entrance of the harbor; an irregular form, built of brick, presenting a battery of three sides on the sea front, and the whole is enclosed with ramparts, parapets. &c. mounting 40 guns . . . . The barracks are of brick . . . for five hundred.

Castle Pinckney, of an elliptical form, built of brick; has two tiers of guns, and has 30 mounted. . . . . quarters for 200. The work is considered the most important in the harbor.

Fort Mechanic; a temporary battery, built on the point of the city; it makes a cross fire with the Castle at a distance of 900 yards; it mounts seven guns . . . . The site is not ceded to the United States, and is falling to decay . . . .

Beaufort - This work [Fort Marion] is of circular form in front, and a straight line in the rear. It is, at present, only in its foundation four feet high above the ground . . . entirely of tapier.

GEORGIA

Savannah - Fort Jackson, situated in a marsh on the west side of Savannah river, three miles below the town, and 1200 yards from the nearest dry land; an enclosed work of masonry and mud, mounting six heavy guns; . . . a wooden barrack for one company. The work is in an unfinished state.

MOUTH OF THE MISSISSIPPI RIVER

Fort St. Philip, at Placquemines, near the mouth of the river; an enclosed work of masonry and wood, calculated for 20 guns, with a magazine and barracks for one company.

English Turn; an enclosed work (old Fort St. Leon), with two bastions and a battery of masonry, for nine guns, with a magazine, and barracks for one company; nearly finished.

Fort St. Charles, in the city of New Orleans; an enclosed redoubt of five sides of masonry and earth; mounting 19 guns; a magazine and barracks for thirty men.

Bayou St. John; a strong battery of six guns, which commands the passage of Lake Ponchartrain, with barracks for 30 men.

APPENDIX H

COMMANDERS OF SEACOAST FORTIFICATIONS
1794-1812

FORT SULLIVAN, Eastport, Maine

1808-1809 - Capt Moses Swett, RA
1810-1812 - 1st Lt Samuel Maclay, RA

FORT SUMNER, Portland, Maine

1798-1799 - Capt Amos Stoddard, 2A&E
1800-1801 - Capt John Henry, 2A&E
1802-1803 - 1st Lt William Wilson, RA
1804-1807 - (no federal garrison)
1808-1809 - 1st Lt Samuel Page, 4 Inf

FORT PREBLE, Portland, Maine

1808-1809 - Capt Joseph Chandler, LA
1809-1811 - Capt Thomas Pitts, LA

FORT SCAMMEL, Portland, Maine

1808-1809 - 1st Lt Samuel Page, 4 Inf

FORT McCLARY, Kittery Point, Maine
(Harbor of Portsmouth, N.H.)

1809-1810 - Capt Paul Wentworth, 4 Inf
1811-1812 - Capt John DeB.Walbach, RA

FORT CONSTITUTION, Portsmouth, N.H.
(formerly Fort William and Mary)

1798-1799 - (Det Stoddard's Co., 2A&E)
1800-1801 - (no federal garrison)
1802-1803 - Capt Amos Stoddard, RA
1803-1806 - Capt Lemuel Gates, RA
1807-1812 - Capt John DeB.Walbach, RA

FORT PICKERING, Salem, and FORT
SEWALL, Marblehead, Mass.
1804-1808 - (no federal garrison)

1800-1802 - Cpt Alexander D. Pope, 2A&E
1802-1803 - (Det Freeman's Co., RA)

1809-1812 - Capt Stephen Ranney, 4 Inf

FORT INDEPENDENCE, Boston, Mass.
(formerly Castle William)

1798   - Capt George Ingersoll, CA&E
1799-1803 - Maj Daniel Jackson, 2A&E
1803   - Capt Lemuel Gates, RA
1803-1810 - Capt Nemiah Freeman, RA
1810-1811 - Maj Moses Porter, RA
1811-1812 - Capt Nemiah Freeman, RA
1812   - Col Moses Porter, LA

FORT WARREN, Boston, Mass.

1809-1810 - (Det Freeman's Co., RA)
1810-1811 - Capt Moses Whitney, Rifles

ELDRIDGE POINT, New Bedford, Mass.

1810-1811 - Capt James Thomas, Drgns
1811-1812 - 1st Lt Henry Whiting, Drgns

FORT WOLCOTT, Newport, Rhode Island

1798-1799 - Capt William Littlefield, CA&E
1799-1802 - Capt Amos Stoddard, 2A&E
  1802   - Maj William MacRea, RA
1802-1809 - Capt Lloyd Beall, RA
  1810   - Maj Moses Porter, RA
1810-1811 - Capt James House, PA
1811-1812 - Maj Abraham Eustis. LA

FORT ADAMS, Newport, Rhode Island

1799-1800 - Capt John Henry, 2A&E
1800-1802 - Capt William Steele, 2A&E
1802-1809 - (Det Beall's Co, RA)
1809-1811 - Capt Abraham Eustis, LA
  1812   - (Det House's Co., RA)

FORT TRUMBULL, New London, Conn.

  1799   - Capt Decius Wadsworth, 2A&E
1800-1804 - Capt James Stille, 2A&E/RA
1804-1805 - (caretaking detachment)
  1809   - Capt Joel Cook, 4 Inf
1810-1812 - Capt Noah Lester, Drgns

FORT HALE, New Haven, Connecticut

1810-1811 - Cor Elijah Boardman, Drgns

FORT JAY, Governors Island, N.Y.

  1794   - Capt Cornelius R. Sedam, 1SL
1795-1796 -Capt Alexander Thompson, CA&E
1796-1797 - Lieut William Wilson, CA&E
1798-1799 - Capt Frederick Frye, CA&E
  1800   - Capt George Ingersoll, 1A&E
1800-1802 - Maj Decius Wadsworth, 2A&E
1802-1803 - Maj George Ingersoll, RA
1803-1804 - Capt John W. Livingston, RA
1804-1806 - Capt Richard Whiley, RA
  (Fort Jay demolished 1806)

FORT COLUMBUS, Governors Is., N.Y.

1807-1809 - Capt Richard Whiley, RA
1809-1810 - Maj Amos Stoddard, RA
1810-1812 - Col Henry Burbeck, RA

CASTLE WILLIAMS, Governors Is., N.Y.

1811-1812 - (Det Swett's Co., RA)

ELLIS'S ISLAND, New York Harbor
(subsequently FORT WOOD)

1808-1809 - Capt Solomon D. Townsend, LA
1810-1811 - Capt John Johnson, 5 Inf

BEDLOE'S ISLAND, New York Harbor
(subsequently FORT GIBSON)

1809   - Capt Ebenezer Cross, 6 Inf
1810   - Capt William N. Irvine, LA
1810-1811 - Capt David Brearly, Drgns
1812   - Capt George Armistead, RA

FORT MIFFLIN, Philadelphia, Pa.
(formerly Fort Mud)

1795   - Capt James Gamble, CA&E
1795-1796 - Lieut David Hale, CA&E
1791-1798 - Capt Donald G. Mitchell, CA&E
1798-1799 - Capt Ebenezer Massey, CA&E
1799-1800 - Lieut Theodore Meminger, lA&E
1800   - Capt Frederick Frye, 1A&E
1800-1801 - Maj William McRea, 2A&E
1801-1802 - Maj J.J.U. Rivardi, lA&E
1802-1804 - Capt James Bruff, RA
1804-1808 - Capt James Read, PA
1809-1810 - Lt Col William Duane, Rifles
1810-1812 - Capt James Reed, PA
1812   - Capt James S. Swearingen, RA

FORT McHENRY, Baltimore, Maryland
(formerly Whetstone Fort)

1795-1796 - Capt James Bruff, CA&E
1796-1797 - (Det Nicoll's CG., CA&E)
1798   - Capt Staats Morris, CA&E
1799-1800 - Capt James Bruff, CA&E
1800-1801 - Capt Nehemiah Freeman, lA&E
1801   - Capt Staats Morris, lA&E
1801-1802 - Capt Abimael Y. Nicoll, lA&E
1802-1804 - Capt John McClallen, RA
1804-1805 - 1st Lt Samuel T. Dyson, RA
1805-1806 - 1st Lt James House, RA
1807-1812 - Capt George Armistead, RA
1812   - Capt Lloyd Beall, RA

FORT MADISON, Annapolis, Maryland

1809-1812 - 2d Lt Satterlee Clark, RA

FORT WASHINGTON, Warburton, Maryland
(formerly Fort Warburton)

1810   - En Robert Cherry, 2 Inf
1810-1812 - Capt Lloyd Beall, RA

FORT POWHATAN, Hodd's Bluff, Va.

1809-1810 - Col Edward Pasteur, 3 Inf
1810-1811 - Capt John Nicks, 3 Inf

FORT NELSON and FORT NORFOLK, Norfolk, Virginia	1798-1800 - Capt Richard S. Blackburn, lA&E
	1800-1802 - Maj Mahlon Ford, lA&E
	1802-1803 - Maj Richard S. Blackburn, RA
	1803-1808 - Capt John Saunders, RA
	1808-1810 - Maj John Saunders, LA
	1810 - Capt William Wilson, RA
	1810 – Col Edward Pasteur, 3 Inf
	1811-1812 - Lt Col Constant Freeman, RA
FORT JOHNSTON, Smithville, N.C.	1797-1798 - (Det CA&E)
	1799 -Lieut John Fergus Jr, 2A&E
	1800 - Lieut Patrick C. Harris, 2A&E
	1800-1802 - Capt James Bruff, lA&E
	1802-1803 - 1st Lt John F. Powell, RA
	1803-1804 - 1st Lt John Fergus Jr, RA
	1804-1805 - 1st Lt Joseph G. Swift, CE
	1806-1807 - 1st Lt William Cocks, RA
	1808-1809 - 1st Lt Robert Roberts, RA
	1810-1812 - Maj Joseph G. Swift, CE
FORT HAMPTON, Beaufort, N.C.	1811-1812 - Capt John McClelland, 3 Inf
FORT JOHNSON, Charleston, S.C.	1794-1807 - Capt Michael Kalteisen, CA&E
	1808-1809 - Capt Clarence Mulford, RA
	1809-1810 - Capt Addison B. Armistead, RA
	1810-1812 - Capt Clarence Mulford, RA
FORT MOULTRIE, Charleston, S.C.	1799 - Capt Francis K. Huger, 2A&E
	1800-1801 - Capt Jonathan Robeson, lA&E
	1802-1803 - Lt Col Constant Freeman, RA
	1804-1808 - (Det Kalteisen's Co., RA)
	1808-1809 - Lt Col John Smith, 3 lnf
	1810-1812 - Capt Addison B. Armistead, RA
	1812 - Maj James Read, RA
CASTLE PINCKNEY, Charleston, S.C.	1802-180? - (used as marine hospital)
	1809-1812 - (Det Armistead's Co., RA)
FORT GREENE, Cockspur Island, Savannah, Georgia	1796-1801 - Capt Abimael Y. Nicoll, CA&E
	1801-1802 - Cpt Richard S. Blackburn, lA&E
	1802-1804 - Capt Abimael Y. Nicoll, RA
	1804 - Ens J.R.N. Luckett, 2 Inf
	(destroyed by hurricane Sept 1804)

FORT JACKSON, Savannah, Georgia

1808-1809 - Capt Addison B. Armistead, RA
1810-1812 - (no federal garrison)

POINT PETRE, St. Mary's, Georgia

1800-1801 - (Det Nicoll's Co., 1A&E)
1801-1802 - (Det Blackburn's Co., lA&E)
1802-1804 - (Det Nicoll's Co., PA)
1805-1810 - (no federal garrison)
   1811 - Lt Col Thomas A. Smith, Rifles
1811-1812 - Maj Jacint Laval, Drgns

ENGLISH TURN, New Orleans,
Orleans Territory (old Fort St. Leon)

1804-1807 - Lt Col Constant Freeman, RA
1807-180? - Capt James B. Many, RA
180?-1811 - Capt William Cocks, RA

FORT ST. PHILIP, Placquemines,
Orleans Territory

1804-1807 - Lt Col Constant Freeman, RA
1807-1808 - Capt John Fergus Jr, RA
1809-1810 - Maj William MacRea, RA
1811-1812 - Capt James B. Many, RA

INDEX

ARTHUR PEARSON WADE

Arthur Pearson Wade was born in 1921, in Asheville, NC, the son of an artillery officer. Wade graduated from Porter Military Academy in Charleston, SC, in 1938, attended the Citadel for a year, and then was appointed to West Point. Wade graduated with the war time Class of January 1943 and was assigned to the 991st Field Artillery which participated in the West Virginia and Tennessee maneuvers and then landed on Omaha Beach at Normandy in 1944. Lieutenant Wade fought with the 991st across France as an air observer and adjusted the first artillery round to land on German soil. Then, in what would be a portent of the future, Wade was assigned to write an operational history of the artillery. In another important event he met a Red Cross Club-mobile girl from Sheboygan, Wisconsin, Ruth Dieckmann, and they were married in Friedberg.

Wade became a Professor of Military Science and Training in 1947 when the couple returned to the United States, and their son Robert was born two years later. Arthur was next assigned to teach military history at West Point, which determined the focus of his life. After a tour of duty in France he returned to head the History of Military Art program at the academy. Wade enrolled in evening graduate school at Fairleigh Dickinson University and earned his MA in History in 1965. The Wade's son Robert entered West Point the next year, graduating with the Class of 1971 and joining the artillery. Arthur was appointed command historian for General William C. Westmoreland in Vietnam and then served as Pacific Command Historian in Hawaii before retiring in 1972.

That same year Wade enrolled in the Graduate School of Kansas State University, completing his course work in 1975, his doctoral dissertation, "Artillerists and Engineers: The Beginnings of American Seacoast Fortifications, 1794-1815," the next year, and was awarded his PhD in 1977. The Wades joined a group of other retired army couples in Columbia, SC, and Arthur became actively involved in several historical organizations--the Company of Military Historians, the American Military Institute, the Organization of American Historians, the Society of Historians of the Early American Republic, and the Council on America's Military Past. He spent the rest of his life writing military history for conference presentations, encyclopedias and periodicals. Colonel Wade died in 1984 and was buried at the West Point cemetery. His wife Ruth passed away in 1989, and tragically, their son, Lieutenant Colonel Robert R. Wade, was killed in an automobile accident in 1991, and was buried at West Point. He is survived by his wife Melinda and stepchildren Jennifer and Jason.

COAST DEFENSE STUDY GROUP, INC.

The CDSG Press would like to thank the Wade family for allowing the CDSG Press to publish this dissertation as book. We would also like to thank Joel Eastman for his special efforts in bring this book to life and arranging permission for us to publish. Mark Berhow provide his expert skills converting the manuscript into to digital files and working with lulu.com to meet their standards. The CDSG Press is pleased to be able to offer these work that help explains U.S. seacoast defenses from 1794 to 1815.

The CDSG Press, the publishing arm of the CDSG, offers for sale back issues of the CDSG's quarterly publication, Coast Defense Journal/CDSG Journal/CDSG News (since 1985) in electronic PDF format on compact disks. Also, available are the Notes from the CDSG Conferences and Special Tours (since 1987) to various United States coast defenses from around the world. These notes include site plans, engineering drawings, and Report of Completed Works, etc. The CDSG Press also offers an ever-expanding number of key reprint reports and manuals in electronic PDF format on compact disks. This digital library contains Report of Completed Works, Engineer Notebooks, Harbor Defense Projects Annex/Supplements, and many other coast defense items. The CDSG Press offers for sale several reprints of coast defense books. They are: (1) Notes on Seacoast Fortification Construction by Col. Eben E. Winslow (1920, 428-pages, hardcover). The 29 engineering drawings that accompanied the original monograph have been slightly reduced and are bound together as a separate softbound volume. Winslow's book is the most comprehensive reference work on the construction techniques of Endicott and Taft period seacoast fortifications. (2) Seacoast Artillery Weapons by U.S. War Department (1944, 202-pages, hardcover) is a technical manual that covers the basics principles employed in the operation of seacoast artillery used during the World War II period. (3) The Service of Coast Artillery by Frank Hines and Franklin Ward (1910, 736-pages, hardcover) is a textbook that focuses on the principal types of seacoast artillery used during the Endicott period. (4) Permanent Fortifications & Sea-Coast Defences by U.S. Congress (1862, 544-pages, hardcover) originally published by the Committee on Military Affairs - U.S. House of Representatives in 1862, this congressional report (No. 56) provides key documents relating to the design and construction of the third system of U.S. seacoast fortifications. (5) American Coast Artillery Material by Office of the Chief of Ordnance, ODD#2042, 1922. This is one of the most comprehensive and profusely illustrated works on the specifics of early modern United States seacoast artillery weapons. (6) American Seacoast Defenses: A Reference Guide – Second Edition by Mark Berhow (2004, 640-pages, softbound), CDSG Press's first original work, compiles the key data about America's coast defenses in one place otherwise a student of coast defense would need hundreds of government documents to gather the same key information. (7) Endicott Board and Taft Board Reports were originally published by the Government Printing Office in 1886 and 1906 to report to the U.S. Congress the recommendations reached by two civilian-military boards on the future of U.S. coastal defenses (522 pages, hardcover with 59 large plates). To order these books/compact disks and other publications, please contact the CDSG Press at www.cdsg.org or 1700 Oak Lane, McLean, Virginia 22101-332 USA Attn: Terrance McGovern.

COAST DEFENSE STUDY GROUP, INC
1700 Oak Lane
McLean, VA 22101 USA

The Coast Defense Study Group, Inc. (CDSG) is a tax-exempt corporation dedicated to the study of seacoast fortifications. The purposes of the CDSG include educational research and documentation, preservation of historic sites, site interpretation, and assistance to other organizations interested in the preservation and interpretation of coast defense sites. Membership is open to any person or organization interested in the study or history of coast defenses and fortifications. Membership in the CDSG will allow you to attend the annual conference, tours, and receive quarterly newsletter and journal. To find out more about the CDSG or to join the CDSG, please visit the CDSG website at www.cdsg.org or contact us at the address listed above.

LaVergne, TN USA
20 February 2011
217235LV00004B/6/P